INTRODUCTORY READINGS in

GOVERNMENT
and POLITICS

● ● ● ● ● ● ● ● ● ● ● ● ● ● ● ● ● ●

FOURTH EDITION

INTRODUCTORY READINGS in

GOVERNMENT
and POLITICS

• • • • • • • • • • • • • • • • •

FOURTH EDITION

MARK O. DICKERSON

THOMAS FLANAGAN

NEIL NEVITTE

University of Calgary

Nelson Canada

I(T)P An International Thomson Publishing Company

Toronto • Albany • Bonn • Boston • Cincinnati • Detroit • London • Madrid • Melbourne
Mexico City • New York • Pacific Grove • Paris • San Francisco • Singapore • Tokyo • Washington

I(T)P™
International Thomson Publishing
The trademark ITP is used under licence

© Nelson Canada,
A Division of Thomson Canada Limited, 1995

Published in 1995 by
Nelson Canada,
A Division of Thomson Canada Limited
1120 Birchmount Road
Scarborough, Ontario M1K 5G4

Canadian Cataloguing in Publication Data

Main entry under title:

Introductory readings in government and politics

4th ed.
ISBN 0-17-604243-1

1. Comparative government.   2. Political science.
3. Canada – Politics and government.   I. Dickerson, M. O., 1934– .
III. Nevitte, Neil.

JC131.I68   1995   320.3   C95-930271-9

Acquisitions Editor	Andrew Livingston
Production Editor	Tracy Bordian
Senior Production Coordinator	Sheryl Emery
Art Director	Liz Harasymczuk
Cover Design	Peggy Rhodes
Composition Analyst	Nelson Gonzalez

Printed and bound in Canada

98 97 96 95 (WC) 1 2 3 4

CONTENTS

PART FOUR THE POLITICAL PROCESS   257

PREFACE

This reader is designed for use in introductory political science courses in Canada with the purpose of complementing general first-year political science texts. Often, introductory texts pass quickly over important ideas that can be a useful focus of discussion. This reader provides some illustrative material upon which those discussions may be based. It also addresses another concern. Canadian students confronting important political ideas for the first time typically find little reference or application to the Canadian context. As a result, the ideas may appear to be disembodied from Canadian politics, or students may be left to make the connections themselves. While this reader is in no measure a substitute for specific courses in Canadian politics, it does contain some selections that are explicitly relevant to Canadians.

The material is organized into four sections: *Basic Concepts, Ideology, Forms of Government,* and *The Political Process.* This mirrors the structure of Mark O. Dickerson and Thomas Flanagan's *An Introduction to Government and Politics,* 4th ed. (Toronto: Nelson Canada, 1994), and instructors using that text may find this book especially useful.

Each of the four sections has a brief introduction that explains how the readings in that section are related to each other and to the overall topic. This instruction may aid instructors in deciding which readings to assign in their courses. Each selection also has a short introductory note to provide contextual information and to highlight the gist of the reading. Students may find these notes helpful in approaching unfamiliar texts. Full bibliographical information is provided in the acknowledgment section for those students who wish to consult the original source material.

Several principles have guided our selection. None of the pieces demands technical background that cannot readily be explained to first-year students. However, some are more intellectually challenging than others, so instructors can choose from a spectrum of complexity. About a quarter of the material deals explicitly with Canada, enough to give a Canadian flavour to an introductory course without turning it into a study of Canadian politics. We have made a special effort to include selections from well-known authors whose names should become familiar to political science students (e.g., Hobbes, Madison, Mill, Renan, Morgenthau). The readings cover a broad range of topics within the discipline while not pretending to touch upon everything, which would be impossible even in a volume many times this size. By using several criteria for selection, we hope to have produced a flexible collection to serve multiple purposes at the introductory level.

The fourth edition of the reader drops 11 selections from the third edition and adds 11 new ones. As the changes are distributed throughout the book, they do not greatly affect the overall configuration. This ongoing revision is partly a matter of keeping up with the march of world affairs and with developments in the discipline, and partly our continuing attempt to find important readings that "work" at the introductory level. As always, we would welcome any suggestions from the instructors and students who use this book in their courses.

• • • • • • • •

PART

1

**Basic
Concepts**

INTRODUCTION

Part I contains seven readings on some of the most fundamental problems of political science: politics, authority, sovereignty, state and nation, the rule of law, and the relationship between states in the international arena. Our working assumption is that students should "begin at the beginning," i.e., come to grips with basic phenomena of politics that have occurred in political situations all over the world and throughout history.

In Reading 7, Hans J. Morgenthau argues that power is the currency of politics and that there a distinct science, political science, that specializes in the study of power. Politics is the resolution of conflicts through power, as J.D.B. Miller shows in Reading 1. Even if, following the teaching of Thomas Hobbes (Reading 3), power is centralized in sovereign authority, it can be bound by the rule of law as interpreted by impartial courts (Reading 6). Moreover, there must be some sort of community in which power is vested, which in the modern world is most often the nation (Readings 4 and 5). Personal charisma (Reading 2) is not an enduring source of either community or power. Thus, although these readings focus on different concepts, certain themes run through them: the inherent limitations of coercion, the necessity of legitimacy to sustain power, and the tension between reason and passion in the exercise of power.

1

POLITICS

Oddly, no single definition of politics has achieved wide acceptance in the discipline of political science. There seem to be almost as many definitions as there are political scientists. The following reading discusses some of the more obvious meanings of politics and proposes a definition that most students of politics could live with, even if they might wish to express it slightly differently.

The selection is from Chapter 1 of J.D.B. Miller's The Nature of Politics *(1962). Miller is Professor of Politics at Leicester University in England.*

● ● ● ● ● ● ● ● ●

What do we mean when we say that something is political? What kind of human activity have we in mind? Faced with the things that men do, we call them artistic, or economic, or religious, or educational—or political. Why is this?

The vulgar answer is that they are activities connected with the political parties; and this kind of answer is often accompanied by some statement to the effect that "politics" is a dirty game which a gentleman would not play. But this will hardly do. The term is widely used in other contexts than that of the political parties. People are often said to be acting politically in their relations with their bosses and colleagues in an office, or in the management of a club of some kind, or in many other situations in which political parties are not mentioned: to say that a man is a 'real politician' or that such-and-such was a 'good political move' is not to connect what has happened with a party. It is some kind of comment upon particular aims and methods.

A more usual answer is that political activity is something to do with government. This brings us closer to the mark. Not only are political parties intimately concerned with government in the official sense, but the activities of the 'politician' in the club or office are specifically connected with the way it is run, that is, with its government. But are we to say that everything connected with government is political? The clerk in the post office works for the government; but we would not say he was engaged in political activity when he sold us a stamp. In England, Thomas Cook and Son Ltd. became government property when the railways were taken over, but few people would say they were engaged in politics when they booked a holiday. What the postal clerk and the man from Cook's are doing is some routine task of buying and selling, not political in character but analogous to what is done by a shopkeeper or a clerk in a bank. We must look further if we are to isolate a strictly political act. It must be something more than the performance of an agreed piece of routine.

The essence of a political situation, as opposed to one of agreement and routine, is that someone is trying to do something about which there is not agreement; and is trying to use some form of government as a means and as protection. Political situations arise out of disagreement. At their most obvious, they are the situations which arise between ins and outs, yeses and noes, government and opposition, majority and minority. Government is routine up to the point where someone questions it and tries to change it; then it ceases to be routine and becomes a political situation. The questioner may be silenced, or he may prevail, or some way may be found of satisfying him by a change in procedure. Whatever happens, political activity will have begun at the point where he objected, and ceased when quiet is resumed. Politics is about policy, first and foremost; and policy is a matter of either the desire for change or the desire to protect something against change. But it need not be, as it usually is in popular discussion, the policy of some party or set of ministers or mass movement; it may be the policy of a small group in or out of the government, or even of a single man. It may reduce itself to the ambition of an under-secretary. Nor need it be some policy which embraces the whole life of the country; it can be the wish for the smallest change in a regulation or even in the administration of a regulation.

Politics, then, is about disagreement or conflict; and political activity is that which is intended to bring about or resist change, in the face of possible resistance. It is not necessary to suggest that people engaged in politics never agree, or that open and flagrant disagreement is necessary before we can see politics going on; what is important is that we should recognise that conflict lies at the heart of politics. In a world of universal agreement, there would be no room for it.

This attribute of conflict is seen to be true of politics from simple observation, no matter where we look. It is obvious enough at the level of world politics, where sovereign states are seen to be pursuing their own advantage in a variety of spheres. Traditional diplomacy exists to minimise conflict and to see that the politics which arises from it is carried on according to recognised rules which are presumed to lead to the least harm being done to all. It is obvious enough, too, at the national level at election-time. The loudness of the debate, the amounts of money spent by the contending parties, the degree of ill-will shown at election meetings and the like, will all give a fair measure of the degree of conflict and the intensity of political feeling. The harder men contend over policy and position, the more political the situation. This is politics at its more obvious; it becomes most obvious in situations of war and revolution, where the normal methods of conducting arguments have broken down under the strain, and violence takes their place. It is not only in Prussia that war is the extension of politics; it is, as it were, the ultimate form of politics.

However, politics is not necessarily always violent and clearcut. There is politics in the board room, in the inter-departmental conference, in the school staff meeting, and in the annual conference of the dog-lovers' association. To the extent that these consist of more than the reading of the minutes and the adjournment for tea, they constitute political situations. Each will display the clash of policies and the representation of interests. If the bodies concerned consist of people who know each other well and do not differ over fundamentals, the politics of the situation may be confined to polite inquiries about the policies brought forward by the executive, and perhaps to a gentlemanly contest over elections (if elections are part of the institutional framework; they are not always so, and policy and position can be pursued in other contexts than those of election to office). If there is a lack of confidence amongst those concerned, or there have been arguments over policy or the way in which policy has been carried out, or if the body in question has been subjected to disconcerting pressure from outside, the strictly political element will be more obvious: more questions will be asked, much will be made of small issues, votes will be taken more often and will show the existence of factions and groups of various kinds, some permanent and some evanescent. There may be strongly contested elections for office. Even so, the situation may still remain so calm as to look harmonious; conflicts, if they arise, may be short-lived; and the persons who exercise effective government of the body may continue in office with little apparent difficulty. All the same, it will be clear that politics is present. If the body is subjected to significant strain in the shape of some vital change of personnel, or some issue which divides those concerned, or some threat to its existence or its customary mode of procedure, politics will become more and more apparent. Trade unions provide the most obvious examples of such political transition. At any given time, some will be somnolent, with no apparent differences of opinion and no interference with the way they are run; others will be split apart by factions, and conduct their disagreements in full view of the public. Again, any given union is likely to show, in its history, periods of calm and periods of tumult, depending upon the forces present within it and the impact upon it of external conditions.

Political activity, then, arises out of disagreement, and it is concerned with the use of government to resolve conflict in the direction of change or in the prevention of change. It is about policy and position. I am not suggesting that agreement never appears in politics; indeed, the resolution of conflict into some kind of agreement, some state of things which will be preserved for at least some time, is one of the principal aims of political activity. What I am suggesting, however, is that anything which is done without any disagreement at all, from start to finish, it not a political act. Politics, to be distinguished as a recognisable activity, demands some initial disagreement between parties or persons, and the presence of government as a means of resolving the disagreement in some direction.

If I am right, we should have no difficulty in recognising a political situation when we see one. But, so far, we have achieved nothing more than description. I want next to suggest a reason for politics.

One might argue ... that all these disagreements are merely the result of error, and that the people who seem to be in conflict with one another are really in agreement about essentials, if only they knew it. The disagreements might be represented as a series of mistakes, or superficial differences below which one could discern fundamental agreement. This, it seems to me, is quite untrue: what we have to contend with in politics is a variety of perpetual disagreements which arise from fundamental differences of condition, status, power, opinion and aim. Politics is what it is because society is what it is: because men, in their social situation, find themselves divided. They live, it is true, in a society which has some system of law and order, and in which every man's hand is not turned against every other man's; but, in spite of this basically peaceable condition, they differ from each other in such a variety of ways that it would be foolish to expect agreement about everything. For, not only are they divided in terms of their condition of life and their views of what ought to be done; they are also concerned to change things so as to improve their lot or have their policies accepted. Politics is a natural reflex of the divergences between the members of a society. There is nothing in history to suggest that divergences will disappear, even if economic progress is overwhelming, or a single religion triumphs, or a single power gains control of the whole world. We should still be entitled to expect that men's wants would remain insatiable, their capacity to quarrel over doctrine significant, and their urge towards betterment an active one.

Let me indicate some of the social bases for divergence. Most obvious of all is the economic: man exists in a condition of perpetual scarcity, where everyone cannot have all he wants, and where some have more of what they want than others. The processes of production and distribution demand different functions in which men find themselves earning more or less than one another, and in which one group of persons will find itself disadvantaged when compared with another. Countries are unequally provided with resources, and unequally able to exploit these; tension between them is inevitable. Men differ in intelligence, skill and market value; it is inevitable that differences between them should be expressed in terms of some inequality of incomes. In general, the business of economy, with its choices between alternative uses of scarce resources, provides a perpetual reason for social differences; these, in their turn, find political expression.

In another field, that of status in law and custom, society invariably provides some causes for diversity. Married people are treated differently from single ones in certain respects; foreigners may be denied privileges according to citizens; women may be discriminated against in regard to property, employment, divorce, civil rights, and the like; persons of a particular colour or religion may be ostracised, or prevented from following particular trades or owning land.

Again, sheer difference of opinion is a characteristic of all societies except perhaps the most primitive. We cannot say that the difference between the teetotaller and the moderate drinker is necessarily due to institutional causes; it may be a matter of sheer conviction. Similarly, national or religious sentiments may have causes so deep as to be registrable in social terms simply as differences of opinion or belief which are sufficient in themselves to create diversity.

If we look at any society which has developed beyond the entirely customary, we shall see that diversity is the keynote of social conditions and opinion. Differences exist within the society: they do not extend to every conceivable situation, and they are absent in a number of aspects of social life, but they are sufficiently numerous, and sufficiently deep-rooted, to make us say that they are neither accidental nor temporary. People in a society have in common their membership of it, and their acceptance of certain rules which enable the society to hold together. Beyond this, they naturally tend towards diversity; and this tendency is accentuated by their universal urge towards betterment, whether of themselves as individuals, themselves and their associates as groups, or their own area or country as against others. Even if certain diversities become settled, others will arise. The differential character of the economic system and the ambitions of individuals will be sufficient to ensure that no society is ever uniform or even in its texture.

There is a close connection between what I have said about diversity in society and what I maintained earlier about conflict being the essence of politics. Politics occurs because the diversities in society make themselves felt as disagreements about which government can be made to act, or on which it is accustomed to act. Politics is, in a sense, the application of government (or the attempted application, or the attempt to prevent the application) to social situations which will not settle themselves. Some of these are sporadic, others are continual; no matter how the individual diversities change, the fact of diversity is ever-present. If I am right, then politics will never stop, because social reconciliation and agreement will never be complete. Politics keeps happening because changes in social conditions, and changes in opinion, never move uniformly towards agreement, but instead, generate new disagreements which communicate themselves to political forces, and sometimes engender new political forces altogether ....

2

CHARISMA

*P*olitical authority is generally divided into traditional, rational-legal, and charismatic types. This classification comes from the work of Max Weber (1864–1920), considered the foremost theorist of modern sociology. This selection concerns Weber's concept of charisma, which he borrowed from the church historian Rudolf Sohm and applied to leadership in general.

Although Weber believed that charismatic leaders would still appear from time to time in the modern world, he thought that on the whole charisma was bound to become less important over time. He saw a broad evolutionary trend in human affairs in the direction of secularism and rationalism, which would make charismatic outbursts less frequent. He might have changed his view had he lived long enough to observe Benito Mussolini, Adolph Hitler, Joseph Stalin, Mao Zedong, Ho Chi Minh, Fidel Castro, and other charismatic leaders of the 20th century.

These passages are taken from Weber's main work, Economy and Society, as translated in H.H. Gerth and C. Wright Mills, From Max Weber.

• • • • • • • •

Bureaucratic and patriarchal structures are antagonistic in many ways, yet they have in common a most important peculiarity: permanence. In this respect they are both institutions of daily routine. Patriarchal power especially is rooted in the provisioning of recurrent and normal needs of the workaday life. Patriarchal authority thus has its original locus in the economy, that is, in those branches of the economy that can be satisfied by means of normal routine. The patriarch is the 'natural leader' of the daily routine. And in this respect, the bureaucratic structure is only the counter-image of patriarchalism transposed into rationality. As a permanent structure with a system of rational rules, bureaucracy is fashioned to meet calculable and recurrent needs by means of a normal routine.

The provisioning of all demands that go beyond those of everyday routine has had, in principle, an entirely heterogeneous, namely, a *charismatic,* foundation; the further back we look in history, the more we find this to be the case. This means that the 'natural' leaders—in times of psychic, physical, economic, ethical, religious, political distress—have been neither officeholders nor incumbents of an 'occupation' in the present sense of the word, that is, men who have acquired expert knowledge and who serve for remuneration. The natural leaders in distress have been holders of specific gifts of the body and spirit; and these gifts have been believed to be supernatural, not accessible to everybody. The concept of 'charisma' is here used in a completely 'value-neutral' sense ....

In contrast to any kind of bureaucratic organization of offices, the charismatic structure knows nothing of a form or of an ordered procedure of appointment or dismissal. It knows of no regulated 'career,' 'advancement,' 'salary,' or regulated and expert training of the holder of charisma or of his aids. It knows no agency of control or appeal, no local bailiwicks or exclusive functional jurisdictions; nor does it embrace permanent institutions like our bureaucratic 'departments,' which are independent of persons and of purely personal charisma.

Charisma knows only inner determination and inner restraint. The holder of charisma seizes the task that is adequate for him and demands obedience and a following by virtue of his mission. His success determines whether he finds them. His charismatic claim breaks down if his mission is not recognized by those to whom he feels he has been sent. If they recognize him, he is their master—so long as he knows how to maintain recognition through 'proving' himself. But he does not derive his 'right' from their will, in the manner of an election. Rather, the reverse holds: it is the *duty* of those to whom he addresses his mission to recognize him as their charismatically qualified leader ....

In order to do justice to their mission, the holders of charisma, the master as well as his disciples and followers, must stand outside the ties of this world, outside of routine occupations, as well as outside the routine obligations of family life. The statutes of the Jesuit order preclude the acceptance of church offices; the members of orders are forbidden to own property or, according to the original rule of St. Francis, the order as such is forbidden to do so. The priest and the knight of an order have to live in celibacy, and numerous holders of a prophetic or artistic charisma are actually single. All this is indicative of the unavoidable separation from the world of those who partake of charisma. In these respects, the economic conditions of participation in charisma may have an (apparently) antagonistic appearance, depending upon the type of charisma—artistic or religious, for instance—and the way of life flowing from its meaning. Modern charismatic movements of artistic origin represent 'independents without gainful employment' (in everyday language, rentiers). Normally such persons are the best qualified to follow a charismatic leader. This is just as logically consistent as was the medieval friar's vow of poverty, which demanded the very opposite.

By its very nature, the existence of charismatic authority is specifically unstable. The holder may forego his charisma; he may feel 'forsaken by his God,' as Jesus did on the cross; he may prove to his followers that 'virtue is gone out of him.' It is then that his mission is extinguished, and hope waits and searches for a new holder of charisma. The charismatic holder is deserted by his following, however, (only) because pure charisma does not know any 'legitimacy' other than that flowing from personal strength, that is, one which is constantly being proved. The charismatic hero does not deduce his authority from codes and statutes, as is the case with the jurisdiction of office; nor does he deduce authority from traditional custom or feudal vows of faith, as is the case with patrimonial power.

The charismatic leader gains and maintains authority solely by proving his strength in life. If he wants to be a prophet, he must perform miracles; if he wants to be a warlord, he must perform heroic deeds. Above all, however, his divine mission must 'prove' itself in that those who faithfully surrender to him must fare well. If they do not fare well, he is obviously not the master sent by the gods ....

The subjects may extend a more active or passive 'recognition' to the personal mission of the charismatic master. His power rests upon this purely factual recognition and springs from faithful devotion. It is devotion to the extraordinary and unheard-of, to what is strange to all rule and tradition and which therefore is viewed as divine. It is a devotion born of distress and enthusiasm.

Genuine charismatic domination therefore knows of no abstract legal codes and statutes and of no 'formal' way of adjudication. Its 'objective' law emanates concretely from the highly personal experience of heavenly grace and from the god-like strength of the hero. Charismatic domination means a rejection of all ties to any external order in favor of the exclusive glorification of the genuine mentality of the prophet and hero. Hence, its attitude is revolutionary and transvalues everything; it makes a sovereign break with all traditional or rational norms: 'It is written, but I say unto you ....

In the evolution of political charisma, kingship represents a particularly important case in the historical development of the charismatic legitimization of institutions. The king is everywhere primarily a warlord, and kingship evolves from charismatic heroism.

In the form it displays in the history of civilized peoples, kingship is not the oldest evolutionary form of 'political' domination. By 'political' domination is meant a power that reaches beyond and which is, in principle, distinct from domestic authority. It is distinct because, in the first place, it is not devoted to leading the peaceful struggle of man with nature; it is, rather, devoted to leading in the violent conflict of one human community with another.

The predecessors of kingship were the holders of all those charismatic powers that guaranteed to remedy extraordinary external and internal distress, or guaranteed the success of extraordinary ventures ....

No matter how many beginnings may be found in the remote past, in its full development all this is specifically modern. The past has known other bases for authority, bases which, incidentally, extend as survivals into the present. Here we wish merely to outline these bases of authority in a terminological way.

In the following discussions the term 'charisma' shall be understood to refer to an *extraordinary* quality of a person, regardless of whether this quality is actual, alleged, or presumed. 'Charismatic authority,' hence, shall refer to a rule over men, whether predominantly external or predominantly internal, to which the governed submit because of their belief in the extraordinary quality of the specific *person*. The magical sorcerer, the prophet, the leader of hunting and booty expeditions, the warrior chieftain, the so-called 'Caesarist' ruler, and, under certain conditions, the personal head of a party are such types of rulers for their disciples, followings, enlisted troops, parties, et cetera. The legitimacy of their rule rests on the belief in and the devotion to the extraordinary, which is valued because it goes beyond the normal human qualities, and which was originally valued as supernatural. The legitimacy of charismatic rule thus rests upon the belief in magical powers, revelations, and hero worship. The source of these beliefs is the 'proving' of the charismatic quality through miracles, through victories and other successes, that is, through the welfare of the governed. Such beliefs and the claimed authority resting on them therefore disappear, or threaten to disappear, as soon as proof is lacking and as soon as the charismatically qualified person appears to be devoid of his magical power or forsaken by his god. Charismatic rule is not managed according to general norms, either traditional or rational, but, in principle, according to concrete revelations and inspirations, and in this sense, charismatic authority is 'irrational.' It is 'revolutionary' in the sense of not being bound to the existing order: 'It is written—but I say unto you ...!' ...

3

SOVEREIGNTY

In the form of political community known as the "state," which has come to dominate the modern world, an organized structure of government rules a population living within fixed territorial boundaries. The existence of the state requires sovereignty, that is, a highest authority at the pinnacle of governmental organization. Sovereign authority may be distributed between levels of a federal system; it may be divided among a head of state, a ruling committee or parliament, or the people themselves; but it must exist somewhere.

Reading 3, a selection from Thomas Hobbes' Leviathan, is the classic liberal argument for the necessity of sovereignty. Hobbes argued in essence that human beings are naturally predatory upon one another. The only way to keep them in check is for them to agree to form "a common power, to keep them in awe." This common power Hobbes called "the sovereign," and he regarded sovereignty as indispensable to peaceful existence. Without it, life would be in his memorable phrase "solitary, poor, nasty, brutish and short."

Thomas Hobbes (1588–1679) is one of the giants of philosophy in general and political theory in particular. The Leviathan is still read carefully by all students of political thought. The selection printed here is from chapter 17 of the Leviathan, which appears in The English Works of Thomas Hobbes, edited by Sir William Molesworth. The orthography has been modernized following Hobbes Selections, edited by Frederick J.E. Woodbridge.

● ● ● ● ● ● ● ●

The final cause, end, or design of men, who naturally love liberty, and dominion over others, in the introduction of that restraint upon themselves, in which we see them live in commonwealths, is the foresight of their own preservation, and of a more contented life thereby; that is to say, of getting themselves out from that miserable condition of war, which is necessarily consequent, ... to the natural passions of men, when there is no visible power to keep them in awe, and tie them by fear of punishment to the performance of their covenants, and observation of those laws of nature ....

For the laws of nature, as *justice, equity, modesty, mercy*, and in sum, *doing to others, as we would be done to*, of themselves, without the terror of some power, to cause them to be observed, are contrary to our natural passions, that carry us to partiality, pride, revenge, and the like. And covenants, without the sword, are but words, and of no strength to secure a man at all. Therefore notwithstanding the laws of nature, which every one hath then kept, when he has the will to keep them, when he can do it safely, if there be no power erected, or not great enough for our security; every man will, and may lawfully rely on his own strength and art, for caution against all other men. And in all places, where men have lived by small families, to rob and spoil one another, has been a trade, and so far from being reputed against the law of nature, that the greater spoils they gained, the greater was their honour; and men observed no other laws therein, but the laws of honour; that is, to abstain from cruelty, leaving to men their lives, and instruments of husbandry. And as small families did then; so now do cities and kingdoms which are but greater families, for their own security, enlarge their dominions, upon all pretences of danger, and fear of invasion, or assistance that may be given to invaders, and endeavour as much as they can, to subdue, or weaken their neighbours, by open force, and secret arts, for want of other caution, justly; and are remembered for it in after ages with honour.

Nor is it the joining together of a small number of men, that gives them this security; because in small numbers, small additions on the one side or the other, make the advantage of strength so great, as is sufficient to carry the victory; and therefore gives encouragement to an invasion. The multitude sufficient to confide in for our own security, is not determined by any certain number, but by comparison with the enemy we fear; and is then sufficient, when the odds of the enemy is not of so visible and conspicuous moment, to determine the event of war, as to move him to attempt.

And be there never so great a multitude; yet if their actions be directed according to their particular judgments, and particular appetites, they can expect thereby no defence, nor protection, neither against a common enemy, nor against the injuries of one another. For being distracted in opinions concerning the best use and application of their strength, they do not help but hinder one another, and reduce their strength by mutual opposition to nothing: whereby they are easily, not only subdued by a very few that agree together; but also when there is no common enemy, they make war upon each other, for their particular interests. For if we could suppose a great multitude of men to consent in the observation of justice, and other laws of nature, without a common power to keep them all in awe; we might as well suppose all mankind to do the same; and then there neither would be, nor need to be any civil government, or commonwealth at all; because there would be peace without subjection.

Nor is it enough for the security, which men desire should last all the time of their life, that they be governed, and directed by one judgement, for a limited time; as in one battle, or one war. For though they obtain a victory by their unanimous endeavour against a foreign enemy; yet afterwards, when either they have no common enemy, or he that by one part is held for an enemy, is by another part held for a friend, they must needs by the difference of their interest dissolve, and fall again into a war amongst themselves.

It is true, that certain living creatures, as bees, and ants, live sociably one with another, which are therefore by Aristotle numbered amongst political creatures; and yet have no direction, than their particular judgments and appetites; nor speech, whereby one of them can signify to another, what he thinks expedient for the common benefit: and therefore some man may perhaps desire to know, why mankind cannot do the same. To which I answer,

First, that men are continually in competition for honour and dignity, which these creatures are not; and consequently amongst men there ariseth on that ground, envy and hatred, and finally war; but amongst these not so.

Secondly, that amongst these creatures, the common good differeth not from the private; and being by nature inclined to their private, they procure thereby the common benefit. But man, whose joy consisteth in comparing himself with other men, can relish nothing but what is eminent.

Thirdly, that these creatures, having not, as man, the use of reason, do not see, nor think they see any fault, in the administration of their common business; whereas amongst men, there are very many, that think themselves wiser, and able to govern the public better than the rest; and these strive to reform and innovate, one this way, another that way; and thereby bring it into distraction and civil war.

Fourthly, that these creatures, though they have some use of voice, in making known to one another their desires, and other affections; yet they want that art of words, by which some men can represent to others, that which is good, in the likeliness of evil; and evil, in the likeness of good; and augment, or diminish the apparent greatness of good and evil; discontenting men, and troubling their peace at their pleasure.

Fifthly, irrational creatures cannot distinguish between *injury*, and *damage*; and therefore as long as they be at ease, they are not offended with their fellows: whereas man is then most troublesome, when he is most at ease: for then it is that he loves to shew his wisdom, and control the actions of them that govern the commonwealth.

Lastly, the agreement of these creatures is natural; that of men, is by covenant only, which is artificial: and therefore it is no wonder if there be somewhat else required, besides covenant, to make their agreement constant and lasting; which is a common power, to keep them in awe, and to direct their actions to the common benefit.

The only way to erect such a common power, as may be able to defend them from the invasion of foreigners, and the injuries of one another, and thereby to secure them in such sort, as that by their own industry, and by the fruits of the earth, they may nourish themselves and live contently; is, to confer all their power and strength upon one man, or upon one assembly of men, that may reduce all their wills, by plurality of voices, unto one will: which is as much as to say, to appoint one man, or assembly of men, to bear their person; and every one to own, and acknowledge himself to be author of whatsoever he that so beareth their person, shall act, or cause to be acted, in those things which concern the common peace and safety; and therein to submit their wills, every one to his will, and their judgments, to his judgment. This is more than consent, or concord; it is a real unity of them all, in one and the same person, made by covenant of every man with every man, in such manner, as if every man should say to every man, *I authorize and give up my right of governing myself, to this man, or to this assembly of men, on this condition, that thou give up thy right to him, and authorize all his actions in like manner*. This done, the multitude so united in one person, is called a COMMONWEALTH, in Latin CIVITAS. This is the generation of that great LEVIATHAN, to speak more reverently, of that *mortal god*, to which we owe under the *immortal God*, our peace and defence. For by this authority, given him by every particular man in the commonwealth, he hath the use of so much power and strength conferred on him, that by terror thereof, he is enabled to perform the wills of them all, to peace at home, and mutual aid against their enemies abroad. And in him consisteth the essence of the commonwealth; which, to define it, is *one person, of whose acts a great multitude, by mutual covenants one with another, have made themselves every one the author, to the end he may use the strength and means of them all, as he shall think expedient, for their peace and common defence.*

And he that carrieth this person, is called SOVEREIGN, and said to have *sovereign power*; and every one besides, his SUBJECT.

The attaining to this sovereign power, is by two ways. One, by natural force; as when a man maketh his children, to submit themselves, and their children, to his government, as being able to destroy them if they refuse; or by war subdueth his enemies to his will, giving them their lives on that condition. The other, is when men agree amongst themselves, to submit to some man, or assembly of men, voluntarily, on confidence to be protected by him against all others. This latter, may be called a political commonwealth, or commonwealth by *institution*; and the former, a commonwealth by *acquisition* ....

4

WHAT IS A NATION?

*T*he state as a structure exists in tension with the social communities in which we live, of which the most important politically is the nation. As a community of psychological identification, what Ernest Renan in Reading 4 calls "a living soul, a spiritual principle," the nation does not depend upon sovereignty or territory. Renan's essay, one of the earliest and most influential attempts to specify the characteristics of the nation, shows how national identification arises from, but is not limited to, the ties of race, language, religion, and custom. There is a curious dialectic between the state and the nation. Renan's historical analysis shows that the national identities of Europe—English, French, German, Spanish, Italian—grew out of the territorial division of the Roman Empire by the Germanic invaders. It was "the fusion of the populations" in these successor states that produced what we now call nations. It appears that at some stage the existence of a state may help create a nation; but once national identification exists, it is no longer wedded to particular boundaries or a particular government. Thus Poland could emerge again as a state after World War I, after more than a century of partition among Germany, Austria-Hungary, and Russia.

Ernest Renan (1823–1890) was a leading French historian, who wrote on many subjects. This selection is an abridged version of "What is a Nation?" in Poetry of the Celtic Races and Other Essays, which is a translation of Renan's March 11, 1882 lecture at the Sorbonne, entitled "Qu'est-ce qu'une Nation?"

• • • • • • • •

I propose to analyse with you an idea, simple in appearance, but capable of the most dangerous misunderstanding. The forms of human society are of the most varied types. Great conglomerations of people, as in the case of China, of Egypt, of ancient Babylon; the tribe, as in the case of the Hebrews and the Arabs; the city, as in the case of Athens and Sparta; unions of different countries, in the fashion of the Empire of Achaemenes, the Roman Empire, or the Carlovingian Empire; communities of no country, held together by the bond of religion, like the Israelites or the Parsees; nations like France, England, and the majority of modern European autonomies; confederations, as in the case of Switzerland and America; relationships similar to those which race and, in a greater degree, language establish between the different branches of the Teutonic family, the different branches of the Slavs—these are modes of grouping which all exist, or at least have existed, and which cannot be confounded, the one with the other, without the most serious inconvenience. At the time of the French Revolution there was a belief that the institutions of small independent towns, such as Sparta and Rome, could be applied to our great nations of thirty or forty millions of souls. In our own day a still graver error is committed: the race is confounded with the nation, and to racial, or rather to linguistic groups, is attributed a sovereignty analogous to that of really existent peoples. Let us attempt to arrive at some precision in these difficult questions, where the least confusion in the sense of words, at the beginning of the discussion, may produce in the end the most fatal errors ....

I

Since the end of the Roman Empire, or rather since the disruption of the Empire of Charlemagne, Western Europe appears to us divided into nations, of which some, at certain epochs, have sought to exercise a supremacy over others, without any lasting success. What Charles V., Louis XIV., and Napoleon I. were unable to do in the past, is hardly likely to be achieved by any one in the future. The establishment of a new Roman Empire, or a new Carlovingian Empire, has become an impossibility. Europe is too deeply divided for an attempt at universal dominion not to provoke, and that quickly, a coalition which would force the ambitious nation to retire within its natural bounds. A species of equilibrium has long been in existence. France, England, German, Russia will still be, in centuries to come, and in spite of the vicissitudes they will have gone through, historic individualities, essential pieces of a chess-board, the squares of which vary unceasingly in importance and greatness, but are never altogether confused ....

What, then, is the characteristic feature of these different states? It consists in the fusion of the populations which compose them. In the countries that we have just enumerated, there is nothing analogous to what you will find in Turkey, where the Turk, the Slav, the Greek, the Armenian, the Arab, the Syrian, and the Kurd are as distinct now as on the day of their conquest. Two essential circumstances contributed to bring this result to pass. First of all is the fact that the Teutonic tribes adopted Christianity as soon as they had had relations of some little duration with the Greek and Latin peoples. When conqueror and conquered are of the same religion, or rather when the conqueror adopts the religion of the conquered, the Turkish system, the absolute distinction of men according to their respective faiths, can no longer be possible. The second circumstance was the conquerors' forgetfulness of their own language. The grandsons of Clovis, of Alaric, of Gondebaud, of Alboin, and of Rollo were already speaking Romance. This fact was itself the consequence of another important peculiarity, namely, that the Franks, the Burgundians, the Goths, the Lombards, and the Normans had very few women of their own race with them. For several generations the chiefs espoused only Teutonic women; but their concubines were Latin, the nurses of their children were Latin; the whole tribe married Latin women. And so it was that the *Lingua Francica* and the *Lingua Gothica* had a very short existence, after the settlement of the Franks and the Goths in Roman territories. The same was not the case in England, for there can be no doubt that the Anglo-Saxon invaders had women with them; the ancient British population took to flight; and, moreover, Latin was no longer dominant in Britain, indeed it had never been so. Even if Gaulish had been generally spoken in Gaul in the fifth century, Clovis and his followers would not have abandoned Teutonic for it.

From this ensues the important fact, that in spite of the extreme violence of the manners of the Teutonic invaders, the mould that they imposed became, in the course of centuries, the very mould of the nation. France, very legitimately, came to be the name of a country into which only an imperceptible minority of Franks had entered. In the tenth century, in the earliest *Chansons de Geste*, which are such a perfect mirror of the spirit of the age, all the inhabitants of France are Frenchmen. The idea of a difference of races in the population of France, that is so apparent in Gregory of Tours, is not present to any extent in the French writers and poets, posterior to Hugh Capet. The difference between noble and serf is as accentuated as it well can be; but in no respect is the difference an ethnical one; it is a difference in courage, in habits, and in hereditarily transmitted education. The idea, that the beginning of it all may be a conquest, does not occur to anybody. The fictitious theories, according to which nobility owed its origin to privilege, conferred by the king for great services rendered to the state, to such an extent that all nobility is an acquisition, were established as a dogma in the thirteenth century. The same thing was the sequel of nearly all the Norman conquests. At the end of one or two generations, the Norman invaders were no longer to be distinguished from the rest of the population. Their influence had not been the less profound; to the conquered land they had given a nobility, warlike habits, and a patriotism hitherto unexistent.

Forgetfulness, and I shall even say historical error, form an essential factor in the creation of a nation; and thus it is that the progress of historical studies may often be dangerous to the nationality. Historical research, in fact, brings back to light the deeds of violence that have taken place at the commencement of all political formations, even of those the consequences of which have been most beneficial. Unity is ever achieved by brutality. The union of Northern and Southern France was the result of an extermination, and of a reign of terror that lasted for nearly a hundred years. The king of France who was, if I may say so, the ideal type of a secular crystalliser, the king of France who made the most perfect national unity in existence, lost his prestige when seen at too close a distance. The nation that he had formed cursed him; and to-day the knowledge of what he was worth, and what he did, belongs only to the cultured.

It is by contrast that these great laws of the history of Western Europe become apparent. In the undertaking which the King of France, in part by his tyranny, in part by his justice, achieved so admirably, many countries came to disaster. Under the crown of St. Stephen, Magyars and Slavs had remained as distinct as they were eight hundred years ago. Far from combining the different elements in its dominions, the house of Hapsburg has held them apart, and often opposed to one another. In Bohemia the Czech element and the German element are superimposed like oil and water in a glass. The Turkish policy of separation of nationalities according to religion has had much graver results. It has brought about the ruin of the East. Take a town like Smyrna or Salonica; you will find there five or six communities, each with its own memories, and possessing among them scarcely anything in common. But the essence of a nation is, that all its individual members should have many things in common; and also, that all of them should hold many things in oblivion. No French citizen knows whether he is a Burgundian, an Alan, or a Visigoth; every French citizen ought to have forgotten St. Bartholomew, and the massacres of the South in the thirteenth century. There are not ten families in France able to furnish proof of a French origin; and yet, even if such proof were given, it would be essentially defective, in consequence of a thousand unknown crosses, capable of deranging all genealogical systems.

The modern nation is then the historical result of a series of events, converging in the same direction. Sometimes unity had been achieved by a dynasty, as in the case of France; sometimes by the direct will of the provinces, as in the case of Holland, Switzerland, and Belgium; sometimes by a general feeling slowly vanquishing the caprices of feudality, as in the case of Italy and Germany. But a profound *raison d'être* has always governed these formations. The principles in such cases come to light in the most unexpected ways. In our own times we have seen Italy united by her defeats, and Turkey destroyed by her victories. Every defeat advanced the cause of Italy, every victory was a loss to Turkey; for Italy is a nation, Turkey, outside Asia Minor, is not. It is the glory of France to have proclaimed by the French Revolution that a nation exists by itself. We ought not to complain because we find ourselves imitated. Ours is the principle of nations. But what then is a nation? Why is Holland a nation, while Hanover or the Grandy Duchy of Parma is not? How does France persist in being a nation, when the principle which created her has disappeared? How is Switzerland, with three languages, two religions, and three or four races, a nation, while Tuscany, for example, which is homogeneous, is not? Why is Austria a state and not a nation? In what respect does the principle of nationality differ from the principle of races? These are the points upon which a reflective mind must be fixed, if it is to find a satisfactory solution ....

II

In the opinion of certain political theorists a nation is, before all else, a dynasty representing an ancient conquest, a conquest first accepted and then forgotten by the mass of the people. According to the politicians of whom I speak, the grouping of provinces affected by a dynasty, by its ways, by its marriages, or by its treaties, comes to an end with the dynasty which has formed it. It is very true that the majority of modern nations owe their existence to a family of feudal origin, which contracted a marriage with the soil, and was in some measure a nucleus of centralisation. There was nothing natural or necessary about the boundaries of France in 1789. The large zone that the house of Capet added to the narrow limits of the Treaty of Verdun, was in every sense the personal acquisition of that house. At the time when the annexations were made, there was no idea of natural frontiers, or of the rights of nations, or of the will of the provinces. The union of England, Ireland, and Scotland was in like manner a dynastic act. The reason for Italy delaying so long in becoming a nation was that no one of her numerous reigning houses, before the present century, made itself the centre of unity. And it is a strange thing that it is from the obscure island of Sardinia, from territory scarcely Italian, that she has taken a royal title. Holland, which created herself by an act of heroic resolution, has nevertheless contracted a marriage with the house of Orange, and would run real dangers on the day of that union's being compromised.

But is such a law as this absolute? Certainly not. Switzerland and the United States, conglomerations formed by successive additions, have no dynastic base. I shall not discuss the question with regard to France. It would be necessary to have the secret of the future. Let us only say that the great royal house of France had been highly national, that, on the morrow of its fall, the nation was able to stand without its support. And then the eighteenth century had changed everything. Man had returned, after centuries of abasement, to the old spirit, to self-respect, to the idea of his rights. The words "country" and "citizen" had resumed their significance. Thus it was that the boldest operation ever attempted in history was accomplished—an operation which might be compared to what in physiology would be the gift of life and its first identity, to a body from which head and heart had been removed.

It must then be admitted that a nation can exist without a dynastic principle; and even that nations formed by dynasties can separate themselves from them without, for that reason, ceasing to exist. The old principle which held account of no right but that of princes, can no longer be maintained; above the dynastic right there is the national right. On what foundation shall we build up this national right, by what sign shall we know it, from what tangible fact shall we derive it?

(I.) From race, say several with assurance. Artificial divisions resulting from feudality, royal marriages, or diplomatic congresses, are unstable. What does remain firm and fixed is the race of populations. That it is which constitutes right and legitimacy. The Teutonic family, for example, according to this theory, has the right of reclaiming such of its members as are beyond the pale of Teutonism—even when these members do not seek reunion. The right of Teutonism over such a province is greater than the right of the inhabitants of the province over themselves. Thus is created a kind of primordial right, analogous to that of the divine right of kings; for the principle of nations is substituted that of ethnography. This is a very grave error, which, if it became dominant, would cause the ruin of European civilisation. So far as the national principle is just and legitimate, so far is the primordial right of races narrow, and full of danger for true progress ....

Racial considerations have then been for nothing in the constitution of modern nations. France is Celtic, Iberian, Teutonic. Germany is Teutonic, Celtic, and Slavonic. Italy is the country where ethnography is most confused. Gauls, Etruscans, Pelasgians, and Greeks, to say nothing of many other elements, are crossed in an undecipherable medley. The British Isles, as a whole, exhibit a mixture of Celtic and Teutonic blood, the relative proportions of which it is singularly difficult to define.

The truth is that there is no pure race; and that making politics depend upon ethnographical analysis, is allowing it to be borne upon a chimaera. The most noble countries, England, France, Italy, are those where blood is mingled. Is Germany an exception to this rule? Is she purely Teutonic? What an illusion is this! The whole of the South was once Gaulish. The whole of the East beyond the Elbe is Slavonic. And what, in point of fact, are the parts alleged to be really pure? ...

Racial facts, important as they are in the beginning, have a constant tendency to lose their importance. Human history is essentially different from zoology. Race is not everything, as it is in the case of rodents and felines; and we have no right to go about the world feeling the heads of people, then taking them by the throat, and saying, "You are of our blood; you belong to us!" Beyond anthropological characteristics there are reason, justice, truth, and beauty; and these are the same in all. Nay, this ethnographical politics is not even safe. You exploit it to-day on other people; some day you may see it turned against yourselves. Is it certain that the Germans, who have raised the flag of ethnography so high, will not see the Slavs coming to analyse in their turn the names of villages in Saxony and Lusatia, to seek for traces of the Wilzen or the Obotrites, and to ask account of the massacres and slavery which their ancestors suffered at the hands of the Othos? It is good for all to know how to forget ....

(II.) What we have been saying about race must also be said of language. Language invites re-union; it does not force it. The United States and England, Spanish America and Spain, speak the same languages, and do not form single nations. On the contrary, Switzerland, which owes her stability to the fact that she was founded by the assent of her several parts, counts three or four languages. In man there is something superior to language—will. The will of Switzerland to be united, in spite of the variety of her languages, is a much more important fact than a similarity of language, often obtained by persecution.

It is an honourable fact for France, that she has never sought to procure unity of speech by measures of coercion. Can we not have the same feelings and thoughts, and love the same things in different languages? We were speaking just now of the inconvenience of making international politics depend on ethnography. There would not be less in making politics depend on comparative philology. Let us allow the fullest liberty of discussion to these interesting studies; do not let us mingle them with that which would affect their serenity. The political importance attached to languages results from the way in which they are regarded as signs of race. Nothing can be more incorrect. Prussia, where nothing but German is now spoken, spoke Slavonic a few centuries ago; Wales speaks English; Gaul and Spain speak the primitive idiom of Alba Longa; Egypt speaks Arabic; indeed, examples are innumerable. Even at the beginning similarity of speech did not imply similarity of race. Let us take the proto-Aryan or proto-Semitic tribe; there were to be found slaves accustomed to speak the same language as their masters; but nevertheless the slave was then very often of a different race from that of his master. Let us repeat it; these classifications of the Indo-European, Semitic, and other tongues, created with such admirable sagacity by comparative philology, do not coincide with the classifications of anthropology. Languages are historical formations, which give but little indication of the blood of those who speak them; and, in any case, cannot enchain human liberty, when there is a question of determining the family with which we unite ourselves for life and death ....

(III.) Nor can religion offer a sufficient basis for the establishment of a modern nationality. In the beginning religion was essential to the very existence of the social group. The social group was an extension of the family. Religious rites were family rites. The Athenian religion was the cult of Athens itself, of its mythical founders, of its laws and customs. It implied no dogmatic theology. This religion was in every sense of the term a State religion. If any one refused to practise it, he was no longer an Athenian. In reality it was the worship of the personified Acropolis. To swear on the altar of Agraulos was to take an oath to die for one's country. This religion was the equivalent of what drawing lots for military service, or the cult of the flag, is among us. To refuse to participate in such a worship was like a refusal of military service in our modern societies. It was a declaration that one was not an Athenian. From another point of view, it is clear that such a religion had no force for any one who was not an Athenian; and thus no proselytism was exercised to compel aliens to accept it. The slaves in Athens did not practice it ....

What was the right at Sparta and Athens was already no longer so in the kingdoms that originated in Alexander's conquest; above all, was no longer right in the Roman Empire. The persecutions of Antiochus Epiphanes, for the purpose of forcing the worship of the Olympian Jupiter on the East, those of the Roman Empire for the purpose of keeping up a pseudo-State religion, were a mistake, a crime, a veritable absurdity. In our own days the position is perfectly clear. No longer are there masses of people professing a uniform belief. Every one believes and practises after his own fashion, what he can, as he pleases. The state-religion is a thing of the past. One can be a Frenchman, an Englishman, or a German; and at the same time be a Catholic, a Protestant, or a Jew, or else be of no creed at all. Religion has become a matter for the individual; it affects the individual's conscience alone. The division of nations into Catholic and Protestant no longer exists. Religion, which fifty-two years ago was so considerable an element in the formation of Belgium, retains all its importance in the spiritual jurisdiction of each man; but it has almost completely disappeared from the considerations that trace the limits of peoples.

(IV.) Community of interests is assuredly a powerful bond between men. But nevertheless can interests suffice to make a nation? I do not believe it. Community of interests makes commercial treaties. There is a sentimental side to nationality; it is at once body and soul; a *Zollverein* [customs union] is not a fatherland.

(V.) Geography, or what we may call natural frontiers, certainly plays a considerable part in the division of nations. Geography is one of the essential factors of history. Rivers have carried races forward; mountains have checked them. The former have favoured, the latter limited, historic movements. Can it be said, however, that, as certain persons believe, the boundaries of a nation are inscribed upon the map; and that this nation has a right to judge what is necessary, to round off certain contours, to reach some mountain or river, to which a species of *a priori* faculty of limitation is ascribed? I know of no doctrine more arbitrary, or more disastrous. By it all violence is justified. First, let us ask, do mountains or rivers constitute these so-called natural frontiers? It is incontestable that mountains separate; but, on the other hand, rivers unite. And then all mountains cannot cut off states. Which are those that separate, and those that do not separate? From Biarritz to the Tornea there is not a single river-estuary which, more than another, has the character of a boundary. Had history required it, the Loire, the Seine, the Meuse, the Elbe, and the Oder would have, to the same extent as the Rhine, that character of a natural frontier which has caused so many infractions of the fundamental right—the will of men. Strategical considerations are mooted. Nothing is absolute; it is clear that many concessions must be made to necessity. But these concessions need not go too far. Otherwise the whole world would claim its military conveniences; and there would be war without end. No, it is no more the land than the race that makes a nation. The land provides the *substratum*, the field of battle and work; man provides the soul. Man is everything in the formation of that sacred thing which we call a people. Nothing of a material nature suffices for it. A nation is a spiritual principle, the result of profound historical complications, a spiritual family, not a group determined by the configuration of the soil. We have now seen what do not suffice for the creation of such a spiritual principle; race, language, interests, religious affinity, geography, military necessities. What more, then, is necessary?

III

A nation is a living soul, a spiritual principle. Two things, which in truth
are but one, constitute this soul, this spiritual principle. One is in the
past, the other in the present. One is the common possession of a rich
heritage of memories; the other is the actual consent, the desire to live
together, the will to preserve worthily the undivided inheritance which
has been handed down. Man does not improvise. The nation, like the
individual, is the outcome of a long past of efforts, and sacrifices, and
devotion. Ancestor-worship is therefore all the more legitimate; for our
ancestors have made us what we are. A heroic past, great men, glory—I
mean glory of the genuine kind—these form the social capital, upon
which a national idea may be founded. To have common glories in the
past, a common will in the present; to have done great things together,
to will to do the like again—such are the essential conditions for the
making of a people. We love in proportion to the sacrifices we have
consented to make, to the sufferings we have endured. We love the
house that we have built, and will hand down to our descendants. The
Spartan hymn, "We are what you were; we shall be what you are," is in
its simplicity the national anthem of every land.

In the past an inheritance of glory and regrets to be shared, in the
future a like ideal to be realised; to have suffered, and rejoiced, and
hoped together; all these things are worth more than custom-houses in
common, and frontiers in accordance with strategical ideas; all these can
be understood in spite of diversities of race and language. I said just now,
"to have suffered together," for indeed suffering in common is a greater
bond of union than joy. As regards national memories, mournings are
worth more than triumphs; for they impose duties, they demand
common effort.

A nation is then a great solidarity, constituted by the sentiment of
the sacrifices that its citizens have made, and of those that they feel
prepared to make once more. It implies a past; but it is summed up in
the present by a tangible fact—consent, the clearly expressed desire to
live a common life. A nation's existence is—if you will pardon the
metaphor—a daily plebiscite, as the individual's existence is a perpetual
affirmation of life. I know very well that this is less metaphysical than
divine right, less brutal than pseudo-historic right. In the order of ideas
that I submit to you, a nation has no more right than a king to say to a
province, "Thou art mine; I take thee unto myself." For us, a province
means its inhabitants; and if any one has a right to be consulted in such
an affair, it is the inhabitants. A nation never favours its true interests
when it annexes or retains a country, regardless of the latter's wishes.
The will of nations is then the only legitimate criterion; and to it we
must always return ....

The nations are not something eternal. They have had their beginnings, they shall have their end. A European confederation will probably take their place. But such is not the law of the age in which we live. At the present hour, the existence of nations is good, even necessary. Their existence is the guarantee of liberty, which would be lost if the world had but one law and one master.

By their diverse and often antagonistic faculties, the nations take part in the common work of civilisation; each brings a note to that great chorus of humanity, which in sum is the highest ideal reality to which we attain. Isolated, their parts are feeble. I often tell myself that an individual who should have the faults regarded by nations as good qualities, who should feed himself with vain glory, who should be in the same way jealous, egoistical, and quarrelsome, who should be able to bear nothing without drawing the sword, would be the most unsupportable of men. But all these discords of detail disappear in the mass. Poor humanity, how much thou hast suffered! How many trials await thee still! May the spirit of wisdom be thy guide, and preserve thee from the countless perils with which thy path is sown!

But to resume: man is neither enslaved by his race, nor by his language, nor by his religion, nor by the course of rivers, nor by the direction of mountain ranges. A great aggregation of men, sane of mind, and warm of heart, creates a moral consciousness, which is called a nation. So far as this moral consciousness proves its strength, through the sacrifices exacted by the individual's abdication for the good of the community, it is legitimate and has a right to exist. If doubts arise concerning frontiers, consult the populations in dispute. They have a very good right to have a voice in the matter. This no doubt will bring a smile to the transcendentalists of politics, those infallible beings who pass their lives in self-deception, and from the height of their superior principles look down in pity upon our modest views. "Consult the populations, indeed! What artlessness! These are the pitiful French ideas, which would replace diplomacy and war by an infantine simplicity." Let us wait; let us suffer the reign of the transcendentalists to pass away; let us know how to submit to the disdain of the strong. It may be that after much unfruitful groping the world will return to our modest empirical solutions. At certain times, the way to be right in the future consists in knowing how to resign ourselves to being out of the fashion in the present.

5

THE NATION-STATE

"Nation," "state," and "nation-state" are notoriously slippery terms; although they are used interchangeably sometimes, important differences of meaning are often implied in the choice of word. In Reading 5, Bert Rockman focuses on the concept of the state. He suggests two ways of viewing the state. In terms of state power, or sovereignty, the state's role in society may be extensive, or it may be limited. Over the past 40 years, for example, state activities increased significantly, whereas today they are diminishing. However, the concept of the state is also seen as an analytical tool, a way of analyzing society-state relations. In their analysis today, political scientists certainly have reintroduced the state as a significant factor in modern politics. Rockman provides three different ways of conceptualizing the state, suggesting that they offer a more concrete way of understanding the role of what is often seen as a rather abstract idea.

Bert Rockman is a professor of political science at the University of Pittsburgh, Pennsylvania. The following reading is taken from his "Minding the State—or a State of Mind? Issues in Comparative Conceptualization of the State," from The Elusive State: International and Comparative Perspectives, *edited by James A. Caporaso, Gage Publications, 1989.*

• • • • • • • •

THE RESURGENT (YET POSSIBLY RECEDING) STATE

It is ironic that just as liberal neoclassical economics has experienced a tremendous resurgence in the 1980s, the concept of the state, also, has experienced a spectacular renewal in its centrality to political theory. While state activities are bring trimmed or at least reordered, the state itself has burgeoned as an organizing concept in the analysis of society. "Bringing the state back in" and "state-centered theory" have been the marching themes of scholars seeking to understand the intricate and causally ambiguous connections between public authority and private interest—or, in language more apt to be employed by aficionados of the concept, the relations between the state and civil society ....

Much of the contemporary resurgence of the state in political theory obviously is constructed around the connections between the organization of state authority and the organization of society, most especially the organization of collective action—social classes, the organization and mobilization of labor, the organization and mobilization of capital, and other forms of interest expression ....

CONCEPTIONS OF THE STATE

There are three conceptions of the state that I want to emphasize in the remainder of this paper that I think help address the issue of state capability. These are: (1) the role of the state as an authoritative policy-making system (the decision-making state); (2) the role of the state as a provider of collective and distributional goods (the production state); and (3) the role of the state as a repository, creator, and mediator of societal interests (the intermediary state). There is inherently some spillover in the reality of these state functions. The relationship between the first and third functions of the state is especially notable because the organization of state authority also influences the organization of private interests (Wilson, 1976). And, each of these conceptions, in turn, is related to how it is the state supplies goods—and to whom (Malloy & Parodi, 1988).

The first conception of the state, which Karl Deutsch (1986) calls the enforcement/decision state, has to do with the internal configuration of authority relations between the agents of the state—its decision-making capability. This capability we may think of as the political capability of the state, and it most obviously reflects the formal constitutional order and the organization of institutions and behavior that develops around it. Richard Rose's article (1969), on "The Variability of Party Government," illustrates handsomely how structures for the mobilization of political capacity can differ.

It is often believed, if not necessarily conclusively shown, that the greater the structural unity in the state apparatus for making decisions, the more conclusive such decisions will be for the society. Whether or not this proposition is true is debatable, but its logic is twofold: (1) a unified state purportedly can arrive at decisions more rapidly; and (2) a unified state also will have fewer possibilities for the losers in any given situation to appeal the decision (Rockman, 1988). In this respect, Wilsford (1988) notes that the French state enjoys particular tactical advantages and yet, precisely because opportunities for institutional appeal are limited, disagreement with decisions frequently leads to street protests.

The constituted structures of political authority are a better place to begin than to end, however. For these provide a frame for the exercise of political authority, but the frame itself lacks a dynamic. For as Malloy and Parodi (1988) aptly point out "One task in the analysis of statecraft is to chart how the capacity moves over time and develop explanations as to how and why it is concentrated or dispersed, where it is lodged, the consequences of particular patterns, etc." (1988: 5).

The second conception of the state has to do with its commitments—its scope, functions, size, activities, and the way these are organized. It is precisely this aspect of the state that is at the heart of the belief that the state is receding; that is, the notion that the scope of the state in producing societal goods has reached an upper limit. The issue of the size of the state and the activities it is engaged in is thought to be, in some sense, also related to the scope of the state. Free market liberals, for instance, have seen in the expansion of state production insidious encroachments on the sphere of society by the state. And certainly, states with centrally controlled economies also usually have centrally controlled organizations reputing to speak for a conflictless (and thus libertyless) society. A distinctly alternate perception sees the expansion of state policies as proliferating social organizations, which then create new interdependencies between state and society, and ultimately shift decision capacity from its initial point of origin (Malloy & Parodi, 1988). This particular condition is often characterized as the bloated state—big, but incapable of system-wide direction.

Yet a small state also can be a powerful one if it is able to monopolize the instruments of coercion—not merely legally, but actually. The hangman's noose may be the major production function of a state with few other goods to produce. (One might consider Haiti, for example.) But that is entirely sufficient to make for a powerful state.

The third conception of the state, the intermediary function, defines the bargaining and control milieu for state/society relations. There are interlocking, yet causally ambiguous, linkages between the first two functions of the state and this third one. Only certain arrangements of political authority appear to be compatible with a system-wide organization of societal interests, and, thus, can accommodate system-wide bargaining such as that posed in the model of societal corporatism. These organizational relationships also can influence the character of the state's production functions—how, for example, it is that social policy is organized; what instruments are available for forging "social contracts" and for managing the economy (Katzenstein, 1985; Hall, 1986); or even what incentives exist to oversupply public goods (Niskanen, 1971; Fiorina, 1977). These state/societal relationships can be shaped and sometimes created, in turn, by the production functions of the state, as Theodore Lowi (1972) noted in setting forth his famous typology of policies and politics ....

THE DECISION-MAKING STATE

How diffuse or concentrated is the decision-making capability of the state? This is an important question (at least constitution makers think so), but it is not equivalent to asking what is the power of the state to mold society, or even how large and varied is the state's production function. Obviously, in the extreme ranges, a state in which power is very concentrated (Stalinism, for instance) will have great impact over society if in no other way than in its repressive functions. Alternatively, a state in which the power to decide is rampantly diffused risks the prospect of stalemate and anarchy. Raymond Aron (1950: 143) observed that unity in the rulership of the state created large dangers to the maintenance of civil freedom, whereas the absence of such unity brought risks to the maintenance of the state itself.

While the relative scope and penetration of the state into society and its ability to resist particular types of societal pressures may be connected to the political or decision-making capacities of the state, the issue here is how clearly can power be mobilized within government? What, in other words, are the relevant relations between the constituted agents of the state?

From a formal standpoint, two obvious dimensions define relationships between agents of the state. The first is the territorial or spatial dimension of power resources; the second is the interinstitutional and intrainstitutional organization of power. The most obvious way of thinking about the vertical arrangement of power is the federalism/unitary state distinction. In theory, the former creates diversity while the latter imposes uniformity. Certainly, the potential for different units of government to be operating at cross-purposes is considerably greater under federal than unitary systems.

In the first years of the Reagan administration in the U.S., for instance, it busily cut taxes and social programs administered by the Federal government. The tax cuts, in part, were done for macroeconomic reasons (so-called supply-side economics) but also because of Reagan's belief that the extractive arm of government should be lessened at all levels. Many states, in fact, faced dramatic cuts in programs maintained by Federal assistance, and, in the face of this, raised taxes. Unfortunately, there is no clear evidence on the macroeconomic effects of these counteractions for the supply-side strategy of freeing capital from the grasp of government, but it is clear that the President's ideological objectives of reducing government at all levels were not completely satisfied.

By way of contrast, in the British unitary state the Thatcher government has reached down into local government to uproot councils whose behavior struck the Prime Minster as unruly, frivolous, and radical (Jones, 1988) ....

At face value, the mechanisms for concerted action are assuredly weaker in federal than in unitary systems, and they are especially so in the American system of federalism where the American constitution provides for all nonspecified powers to reside at the state level (the so-called Doctrine of Residual Powers). The great growth in public employment in the United States also throughout recent decades has been at the state and local levels rather than the Federal government. Peters (1985) shows, for example, that during a 30-year period (1952–82), the percentage of government employees at the Federal level dropped from 57% of the total in 1952 to a mere 24% in 1982. Some of this decrease at the Federal level is reflected in the conversion of a previously direct and labor-intensive function (postal services) to a public corporation.

Ultimately, though, the key resource commanded by the center is much less its percentage of state employment or even its percentage of the total tax take (though the latter is not to be discounted) than it is the ability to make national policy. There is no doubt that this has something to do with the leverage that local or regional governments can exert, and also with the institutions at the national level through which interests are articulated.

Whatever else can be said about the state, it is clear that it is not a unified entity (Allison, 1969). Even when all of the bulk of policy capacity is lodged in instrumentalities of the state, such capacity may be dispersed among its various instrumentalities in such a way as to checkmate decisional power (Malloy & Parodi, 1988). The state, in other words, almost never is a coherent and encompassing unit of action. Instead, the governing bodies and authorities of the state represent a number of units of action—their relative autonomy or interdependence or dependence being shaped by constitutional law. Yet, actual behavior in the struggle between units of government to gain needed resources or fair share allotments, or simply to acquire freedom of action often rests upon factors outside of the purely legal domain, for example, elite networks, salient constituencies or interest organizations, entrepreneurial skills, and the principal values of the political culture ....

In these respects, it appears to be the case that the government of the British state has great decision-making or political capacity, yet relatively modest steering or guidance capacity toward society overall. Writing, for example, in the context of environmental and industrial regulatory policies in Britain, David Vogel (1986) observes that "The government is unable to implement policies in either area without securing the consent and cooperation of the companies affected by their decisions" (1986:284). In other words, while central authority in British government "is more powerful than that of any other democracy ..., the relative power of the British state vis-à-vis British society is sharply limited" (1986:287).

The American system of dispersing political authority is nearly at the other extreme to the British case. The American system is purposefully designed as a form of government to be in perpetual conflict with itself. The design of American political structure is to inhibit the possibilities for decision making in the absence of transinstitutional agreements. The nature of British political organization, alternatively, reinforces centrism. American political organization, however, has made authority even more diffuse in the United States. Lowi points out that American political parties represent a case of incomplete development; their prime organizational moment (outside of the legislative body) came in the latter part of the nineteenth and early twentieth centuries when American politics was denationalized and the influx of new populations into urban centers made the party organizations into little more than effective patronage dispensing machines. Thus, American political organization traditionally has catered to the already ample centrifugal tendencies of American government. Over the years, these tendencies changed from local and often corrupt mechanisms of political control to providing virtually no mechanisms for such control. The advent of mass political processes in the selection of a party's candidates to stand for office has produced an especially individualistic form of politics. This often exacerbates the problem of decision making in American government, by promoting the independence of officeholders, and makes resisting constituent and group pressures on the part of officeholders particularly difficult ....

... Even within this limitation, the structure of relations between the agents of the state are as much influenced by the organization of informal organizations (such as parties) that have wrapped themselves around the state as they are a product of the formally constituted structures. The joint effect of both formal and informal organizational structures still does not explain many of the important ways in which the state connects to society. The sociocultural elements of politics, the implicit and tacit understandings that permeate its operations, as well as the historical development of social organization are essential ingredients for comprehending the forms this connection takes. Yet, a theory of incentives also is necessary for understanding the strategic choices that are available in these relations.

THE PRODUCTION STATE

One of the major themes about the state emanating particularly from the literature of the 1970s and early 1980s is that of the *overburdened state*. Following upon the great prosperity of the 1960s in Western Europe and the expansion of programs and public expenditure commitments made then, the economic stagflation that arose by the end of the 1970s coincided with a realization that an ever more vast set of spending pressures on governments would be created by the logic of these expanded commitments and of the demographic tendencies spurring the demand for pensions and medical care.

Three sets of explanations for this alleged overburden can be readily identified. Behind at least two of them is the idea that the state oversupplies public goods because of systematic biases in the way in which demands for these goods are represented in the polity.

At the most microcosmic level Niskanen's effort (1971) to apply the theory of the firm to the bureau stipulates that public goods are oversupplied because both their supply and the demand for them are monopolized. This monopoly conceals a true aggregate demand function that, if known, would constrain supply. Thus, a noncompetitive bureau has incentives to maximize its budget resources, and clientele groups with intense preferences for the goods the bureau supplies demand their production while diverting their cost onto the general public ....

A rather different kind of argument, represented in the early literature on "overload," emphasized the declining capabilities for governance as more and more interests acquired a stake in public policy. Whereas the theory of oversupply emphasizes the symbiotic relationship (stemming from matched incentives) between subgovernmental elites and interest group elites, the syndrome of "overload" explanations stresses the role of public demand. To put it in slightly different language, *oversupply* is a supply-side argument, where *overload* is a demand-side argument. The logic of demand-side politics, in this view, stemmed from an apparently insatiable appetite for the supply of public goods that would outstrip the capacity of governments to generate policies with short-term costs ....

In any event, the clear supposition behind this literature and the concern it expresses for the legitimacy of public authority is that more demands are being put on government than governments can deliver. Given the constraints of democratic politics, more expenditure demands are made on government than governments are willing to pay for. This is presumably because citizens are tax minimizers and politicians are vote maximizers.

Yet a third emphasis on the "overburdened state," though not necessarily inconsistent with the other two, focuses on the steady accretion of past commitments as being chiefly responsible for the growth in public expenditure (Rose & Peters, 1978; Rose, 1984b). The truly large and accumulating expenditures with nearly untouchable political status are principally the consequence of relatively early commitments to social welfare, such as pensions and medical care which, however, also were adjusted through the 1970s. Left undisturbed, the inertial effects of these commitments produce what Rose and Peters (1979) call the *juggernaut of incrementalism*.

The consequences of all of these notions about the overburdened state is that in the end the oversupply of public goods and the undersupply of public authority and state capacity will lead either to an erosion in standards of living and, hence, a crisis of legitimacy or, in the shorter term, a crisis of capital accumulation (O'Connor, 1973). Depending upon how indebtedness is financed, the state may be rendered increasingly vulnerable to international capital flows or, at considerable political cost, must impose policies of domestic austerity ....

A further conception of the production function of the state, emphasizing the role of statecraft, is that of the *expert state*. Expertise presumably is agnostic about ideological presuppositions. It may be interventionist or market focused, but state guidance on the part of a technocratic elite with accessibility to political and economic power is the essential characteristic of the expert state. The administrative elites in France (Suleiman, 1974; 1978), Japan (Johnston, 1975; 1982), and Sweden (Anton, Linde, & Melbourn, 1973), among others, are reputed to be a strategically located elite of this sort ....

This struggle between the convoluted organization of the production functions of the state and its financial management is frequently defined in terms of a struggle between the whole and the parts of government. Increasingly, in times of fiscal stress (which are most times), the political leadership at the center identifies with the finance officer rather than the production line, whereas the political constituencies upon whom the central leadership depends identify with the production functions rather than their financial management ....

The irony here is that the greater the expanse of state functions, the greater the sprawl of its administrative apparatus, thus, the greater its proliferation of societal constituents, and the less able the state is to impose (except through financial management) a unified course or vision. An intriguing implication of this is that the state can retain such a unity only when its functions are relatively limited to the production of collective goods. If that is the case, then the irony is complete. For then, the real state-builders appear to be named Thatcher and Reagan, each of whom, but especially Thatcher, is devoted to a leaner, yet morally purposeful state.

THE INTERMEDIARY STATE

The major focus of state-centered theory lies in the relationship between the organizations and institutions of the state and those of society. The prevailing supposition of state-centered theory is that state organization influences the aggregation of social interests.

These relationships, however, Peter Hall (1986) and Esping-Andersen (1985) point out, are not static. When existing equilibria become unsatisfactory, the regime will seek to manipulate or counter the organization of relevant social aggregates. For example, the Reagan administration in 1981 successfully altered funding formulas of health and other assistance programs so as to decentralize the discretion for decision-making. One key objective was to dissipate the influence of the interests who were organized around the existing administration of these programs.

Yet the organization of social aggregates (especially as peak organizations) also is held together by some pattern of marginal benefit to the members. When such benefits decline, the stability of existing organization also comes under pressure. Thus, there is a dual dynamic—an internal organizational one, and one that exists between the organization of the state and the social aggregates ....

The link between state authority and social fabric, however, is frequently so tightly woven that it is difficult to extricate clear causal patterns. Indeed, the weave more nearly has the quality of a seamless web. The problem, as Peter Hall correctly argues, is that:

> The capacities of the state to implement a program tend to depend as much on the configuration of the society as of the state .... The state appears as a network of institutions, deeply embedded within a

constellation of ancillary institutions associated with society and the economic system (1986, 17) ....

The shape of the state and its mechanisms for decision making clearly influence the structure and organization of societal interests. Not surprisingly, the American system which is predicated on the individualistic and institutionalized notion of countering ambition with ambition makes it difficult to organize cooperation system-wide and, thus, ultimately makes it easier to develop narrow distributional coalitions. These subgovernmental coalitions both reinforce the problem of aggregating decisions while potentially increasing the aggregative costs for the society of indecision.

To the extent that the central leadership of the state is able to shape the bargaining game, its interests lie in depoliticizing it. One of the elements of that strategy is the creation of large aggregates to displace a larger number of smaller ones so as to absorb parochial and less manageable interests into larger and presumably more manageable national ones. The latter condition conduces to providing the state leadership with more tools for the management of the economy and public finance. When, however, the institutions of the state and the organization of society are noncentralized and relatively mature (as in the United States), the prospects for producing this level of aggregation are highly improbable ....

CONCLUSION

The state is a concept that is simultaneously alluring and protean. Part of its allure apparently rests on its protean character—the ability to be molded into whatever shape the analyst finds useful. Of the various ways in which the state can be conceptualized, I have focused in this paper on three: (1) the decision-making state; (2) the production state; and (3) the intermediary state. These conceptualizations of the state are all relevant to the even broader, if highly ambiguous, notion of state capacity.

Characterizing the state as a decisional entity helps us to focus on the bargaining (and command) relationships that exist among its officers. It helps to define the terms of the "game" that the agents of the state play. Whether the apparatus of the state has a center or not can suggest to us how complicated these bargains may be. They do not necessarily tell us how the state may influence society, but they may tell us how society organizes to try to influence the state.

Describing the state in the context of its production functions helps us to focus on its assets and liabilities and problems of liquidity. It also can lead us to focus on how these production functions are organized so as to enable a clearer understanding of the state as both decisional entity and as intermediary with society. The organization of these production functions, in fact, is very much linked to the decisional structure of the state and the organization of society. Rationalization of the production function typically is associated with centristic control which clearly represents a vital means of building state authority. Today, the financial management function seems to be ascendant, and its rationalization dictates both growing centrism within the state apparatus and growing insulation from demand-oriented societal groups.

Finally, analysis of the intermediary functions of the state necessarily leads us to focus on the organization of society and the opportunities thus given to state authorities to steer society. It is helpful to look at these relations in the form of a dynamic equilibrium. Thus, we need to know the terms of the "game" played between the state authorities and significant social aggregates. These, in turn, also help us to understand how some state actors must interact with others—for example, whether or not, and to what extent, public investment is dependent on private financial markets (Sbragia, 1986).

Overall, the state lacks uniqueness as a concept because it assumes so many definitions. It lacks, therefore, a universalized specificity of meaning. Rather, its meaning and utility appear to derive from different cultural, political, and developmental traditions. Particularly in Latin traditions, the state takes on the Hegelian conception of being the highest expression of the community over whom its authority is exercised. In theory, if not reality, this provides the logic for the so-called autonomous state, which expresses a unity that is greater than the sum of the constituent parts of the society it governs ....

My own view as to why the state has been theoretically resurgent (even as it has in certain regards mildly receded) is that it brings together the most important macrolevel connections of the polity, the society, and the economy, which cannot be adequately analyzed in isolation from one another. The monopoly of legal authority gives the state (and statesmen) the responsibility for the maintenance of social peace and the production of collective goods. These, of course, may be operationalized in wildly different ways—the peace may be kept by the policeman's truncheon or it may be kept through the so-called social contract. The peace may be seen by Marxists as a means for the maintenance of a dominant (if not always ruling) class. Or it may be seen by social integration theorists, such as Talcott Parsons, as the most extraordinary outcome of complex social processes.

The state, above all, provides a means for the study of statecraft within a given constellation of institutional and interest formations and public cultures. Statecraft, in this conception, is more than the leadership of single individuals. It does and certainly must focus attention on the means of building political support within the state apparatus itself (the decision-making state), but also must focus on the manipulations between the state (and its internal elements) and social aggregates (the intermediating state). Above all, it seems to me that a theory of the state also must provide for a dynamic—that is, a theory of equilibrium and disequilibrium. Ironically, both Marxist and the neoliberal market theorists share, at one level, similar theoretical premises about the internal contradictions of the capitalist-welfare state: the problem of its liquidity and its legitimation ....

Within the context, then, of a theoretical dynamic that provides for an inner logic of change, statecraft is vital. The role of statecraft is to manipulate the equilibrium to ensure (for a time) a favorable balance on behalf of the fundamental functions of the state. To achieve this, bargains are made with elements of civil society. From the perspective of the steering capacity of the state, some of these bargains are Machiavellian; others, it is later discovered, are Faustian.

REFERENCES

Allison, G. T. (1969). Conceptual models and the Cuban missile crisis. *American Political Science Review, 63* (September), 689–718.

Anton, T. J., Linde, C., and Melbourne, A. (1973). Bureaucrats in politics: A profile of the Swedish administrative elite. *Canadian Public Administration, 16,* 627–651.

Aron, R. (1950). Social structure and the ruling class. *British Journal of Sociology* (Parts 1 and 2), *1* (March and June), 1–16; 126–143.

Deutsch, K. W. (1986). State functions and the future of the state. *International Political Science Review, 7* (2), 209–222.

Esping-Andersen, G. (1985). *Politics against markets: The social democratic road to power.* Princeton, NJ: Princeton University Press.

Fiorina, M. P. (1977). *Congress: Keystone of the Washington establishment.* New Haven, CT: Yale University Press.

Hall, P. (1986). *Governing the economy: The economics of state intervention in Britain and France.* New York: Oxford University Press.

Johnson, C. (1975). Japan: Who governs? An essay on official bureaucracy. *Journal of Japanese Studies, 2* (Autumn), 1–28.

Jones, G. (1988). The crisis in British central-local government relationships. *Governance, 1* (April), 162–183.

Katzenstein, P. (1985). *Small states in world markets: Industrial policy in Europe.* Ithaca, NY: Cornell University Press.

Lowi, T. J. (1972). Four systems of policy, politics and choice. *Public Administration Review, 32* (July/August), 298–310.

Malloy, J. M. & Parodi, C. A. (1988). *Statecraft, social policy and regime transition in Brazil.* Paper presented at the 14th International Congress of the Latin American Studies Association, New Orleans, Louisiana.

Niskanen, W. A., Jr. (1971). *Bureaucracy and representative government.* Chicago: Aldine-Atherton.

O'Connor, J. (1973). *The fiscal crisis of the state.* New York: St. Martin's Press.

Peters, B. G. (1985). The United States: Absolute change and relative stability, pp. 228–261. In R. Rose (Ed.) *Public employment in western nations.* Cambridge: Cambridge University Press.

_____ (1988). *Centrism without a center—The development of American presidentialism.* Paper prepared for the Roundtable on L'Etat aux Etats Unis, Chantilly, France.

Rose, R. (1969). The variability of party government. *Political Studies, 17* (December), 413–445.

_____ (1984a). *The capacity of the president: A comparative analysis* (Studies in Public Policy, #130). Glasgow: Center for the Study of Public Policy, University of Strathclyde.

Rose, R. & Peters, G. (1978). *Can governments go bankrupt?* New York: Basic Books.

_____ (1979). *The juggernaut of incrementalism* (Studies in Public Policy, #63). Glasgow: Center for the Study of Public Policy, University of Strathclyde.

Sbragia, A. (1979). Not all roads lead to Rome: Local housing policy in the unitary Italian state. *British Journal of Political Science, 9* (July), 315–339.

Suleiman, E. N. (1974). *Politics, power, and bureaucracy in France: The administrative elite.* Princeton, NJ: Princeton University Press.

_____ (1978). *Elites in French society: The politics of survival.* Princeton, NJ: Princeton University Press.

Vogel, D. (1986). *National styles of regulation: Environmental policy in Great Britain and the United States.* Ithaca, NY: Cornell University Press.

Wilsford, D. (1988). Tactical advantages versus administrative heterogeneity: The strengths and the limits of the French state. *Comparative Political Studies, 21* (April), 126–168.

Wilson, J. Q. (1976). The rise of the bureaucratic state, pp. 77–103. In N. Glazer & I. Kristol (Eds.) *The American commonwealth—1976.* New York: Basic Books.

6   THE RULE OF LAW

*T*he Manitoba Act, 1870 *created the province of Manitoba and provided for its admission into the Canadian Confederation; this federal statute is, in effect, the constitution of the province. Its constitutional status was further entrenched by means of the* Constitution Act, 1982, *the appendix to which lists the* Manitoba Act *as one of the parts of Canada's written Constitution.*

Section 23 of the Manitoba Act *provided for a limited degree of bilingualism in the province: "That the English and French languages be common in the Legislature, and in the courts, and that all public documents, as well as all Acts of the Legislature, be published in both languages." Notwithstanding Section 23, the legislature of Manitoba provided in the* Official Language Act, 1890 *that provincial laws should only be printed in English; and from that point on, French publication of statutes ceased.*

In 1979, the Supreme Court of Canada, in the Forest *case, held that the* Official Language Act *was null and void because it conflicted with Section 23 of the* Manitoba Act, *which, as part of the Constitution of Canada, could not be amended by a simple act of the Manitoba legislature. Subsequent to this decision, the Manitoba legislature began to publish new statutes in French, but it did nothing to translate existing provincial laws. Further legal challenges to the validity of statutes that had been passed only in English led the federal cabinet to "refer" this question to the Supreme Court of Canada (the "reference" procedure allows the cabinet to approach the Supreme Court directly for an opinion without having to wait for a lawsuit to run its normal course of appeals).*

In 1985, the Supreme Court held that all Manitoba laws not published in French were invalid, but how was this decision to be implemented? To strike down almost all existing provincial laws in one blow would produce chaos. Laws governing traffic safety, mortgages, contracts, and many other aspects of daily life would suddenly cease to exist. In a piece of interesting and important reasoning, the court held that the enforcement of the Constitution could not be allowed to undermine the rule of law, since the whole point of having a written constitution is to strengthen the law. This case represents the most recent and authoritative statement by the Supreme Court of what the rule of law means.

Below are the relevant excerpts from the Supreme Court's opinion in the Reference re Manitoba Language Rights *[1985] 2 S.C.R. 347, reprinted in the series* Leading Constitutional Decisions of the Supreme Court of Canada *(University of Calgary, Research Unit for Socio-Legal Studies).*

• • • • • • • • •

1. THE PRINCIPLE

The difficulty with the fact that the unilingual Acts of the Legislature of Manitoba must be declared invalid and of no force or effect is that, without going further, a legal vacuum will be created with consequent legal chaos in the Province of Manitoba. The Manitoba Legislature has, since 1890, enacted nearly all of its laws in English only. Thus, to find that the unilingual laws of Manitoba are invalid and of no force or effect would mean that only laws enacted in both French and English *before 1890*, would continue to be valid, and would still be in force even if the law had purportedly been repealed or amended by a post-1890 unilingual statute; matters that were not regulated by laws enacted before 1890 would now be unregulated by law ....

The situation of the various institutions of provincial government would be as follows: the courts, administrative tribunals, public officials, municipal corporations, school boards, professional governing bodies, and all other bodies created by law, to the extent that they derive their existence from or purport to exercise powers conferred by Manitoba laws enacted since 1890 in English only, would be acting without legal authority.

Questions as to the validity of the present composition of the Manitoba Legislature might also be raised. Under the **Manitoba Act, 1870**, the Legislative Assembly was to be composed of 24 members (s. 14), and voters were to be male and over 21 (s. 17). By laws enacted in 1890 in English only, the size of the Legislative Assembly was increased to 57 members, and all persons, both women and men, over 18 were granted the right to vote .... If these laws are invalid and of no force or effect, the present composition of the Manitoba Legislature might be invalid ....

Finally, all legal rights, obligations and other effects which have purportedly arisen under all Acts of the Manitoba Legislature since 1890 would be open to challenge to the extent that their validity and enforceability depends upon a regime of unconstitutional unilingual laws.

In the present case, declaring the Acts of the Legislature of Manitoba invalid and of no force or effect would, without more, undermine the principle of the Rule of Law. The Rule of Law, a fundamental principle of our Constitution, must mean at least two things. First, that the law is supreme over officials of the government as well as private individuals, and thereby preclusive of the influence of arbitrary power. Indeed, it is because of the supremacy of law over the government, as established in s. 23 of the **Manitoba Act, 1870** and s. 52 of the **Constitution Act, 1982**, that this Court must find the unconstitutional laws of Manitoba to be invalid and of no force and effect.

Second, the Rule of Law requires the creation and maintenance of an actual order of positive laws which preserves and embodies the more general principle of normative order. Law and order are indispensable elements of civilized life. "The Rule of Law in this sense implied ... simply the existence of public order." ... As John Locke once said, "A government without laws is, I suppose, a mystery in politics, inconceivable to human capacity and inconsistent with human society." ...

It is this second aspect of the Rule of Law that is of concern in the present situation. The conclusion that the Acts of the Legislature of Manitoba are invalid and of no force or effect means that the positive legal order which has purportedly regulated the affairs of the citizens of Manitoba since 1890 will be destroyed and the rights, obligations and other effects arising under these laws will be invalid and unenforceable. As for the future, since it is reasonable to assume that it will be impossible for the Legislature of Manitoba to rectify *instantaneously* the constitutional defect, the Acts of the Manitoba Legislature will be invalid and of no force or effect until they are translated, re-enacted, printed and published in both languages ....

The constitutional status of the Rule of Law is beyond question. The preamble to the **Constitution Act, 1982** states:

> Whereas Canada is founded upon principles that recognize the supremacy of God and the *rule of law*. [Emphasis added.]

This is explicit recognition that "the rule of law [is] a fundamental postulate of our constitutional structure (*per* Rand. J. **Roncarelli v. Duplessis** [1959] S.C.R. 121, at p. 142). The Rule of Law has always been understood as the very basis of the English Constitution characterising the political institutions of England from the time of the Norman Conquest (A.V. Dicey, **The Law of the Constitution**, 10th ed., 1959, at p. 183). It becomes a postulate of our own constitutional order by way of the preamble to the **Constitution Act 1982**, and its implicit inclusion in the preamble to the **Constitution Act, 1867** by virtue of the words "with a constitution similar in principle to that of the United Kingdom."

Additional to the inclusion of the Rule of Law in the preambles of the **Constitution Acts** of 1867 and 1982, the principle is clearly implicit in the very nature of a Constitution. The Constitution, as the Supreme Law, must be understood as a purposive ordering of social relations providing a basis upon which an actual order of positive laws can be brought into existence. The founders of this nation must have intended, as one of the basic principles of nation building, that Canada be a society of legal order and normative structure: one governed by Rule of Law. While this is not set out in a specific provision, the principle of the Rule of Law is clearly a principle of our Constitution.

This Court cannot take a narrow and literal approach to constitutional interpretation. The jurisprudence of the Court evidences a willingness to supplement textual analysis with historical, contextual and purposive interpretation in order to ascertain the intent of the makers of our Constitution.

The Court has in the past inferred constitutional principles from the preambles to the Constitution Acts and the general object and purpose of the Constitution. In the **Patriation Reference**, *supra*, the Court found the federal principle to be inherent in the Constitution in this way ....

... In other words, in the process of Constitutional adjudication, the Court may have regard to unwritten postulates which form the very foundation of the Constitution of Canada. In the case of the **Patriation Reference**, *supra*, this unwritten postulate was the principle of federalism. In the present case it is the principle of Rule of Law.

2. APPLICATION OF THE PRINCIPLE OF THE RULE OF LAW

It is clear from the above that: (i) the law as stated in s. 23 of the **Manitoba Act, 1870** and s. 52 of the **Constitution Act, 1982** requires that the unilingual Acts of the Manitoba Legislature be declared to be invalid and of no force or effect, and (ii) without more, such a result would violate the Rule of Law. The task the Court faces is to recognize the unconstitutionality of Manitoba's unilingual laws and the Legislature's duty to comply with the "supreme law" of this country, while avoiding a legal vacuum in Manitoba and ensuring the continuity of the Rule of Law.

A number of the parties and interveners have suggested that the Court declare the unilingual Acts of the Manitoba legislature to be invalid and of no force or effect and leave it at that, relying on the legislatures to work out a constitutional amendment. This approach because it would rely on a future and uncertain event, would be inappropriate. A declaration that the laws of Manitoba are invalid and of no legal force or effect would deprive Manitoba of its legal order and cause a transgression of the Rule of Law. For the Court to allow such a situation to arise and fail to resolve it would be an abdication of its responsibility as protector and preserver of the Constitution.

Other solutions suggested by the parties and interveners are equally unsatisfactory. Counsel for the Attorney General of Manitoba argues that the linguistic rights guaranteed by s. 23 of the **Manitoba Act, 1870** can be protected by the Lieutenant Governor of the province, who can either withhold Royal Assent to a unilingual bill or reserve the bill for the signification of the Governor General's pleasure. **Constitution Act, 1867** ss. 55, 57, 90. See also **Manitoba Act, 1870**, s. 2. Though this legal power continues to exist, it has not been exercised in recent years. See, **Reference re Disallowance and Reservation**, [1938] S.C.R. 71.

The fundamental difficulty with the Attorney General of Manitoba's suggestion is that it would make the executive branch of the federal government, rather than the courts, the guarantor of constitutionally entrenched language rights. It should be noted that a decision of a provincial Lieutenant Governor as to whether to withhold assent or reserve a bill is not reviewable by the courts. **Reference re Disallowance and Reservation**, *supra*, at p. 95. The overall effect of implementing the suggestion of the Attorney General of Manitoba would be to insulate the Legislature's failure to comply with s. 23 of the **Manitoba Act, 1870** from judicial review. Such a result would be entirely inconsistent with the judiciary's duty to uphold the Constitution ....

The only appropriate resolution to this Reference is for the Court to fulfill its duty under s. 52 of the **Constitution Act, 1982** and declare all the unilingual Acts of the Legislature of Manitoba to be invalid and of no force and effect and then to take such steps as will ensure the Rule of Law in the Province of Manitoba.

There is no question that it would be impossible for all the Acts of the Manitoba Legislature to be translated, re-enacted, printed and published overnight. There will necessarily be a period of time during which it would not be possible for the Manitoba Legislature to comply with its constitutional duty under s. 23 of the **Manitoba Act, 1870.**

The vexing question, however, is what will be the legal situation in the Province of Manitoba for the duration of this period. The difficulties faced by the Province of Manitoba are two-fold: first, all of the rights, obligations and other effects which have arisen under the repealed, spent and current Acts of the Manitoba Legislature will be open to challenge, since the laws under which they purportedly arise are invalid and of no force or effect; and, second, the Province of Manitoba has an invalid and therefore ineffectual legal system until the Legislature is able to translate, re-enact, print and publish its current Acts ....

The only appropriate solution for preserving the rights, obligations and other effects which have arisen under invalid Acts of the Legislature of Manitoba and which are not saved by the *de facto* or other doctrines is to declare that, in order to uphold the Rule of Law, these rights, obligations and other effects have, and will continue to have, the same force and effect they would have had if they had arisen under valid enactments, for that period of time during which it would be impossible for Manitoba to comply with its constitutional duty under s. 23 of the **Manitoba Act, 1870.** The Province of Manitoba would be faced with chaos and anarchy if the legal rights, obligations and other effects which have been relied upon by the people of Manitoba since 1890 were suddenly open to challenge. The constitutional guarantee of Rule of Law will not tolerate such chaos and anarchy.

Nor will the constitutional guarantee of Rule of Law tolerate the Province of Manitoba being without a valid and effectual legal system for the present and future. Thus, it will be necessary to deem temporarily valid and effective the unilingual Acts of the Legislature of Manitoba which would be currently in force, were it not for their constitutional defect, for the period of time during which it would be impossible for the Manitoba Legislature to fulfill its constitutional duty. Since this temporary validation will include the legislation under which the Manitoba Legislature is presently constituted, it will be legally able to re-enact, print and publish its laws in conformity with the dictates of the Constitution once they have been translated.

Analogous support for the measures can be found in cases which have arisen under the doctrine of state necessity. Necessity in the context of governmental action provides a justification for the otherwise illegal conduct of a government during a public emergency. In order to ensure Rule of Law, the Courts will recognize as valid the constitutionally invalid Acts of the Legislature ....

The doctrine of necessity is not used in these cases to support some law which is above the Constitution; it is, instead used to ensure the unwritten but inherent principle of Rule of Law which must provide the foundation of any constitution.

In every case in which the doctrine of state necessity has been applied it has been either the executive or the legislative branch of government which has responded to the necessitous circumstances, later to have its actions tested in the courts. This fact does not, however, detract from the general relevance of these cases in demonstrating that the courts will not allow the Constitution to be used to create chaos and disorder.

Turning back to the present case, because of the Manitoba Legislature's persistent violation of the constitutional dictates of the **Manitoba Act, 1870** the Province of Manitoba is in a state of emergency: all of the Acts of the Legislature of Manitoba, purportedly repealed, spent and current (with the exception of those recent laws which have been enacted, printed and published in both languages), are and always have been invalid and of no force or effect, and the legislature is unable to immediately re-enact these unilingual laws in both languages. The Constitution will not suffer a province without laws. Thus the Constitution requires that temporary validity and force and effect be given to the current Acts of the Manitoba Legislature from the date of this judgment, and that rights, obligations and other effects which have arisen under these laws and the repealed and spent laws of the Province prior to the date of this judgment, which are not saved by the *de facto* or some other doctrine, are deemed temporarily to have been and continue to be effective and beyond challenge. It is only in this way that legal chaos can be avoided and the Rule of Law preserved.

To summarize, the legal situation in the Province of Manitoba is as follows. All unilingually enacted Acts of the Manitoba Legislature are, and always have been, invalid and of no force or effect.

All Acts of the Manitoba Legislature which would currently be valid and of force and effect, were it not for their constitutional defect, are deemed temporarily valid and effective from the date of this judgement to the expiry of the minimum period necessary for translation, re-enactment, printing and publishing ....

All rights, obligations and any other effects which have arisen under Acts of the Manitoba Legislature which are purportedly repealed, spent, or would currently be in force were it not for their constitutional defect, and which are *not* saved by the *de facto* doctrine, or doctrines such as *res judicata* and mistake of law, are deemed temporarily to have been, and to continue to be, enforceable and beyond challenge from the date of their creation to the expiry of the minimum period of time necessary for translation, re-enactment, printing and publishing of these laws. At the termination of the minimum period these rights, obligations and other effects will cease to have force and effect unless the Acts under which they arose have been translated, re-enacted, printed and published in both languages ....

As concerns the future, the Constitution requires that, from the date of this judgment, all new Acts of the Manitoba Legislature be enacted, printed and published in both French and English. Any Acts of the Legislature that do not meet this requirement will be invalid and of no force and effect ....

7

REALISM

*O*nce states come into existence, the question arises as to how they will deal with one another. Broadly speaking, there are two schools of thought on this question in political science. The "realist" position holds that, in the absence of a supranational sovereign power to enforce international law, states will be guided by their own national interest, with self-preservation as their highest priority. Thus we cannot expect leaders of states to conduct foreign policy as if other states would always act morally. States must expect the worst and be prepared for it. Consequently, the highest virtue in international politics is prudence, and the test of morality is real-world consequences, not good intentions. In contrast, the "idealist" or "liberal" position holds that states can be bound by international law, and that morality can triumph over Realpolitik. Because history seems to offer greater support for realism, advocates of idealism usually postulate the necessity of some fundamental structural change, such as the creation of the League of Nations or the United Nations, as a precondition for more moral behaviour in the future. Without denying the value of such changes, realists note that it is not easy to alter the predatory aspects of human nature nor the logic of the state system, which pits states against one another in a Hobbesian "war of all against all."

Hans J. Morgenthau (1904–1980) was a German-Jewish refugee from fascism. For many years a professor of political science at the University of Chicago, he was a distinguished exponent of realism. He became an early opponent of American involvement in the Vietnam War, not because he shared the naive illusion that the Viet Cong were noncommunist agrarian reformers, but because he thought that

Vietnam was too close to China for a Western power to be able to win the war. This selection is from chapter 1 of Morgenthau's well-known textbook of international relations, Politics among Nations: The Struggle for Power and Peace.

· · · · · · · · ·

The history of modern political thought is the story of a contest between two schools that differ fundamentally in their conceptions of the nature of man, society, and politics. One believes that a rational and moral political order, derived from universally valid abstract principles, can be achieved here and now. It assumes the essential goodness and infinite malleability of human nature, and blames the failure of the social order to measure up to the rational standards on lack of knowledge and understanding, obsolescent social institutions, or the depravity of certain isolated individuals or groups. It trusts in education, reform, and the sporadic use of force to remedy these defects.

The other school believes that the world, imperfect as it is from the rational point of view, is the result of forces inherent in human nature. To improve the world one must work with these forces, not against them. This being inherently a world of opposing interests and of conflict among them, moral principles can never be fully realized, but must at best be approximated through the ever temporary balancing of interests and the ever precarious settlement of conflicts. This school, then, sees in a system of checks and balances a universal principle for all pluralist societies. It appeals to historic precedent rather than to abstract principles, and aims at the realization of the lesser evil rather than of the absolute good.

This theoretical concern with human nature as it actually is, and with the historic processes as they actually take place, has earned for the theory presented here the name of realism. What are the tenets of political realism? No systematic exposition of the philosophy of political realism can be attempted here; it will suffice to single out six fundamental principles, which have frequently been misunderstood.

SIX PRINCIPLES OF POLITICAL REALISM

1. Political realism believes that politics, like society in general, is governed by objective laws that have their roots in human nature. In order to improve society it is first necessary to understand the laws by which society lives. The operation of these laws being impervious to our preferences, men will challenge them only at the risk of failure.

Realism, believing as it does in the objectivity of the laws of politics, must also believe in the possibility of developing a rational theory that reflects, however imperfectly and one-sidedly, these objective laws. It believes also, then, in the possibility of distinguishing in politics between truth and opinion—between what is true objectively and rationally, supported by evidence and illuminated by reason, and what is only a subjective judgment, divorced from the facts as they are and informed by prejudice and wishful thinking.

Human nature, in which laws of politics have their roots, has not changed since the classical philosophies of China, India, and Greece endeavored to discover these laws. Hence, novelty is not necessarily a virtue in political theory, nor is old age a defect. The fact that a theory of politics, if there be such a theory, has never been heard of before tends to create a presumption against, rather than in favor of, its soundness. Conversely, the fact that a theory of politics was developed hundreds or even thousands of years ago—as was the theory of the balance of power—does not create a presumption that it must be outmoded and obsolete. A theory of politics must be subjected to the dual test of reason and experience. To dismiss such a theory because it had its flowering in centuries past is to present not a rational argument but a modernistic prejudice that takes for granted the superiority of the present over the past. To dispose of the revival of such a theory as a "fashion" or "fad" is tantamount to assuming that in matters political we can have opinions but no truths ....

2. The main signpost that helps political realism to find its way through the landscape of international politics is the concept of interest defined in terms of power. This concept provides the link between reason trying to understand international politics and the facts to be understood. It sets politics as an autonomous sphere of action and understanding apart from other spheres, such as economics (understood in terms of interest defined as wealth), ethics, aesthetics, or religion. Without such a concept a theory of politics, international or domestic, would be altogether impossible, for without it we could not distinguish between political and nonpolitical facts, nor could we bring at least a measure of systematic order to the political sphere.

We assume that statesmen think and act in terms of interest defined as power, and the evidence of history bears that assumption out. That assumption allows us to retrace and anticipate, as it were, the steps a statesman—past, present or future—has taken or will take on the political scene. We look over his shoulder when he writes his dispatches; we listen in on his conversation with other statesmen; we read and anticipate his very thoughts. Thinking in terms of interest defined as power, we think as he does, and as disinterested observers we understand his thoughts and actions perhaps better than he, the actor on the political scene, does himself.

The concept of interest defined as power imposes intellectual discipline upon the observer, infuses rational order into the subject matter of politics, and thus makes the theoretical understanding of politics possible. On the side of the actor, it provides for rational discipline in action and creates that astounding continuity in foreign policy which makes American, British, or Russian foreign policy appear as an intelligible, rational continuum, by and large consistent within itself, regardless of the different motives, preferences, and intellectual and moral qualities of successive statesmen. A realist theory of international politics, then, will guard against two popular fallacies: the concern with motives and the concern with ideological preferences.

To search for the clue to foreign policy exclusively in the motives of statesmen is both futile and deceptive. It is futile because motives are the most illusive of psychological data, distorted as they are, frequently beyond recognition, by the interests and emotions of actor and observer alike. Do we really know what our own motives are? And what do we know of the motives of others? ...

We cannot conclude from the good intentions of a statesman that his foreign policies will be either morally praiseworthy or politically successful. Judging his motives, we can say that he will not intentionally pursue policies that are morally wrong, but we can say nothing about the probability of their success. If we want to know the moral and political qualities of his actions, we must know them, not his motives. How often have statesmen been motivated by the desire to improve the world, and ended by making it worse? And how often have they sought one goal, and ended by achieving something they neither expected nor desired?

Neville Chamberlain's politics of appeasement were, as far as we can judge, inspired by good motives; he was probably less motivated by considerations of personal power than were many other British prime ministers, and he sought to preserve peace and to assume the happiness of all concerned. Yet his policies helped to make the Second World War inevitable, and to bring untold miseries to millions of men. Sir Winston Churchill's motives, on the other hand, have been much less universal in scope and much more narrowly directed toward personal and national power, yet the foreign policies that sprang from these inferior motives were certainly superior in moral and political quality to those pursued by his predecessor. Judged by his motives, Robespierre was one of the most virtuous men who ever lived. Yet it was the utopian radicalism of that very virtue that made him kill those less virtuous than himself, brought him to the scaffold, and destroyed the revolution of which he was a leader.

A realist theory of international politics will also avoid the other popular fallacy of equating the foreign policies of a statesman with his philosophic or political sympathies, and of deducing the former from the latter. Statesmen, especially under contemporary conditions, may well make a habit of presenting their foreign policies in terms of their philosophic and political sympathies in order to gain popular support for them. Yet they will distinguish with Lincoln between their "*official* duty," which is to think and act in terms of the national interest, and their "*personal* wish," which is to see their own moral values and political principles realized throughout the world. Political realism does not require, nor does it condone, indifference to political ideals and moral principles, but it requires indeed a sharp distinction between the desirable and the possible—between what is desirable everywhere and at all times and what is possible under the concrete circumstances of time and place.

It stands to reason that not all foreign policies have always followed so rational, objective, and unemotional a course. The contingent elements of personality, prejudice, and subjective preference, and of all the weaknesses of intellect and will which flesh is heir to, are bound to deflect foreign policies from their rational course. Especially where foreign policy is conducted under the conditions of democratic control, the need to marshal popular emotions to the support of foreign policy cannot fail to impair the rationality of foreign policy itself. Yet a theory of foreign policy which aims at rationality must for the time being, as it were, abstract from these irrational elements and seek to paint a picture of foreign policy which presents the rational essence to be found in experience, without the contingent deviations from rationality which are also found in experience ....

3. Realism does not endow its key concept of interest defined as power with a meaning that is fixed once and for all. The idea of interest is indeed of the essence of politics and is unaffected by the circumstances of time and place. Thucydides' statement, born of the experiences of ancient Greece, that "identity of interests is the surest of bonds whether between states or individuals" was taken up in the nineteenth century by Lord Salisbury's remark that "the only bond of union that endures" among nations is "the absence of all clashing interests." It was erected into a general principle of government by George Washington:

A small knowledge of human nature will convince us, that, with far the greatest part of mankind, interest is the governing principle; and that almost every man is more or less, under its influence. Motives of public virtue may for a time, or in particular instances, actuate men to the observance of a conduct purely disinterested; but they are not of themselves sufficient to produce persevering conformity to the refined dictates and obligations of social duty. Few men are capable of making a continual sacrifice of all views of private interest, or advantage, to the common good. It is vain to exclaim against the depravity of human nature on this account; the fact is so, the experience of every age and nation has proved it and we must in a great measure, change the constitution of man, before we can make it otherwise. No institution, not built on the presumptive truth of these maxims can succeed ....

Yet the kind of interest determining political action in a particular period of history depends upon the political and cultural context within which foreign policy is formulated. The goals that might be pursued by nations in their foreign policy can run the whole gamut of objectives any nation has ever pursued or might possibly pursue ....

The realist parts company with other schools of thought before the all-important question of how the contemporary world is to be transformed. The realist is persuaded that his transformation can be achieved only through the workmanlike manipulation of the perennial forces that have shaped the past as they will the future. The realist cannot be persuaded that we can bring about that transformation by confronting a political reality that has its own laws with an abstract ideal that refuses to take those laws into account.

4. Political realism is aware of the moral significance of political action. It is also aware of the ineluctable tension between the moral command and the requirements of successful political action. And it is unwilling to gloss over and obliterate that tension and thus to obfuscate both the moral and the political issue by making it appear as though the stark facts of politics were morally more satisfying than they actually are, and the moral law less exacting than it actually is.

Realism maintains that universal moral principles cannot be applied to the actions of states in their abstract formulation, but that they must be filtered through the concrete circumstances of time and place. The individual may say for himself: *"Fiat justitia, pereat mundus* (Let justice be done, even if the world perish)," but the state has no right to say so in the name of those who are in its care. Both individual and state must judge political action by universal moral principles, such as that of liberty. Yet while the individual has a moral right to sacrifice himself in defense of such a moral principle, the state has no right to let its moral disapprobation of the infringement of liberty get in the way of successful political action, itself inspired by the moral principle of national survival. There can be no political morality without prudence; that is, without consideration of the political consequences of seemingly moral action. Realism, then, considers prudence—the weighing of the consequences of alternative political actions—to be the supreme virtue in politics. Ethics in the abstract judges action by its conformity with the moral law; political ethics judges action by its political consequences. Classical and medieval philosophy knew this, and so did Lincoln when he said:

> I do the very best I know how, the very best I can, and I mean to keep doing so until the end. If the end brings me out all right, what is said against me won't amount to anything. If the end brings me out wrong, ten angels swearing I was right would make no difference.

5. Political realism refuses to identify the moral aspirations of a particular nation with the moral laws that govern the universe. As it distinguishes between truth and opinion, so it distinguishes between truth and idolatry. All nations are tempted—and few have been able to resist the temptation for long—to clothe their own particular aspirations and actions in the moral purposes of the universe. To know that nations are subject to the moral law is one thing, while to pretend to know with certainty what is good and evil in the relations among nations is quite another. There is a world of difference between the belief that all nations stand under the judgment of God, inscrutable to the human mind, and the blasphemous conviction that God is always on one's side and that what one wills oneself cannot fail to be willed by God also.

The lighthearted equation between a particular nationalism and the counsels of Providence is morally indefensible, for it is that very sin of pride against which the Greek tragedians and the Biblical prophets have warned rulers and ruled. That equation is also politically pernicious, for it is liable to engender the distortion in judgment which, in the blindness of crusading frenzy, destroys nations and civilization—in the name of moral principle, ideal, or God himself.

On the other hand, it is exactly the concept of interest defined in terms of power that saves us from both that moral excess and that political folly. For if we look at all nations, our own included, as political entities pursuing their respective interests defined in terms of power, we are able to do justice to all of them. And we are able to do justice to all of them in a dual sense: We are able to judge other nations as we judge our own and, having judged them in this fashion, we are then capable of pursuing policies that respect the interests of other nations, while protecting and promoting those of our own. Moderation in policy cannot fail to reflect the moderation of moral judgment.

6. The difference, then, between political realism and other schools of thought is real, and it is profound. However much the theory of political realism may have been misunderstood and misinterpreted, there is

no gainsaying its distinctive intellectual and moral attitude to matters political.

Intellectually, the political realist maintains the autonomy of the political sphere, as the economist, the lawyer, the moralist maintain theirs. He thinks in terms of interest defined as power, as the economist thinks in terms of interest defined as wealth; the lawyer, of the conformity of action with legal rules; the moralist, of the conformity of action with moral principles. The economist asks: "How does this policy affect the wealth of society, or a segment of it?" The lawyer asks: "Is this policy in accord with the rules of law?" The moralist asks: "Is this policy in accord with moral principles?" And the political realist asks: "How does this policy affect the power of the nation?" ...

The political realist is not unaware of the existence and relevance of standards of thought other than political ones. As political realist, he cannot but subordinate these other standards to those of politics. And he parts company with other schools when they impose standards of thought appropriate to other spheres upon the political sphere. It is here that political realism takes issue with the "legalistic-moralistic approach" to international politics. That this issue is not, as has been contended, a mere figment of the imagination, but goes to the very core of the controversy, can be shown from many historical examples. Three will suffice to make the point.

In 1939 the Soviet Union attacked Finland. This action confronted France and Great Britain with two issues, one legal, the other political. Did that action violate the Covenant of the League of Nations and, if it did, what countermeasures should France and Great Britain take? The legal question could easily be answered in the affirmative, for obviously the Soviet Union had done what was prohibited by the Covenant. The answer to the political question depended, first, upon the manner in which the Russian action affected the interests of France and Great Britain; second, upon the existing power of distribution between France and Great Britain, on the one hand, and the Soviet Union and the other potentially hostile nations, especially Germany, on the other; and third, upon the influence that the countermeasures were likely to have upon the interests of France and Great Britain and the future distribution of power. France and Great Britain, as the leading members of the League of Nations, saw to it that the Soviet Union was expelled from the League, and they were prevented from joining Finland in the war against the Soviet Union only by Sweden's refusal to allow their troops to pass through Swedish territory on their way to Finland. If this refusal by Sweden had not saved them, France and Great Britain would shortly have found themselves at war with the Soviet Union and Germany at the same time.

The policy of France and Great Britain was a classic example of legalism in that they allowed the answer to the legal question, legitimate within its sphere, to determine their political actions. Instead of asking both questions, that of law and that of power, they asked only the question of law; and the answer they received could have no bearing on the issue that their very existence might have depended upon.

The second example illustrates the "moralistic approach" to international politics. It concerns the international status of the Communist government of China. The rise of that government confronted the Western world with two issues, one moral, the other political. Were the nature and policies of that government in accord with the moral principles of the Western world? Should the Western world deal with such a government? The answer to the first question could not fail to be in the negative. Yet it did not follow with necessity that the answer to the second question should also be in the negative. The standard of thought applied to the first—the moral—question was simply to test the nature and the policies of the Communist government of China by the principles of Western morality. On the other hand, the second—the political—question had to be subjected to the complicated test of the interests involved and the power available on either side, and of the bearing of one or the other course of action upon these interests and power. The application of this test could well have led to the conclusion that it would be wiser not to deal with the Communist government of China. To arrive at this conclusion by neglecting this test altogether and answering the political question in terms of the moral issue was indeed a classic example of the "moralistic approach" to international politics.

The third case illustrates strikingly the contrast between realism and the legalistic-moralistic approach to foreign policy. Great Britain, as one of the guarantors of the neutrality of Belgium, went to war with Germany in August 1914 because Germany had violated the neutrality of Belgium. The British action could be justified either in realistic or legalistic-moralistic terms. That is to say, one could argue realistically that for centuries it had been axiomatic for British foreign policy to prevent the control of the Low Countries by a hostile power. It was then not so much the violation of Belgium's neutrality per se as the hostile intentions of the violator which provided the rationale for British intervention. If the violator had been another nation but Germany, Great Britain might well have refrained from intervening ....

This realist defense of the autonomy of the political sphere against its subversion by other modes of thought does not imply disregard for the existence and importance of these other modes of thought. It rather implies that each should be assigned its proper sphere and function. Political realism is based upon a pluralistic conception of human nature.

Real man is a composite of "economic man," "political man," "moral man," "religious man," etc. A man who was nothing but "religious man" would be a saint, for he would be completely lacking in worldly desires ....

It is in the nature of things that a theory of politics which is based upon such principles will not meet with unanimous approval—nor does, for that matter, such a foreign policy. For theory and policy alike run counter to two trends in our culture which are not able to reconcile themselves to the assumptions and results of a rational, objective theory of politics. One of these trends disparages the role of power in society on grounds that stem from the experience and philosophy of the nineteenth century; ... The other trend, opposed to the realistic theory and practice of politics, stems from the very relationship that exists, and must exist, between the human mind and the political sphere .... the human mind in its day-by-day operations cannot bear to look the truth of politics straight in the face. It must disguise, distort, belittle, and embellish the truth—the more so, the more the individual is actively involved in the processes of politics, and particularly in those of international politics. For only by deceiving himself about the nature of politics and the role he plays on the political scene is man able to live contentedly as a political animal with himself and his fellow men.

Thus it is inevitable that a theory which tries to understand international politics as it actually is and as it ought to be in view of its intrinsic nature, rather than as people would like to see it, must overcome a psychological resistance that most other branches of learning need not face.

Ideology

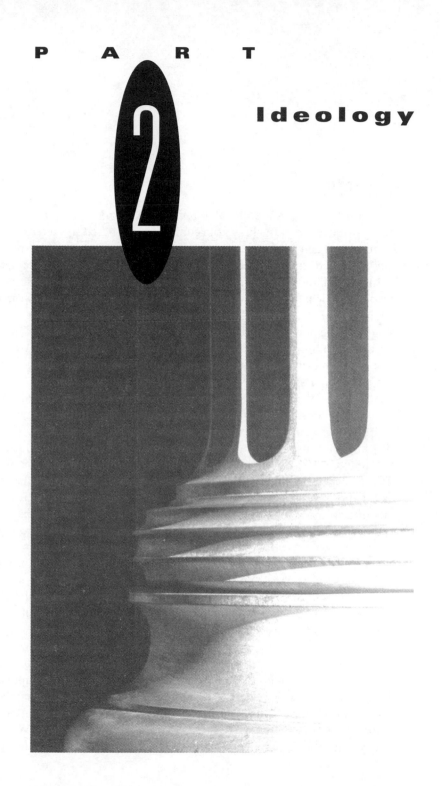

INTRODUCTION

That human beings are political animals in Aristotle's sense means that their participation in the life of the community is based upon reason and discussion. Their action/reaction toward one another is also "interaction" founded upon reflective consideration of common problems. Politics, therefore, always has intellectual and moral dimensions. As we reason and debate about which course of action to pursue, we make judgments of desirability based on concepts of right and wrong, on images of the sort of life that we do and should lead. Inevitably these reflections about the ends of political action and about the proper means to attain those ends do not remain mere random thoughts but cluster into patterns or systems of interrelated ideas.

"Ideology" is the term most commonly used today to designate such a system of ideas about the purpose and proper function of political institutions. In some ways the term is unfortunate because it is fraught with implications stemming from its history. It was coined in 1796 by the French writer Antoine Destutt de Tracy to mean the "science of the mind." Marx and Engels picked up the term after it had fallen into disuse and gave it quite another meaning. For them it did not imply a scientific study of ideas but referred to particular sets of ideas that they regarded as reflections of economic conditions or dominant economic forces.

Our use of the term "ideology" is not intended to carry with it any of these special implications. We merely follow the increasingly common tendency in the literature of social science to use "ideology" as a neutral label for sets of political ideas that are at least partially integrated, that have some mass acceptance, that place politics in a moral context, and that are not purely theoretical but provide guidance for practical action.

Part II of this book contains readings about the four most important ideologies of our age: liberalism, conservatism, socialism, and nationalism. Although these four "isms" do not exhaust the infinite variety of political thought, they have dominated political discussion in Western society since the French Revolution—and with the influence of the West over the rest of the world, they have now supplanted, if not wholly replaced, more traditional modes of thought in other societies. Anyone who becomes acquainted with the main tenets of these four ideologies will be able to follow most of the political debates of our time.

We also try to take into account the internal variety within ideological families. We thus present an example of classical liberalism—John Stuart Mill in Reading 8—followed by an example of reform liberalism—T.H. Green in Reading 9. The two readings contrast sharply in their understanding of freedom, leading to rather different views about the role of government in society. Similarly, we present two versions of conservatism—Readings 10 and 11—as well as examples of the two major wings of socialism: Marx and Engels (Reading 12) as an instance of revolutionary socialism, and the Regina Manifesto (Reading 13) as an example of social democracy. We offer Benito Mussolini (Reading 15) as an extreme exponent of nationalism, balanced by Michael Ignatieff's discussion of ethnic nationalism and civic nationalism (Reading 14) to show that nationalism is not necessarily an aggressive, militaristic doctrine.

Finally, we offer two interpretive works on ideology in Canada. Gad Horowitz's famous essay (Reading 16), applying Hartzian fragment theory to Canada, is still the starting point of all discussion in this field. Neil Nevitte's discussion of the "new politics" in Reading 17 deals with recent ideological developments in Canada in the context of similar trends throughout the Western world. Drawing on the "postmaterialism" thesis made famous by Ronald Inglehart, Nevitte shows how new ideologies such as environmentalism and feminism are becoming increasingly important in Canadian politics.

The postmaterialist thesis holds that liberalism, conservatism, and socialism were ideologies of the industrial age, which was characterized by economic growth and struggles over distribution of wealth. Now that a high standard of material prosperity exists in Western nations, attention has increasingly shifted to "quality of life" issues such as the environment and the status of women. The older ideologies are being decisively reshaped, perhaps even rendered obsolete, by this profound social change. Such developments illustrate the fluid nature of ideologies and the mistake of thinking of them as rigid systems. They are tendencies of thought in constant flux, reflecting the ceaseless changes in our social milieu.

8

CLASSICAL LIBERALISM

The central concept of classical liberalism is freedom, understood as the absence of coercion. According to this view, we are free when no one uses force to interfere with our actions. Freedom, then, means acting according to our own will without encountering violence or threats of violence from others.

John Stuart Mill (1806–1873) worked out the implications of this view in his famous essay On Liberty, *published in 1859. In particular, he addressed the question of what limits can justifiably be placed upon individual freedom. His answer was that we (or government acting on our behalf) are justified in using coercion only to protect our rights from invasion by others. We can coerce others to protect ourselves and our legitimate interests from those who would violate them, but we cannot coerce others in the name of their interests. Mill thus developed a liberal theory of the state as a protective device in contrast to the doctrine of paternalism, which would allow the state to look after the interests of individuals even against their own wishes.*

Mill's version of classical liberalism requires a distinction to be drawn between "self-regarding" and "other-regarding" actions. Government has a legitimate right to regulate the latter, but not the former. Reading 8 illustrates Mill's attempt to draw this distinction. He was confident that he had succeeded in reducing the matter to "one very simple principle," but later generations have not found it so simple. Argument rages to this day over whether Mill's distinction between self-regarding and other-regarding behaviour tells us anything useful about the role of government in society. But regardless of where one stands in this argument, it is almost always conducted in the terms set by Mill.

The sections printed here are from the end of chapter 1 and the beginning of chapter 4 of On Liberty, *as reprinted in* Utilitarianism and Other Writings.

• • • • • • • • •

The object of this Essay is to assert one very simple principle, as entitled to govern absolutely the dealings of society with the individual in the way of compulsion and control, whether the means used be physical force in the form of legal penalties, or the moral coercion of public opinion. That principle is, that the sole end for which mankind are warranted, individually or collectively, in interfering with the liberty of action of any of their number, is self-protection. That the only purpose for which power can be rightfully exercised over any member of a civilised community, against his will, is to prevent harm to others. His own good, either physical or moral, is not a sufficient warrant. He cannot rightfully be compelled to do or forbear because it will be better for him to do so, because it will make him happier, because, in the opinions of others, to do so would be wise, or even right. These are good reasons for remonstrating with him, or reasoning with him, or persuading him, or entreating him, but not for compelling him, or visiting him with any evil in case he do otherwise. To justify that, the conduct from which it is desired to deter him must be calculated to produce evil to some one else. The only part of the conduct of any one, for which he is amenable to society, is that which concerns others. In the part which merely concerns himself, his independence is, of right, absolute. Over himself, over his own body and mind, the individual is sovereign.

It is, perhaps, hardly necessary to say that this doctrine is meant to apply only to human beings in the maturity of their faculties. We are not speaking of children, or of young persons below the age which the law may fix as that of manhood or womanhood. Those who are still in a state to require being taken care of by others must be protected against their own actions as well as against external injury. For the same reason, we may leave out of consideration those backward states of society in which the race itself may be considered as in its nonage. The early difficulties in the way of spontaneous progress are so great, that there is seldom any choice of means for overcoming them; and a ruler full of the spirit of improvement is warranted in the use of any expedients that will attain an end, perhaps otherwise unattainable. Despotism is a legitimate mode of government in dealing with barbarians, provided the end be their improvement, and the means justified by actually effecting that end. Liberty, as a principle, has no application to any state of things anterior to the time when mankind have become capable of being improved by free and equal discussion. Until then, there is nothing for them but implicit obedience to an Akbar or a Charlemagne, if they are so fortunate as to find one. But as soon as mankind have attained the capacity of being guided to their own improvement by conviction or persuasion (a period long since reached in all nations with whom we need here concern ourselves), compulsion, either in the direct form or in that of pains and penalties for non-compliance, is no longer admissible as a means to their own good, and justifiable only for the security of others.

It is proper to state that I forego any advantage which could be derived to my argument from the idea of abstract right, as a thing independent of utility. I regard utility as the ultimate appeal on all ethical questions; but it must be utility in the largest sense, grounded on the permanent interests of a man as a progressive being. Those interests, I contend, authorise the subjection of individual spontaneity to external control, only in respect to those actions of each, which concern the interest of other people. If any one does an act hurtful to others, there is a *prima facie* case for punishing him, by law, or, where legal penalties are not safely applicable, by general disapprobation. There are also many positive acts for the benefit of others, which he may rightfully be compelled to perform; such as to give evidence in a court of justice; to bear his fair share in the common defence, or in any other joint work necessary to the interest of the society of which he enjoys the protection; and to perform certain acts of individual beneficence, such as saving a fellow-creature's life, or interposing to protect the defenceless against ill-usage, things which whenever it is obviously a man's duty to do, he may rightfully be made responsible to society for not doing. A person may cause evil to others not only by his actions but by his inaction, and in either case he is justly accountable to them for the injury. The latter case, it is true, requires a much more cautious exercise of compulsion than the former. To make any one answerable for doing evil to others is the rule; to make him answerable for not preventing evil is, comparatively speaking, the exception. Yet there are many cases clear enough and grave enough to justify that exception. In all things which regard the external relations of the individual, he is *de jure* amenable to those whose interests are concerned, and, if need be, to society as their protector. There are often good reasons for not holding him to the responsibility; but these reasons must arise from the special expediencies of the case: either because it is a kind of case in which he is on the whole likely to act better, when left to his own discretion, than when controlled in any way in which society have it in their power to control him; or because the attempt to exercise control would produce other evils, greater than those which it would prevent. When such reasons as these preclude the enforcement of responsibility, the conscience of the agent himself should step into the vacant judgement seat, and protect those interests of others which have no external protection; judging himself all the more rigidly, because the case does not admit of his being made accountable to the judgment of his fellow-creatures.

But there is a sphere of action in which society, as distinguished from the individual, has, if any, only an indirect interest; comprehending all that portion of a person's life and conduct which affects only himself, or if it also affects others, only with their free, voluntary, and undeceived consent and participation. When I say only himself, I mean directly, and in the first instance; for whatever affects himself, may affect others through himself; and the objection which may be grounded on this contingency, will receive consideration in the sequel. This, then, is the appropriate region of human liberty. It comprises, first, the inward domain of consciousness; demanding liberty of conscience in the most comprehensive sense; liberty of thought and feeling; absolute freedom of opinion and sentiment on all subjects practical or speculative, scientific, moral, or theological. The liberty of expressing and publishing opinions may seem to fall under a different principle, since it belongs to that part of the conduct of an individual which concerns other people; but, being almost of as much importance as the liberty of thought itself, and resting in great part on the same reasons, is practically inseparable from it. Secondly, the principle requires liberty of tastes and pursuits; of framing the plan of our life to suit our own character; of doing as we like, subject to such consequences as may follow: without impediment from our fellow-creatures, so long as what we do does not harm them, even though they should think our conduct foolish, perverse, or wrong. Thirdly, from this liberty of each individual, follows the liberty, within the same limits, of combination among individuals; freedom to unite, for any purpose not involving harm to others: the persons combining being supposed to be of full age, and not forced or deceived.

No society in which these liberties are not, on the whole, respected, is free, whatever may be its form of government; and none is completely free in which they do not exist absolute and unqualified. The only freedom which deserves the name, is that of pursuing our own good in our own way, so long as we do not attempt to deprive others of theirs, or impede their efforts to obtain it. Each is the proper guardian of his own health, whether bodily, *or* mental and spiritual. Mankind are greater gainers by suffering each other to live as seems good to themselves, than by compelling each to live as seems good to the rest ....

What, then, is the rightful limit to the sovereignty of the individual over himself? Where does the authority of society begin? How much of human life should be assigned to individuality, and how much to society?

Each will receive its proper share, if each has that which more particularly concerns it. To individuality should belong the part of life in which it is chiefly the individual that is interested; to society, the part which chiefly interests society.

Though society is not founded on a contract, and though no good purpose is answered by inventing a contract in order to deduce social obligations from it, every one who receives the protection of society owes a return for the benefit, and the fact of living in society renders it indispensable that each should be bound to observe a certain line of conduct towards the rest. This conduct consists, first, in not injuring the interests of one another; or rather certain interests, which, either by express legal provision or by tacit understanding, ought to be considered as rights; and secondly, in each person's bearing his share (to be fixed on some equitable principle) of the labours and sacrifices incurred for defending the society or its members from injury and molestation. These conditions society is justified in enforcing, at all costs to those who endeavour to withhold fulfillment. Nor is this all that society may do. The acts of an individual may be hurtful to others, or wanting in due consideration for their welfare, without going to the length of violating any of their constituted rights. The offender may then be justly punished by opinion, though not by law. As soon as any part of a person's conduct affects prejudicially the interests of others, society has jurisdiction over it, and the question whether the general welfare will or will not be promoted by interfering with it, becomes open to discussion. But there is no room for entertaining any such question when a person's conduct affects the interests of no persons besides himself, or needs not affect them unless they like (all the persons concerned being of full age, and the ordinary amount of understanding). In all such cases, there should be perfect freedom, legal and social, to do the action and stand the consequences.

It would be a great misunderstanding of this doctrine to suppose that it is one of selfish indifference, which pretends that human beings have no business with each other's conduct in life, and that they should not concern themselves about the well-doing or well-being of one another, unless their own interest is involved. Instead of any diminution, there is need of a great increase of disinterested exertion to promote the good of others. But disinterested benevolence can find other instruments to persuade people to their good than whips and scourges, either of the literal or the metaphorical sort. I am the last person to undervalue the self-regarding virtues; they are only second in importance, if even second, to the social. It is equally the business of education to cultivate both. But even education works by conviction and persuasion as well as by compulsion, and it is by the former only that, when the period of education is passed, the self-regarding virtues should be inculcated. Human beings owe to each other help to distinguish the better from the worse, and encouragement to choose the former and avoid the latter. They should be for ever stimulating each other to increased exercise of their higher faculties, and increased direction of their feelings and aims towards wise instead of foolish, elevating instead of degrading, objects and contemplations. But neither one person, nor any number of persons, is warranted in saying to another human creature of ripe years, that he shall not do with his life for his own benefit what he chooses to do with it. He is the person most interested in his own well-being; the interest which any other person, except in cases of strong personal attachment, can have in it, is trifling, compared with that which he himself has; the interest which society has in him individually (except as to his conduct to others) is fractional, and altogether indirect; while with respect to his own feelings and circumstances, the most ordinary man or woman has means of knowledge immeasurably surpassing those that can be possessed by any one else. The interference of society to overrule his judgment and purposes in what only regards himself must be grounded on general presumption; which may be altogether wrong, and even if right, are as likely as not to be misapplied to individual cases, by persons no better acquainted with the circumstances of such cases than those are who look at them merely from without. In this department, therefore, of human affairs, Individuality has its proper field of action. In the conduct of human beings toward one another it is necessary that general rules should for the most part be observed, in order that people may know what they have to expect: but in each person's own concerns his individual spontaneity is entitled to free exercise. Considerations to aid his judgment, exhortations to strengthen his will, may be offered to him, even obtruded on him, by others: but he himself is the final judge. All errors which he is likely to commit against advice and warning are far outweighed by the evil of allowing others to constrain him to what they deem his good.

I do not mean that the feelings with which a person is regarded by others ought not to be in any way affected by his self-regarding qualities or deficiencies. This is neither possible nor desirable. If he is eminent in any of the qualities which conduce to his own good, he is, so far, a proper object of admiration. He is so much the nearer to the ideal perfection of human nature. If he is grossly deficient in those qualities, a sentiment the opposite of admiration will follow ....

9 REFORM LIBERALISM

Classical liberalism's understanding of freedom as the absence of coercion led to a strictly limited view of the role of government in society. By the end of the nineteenth century, many thinkers who thought of themselves as liberals began to question this restrictive view of state action. They particularly believed that government intervention would be necessary to lift the industrial working class out of poverty and degradation.

Typical of this new generation of liberal writers was Thomas Hill Green (1836–1882), a professor of philosophy at Oxford and an active member of the Liberal Party of Great Britain. In seeking to justify an interventionist, reforming role for government, Green rethought the classical liberal definition of freedom, turning it into a much broader concept: "a positive power or capacity of doing or enjoying something worth doing or enjoying, and that, too, something that we do or enjoy in common with others." He saw this new understanding of freedom as justifying a much more activist use of government to help people fulfil their capacities.

A striking result of Green's revised liberalism was the demand to prohibit the sale of alcoholic beverages in the name of obtaining a higher freedom, which may in fact conflict with what people think they want. In comparison with the classical liberalism of John Stuart Mill, Green's reform liberalism contained a strong dose of paternalism, generating controversies that continue to reverberate in the modern welfare state.

Reading 9 is extracted from Green's "Lecture on Liberal Legislation and Freedom of Contract," delivered at Leicester in 1881 and subsequently published in The Works of Thomas Hill Green.

• • • • • • • •

... [T]he most pressing political questions of our time are questions of which the settlement, I do not say necessarily involves an interference with freedom of contract, but is sure to be resisted in the sacred name of individual liberty, not only by all those who are interested in keeping things as they are, but by others to whom freedom is dear for its own sake, and who do not sufficiently consider the conditions of its maintenance in such a society as ours. In this respect there is a noticeable difference between the present position of political reformers and that in which they stood a generation ago. Then they fought the fight of reform in the name of individual freedom against class privilege. Their opponents could not with any plausibility invoke the same against them. Now, in appearance—though, as I shall try to show, not in reality—the case is changed. The nature of the genuine political reform is perhaps always the same. The passion for improving mankind, in its ultimate object, does not vary. But the immediate object of reformers, and the forms of persuasion by which they seek to advance them, vary much in different generations. To a hasty observer they might even seem contradictory, and to justify the notion that nothing better than a desire for change, selfish or perverse, is at the bottom of all reforming movements. Only those who will think a little longer about it can discern the same old cause of social good against class interests, for which, under altered names, liberals are fighting now as they were fifty years ago.

Our political history since the first reform act naturally falls into three divisions. The first, beginning with the reform of parliament, and extending to Sir R. Peel's administration, is marked by the struggle of free society against close privileged corporations. Its greatest achievement was the establishment of representative municipal governments in place of the close bodies which had previously administered the affairs of our cities and boroughs; a work which after an interval of nearly half a century we hope shortly to see extended to the rural districts. Another important work was the overhauling of the immense charities of the country, and the placing them under something like adequate public control. And the natural complement of this was the removal of the grosser abuses in the administration of the church, the abolition of pluralities and sinecures, and the reform of cathedral chapters. In all this, while there was much that contributed to the freedom of our civil life, there was nothing that could possibly be construed as an interference with the rights of the individual. No one was disturbed in doing what he would with his own. Even those who had fattened on abuses had their vested interests duly respected, for the house of commons then as now had 'quite a passion for compensation.' With the ministry of Sir R. Peel began the struggle of society against monopolies; in other words, the liberation of trade. Some years later Mr. Gladstone, in his famous budgets, was able to complete the work which his master began, and it is now some twenty years since the last vestige of protection for any class of traders or producers disappeared. The taxes on knowledge, as they were called, followed the taxes on food, and since most of us grew up there has been no exchangeable commodity in England except land—no doubt a large exception—of which the exchange has not been perfectly free.

The realisation of complete freedom of contract was the special object of this reforming work. It was to set men at liberty to dispose of what they had made their own that the free-trader worked. He only interfered to prevent interference. He would put restraint on no man in doing anything that did not directly check the free dealing of some one in something else. But of late reforming legislation has taken, as I have pointed out, a seemingly different direction. It has not at any rate been so readily identifiable with the work of liberation. In certain respects it has put restraints on the individual in doing what he will with his own. And it is noticeable that this altered tendency begins, in the main, with the more democratic parliament of 1868. It is true that the earlier factory acts, limiting as they do by law the conditions under which certain kinds of labour may be bought and sold, had been passed some time before. The first approach to an effectual factory act dates as far back as the time of the first reform act, but it only applied to the cotton industry, and was very imperfectly put in force. It aimed at limiting the hours of labour for children and young persons ....

... [N]ow we have a system of law by which, in all of our chief industries except the agricultural, the employment of children as half-timers is effectually prevented, the employment of women and young persons is effectually restricted to ten hours a day, and in all places of employment health and bodily safety have all the protection which rules can give them.

If factory regulation had been attempted, though only in a piecemeal way, some time before we had a democratic house of commons, the same cannot be said of education law. It was the parliament elected by a more popular suffrage in 1868 that passed, as we know, the first great education act. That act introduced compulsory schooling. It left the compulsion, indeed, optional with local school-boards, but compulsion is the same in principle, is just as much compulsion by the state, whether exercised by the central government or delegated by that government to provincial authorities ....

The principle was established once for all that parents were not to be allowed to do as they willed with their children, if they willed either to set them to work or to let them run wild without elementary education. Freedom of contract in respect of all dealings with the labour of children was so far limited ....

The most mature man is prohibited by law from contracting to labour in factories, or pits, or workshops, unless certain rules for the protection of health and limb are complied with. In like manner he is prohibited from living in a house which the sanitary inspector pronounces unwholesome. The free sale or letting of a certain kind of commodity is thereby prevented. Here, then, is a great system of restriction, which yet hardly any impartial person wishes to see reversed; which many of us wish to see made more complete. Perhaps, however, we have never thoroughly considered the principles on which we approve it. It may be well, therefore, to spend a short time in ascertaining these principles. We shall then be on surer ground in approaching those more difficult questions of legislation which must shortly be dealt with, and of which the settlement is sure to be resisted in the name of individual liberty.

We shall probably all agree that freedom, rightly understood, is the greatest of blessings; that its attainment is the true end of all our effort as citizens. But when we thus speak of freedom, we should consider carefully what we mean by it. We do not mean merely freedom from restraint or compulsion. We do not mean merely freedom to do as we like irrespectively of what it is that we like. We do not mean a freedom that can be enjoyed by one man or one set of men at the cost of a loss of freedom to others. When we speak of freedom as something to be so highly prized, we mean a positive power or capacity of doing or enjoying something worth doing or enjoying, and that, too, something that we do or enjoy in common with others. We mean by it a power which each man exercises through the help or security given him by his fellow-men, and which he in turn helps to secure for them. When we measure the progress of a society by its growth in freedom, we measure it by the increasing development and exercise on the whole of those powers of contributing to social good with which we believe the members of the society to be endowed; in short, by the greater power on the part of the citizens as a body to make the most and best of themselves. Thus, though of course there can be no freedom among men who act not willingly but under compulsion, yet on the other hand the mere removal of compulsion, the mere enabling a man to do as he likes, is in itself no contribution to true freedom. In one sense no man is so well able to do as he likes as the wandering savage. He has no master. There is no one to say to him nay. Yet we do not count him really free, because the freedom of savagery is not strength, but weakness. The actual powers of the noblest savage do not admit of comparison with those of the humblest citizen of a law-abiding state. He is not the slave of man, but he is the slave of nature. Of compulsion by natural necessity he has plenty of experience, though of restraint by society none at all. Nor can he deliver himself from that compulsion except by submitting to this restraint. So to submit is the first step in true freedom, because the first step towards the full exercise of the faculties with which man is endowed. But we rightly refuse to recognise the highest development on the part of an exceptional individual or exceptional class, as an advance towards the true freedom of man, if it is founded on a refusal of the same opportunity to other men. The powers of the human mind have probably never attained such force and keenness, the proof of what society can do for the individual has never been so strikingly exhibited, as among the small groups of men who possessed civil privileges in the small republics of antiquity. The whole framework of our political ideas, to say nothing of our philosophy, is derived from them. But in them this extraordinary efflorescence of the privileged class was accompanied by the slavery of the multitude. That slavery was the condition on which it depended, and for that reason it was doomed to decay. There is no clearer ordinance of that supreme reason, often dark to us, which governs the course of man's affairs, than that no body of men should in the long run be able to strengthen itself at the cost of others' weakness. The civilisation and freedom of the ancient world were shortlived because they were partial and exceptional. If the ideal of true freedom is the maximum of power for all members of human society alike to make the best of themselves, we are right in refusing to ascribe the glory of freedom to a state in which the apparent elevation of the few is founded on the degradation of the many, and in ranking modern society, founded as it is on free industry, with all its confusion and ignorant licence and waste of effort, above the most splendid of ancient republics.

If I have given a true account of that freedom which forms the goal of social effort, we shall see that freedom of contract, freedom in all the forms of doing what one will with one's own, is valuable only as a means to an end. That end is what I call freedom in the positive sense: in other words, the liberation of the powers of all men equally for contributions to a common good. No one has a right to do what he will with his own in such a way as to contravene this end. It is only through the guarantee which society gives him that he has property at all, or, strictly speaking, any right to his possessions. This guarantee is founded on a sense of common interest. Every one has an interest in securing to every one else the free use and enjoyment and disposal of his possessions, so long as that freedom on the part of one does not interfere with a like freedom on the part of others, because such freedom contributes to that equal development of the faculties of all which is the highest good for all. This is the true and the only justification of rights of property. Rights of property, however, have been and are claimed which cannot be thus justified. We are all now agreed that men cannot rightly be the property of men.

The institution of property being only justifiable as a means to the free exercise of the social capabilities of all, there can be no true right to property of a kind which debars one class of men from such free exercise altogether. We condemn slavery no less when it arises out of a voluntary agreement on the part of the enslaved person. A contract by which any one agreed for a certain consideration to become the slave of another we should reckon a void contract. Here, then, is a limitation upon freedom of contract which we all recognise as rightful. No contract is valid in which human persons, willingly or unwillingly, are dealt with as commodities, because such contracts of necessity defeat the end for which alone society enforces contracts at all.

Are there no other contracts which, less obviously perhaps but really, are open to the same objection? In the first place, let us consider contracts affecting labour. Labour, the economist tells us, is a commodity exchangeable like other commodities. This is in a certain sense true, but it is a commodity which attaches in a peculiar manner to the person of man. Hence restrictions may need to be placed on the sale of this commodity which would be unnecessary in other cases, in order to prevent labour from being sold under conditions which make it impossible for the person selling it ever to become a free contributor to social good in any form. This is most plainly the case when a man bargains to work under conditions fatal to health, e.g., in an unventilated factory. Every injury to the health of the individual is, so far as it goes, a public injury. It is an impediment to the general freedom; so much deduction from our power, as members of society, to make the best of ourselves. Society is, therefore, plainly within its right when it limits freedom of contract for the sale of labour, so far as is done by our laws for the sanitary regulations of factories, workshops, and mines. It is equally within its right in prohibiting the labour of women and young persons beyond certain hours. If they work beyond those hours, the result is demonstrably physical deterioration; which, as demonstrably, carries with it a lowering of the moral forces of society. For the sake of that general freedom of its members to make the best of themselves, which it is the object of civil society to secure, a prohibition should be put by law, which is the deliberate voice of society, on all such contracts of service as in a general way yield such a result. The purchase or hire of unwholesome dwellings is properly forbidden on the same principle. Its application to compulsory education may not be quite so obvious, but it will appear on a little reflection. Without a command of certain elementary arts and knowledge, the individual in modern society is as effectually crippled as by the loss of a limb or a broken constitution. He is not free to develop his faculties. With a view to securing such freedom among its members it is as certainly within the province of the state to prevent children from growing up in that kind of ignorance which practically excludes them from a free career in life, as it is within its province to require the sort of building and drainage necessary for public health.

Our modern legislation, then with reference to labour, and education, and health, involving as it does manifold interference with freedom of contract, is justified on the ground that it is the business of the state, not indeed directly to promote moral goodness, for that, from the very nature of moral goodness, it cannot do, but to maintain the conditions without which a free exercise of the human faculties is impossible ....

Now, we shall probably all agree that a society in which the public health was duly protected, and necessary education duly provided for, by the spontaneous action of individuals, was in a higher condition than one in which the compulsion of law was needed to secure these ends. But we must take men as we find them. Until such a condition of society is reached, it is the business of the state to take the best security it can for the young citizens' growing up in such health and with so much knowledge as is necessary for their real freedom. In so doing it need not at all interfere with the independence and self-reliance of those whom it requires to do what they would otherwise do for themselves. The man who, of his own right feeling, saves his wife from overwork and sends his children to school, suffers no moral degradation from a law which, if he did not do this for himself, would seek to make him do it. Such a man does not feel the law as constraint at all. To him it is simply a powerful friend. It gives him security for that being done efficiently which, with the best wishes, he might have much trouble in getting done efficiently if left to himself. No doubt it relieves him from some of the responsibility which would otherwise fall to him as head of a family, but, if he is what we are supposing him to be, in proportion as he is relieved of responsibilities in one direction he will assume them in another. The security which the state gives him for the safe housing and sufficient schooling of his family will only make him the more careful for their well-being in other respects, which he is left to look after for himself. We need have no fear, then, of such legislation having an ill effect on those who, without the law, would have seen to that being done, though probably less efficiently, which the law requires to be done. But it was not their case that the laws we are considering were especially meant to meet. It was the overworked women, the ill-housed and untaught families, for whose benefit they were intended. And the question is whether without these laws the suffering classes could have been delivered quickly or slowly from the condition they were in. Could the enlightened self-interest or benevolence of individuals, working under a system of unlimited freedom of contract, have ever brought them into a state compatible with the free development of the human faculties? No one considering the facts can have any doubt as to the answer to this question. Left to itself, or to the operation of casual benevolence, a degraded population perpetuates and increases itself. Read any of the authorised accounts, given before royal or parliamentary commissions, of the state of the labourers, especially of the women and children, as they were in our great industries before the law was first brought to bear on them, and before freedom of contract was first interfered with in them. Ask yourself what chance there was of a generation, born and bred under such conditions, ever contracting itself out of them. Given a certain standard of moral and material well-being, people may be trusted not to sell their labour, or the labour of their children, on terms which would not allow that standard to be maintained. But with large masses of our population, until the laws we have been considering took effect, there was no such standard. There was nothing on their part, in the way either of self-respect or established demand for comforts, to prevent them from working and living, or from putting their children to work and live, in a way in which no one who is to be a healthy and free citizen can work and live. No doubt there were many high-minded employers who did their best for their workpeople before the days of state-interference, but they could not prevent less scrupulous hirers of labour from hiring it on the cheapest terms. It is true that cheap labour is in the long run dear labour, but it is so only in the long run, and eager traders do not think of the long run. If labour is to be had under conditions incompatible with the health or decent housing or education of the labourer, there will always be plenty of people to buy it under those conditions, careless of the burden in the shape of rates and taxes which they may be laying up for posterity. Either the standard of well-being on the part of the sellers of labour must prevent them from selling their labour under those conditions, or the law must prevent it. With a population such as ours was forty years ago, and still largely is, the law must prevent it and continue the prevention for some generations, before the sellers will be in a state to prevent it for themselves ....

I have left myself little time to speak of the principles on which some of us hold that, in the matter of intoxicating drinks, a further limitation of freedom of contract is needed in the interest of general freedom ....

We justify it on the simple ground of the recognised right on the part of society to prevent men from doing as they like, if, in the exercise of their peculiar tastes in doing as they like, they create a social nuisance. There is no right to freedom in the purchase and sale of a particular commodity, if the general result of allowing such freedom is to detract from freedom in the higher sense, from the general power of men to make the best of themselves. Now with anyone who looks calmly at the facts, there can be no doubt that the present habits of drinking in

England do lay a heavy burden on the free development of man's powers for social good, a heavier burden probably than arises from all other preventible causes put together. It used to be the fashion to look on drunkenness as a vice which was the concern only of the person who fell into it, so long as it did not lead him to commit an assault on his neighbours. No thoughtful man any longer looks on it in this way. We know that, however decently carried on, the excessive drinking of one man means an injury to others in health, purse, and capability, to which no limits can be placed. Drunkenness in the head of a family means, as a rule, the impoverishment and degradation of all members of the family; and the presence of a drink-shop at the corner of a street means, as a rule, the drunkenness of a certain number of heads of families in that street. Remove the drink-shops, and, as the experience of many happy communities sufficiently shows, you almost, perhaps in time altogether, remove the drunkenness. Here, then, is a wide-spreading social evil, of which society may, if it will, by a restraining law, to a great extent, rid itself, to the infinite enhancement of the positive freedom enjoyed by its members. All that is required for the attainment of so blessed a result is so much effort and self-sacrifice on the part of the majority of citizens as is necessary for the enactment and enforcement of the restraining law. The majority of citizens may still be far from prepared for such an effort. That is a point on which I express no opinion. To attempt a restraining law in advance of the social sentiment necessary to give real effect to it, is always a mistake. But to argue that an effectual law in restraint of the drink-traffic would be a wrongful interference with individual liberty, is to ignore the essential condition under which alone every particular liberty can rightly be allowed to the individual, the condition, namely, that the allowance of that liberty is not, as a rule, and on the whole, an impediment to social good.

The more reasonable opponents of the restraint for which I plead, would probably argue not so much that it was necessarily wrong in principle, as that it was one of those short cuts to a good end which ultimately defeat their own object. They would take the same line that has been taken by the opponents of state-interference in all its forms. 'Leave the people to themselves,' they would say; 'as their standard of self-respect rises, as they become better housed and better educated, they will gradually shake off the evil habit. The cure so effected may not be so rapid as that brought by a repressive law, but it will be more lasting. Better that it should come more slowly through the spontaneous action of individuals, than more quickly through compulsion.'

But here again we reply that it is dangerous to wait. The slower remedy might be preferable if we were sure that it was a remedy at all, but we have no such assurance. There is strong reason to think the contrary. Every year that the evil is left to itself, it becomes greater. The vested interest in the encouragement of the vice becomes larger, and the persons affected by it more numerous. If any abatement of it has already taken place, we may fairly argue that this is because it has not been altogether left to itself; for the licensing law, as it is, is much more stringent and more stringently administered than it was ten years ago. A drunken population naturally perpetuates and increases itself. Many families, it is true, keep emerging from the conditions which render them specially liable to the evil habit, but on the other hand descent through drunkenness from respectability to squalor is constantly going on. The families of drunkards do not seem to be smaller than those of sober men, though they are shorter-lived; and that the children of a drunkard should escape from drunkenness is what we call almost a miracle. Better education, better housing, more healthy rules of labour, no doubt lessen the temptations to drink for those who have the benefit of these advantages, but meanwhile drunkenness is constantly recruiting the ranks of those who cannot be readily educated, and who will not be better housed, who make their employments dangerous and unhealthy. An effectual liquor law in short is the necessary complement of our factory acts, our education acts, our public health acts. Without it the full measure of their usefulness will never be attained ....

The danger of legislation, either in the interests of a privileged class or for the promotion of particular religious opinions, we may fairly assume to be over. The popular jealousy of law, once justifiable enough, is therefore out of date. The citizens of England now make its law. We ask them by law to put a restraint on themselves in the matter of strong drink. We ask them further to limit, or even altogether to give up, the not very precious liberty of buying and selling alcohol, in order that they may become more free to exercise the faculties and improve the talents which God has given them.

10 TRADITIONAL CONSERVATISM

The chief source of conservative thought is the Anglo-Irish parliamentarian Edmund Burke (1729–1797), who argued that government ought to be based on respect for tradition, which is a repository of the wisdom of the past. This selection, taken from Russell Kirk's book, The Conservative Mind: From Burke to Elliott, *offers a short summary of the main principles of Burkean conservatism.*

Kirk is a well-known American writer on politics and literature. He has often contributed to William F. Buckley's periodical, National Review, *the oldest and still one of the most widely read conservative magazines in the United States. The* Conservative Mind, *first published in 1953, was a major intellectual force in generating a conservative movement in postwar America. This selection is taken from the third edition (1960).*

• • • • • • • •

... Any informed conservative is reluctant to condense profound and intricate intellectual systems to a few pretentious phrases; he prefers to leave that technique to the enthusiasm of radicals. Conservatism is not a fixed and immutable body of dogma, and conservatives inherit from Burke a talent for re-expressing their convictions to fit the time. As a working premise, nevertheless, one can observe here that the essence of social conservatism is preservation of the ancient moral traditions of humanity. Conservatives respect the wisdom of their ancestors (this phrase was Strafford's and Hooker's, before Burke illuminated it); they are dubious of wholesale alteration. They think society is a spiritual reality, possessing an eternal life but a delicate constitution: it cannot be scrapped and recast as if it were a machine. "What is conservatism?" Abraham Lincoln inquired once. "Is it not adherence to the old and tried, against the new and untried?" It is that, but it is more. Professor Hearnshaw, in his *Conservatism in England*, lists a dozen principles of conservatives, but possibly these may be comprehended in a briefer catalogue. I think that there are six canons of conservative thought—

(1) Belief that a divine intent rules society as well as conscience, forging an eternal chain of right and duty which links great and obscure, living and dead. Political problems, at bottom, are religious and moral problems. A narrow rationality, what Coleridge calls the Understanding, cannot of itself satisfy human needs. "Every Tory is a realist," says Keith Feiling: "he knows that there are great forces in heaven and earth that man's philosophy cannot plumb or fathom. We do wrong to deny it, when we are told that we do not trust human reason: we do not and we may not. Human reason set up a cross on Calvary, human reason set up the cup of hemlock, human reason was canonised in Nôtre Dame." Politics is the art of apprehending and applying the Justice which is above nature.

(2) Affection for the proliferating variety and mystery of traditional life, as distinguished from the narrowing uniformity and equalitarianism and utilitarian aims of most radical systems. This is why Quintin Hogg (Lord Hailsham) and R. J. White describe conservatism as "enjoyment." It is this buoyant view of life which Walter Bagehot called "the proper source of an animated Conservatism."

(3) Conviction that civilized society requires orders and classes. The only true equality is more equality; all other attempts at levelling lead to despair, if enforced by positive legislation. Society longs for leadership, and if a people destroy natural distinctions among men, presently Buonaparte fills the vacuum.

(4) Persuasion that property and freedom are inseparably connected, and that economic levelling is not economic progress. Separate property from private possession, and liberty is erased.

(5) Faith in prescription and distrust of "sophisters and calculators." Man must put a control upon his will and his appetite, for conservatives know man to be governed more by emotion than by reason. Tradition and sound prejudice provide checks upon man's anarchic impulse.

(6) Recognition that change and reform are not identical, and that innovation is a devouring conflagration more often than it is a torch of progress. Society must alter, for slow change is the means of its conservation, like the human body's perpetual renewal; but Providence is the proper instrument for change, and the test of a statesman is his cognizance of the real tendency of Providential social forces.

Various deviations from this system of ideas have occurred, and there are numerous appendages to it; but in general conservatives have adhered to these articles of belief with a consistency rare in political history. To catalogue the principles of their opponents is more difficult.

At least five major schools of radical thought have competed for public favor since Burke entered politics: the rationalism of the *philosophes,* the romantic emancipation of Rousseau and his allies, the utilitarianism of the Benthamites, the positivism of Comte's school, and the collectivistic materialism of Marx and other socialists. This list leaves out of account those scientific doctrines, Darwinism chief among them, which have done so much to undermine the first principles of a conservative order. To express these several radicalisms in terms of a common denominator probably is presumptuous, foreign to the philosophical tenets of conservatism. All the same, in a hastily generalizing fashion one may say that radicalism since 1790 has tended to attack the prescriptive arrangement of society on the following grounds—

(1) The perfectability of man and the illimitable progress of society: meliorism. Radicals believe that education, positive legislation, and alteration of environment can produce men like gods; they deny that humanity has a natural proclivity toward violence and sin.

(2) Contempt for tradition. Reason, impulse, and materialistic determinism are severally preferred as guides to social welfare, trustier than the wisdom of our ancestors. Formal religion is rejected and a variety of anti-Christian systems are offered as substitutes.

(3) Political levelling. Order and privilege are condemned; total democracy, as direct as practicable, is the professed radical ideal. Allied with this spirit, generally, is a dislike of old parliamentary arrangements and an eagerness for centralization and consolidation.

(4) Economic levelling. The ancient rights of property, especially property in land, are suspect to almost all radicals; and collectivistic reformers hack at the institution of private property root and branch.

As a fifth point, one might try to define a common radical view of the state's function; but here the chasm of opinion between the chief schools of innovation is too deep for any satisfactory generalization. One can only remark that radicals unite in detesting Burke's description of the state as a divinely ordained moral essence, a spiritual union of the dead, the living, and those yet unborn ....

In a revolutionary epoch, sometimes men taste every novelty, sicken of them all, and return to ancient principles so long disused that they seem refreshingly hearty when they are rediscovered. History often appears to resemble a roulette wheel; there is truth in the old Greek idea of cycles, and round again may come the number which signifies a conservative order. One of those flaming clouds which we deny to the Deity but arrogate to our own employment may erase our present elaborate constructions as abruptly as the tocsin in the Faubourg St. Germain terminated an age equally tired of itself. Yet this roulette-wheel simile would be repugnant to Burke (or to John Adams), who knew history to be the unfolding of a Design. The true conservative thinks of this process, which looks like chance or fate, as, rather, the Providential operation of a moral law of polarity. And Burke, could he see our century, never would concede that a consumption-society, so near to suicide, is the end for which Providence has prepared man. If a conservative order is indeed to return, we ought to know the tradition which is attached to it, so that we may rebuild society; if it is not to be restored, still we ought to understand conservative ideas so that we may rake from the ashes what scorched fragments of civilization escape the conflagration of unchecked will and appetite.

11

NEOCONSERVATISM

*T*he *following selection summarizes the program of political and economic reform undertaken by Conservative governments in Great Britain, beginning in 1979 under Margaret Thatcher and continuing under her successor, John Major. The nature of the program illustrates the ambiguity of conservatism in the late 20th century. Although conservatives claim to be guided by the inherited wisdom of the past, many who call themselves "conservatives" now propose major alterations to the institutions of the welfare state developed by reform-liberal and social-democratic governments. Moreover, these reforms are conceived in the spirit of classical liberalism—smaller government, individual freedom, open markets. This is certainly true of the four main proposals discussed in this reading: privatization of state-owned industries; creation of internal markets for services, such as education and health care, that continue to be provided in the public sector; a "Citizen's Charter" to set standards for the delivery of public services; and the transformation of government departments into "agencies" that act almost as private businesses contracting with policy-makers to provide specified services to the state. The term "neoconservatism" is now often used to describe those contemporary currents of conservative thought that are based more on abstract ideas, such as the market and individual freedom, than on Burkean respect for tradition and continuity.*

The author of this selection, Dr. Madsen Pirie, was previously a professor of philosophy and is now president of the Adam Smith Institute in England. As an advisor to the Thatcher government, he helped design many of the policies described here. The text is taken from his 1993 book Blueprint for a Revolution, *distributed in Canada by the National Citizens' Coalition, a conservative advocacy group.*

• • • • • • • • •

Four of the most important initiatives undertaken by the governments elected since 1979 have been concerned with a transfer of power in society. Although they might seem to outsiders to be unrelated activities, in fact the policies of *privatization, internal markets, the Citizen's Charter, and restructuring the bureaucracy* form part of a common approach to the public sector. They aim to redistribute power downwards from government and its bureaucracy, and into the hands of ordinary citizens.

Of the four, privatization was the earliest and the most dramatic in terms of the results it achieved. It has enabled several dozen state industries and utilities in Britain to be taken out of the public sector and turned into private sector businesses. Although its economic benefits have been manifold, it could be argued that its social impact has been wider. In taking industries out of state hands and putting them into the sector where profits, costs and consumers have to be attended to, privatization has demonstrated very vividly that state control is a dead end. It ultimately destroys the industries it intends to operate for the public good.

Margaret Thatcher, who as Prime Minster presided over the first two of these policies, once remarked that the public control the private sector, but nobody controls the public sector. This is a truism. The public have more control over the output of private corporations than they do over that of the state industries. This happens because the private firms need their custom in order to survive and prosper, whereas the state industries do not. Financed from taxation, they have a lien on the public purse which makes them largely independent of consumer choices.

Although the state industries are theoretically controlled through the political process, experience has shown this control to be ineffective. The public sector has a life of its own which defies political control, as successive governments learned while trying to make them less costly and more efficient.

Privatization cut like a knife through the political problems which beset state industries. In returning them to the private sector, it returned them to the influence of consumers. Making them competitive wherever possible, and commercial always, it made them behave in ways which responded to the pressures of the market instead of those in the political process.

The experience which Britain gained by the application of this policy has proved hugely beneficial to other countries heading down the same road. The implications for the developing world were spotted early on. Many of them had seen their economies ruined by state control and state ownership, much of it learned, it should be said, from the British universities which their future leaders had attended. If privatization could unloose the stranglehold which state intervention had locked upon them, then their economies could perhaps develop and prosper in the free market. Britain offered not only the rationale behind the rejection of state control, but the mechanisms by which it could be undone.

The result of this was that British expertise in privatization became a major export industry, with British advisers leading the world as those with the skills and the experience to oversee the transfer of industries from government to private hands. As the numbers of countries following this course mounted, it became increasingly hard to name countries where privatization is not a fact of economic life. They now include Cuba, Iran and North Korea, and few others.

While the impact upon the developing world was anticipated, no one expected the communist countries to become the chief centres of privatization in the 1990s. Since the collapse of socialism across the world, though, it has been the post communist countries who have embraced privatization most eagerly. With economies crippled by decades of socialism, they have the greatest need to restore private sector initiatives and to get a private market operating again as quickly as possible. Of all the international customers for privatization, the post communists have proved to be amongst the most enthusiastic. They know, after all, what socialism and central planning mean in practice.

The demise of socialism on the world stage has critically blunted the enthusiasm of those in Britain who argued for state ownership. They feel unable to sustain the drive at home for something which has been so thoroughly discredited on the world stage. By driving out communism from their own countries, the peoples of central and Eastern Europe have driven the threat of socialism from ours. The reformed Labour Party in Britain no longer threatens to undo what privatization has achieved.

It should be pointed out that privatization only became a popular policy after it succeeded. Virtually no individual sale commanded popular support in advance. Only when it was done and had been seen to succeed did it attract popular support. It takes a brave government to lead so determinedly from the front, and Britain had the advantage of a brave leadership during this period. Other countries which try to gain popular support for privatization in advance find their leaders cowering behind opinion polls when they could be leading the way. Privatization won its support in practice, not in theory. Its transformation of ailing state industries into vibrant private ones is what won it support.

The leadership, brave as it was, did not attempt the privatization of the human services in Britain. The process of reforming them started with the probably correct assumption that they could not be privatized in the conventional sense. People had grown so used to "free" health and "free" education that any attempt to make people pay in a private market was thought to be doomed to political defeat. Even if people were better off as a result, even manifestly better off, still it was thought that "free" human services were totems too holy to be assaulted.

In the absence of privatization, government settled for internal markets in education and health. The markets were "internal" in the sense that people did not pay with their own money. The services remained free to users at the point of consumption, and financed out of taxation. But where the allocation of resources had flowed through a bureaucratic network, it was now changed to follow from consumer choices. In selecting a school or a doctor, individual members of the public were now making decisions which had financial consequences. The state money followed in the wake of those decisions.

The innovative aspect of internal markets was that people were allocating resources when they made decisions, even though those resources were not their own. The new structure meant that the state's money followed the individual's choice.

Although internal markets have only just started in Britain, it is already apparent that they have succeeded in making the human services responsive. They are bringing those state services into the realm of activities which people control by their decisions. In place of a uniform state supply which emanated from the centre, there is now a reactive system which responds to the demands made upon it, and in which the supply has to be constantly geared to what members of the public ask of it.

The paternalist state, which gave the public the education and health services which it thought were best for them (and which were often best for the producers of the same) is being replaced by the entrepreneurial state, in which public sector producers vie with each other to make their product more attractive to a public which can not only choose between them, but can determine by its choice where the funding is to be directed.

In both education and health the internal markets are in their early stages, and will require subsequent measures to improve them. But the principle is already well established: that people make choices, and that those choices have financial consequences upon producers.

The third of the policy initiatives which form part of this strategy of reforming the public sector is that which is now known as the Citizen's Charter. Essentially it represents an attempt to make the state industries behave more responsively toward their customers. They do not face the commercial and competitive pressures which make the private sector behave in this way, so other pressures are applied.

The Citizen's Charter uses legislation and statute to require appropriate behaviour from the public services. Specifically, it draws up a contract between each state service and its public, a contract which contains mechanisms to make it enforceable. In place of a vague public duty to provide some undefined and unspecified level of performance, the Charter substitutes specific performance targets which each service is pledged to achieve. These are qualified in terms of waiting periods and maximum acceptable delays.

Furthermore, the Charter requires each of these contracts to have built into it a mechanism under which members of the public have access to some form of redress if the promised performance does not materialize. That redress may range from a formal apology to financial compensation; the important thing is that the procedure for making complaints and following them through must be a simple one which members of the public will have no difficulty in using.

The Citizen's Charter is even more recent than internal markets, yet it, too, has already shown signs that it can achieve at least a part of what it was designed to achieve. The public services have already responded with key initiatives to upgrade their levels of service and their accessibility to the general public. They are becoming more user friendly.

The fourth reform, one of the most dramatic and far-reaching, is the fundamental overhaul of the Civil Service through the introduction of agencies. It has restructured the machinery of government itself.

This reform involved breaking up the bureaucracy's unified management structure and delegating the functions of the Civil Service to discrete functional units. These units have independent management, full delegation of responsibility and clearly delineated boundaries.

The Civil Service becomes a much smaller core surrounded by independent agencies, each of which performs work according to policy guidelines set up by the Minister, with the resources allocated to them.

In effect, these agencies perform very much like private firms performing government work under contract. The price is set, the work agreed and then the agency is left to get on with the job.

Targets for improved financial performance, efficiency and service quality have been set and largely met or exceeded by the agencies.

By May, 1993, there were 89 agencies with about 350,000 staff or half of the Civil Service. This total will rise shortly as more agencies come though the pipeline.

The test of internal markets, the Citizen's Charter and agencies will be the same as it was for privatization. They will be judged on what they achieve in practice. While the early indicators are good, it will be some years before anything other than an interim verdict can be given. That interim verdict suggests for the moment that, like privatization, they are proving effective in reversing the top-down structure of the state industries. In its place they are substituting structures which send signals from consumers and enable members of the public to have a direct influence on their output and performance.

The common thread linking the four policies is Public Choice Theory. They arise from a desire to make society interactive and spontaneous instead of command driven, but the methods they choose are specifically linked to an analysis of society which applied the methods of economics to social affairs. Public Choice Theory uses the premise that politicians, civil servants, interest groups and ordinary electors, behave as if they were economic participants, each trying to maximize their advantage, and acting rationally to secure their objectives.

Many political reforms are thwarted, despite their apparent worthiness, because they are seen as hostile to interest groups sufficiently powerful to derail them. Governments which fail to push through their reforms in such circumstances are frequently derided as "too weak," whereas a more valid criticism might be that they are using the wrong methods. However strong willed a government might be, there are limits to its ability to ignore political reality.

It is all very well saying "make government smaller," but if the pressures are all conspiring to make government larger, and if most of the key interest groups see a bigger government as one which enhances their own advantage, strength of will by itself is probably not enough to overcome those tendencies.

The policies which are formulated in the light of Public Choice Theory are more complex and more sophisticated than their rivals precisely because they take account of interest groups and attempt to circumvent the opposition which might be generated by them in the normal course of events. Like antibodies, these policies have elements designed to target those interest groups and to neutralize their opposition.

The policies of privatization, internal markets, the Citizen's Charter and agencies are all horses from the same stable; they have arisen in the light of Public Choice analysis. They all attempt to engineer a society which will be determined spontaneously by the interaction of its citizens, and to transform those elements of it which are planned and directed from the centre.

That these policies have proved effective in Britain and have enjoyed considerable success there since 1979 is now a matter of historical record. That they could succeed in achieving similar objectives in other countries is less certain, but there are few reasons to suppose that they could not. Certainly, privatization has now spread to the world stage with some striking successes.

In the 1980s representatives of other countries came to Britain to learn about privatization and to see how it might be applied in their own countries. It is significant that a similar interest is now being shown in internal markets, the Citizen's Charter and agencies. Several countries have launched studies to see how the British experience might be used to advantage to develop similar policies suited to their own circumstances.

It would well be that, just as privatization became a world phenomenon, so too could the other three policies which followed in its wake in pursuit of similar objectives. Internal markets in health and education, a Citizen's Charter for public services and the restructuring of the bureaucracy through agencies could well become the normal means by which most countries seek to control an overgrown and unresponsive public sector.

REVOLUTIONARY SOCIALISM

*K*arl Marx (1818–1883) and Friedrich Engels (1820–1895), the most important socialist writers of the nineteenth century, were ambiguous about the way in which socialism would come to power. At times, they spoke as if a violent revolution were the only way to attain power. Reading 12, an excerpt from the Communist Manifesto, sketches their famous theory of "historical materialism," which was supposed to make this revolution inevitable. According to Marx and Engels, history is the story of class struggle. Each era, each economic and social system, sees an internal contest between a ruling class that owns the means of production and an exploited class that languishes under its domination. But history is not endless cyclical recurrence; it is a progressive story with a happy ending. The last system—"capitalism"—destroys itself utterly through class warfare between bourgeoisie and proletariat. When the proletariat seizes power in a world revolution, it abolishes private property and uses the state to ratify the social changes that have already occurred. Society can become "classless" because other classes like the peasantry and middle classes, already reduced through relentless competition, lose their economic basis of private ownership. Once the numerically small bourgeoisie is dispossessed, there remains only the world proletariat. But a single-class society is essentially classless, for there is no longer a division based on wealth or power.

Reading 13 is excerpted from Karl Marx and Friedrich Engels' Manifesto of the Communist Party. Marx drafted most of this document with some help from Engels. Begun in 1847 as the programmatic statement of the Communist League, a rather shadowy revolutionary organization, it was first published in Germany early *in 1848. It played no important role in the series of revolutions that swept across Europe in that year, but it later became a standard text of the socialist movement.*

• • • • • • • • •

A spectre is haunting Europe—the spectre of Communism. All the Powers of old Europe have entered into a holy alliance to exorcise this spectre: Pope and Czar, Metternich and Guizot, French Radicals and German police spies.

Where is the party in opposition that has not been decried as Communistic by its opponents in power? Where the Opposition that has not hurled back the branding reproach of Communism, against the more advanced opposition parties, as well as against its reactionary adversaries?

Two things result from this fact:

I. Communism is already acknowledged by all European Powers to be itself a Power.

II. It is high time that Communists should openly, in the face of the whole world, publish their views, their aims, their tendencies, and meet this nursery tale of the Spectre of Communism with a Manifesto of the party itself.

To this end, Communists of various nationalities have assembled in London, and sketched the following Manifesto, to be published in the English, French, German, Italian, Flemish, and Danish languages.

BOURGEOIS AND PROLETARIANS

The history of all hitherto existing society is the history of class struggles.

Freeman and slave, patrician and plebeian, lord and serf, guild-master and journeyman, in a word, oppressor and oppressed, stood in constant opposition to one another, carried on an uninterrupted, now hidden, now open fight, a fight that each time ended, either in revolutionary reconstitution of society at large, or in the common ruin of the contending classes.

In the earlier epochs of history, we find almost everywhere a complicated arrangement of society into various orders, a manifold gradation of social rank. In ancient Rome we have patricians, knights, plebeians, slaves; in the Middle Ages, feudal lords, vassals, guild-masters, journeymen, apprentices, serfs; in almost all of these classes, again, subordinate gradations.

The modern bourgeois society that has sprouted from the ruins of feudal society has not done away with class antagonisms. It has but established new classes, new conditions of oppression, new forms of struggle in place of the old ones.

Our epoch, the epoch of the bourgeoisie, possesses, however, this distinctive feature: it has simplified the class antagonisms. Society as a whole is more and more splitting up into two great hostile camps, into two great classes directly facing each other: Bourgeoisie and Proletariat.

From the serfs of the Middle Ages sprang the chartered burghers of the earliest towns. From these burgesses the first elements of the bourgeoisie were developed.

The discovery of America, the rounding of the Cape, opened up fresh ground for the rising bourgeoisie. The East-Indian and Chinese markets, the colonization of America, trade with the colonies, the increase in the means of exchange and in commodities generally, gave to commerce, to navigation, to industry, an impulse never before known, and thereby, to the revolutionary element in the tottering feudal society, a rapid development.

The feudal system of industry, under which industrial production was monopolized by closed guilds, now no longer sufficed for the growing wants of the new markets. The manufacturing system took its place. The guild-masters were pushed on one side by the manufacturing middle class; division of labour between the different corporate guilds vanished in the face of division of labour in each single workshop.

Meantime the markets kept ever growing, the demand ever rising. Even manufacture no longer sufficed. Thereupon, steam and machinery revolutionized industrial production. The place of manufacture was taken by the giant, Modern Industry, the place of the industrial middle class, by industrial millionaires, the leaders of the whole industrial armies, the modern bourgeois.

Modern industry has established the world market, for which the discovery of America paved the way. This market has given an immense development to commerce, to navigation, to communication by land. This development has, in its turn, reacted on the extension of industry; and in proportion as industry, commerce, navigation, railways extended, in the same proportion the bourgeoisie developed, increased its capital, and pushed into the background every class handed down from the Middle Ages.

We see, therefore, how the modern bourgeoisie is itself the product of a long course of development, of a series of revolutions in the modes of production and of exchange.

Each step in the development of the bourgeoisie was accompanied by a corresponding political advance of that class. An oppressed class under the sway of the feudal nobility, an armed and self-governing association in the medieval commune; here independent urban republic (as in Italy and Germany), there taxable "third estate" of the monarchy (as in France), afterwards, in the period of manufacture proper, serving either the semifeudal or the absolute monarchy as a counterpoise against the nobility, and, in fact, corner-stone of the great monarchies in general, the bourgeoisie has at last, since the establishment of Modern Industry and of the world market, conquered for itself, in the modern representative State, exclusive political sway. The executive of the modern State is but a committee for managing the common affairs of the whole bourgeoisie.

The bourgeoisie, historically, has played a most revolutionary part.

The bourgeoisie, wherever it has got the upper hand, has put an end to all feudal, patriarchal, idyllic relations. It has pitilessly torn asunder motley feudal ties that bound man to his "natural superiors," and has left remaining no other nexus between man and man than naked self-interest, than callous "cash payment." It has drowned the most heavenly ecstasies of religious fervour, of chivalrous enthusiasm, of philistine sentimentalism, in the icy water of egotistical calculation. It has resolved personal worth into exchange value, and in place of the numberless indefeasible chartered freedoms, has set up that single, unconscionable freedom—Free Trade. In one word, for exploitation, veiled by religious and political illusions, it has substituted naked, shameless, direct, brutal exploitation.

The bourgeoisie has stripped of its halo every occupation hitherto honoured and looked up to with reverent awe. It has converted the physician, the lawyer, the priest, the poet, the man of science, into its paid wage labourers.

The bourgeoisie has torn away from the family its sentimental veil, and has reduced the family relation to a mere money relation.

The bourgeoisie has disclosed how it came to pass that the brutal display of vigour in the Middle Ages, which Reactionists so much admire, found its fitting complement in the most slothful indolence. It has been the first to show what man's activity can bring about. It has accomplished wonders far surpassing Egyptian pyramids, Roman aqueducts, and Gothic cathedrals; it has conducted expeditions that put in the shade all former Exoduses of nations and crusades.

The bourgeoisie cannot exist without constantly revolutionizing the instruments of production, and thereby the relations of production, and with them the whole relations of society. Conservation of the old modes of production in unaltered form, was, on the contrary, the first condition of existence for all earlier industrial classes. Constant revolutionizing of production, uninterrupted disturbance of all social conditions, everlasting uncertainty and agitation distinguish the bourgeois epoch from all earlier ones. All fixed, fast-frozen relations, with their train of ancient and venerable prejudices and opinions are swept away, all new-formed ones become antiquated before they can ossify. All that is solid melts into air, all that is holy is profaned, and man is at last compelled to face with sober senses, his real conditions of life, and his relations with his kind.

The need of a constantly expanding market for its products chases the bourgeoisie over the whole surface of the globe. It must nestle everywhere, settle everywhere, establish connexions everywhere.

The bourgeoisie has through its exploitation of the world market given a cosmopolitan character to production and consumption in every country. To the great chagrin of Reactionists, it has drawn from under the feet of industry the national ground on which it stood. All old-established national industries have been destroyed or are daily being destroyed. They are dislodged by new industries, whose introduction becomes a life and death question for all civilized nations, by industries that no longer work up indigenous raw material, but raw material drawn from the remotest zones; industries whose products are consumed, not only at home, but in every quarter of the globe. In place of the old wants, satisfied by the productions of the country, we find new wants, requiring for their satisfaction the products of distant lands and climes. In place of the old local and national seclusion and self-sufficiency, we have intercourse in every direction, universal inter-dependence of nations. And as in material, so also in intellectual production. The intellectual creations of individual nations become common property. National one-sidedness and narrow-mindedness become more and more impossible, and from the numerous national and local literatures, there arises a world literature.

The bourgeoisie, by the rapid improvement of all instruments of production, by the immensely facilitated means of communication, draws all, even the most barbarian, nations into civilization. The cheap prices of its commodities are the heavy artillery with which it batters down all Chinese walls, with which it forces the barbarians' intensely obstinate hatred of foreigners to capitulate. It compels all nations, on pain of extinction, to adopt the bourgeois mode of production; it compels them to introduce what it calls civilization into their midst, i.e., to become bourgeois themselves. In one word, it creates a world after its own image.

The bourgeoisie has subjected the country to the rule of the towns. It has created enormous cities, has greatly increased the urban population as compared with the rural, and has thus rescued a considerable part of the population from the idiocy of rural life. Just as it has made the country dependent on the towns, so it has made barbarian and semi-barbarian countries dependent on the civilized ones, nations of peasants on nations of bourgeois, the East on the West.

The bourgeoisie keeps more and more doing away with the scattered state of the population, of the means of production, and of property. It has agglomerated population, centralized means of production, and has concentrated property in a few hands. The necessary consequence of this was political centralization. Independent, or but loosely connected, provinces with separate interests, laws, governments and systems of taxation, became lumped together into one nation, with one government, one code of laws, one national class-interest, one frontier and one customs-tariff.

The bourgeoisie, during its rule of scarce one hundred years, has created more massive and more colossal productive forces than have all preceding generations together. Subjection of Nature's forces to man, machinery, application of chemistry to industry and agriculture, steam navigation, railways, electric telegraphs, clearing of whole continents for cultivation, canalization of rivers, whole populations conjured out of the ground—what earlier century had even a presentiment that such productive forces slumbered in the lap of social labour?

We see then: the means of production and of exchange, on whose foundation the bourgeoisie built itself up, were generated in feudal society. At a certain stage in the development of these means of production and of exchange, the conditions under which feudal society produced and exchanged, the feudal organization of agriculture and manufacturing industry, in one word, the feudal relations of property became no longer compatible with the already developed productive forces; they became so many fetters. They had to be burst asunder; they were burst asunder.

Into their place stepped free competition, accompanied by a social and political constitution adapted to it, and by the economical and political sway of the bourgeois class.

A similar movement is going on before our own eyes. Modern bourgeois society with its relations of production, of exchange and of property, a society that has conjured up such gigantic means of production and of exchange, is like the sorcerer, who is no longer able to control the powers of the nether world whom he has called up by his spells. For many a decade past the history of industry and commerce is but the history of the revolt of modern productive forces against modern conditions of production, against the property relations that are the conditions for the existence of the bourgeoisie and of its rule. It is enough to mention the commercial crises that by their periodical return put on its trial, each time more threateningly, the existence of the entire bourgeois society. In these crises a great part not only of the existing products, but also of the previously created productive forces, are periodically destroyed. In these crises there breaks out an epidemic that, in all earlier epochs, would have seemed an absurdity—the epidemic of overproduction. Society suddenly finds itself put back into a state of momentary barbarism; it appears as if a famine, a universal war of devastation had cut off the supply of every means of subsistence; industry and commerce seem to be destroyed; and why? Because there is too much civilization, too much means of subsistence, too much industry, too much commerce. The productive forces at the disposal of society no longer tend to further the development of the conditions of bourgeois property; on the contrary, they have become too powerful for these conditions, by which they are fettered, and so soon as they overcome these fetters, they bring disorder into the whole of bourgeois society, endanger the existence of bourgeois property. The conditions of bourgeois society are too narrow to comprise the wealth created by them. And how does the bourgeoisie get over these crises? On the one hand by enforced destruction of a mass of productive forces; on the other, by the conquest of new markets, and by the more thorough exploitation of the old ones. That is to say, by paving the way for more extensive and more destructive crises, and by diminishing the means whereby crises are prevented.

The weapons with which the bourgeoisie felled feudalism to the ground are now turned against the bourgeoisie itself.

But not only has the bourgeoisie forged the weapons that bring death to itself; it has also called into existence the men who are to wield those weapons—the modern working class—the proletarians.

In proportion as the bourgeoisie, i.e., capital, is developed, in the same proportion is the proletariat, the modern working class, developed—a class of labourers, who live only so long as they find work, and who find work only so long as their labour increases capital. These labourers, who must sell themselves piecemeal, are a commodity, like every other article of commerce, and are consequently exposed to all the vicissitudes of competition, to all the fluctuations of the market.

Owing to the extensive use of machinery and to division of labour, the work of the proletarians has lost all individual character, and, consequently, all charm for the workman. He becomes an appendage of the machine, and it is only the most simple, most monotonous, and most easily acquired knack, that is required of him. Hence, the cost of production of a workman is restricted, almost entirely, to the means of subsistence that he requires for his maintenance, and for the propagation of his race. But the price of a commodity, and therefore also of labour, is equal to its cost of production. In proportion, therefore, as the repulsiveness of the work increases, the wage decreases. Nay more, in proportion as the use of machinery and division of labour increases, in the same proportion the burden of toil also increases, whether by prolongation of the working hours, by increase of the work exacted in a given time or by increased speed of the machinery, etc.

Modern industry has converted the little workshop of the patriarchal master into the great factory of the industrial capitalist. Masses of labourers, crowded into the factory, are organized like soldiers. As privates of the industrial army they are placed under the command of a perfect hierarchy of officers and sergeants. Not only are they slaves of the bourgeois class, and of the bourgeois State; they are daily and hourly enslaved by the machine, by the overlooker, and, above all, by the individual bourgeois manufacturer himself. The more openly this despotism proclaims gain to be its end and aim, the more petty, the more hateful and the more embittering it is.

The less the skill and exertion of strength implied in manual labour, in other words, the more modern industry becomes developed, the more is the labour of men superseded by that of women. Differences of age and sex have no longer distinctive social validity for the working class. All are instruments of labour, more or less expensive to use, according to their age and sex.

No sooner is the exploitation of the labourer by the manufacturer, so far, at an end, that he receives his wages in cash, than he is set upon by the other portions of the bourgeoisie, the landlord, the shopkeeper, the pawnbroker, etc.

The lower strata of the middle class—the small tradespeople, shopkeepers, and retired tradesman generally, the handicraftsmen and peasants—all these sink gradually into the proletariat, partly because their diminutive capital does not suffice for the scale on which Modern Industry is carried on, and is swamped in the competition with the large capitalists, partly because their specialized skill is rendered worthless by new methods of production. Thus the proletariat is recruited from all classes of the population.

The proletariat goes through various stages of development. With its birth begins its struggle with the bourgeoisie. At first the contest is carried on by individual labourers, then by the work-people of a factory, then by the operatives of one trade, in one locality, against the individual bourgeois who directly exploits them. They direct their attacks not against the bourgeois conditions of production, but against the instruments of production themselves; they destroy imported wares that compete with their labour, they smash to pieces machinery, they set factories ablaze, they seek to restore by force the vanished status of the workman of the Middle Ages.

At this stage the labourers still form an incoherent mass scattered over the whole country, and broken up by their mutual competition. If anywhere they unite to form more compact bodies, this is not yet the consequence of their own active union, but of the union of the bourgeoisie, which class, in order to attain its own political ends, is compelled to set the whole proletariat in motion, and is moreover yet, for a time, able to do so. At this stage, therefore, the proletarians do not fight their enemies, but the enemies of their enemies, the remnants of absolute monarchy, the landowners, the non-industrial bourgeois, the petty bourgeoisie. Thus the whole historical movement is concentrated in the hands of the bourgeoisie; every victory so obtained is a victory for the bourgeoisie.

But with the development of industry the proletariat not only increases in number; it becomes concentrated in greater masses, its strength grows, and it feels that strength more. The various interests and conditions of life within the ranks of the proletariat are more and more equalized, in proportion as machinery obliterates all distinctions of labour, and nearly everywhere reduces wages to the same low level. The growing competition among the bourgeois, and the resulting commercial crises, make the wages of the workers even more fluctuating. The increasing improvement of machinery, ever more rapidly developing, makes their livelihood more and more precarious; the collisions between individual workmen and individual bourgeois take more and more the character of collisions between two classes. Thereupon the workers begin to form combinations (Trades Unions) against the bourgeois; they club together in order to keep up the rate of wages; they found permanent associations in order to make provision before for these occasional revolts. Here and there the contest breaks out into riots.

Now and then the workers are victorious, but only for a time. The real fruit of their battles lies, not in the immediate result, but in the ever-expanding union of the workers. This union is helped on by the improved means of communication that are created by modern industry and that place the workers of different localities in contact with one another. It was just this contact that was needed to centralize the numerous local struggles, all of the same character, into one national struggle between classes. But every class struggle is a political struggle. And that union, to attain which the burghers of the Middle Ages, with their miserable highways, required centuries, the modern proletarians, thanks to railways, achieve in a few years.

This organization of the proletarians into a class, and consequently into a political party, is continually being upset again by the competition between the workers themselves. But it ever rises up again, stronger, firmer, mightier. It compels legislative recognition of particular interests of the workers, by taking advantage of the divisions among the bourgeoisie itself. Thus the Ten Hours bill in England was carried.

Altogether collisions between the classes of the old society further, in many ways, the course of development of the proletariat. The bourgeoisie finds itself involved in a constant battle. At first with the aristocracy; later on, with those portions of the bourgeoisie itself, whose interests have become antagonistic to the progress of industry; at all times, with the bourgeoisie of foreign countries. In all these battles it sees itself compelled to appeal to the proletariat, to ask for its help, and thus, to drag it into the political arena. The bourgeoisie itself, therefore, supplies the proletariat with its own elements of political and general education, in other words, it furnishes the proletariat with weapons for fighting the bourgeoisie.

Further, as we have already seen, entire sections of the ruling classes are, by the advance of industry, precipitated into the proletariat, or are at least threatened in their conditions of existence. These also supply the proletariat with fresh elements of enlightenment and progress.

Finally, in times when the class struggle nears the decisive hour, the process of dissolution going on within the ruling class, in fact within the whole range of old society, assumes such a violent, glaring character, that a small section of the ruling class cuts itself adrift, and joins the revolutionary class, the class that holds the future in its hands. Just as, therefore, at an earlier period, a section of the nobility went over to the bourgeoisie, so now a portion of the bourgeoisie goes over to the prole-tariat, and in particular, a portion of the bourgeois ideologists, who have raised themselves to the level of comprehending theoretically the histor-ical movement as a whole.

Of all the classes that stand face to face with the bourgeoisie today, the proletariat alone is a really revolutionary class. The other classes decay and finally disappear in the face of modern industry; the prole-tariat is its special and essential product.

The lower middle class, the small manufacturer, the shopkeeper, the artisan, the peasant, all these fight against the bourgeoisie, to save from extinction their existence as fractions of the middle class. They are therefore not revolutionary, but conservative. Nay more, they are reac-tionary, for they try to roll back the wheel of history. If by chance they are revolutionary, they are so only in view of their impending transfer into the proletariat; they thus defend not their present, but their future interests, they desert their own standpoint to place themselves at that of the proletariat.

The "dangerous class," the social scum, that passively rotting mass thrown off by the lowest layers of old society, may, here and there, be swept into the movement by a proletarian revolution; its conditions of life, however, prepare it far more for the part of a bribed tool of reac-tionary intrigue.

In the conditions of the proletariat, those of old society at large are already virtually swamped. The proletarian is without property; his rela-tion to his wife and children has no longer anything in common with the bourgeois family relations; modern industrial labour, modern subjection to capital, the same in England as in France, in America as in Germany, has stripped him of every trace of national character. Law, morality, religion, are to him so many bourgeois prejudices, behind which lurk in ambush just as many bourgeois interests.

All the preceding classes that got the upper hand sought to fortify their already acquired status by subjecting society at large to their conditions of appropriation. The proletarians cannot become masters of the productive forces of society, except by abolishing their own previous mode of appropriation, and thereby also every other previous mode of appropriation. They have nothing of their own to secure and to fortify; their mission is to destroy all previous securities for, and insurances of, individual property.

All previous historical movements were movements of minorities, or in the interest of minorities. The proletarian movement is the self-conscious, independent movement of the immense majority, in the interest of the immense majority. The proletariat, the lowest stratum of our present society, cannot stir, cannot raise itself up, without the whole superincumbent strata of official society being sprung into the air.

Though not in substance, yet in form, the struggle of the proletariat with the bourgeoisie is at first a national struggle. The proletariat of each country must, of course, first all settle matters with its own bourgeoisie.

In depicting the most general phases of the development of the proletariat, we traced the more or less veiled civil war, raging within existing society, up to the point where that war breaks out into open revolution, and where the violent overthrow of the bourgeoisie lays the foundation for the sway of the proletariat.

Hitherto, every form of society has been based, as we have already seen, on the antagonism of oppressing and oppressed classes. But in order to oppress a class, certain conditions must be assured to it under which it can, at least, continue its slavish existence. The serf, in the period of serfdom, raised himself to membership in the commune, just as the petty bourgeois, under the yoke of feudal absolutism, managed to develop into a bourgeois. The modern labourer, on the contrary, instead of rising with the progress of industry, sinks deeper and deeper below the conditions of existence of his own class. He becomes a pauper, and pauperism develops more rapidly than population and wealth. And here it becomes evident that the bourgeoisie is unfit any longer to be the ruling class in society, and to impose its conditions of existence upon society as an overriding law. It is unfit to rule because it is incompetent to assure an existence to its slave within his slavery, because it cannot help letting him sink into such a state, that it has to feed him, instead of being fed by him. Society can no longer live under this bourgeoisie, in other words, its existence is no longer compatible with society.

The essential condition for the existence, and for the sway of the bourgeois class, is the formation and augmentation of capital; the condition for capital is wage labour. Wage labour rests exclusively on competition between the labourers. The advance of industry, whose involuntary promoter is the bourgeoisie, replaces the isolation of labourers, due to competition, by their revolutionary combination, due to association. The development of Modern Industry, therefore, cuts from under its feet the very foundation on which the bourgeoisie produces and appropriates products. What the bourgeoisie, therefore, produces, above all, is its own gravediggers. Its fall and the victory of the proletariat are equally inevitable.

13 SOCIAL DEMOCRACY

Although an apocalyptic vision of world destruction and renewal pervades the Communist Manifesto, Marx and Engels spoke at other times in more sober tones of a gradual accession to political power through the democratic political systems that had come into being in Western Europe and North America. This gradualist strategy is the source of the less radical wing of socialism now known as social democracy or democratic socialism. Along with the idea of revolution, social democrats have abandoned the withering away of the state, the classless society, and other characteristic Marxian speculations.

Reading 13, the Regina Manifesto, is an important Canadian example of social democracy. Adopted by the Co-operative Commonwealth Federation (CCF) in 1933 during the worst of the Depression, it was unremittingly hostile in tone to capitalism, calling for its eradication and replacement by a "full programme of socialized planning." Significantly, however, the Manifesto did not call for complete public ownership of the means of production; only certain key industries—finance, transportation, communications, utilities, and natural resources—were to be nationalized. Large areas of the economy, such as agriculture, manufacturing, wholesaling, retailing, and personal services, were to be left in private hands. Beyond this rather diluted program of socialization, the Manifesto's other proposals were similar in principle to reform liberalism: social security, protection of workers, socialized medicine, and redistribution through progressive taxation. All this was to be accomplished by constitutional means: "we do not believe in violence."

The Regina Manifesto was drafted in June 1933 by Frank Underhill, a history professor at the University of Toronto, and revised with the assistance of Eugene Forsey, F.R. Scott, and other colleagues in the League for Social Reconstruction, an association of socialist intellectuals modelled on the British Fabian Society and associated with the CCF. The Manifesto remained the CCF's major statement of principles until the party adopted a new declaration, much less openly socialist in tone, at the Winnipeg convention of 1956.

• • • • • • • • •

The CCF is a federation of organizations whose purpose is the establishment in Canada of a Co-operative Commonwealth in which the principle regulating production, distribution and exchange will be the supplying of human needs and not the making of profits.

We aim to replace the present capitalist system, with its inherent injustice and inhumanity, by a social order from which the domination and exploitation of one class by another will be eliminated, in which economic planning will supersede unregulated private enterprise and competition, and in which genuine democratic self-government, based upon economic equality will be possible. The present order is marked by glaring inequalities of wealth and opportunity, by chaotic waste and instability; and in an age of plenty it condemns the great mass of the people to poverty and insecurity. Power has become more and more concentrated into the hands of a small, irresponsible minority of financiers and industrialists and to their predatory interests the majority are habitually sacrificed. When private profit is the main stimulus to economic effort, our society oscillates between periods of feverish prosperity in which the main benefits go to speculators and profiteers, and of catastrophic depression, in which the common man's normal state of insecurity and hardship is accentuated. We believe that these evils can be removed only in a planned and socialized economy in which our natural resources and the principal means of production and distribution are owned, controlled and operated by the people.

The new social order at which we aim is not one in which individuality will be crushed out by a system of regimentation. Nor shall we interfere with cultural rights of racial or religious minorities. What we seek is a proper collective organization of our economic resources such as will make possible a much greater degree of leisure and a much richer individual life for every citizen.

This social and economic transformation can be brought about by political action, through the election of a government inspired by the ideal of a Co-operative Commonwealth and supported by a majority of the people. We do not believe in change by violence. We consider that both the old parties in Canada are the instruments of capitalist interests and cannot serve as agents of social reconstruction, and that whatever the superficial differences between them, they are bound to carry on government in accordance with the dictates of the big business interests who finance them. The CCF aims at political power in order to put an end to this capitalist domination of our political life. It is a democratic movement, a federation of farmer, labor, and socialist organizations, financed by its own members and seeking to achieve its ends solely by constitutional methods. It appeals for support to all who believe the time has come for a far-reaching reconstruction of our economic and political institutions and who are willing to work together for the carrying out of the following policies:

1. PLANNING

The establishment of a planned, socialized economic order, in order to make possible the most efficient development of the national resources and the most equitable distribution of the national income.

The first step in this direction will be the setting up of a National Planning Commission consisting of a small body of economists, engineers and statisticians assisted by an appropriate technical staff.

The task of the commission will be to plan for the production, distribution and exchange of all goods and services necessary to the efficient functioning of the economy; to co-ordinate the activities of the socialized industries; to provide for a satisfactory balance between the producing and consuming power; and to carry on continuous research into all branches of the national economy in order to acquire the detailed information necessary to efficient planning.

The Commission will be responsible to the Cabinet and will work in co-operation with the Managing Boards of the Socialized Industries.

It is now certain that in every industrial country some form of planning will replace the disintegrating capitalist system. The CCF will provide that in Canada the planning shall be done, not by a small group of capitalist magnates in their own interests, but by public servants acting in the public interest and responsible to the people as a whole.

2. SOCIALIZATION OF FINANCE

Socialization of all financial machinery—banking, currency, credit, and insurance, to make possible the effective control of currency, credit and prices, and the supplying of new productive equipment for socially desirable purposes.

Planning by itself will be of little use if the public authority has not the power to carry its plans into effect. Such power will require the control of finance and of all those vital industries and services, which, if they remain in private hands, can be used to thwart or corrupt the will of the public authority. Control of finance is the first step in the control of the whole economy. The chartered banks must be socialized and removed from the control of private profit-seeking interests; and the national banking system thus established must have at its head a Central Bank to control the flow of credit and the general price level, and to regulate foreign-exchange operations. A National Investment Board must also be set up, working in co-operation with the socialized banking system to mobilize and direct the unused surpluses of production for socially desired purposes as determined by the Planning Commission.

Insurance Companies, which provide one of the main channels for the investment of individual savings and which, under their present competitive organization, charge needlessly high premiums for the social services that they render, must also be socialized.

3. SOCIAL OWNERSHIP

Socialization (Dominion, Provincial or Municipal) of transportation, communications, electric power and all other industries and services essential to social planning, and their operation under the general direction of the Planning Commission by competent managements freed from day-to-day political interference.

Public utilities must be operated for the public benefit and not for the private profit of a small group of owners or financial manipulators. Our natural resources must be developed by the same methods. Such a programme means the continuance and extension of the public ownership enterprises in which most governments in Canada have already gone some distance. Only by such public ownership, operated on a planned economy, can our main industries be saved from the wasteful competition of the ruinous over-development and over-capitalization which are the inevitable outcome of capitalism. Only in a regime of public ownership and operation will the full benefits accruing from the centralized control and mass production be passed on to the consuming public.

Transportation, communication and electric power must come first in a list of industries to be socialized. Others, such as mining, pulp and paper, and the distribution of milk, bread, coal and gasoline, in which exploitation, waste, or financial malpractices are particularly prominent, must next be brought under social ownership and operation.

In restoring to the community its natural resources and in taking over industrial enterprises from private into public control we do not propose any policy of outright confiscation. What we desire is the most stable and equitable transition to the Co-operative Commonwealth. It is impossible to decide the policies to be followed in particular cases in an uncertain future, but we insist upon certain broad principles. The welfare of the community must take supremacy over the claims of private wealth. In times of war, human life has been conscripted. Should economic circumstances call for it, conscription of wealth would be more justifiable. We recognize the need for compensation in the case of individuals and institutions which must receive adequate maintenance during the transitional period before the planned economy becomes fully operative. But a CCF government will not play the role of rescuing bankrupt private concerns for the benefit of promoters and of stock and bond holders. It will not pile up a deadweight burden of unremunerative debt which represents claims upon the public treasury of a functionless owner class.

The management of publicly owned enterprises will be vested in boards who will be appointed for their competence in the industry and will conduct each particular enterprise on efficient economic lines. The machinery of management may well vary from industry to industry, but the rigidity of Civil Service rules should be avoided and likewise the evils of the patronage system as exemplified in so many departments of the Government today. Workers in these public industries must be free to organize in trade unions and must be given the right to participate in the management of the industry.

4. AGRICULTURE

Security of tenure for the farmer upon his farm on conditions to be laid down by individual provinces; insurance against unavoidable crop failure; removal of the tariff burden from the operations of agriculture; encouragement of producers' and consumers' co-operatives; the restoration and maintenance of an equitable relationship between prices of agricultural products and those of other commodities and services; and improving the efficiency of export trade in farm products.

The security of tenure for the farmer upon his farm which is imperilled by the present disastrous situation of the whole industry, together with adequate social insurance, ought to be guaranteed under equitable conditions.

The prosperity of agriculture, the greatest Canadian industry, depends upon a rising volume of purchasing power of the masses in Canada for all farm goods consumed at home, and upon the maintenance of large-scale exports of the staple commodities at satisfactory prices or equitable commodity exchange.

The intense depression in agriculture today is a consequence of the general world crisis caused by the normal workings of the capitalistic system resulting in: (1) Economic nationalism expressing itself in tariff barriers and other restrictions of world trade; (2) The decreased purchasing power of unemployed and under-employed workers and of the Canadian people in general; (3) The exploitation of both primary producers and consumers by monopolistic corporations who absorb a great proportion of the selling price of farm products. (This last is true, for example, of the distribution of milk and dairy products, the packing industry, and milling.)

The immediate cause of agricultural depression is the catastrophic fall in the world prices of foodstuffs as compared with other prices, this fall being due in large measure to the deflation of currency and credit. To counteract the worst effect of this, the internal price level should be raised so that the farmers' purchasing power may be restored.

We propose therefore:

(1) The improvement of the position of the farmer by the increase of purchasing power made possible by the social control of the financial system. This control must be directed towards the increase of employment as laid down elsewhere and towards raising the prices of farm commodities by appropriate credit and foreign policies.

(2) Whilst the family farm is the accepted basis for agricultural production in Canada the position of the farmer may be much improved by:
    (a) The extension of consumers' co-operatives for the purchase of farm supplies and domestic requirements; and
    (b) The extension of co-operative institutions for the processing and marketing of farm products.
    Both of the foregoing to have suitable state encouragement and assistance.

(3) The adoption of a planned system of agricultural development based upon scientific soil surveys directed towards better land utilization, and a scientific policy of agricultural development for the whole of Canada.

(4) The substitution for the present system of foreign trade, of a system of import and export boards to improve the efficiency of overseas marketing, to control prices, and to integrate the foreign trade policy with the requirements of the national economic plan.

5. EXTERNAL TRADE

The regulation in accordance with the National plan of external trade through import and export boards.

Canada is dependent on external sources of supply for many of her essential requirements of raw materials and manufactured products. These she can obtain only by large exports of the goods she is best fitted to produce. The strangling of our export trade by insane protectionist policies must be brought to an end. But the old controversies between free traders and protectionists are now largely obsolete. In a world of nationally organized economies Canada must organize the buying and selling of her main imports and exports under public boards, and take steps to regulate the flow of less important commodities by a system of licenses. By so doing she will be enabled to make the best trade agreements possible with foreign countries, put a stop to the exploitation of both primary producer and ultimate consumer, make possible the coordination of internal processing, transportation, and marketing of farm products, and facilitate the establishment of stable prices for such export commodities.

6. CO-OPERATIVE INSTITUTIONS

The encouragement by the public authority of both producers' and consumers' co-operative institutions.

In agriculture, as already mentioned, the primary producer can receive a larger net revenue through co-operative organization of purchases and marketing. Similarly in retail distribution of staple commodities such as milk, there is room for development both of public municipal operation and of consumers' co-operatives, and such co-operative organization can be extended into wholesale distribution and into manufacturing. Co-operative enterprises should be assisted by the state through appropriate legislation and through the provision of adequate credit facilities.

7. LABOUR CODE

A National Labour Code to secure for the worker maximum income and leisure, insurance covering illness, accident, old age, and unemployment, freedom of association and effective participation in the management of his industry or profession.

The spectre of poverty and insecurity which still haunts every worker, though technological developments have made possible a high standard of living for everyone, is a disgrace which must be removed from our civilization. The community must organize its resources to effect progressive reduction of the hours of work in accordance with technological development and to provide a constantly rising standard of life to everyone who is willing to work. A labor code must be developed which will include state regulation of all wages, equal reward and equal opportunity of advancement for equal services, irrespective of sex; measures to guarantee the right to work or the right to maintenance through stabilization of employment and through unemployment insurance; social insurance to protect workers and their families against the hazards of sickness, death, industrial accident and old age; limitation of hours of work and protection of health and safety in industry. Both wages and insurance benefits should be varied in accordance with family needs.

In addition workers must be guaranteed the undisputed right to freedom of association, and should be encouraged and assisted by the state to organize themselves in trade unions. By means of collective agreements and participation in works councils, the workers can achieve fair working rules and share in the control of industry and profession; and their organizations will be indispensable elements in a system of genuine industrial democracy.

The labor code should be uniform throughout the country. But the achievement of this end is difficult so long as jurisdiction over labor legislation under the BNA Act is mainly in the hands of the provinces. It is urgently necessary, therefore that the BNA Act be amended to make such a national labor code possible.

8. SOCIALIZED HEALTH SERVICES

Publicly organized health, hospital and medical services.

With the advance of medical science the maintenance of a healthy population has become a function for which every civilized community should undertake responsibility. Health services should be made at least as freely available as are educational services today. But under a system which is still mainly one of private enterprise the costs of proper medical care, such as the wealthier members of society can easily afford, are at present prohibitive for great masses of the people. A properly organized system of public health services including medical and dental care, which would stress the prevention rather than the cure of illness should be extended to all our people in both rural and urban areas. This is an enterprise in which Dominion, Provincial and Municipal authorities, as well as the medical and dental professions, can co-operate.

9. BNA ACT

The amendment of the Canadian Constitution, without infringing upon racial or religious minority rights or upon legitimate provincial claims to autonomy, so as to give the Dominion Government adequate powers to deal effectively with urgent economic problems which are essentially national in scope; the abolition of the Canadian Senate.

We propose that the necessary amendments to the BNA Act shall be obtained as speedily as required, safeguards being inserted to ensure that the existing rights of racial and religious minorities shall not be changed without their own consent. What is chiefly needed today is the placing in the hands of the national government of more power to control national economic development. In a rapidly changing economic environment our political constitution must be reasonably flexible. The present division of powers between Dominion and Provinces reflects the conditions of a pioneer, mainly agricultural, community in 1867. Our constitution must be brought into line with the increasing industrialization of the country and the consequent centralization of economic and financial power—which has taken place in the last two generations. The principle laid down in the Quebec Resolution of the Fathers of Confederation should be applied to the conditions of 1933, that "there be a general government charged with matters of common interest to the whole country and local governments for each of the provinces charged with the control of local matters in their respective sections."

The Canadian Senate, which was originally created to protect provincial rights, but has failed even in this function, has developed into a bulwark of capitalist interests, as is illustrated by the large number of company directorships held by its aged members. In its peculiar composition of a fixed number of members appointed for life it is one of the most reactionary assemblies in the civilized world. It is a standing obstacle to all progressive legislation, and the only permanently satisfactory method of dealing with the constitutional difficulties it creates is to abolish it.

10. EXTERNAL RELATIONS

A Foreign Policy designed to obtain international economic co-operation and to promote disarmament and world peace.

Canada has a vital interest in world peace. We propose, therefore, to do everything in our power to advance the idea of international co-operation as represented by the League of Nations and the International Labor Organization. We would extend our diplomatic machinery for keeping in touch with the main centres of world interest. But we believe that genuine international co-operation is incompatible with the capitalist regime which is in force in most countries, and that strenuous efforts are needed to rescue the League from its present condition of being mainly a League of capitalist Great Powers. We stand resolutely against all participation in imperialist wars. With the British Commonwealth, Canada must maintain her autonomy as a completely self-governing nation. We must resist all attempts to build up a new economic British Empire in place of the old political one, since such attempts readily lend themselves to the purposes of capitalist exploitation and may easily lead to further world wars. Canada must refuse to be entangled in any more wars fought to make the world safe for capitalism.

11. TAXATION AND PUBLIC FINANCE

A new taxation policy designed not only to raise public revenues but also to lessen the glaring inequalities of income and to provide funds for social services and the socialization of industry; the cessation of the debt creating system of Public Finance.

In the type of economy that we envisage, the need for taxation, as we now understand it, will have largely disappeared. It will nevertheless be essential during the transition period, to use the taxing powers, along with the other methods proposed elsewhere, as a means of providing for the socialization of industry, and for extending the benefits of Social Services.

At the present time capitalist governments in Canada raise a large proportion of their revenues from such levies as customs duties and sales taxes, the main burden of which falls upon the masses. In place of such taxes upon articles of general consumption, we propose a drastic extension of income, corporation and inheritance taxes, steeply graduated according to ability to pay. Full publicity must be given to income tax payments and our tax collection system must be brought up to the English standard of efficiency.

We also believe in the necessity for an immediate revision of the basis of Dominion and Provincial sources of revenues, so as to produce a coordinated and equitable system of taxation throughout Canada.

An inevitable effect of the capitalist system is the debt creating character of public financing. All public debts have enormously increased, and the fixed interest charges paid thereon now amount to the largest single item of so-called uncontrollable public expenditures. The CCF proposes that in future no public financing shall be permitted which facilitates the perpetuation of the parasitic interest-receiving class; that capital shall be provided through the medium of the National Investment Board and free from perpetual interest charges.

We propose that all Public Works, as directed by the Planning Commission, shall be financed by the issuance of credit, as suggested, based upon the National Wealth of Canada.

12. FREEDOM

Freedom of speech and assembly for all; repeal Section 98 of the Criminal Code; amendment of the Immigration Act to prevent the present inhuman policy of deportation; equal treatment before the law of all residents of Canada irrespective of race, nationality or religious or political beliefs.

In recent years, Canada has seen an alarming growth of Fascist tendencies among all governmental authorities. The most elementary rights of freedom of speech and assembly have been arbitrarily denied to workers and to all whose political and social views do not meet with the approval of those in power. The lawless and brutal conduct of the police in certain centres in preventing public meetings and in dealing with political prisoners must cease. Section 98 of the Criminal Code which has been used as a weapon of political oppression by a panic-stricken capitalist government, must be wiped off the statute book and those who have been imprisoned under it must be released. An end must be put to the inhuman practice of deporting immigrants who were brought to this country by immigration propaganda and now, through no fault of their own, find themselves victims of an executive department against whom there is no appeal to the courts of the land. We stand for full economic, political and religious liberty for all.

13. SOCIAL JUSTICE

The establishment of a commission composed of psychiatrists, psychologists, socially minded jurists and social workers, to deal with all matters pertaining to crime and punishment and the general administration of law, in order to humanize the law and to bring it into harmony with the needs of the people.

While the removal of economic inequality will do much to overcome the most glaring injustices in the treatment of those who come into conflict with the law, our present archaic system must be changed and brought into accordance with a modern concept of human relationships. This new system must not be based as is the present one, upon vengeance and fear, but upon an understanding of human behaviour. For this reason its planning and control cannot be left in the hands of those steeped in the outworn legal tradition; and therefore it is proposed that there shall be established a national commission composed of psychiatrists, psychologists, socially minded jurists and social workers whose duty it shall be to devise a system of prevention and correction consistent with other features of the new social order.

14. AN EMERGENCY PROGRAMME

The assumption by the Dominion Government of direct responsibility for dealing with the present critical unemployment situation and for tendering suitable work or adequate maintenance; the adoption of measures to relieve the extremity of the crisis such as a programme of public spending on housing, and other enterprises that will increase the real wealth of Canada, to be financed by the issue of credit based on the national wealth.

The extent of unemployment and the widespread suffering which it has caused, creates a situation with which provincial and municipal governments have long been unable to cope and forces upon the Dominion government direct responsibility for dealing with the crisis as the only authority with financial resources adequate to meet the situation. Unemployed workers must be secured in the tenure of their homes, and the scale and methods of relief, at present altogether inadequate, must be such as to preserve decent human standards of living.

It is recognized that even after a Co-operative Commonwealth Federation Government has come into power, a certain period of time must elapse before the planned economy can be fully worked out. During this brief transitional period, we propose to provide work and purchasing power for those now unemployed by a far-reaching programme of public expenditure on housing, slum clearance, hospitals, libraries, schools, community halls, parks, recreational projects, reforestation, rural electrification, the elimination of grade crossing, and other similar projects in both town and country. This programme, which would be financed by the issuance of credit based on the national wealth, would serve the double purpose of creating employment and meeting recognized social needs. Any steps which the Government takes, under this emergency programme, which may assist private business, must include guarantees of adequate wages and reasonable hours of work, and must be designed to further the advance towards the complete Co-operative Commonwealth.

Emergency measures, however, are of only temporary value, for the present depression is a sign of the mortal sickness of the whole capitalist system, and this sickness cannot be cured by the application of salves. These leave untouched the cancer which is eating at the heart of our society, namely, the economic system in which our natural resources and our principal means of production and distribution are owned, controlled and operated for the private profit of a small proportion of our population.

No CCF Government will rest content until it has eradicated capitalism and put into operation the full programme of socialized planning which will lead to the establishment in Canada of the Co-operative Commonwealth.

14

NATIONALISM

*A*s an emotion, nationalism is a feeling of loyalty to the nation as one's highest political community; as an ideology, it is the belief that the nation should be sovereign, i.e., a nation-state. But within these common parameters, there is much room for variation. This extract from Michael Ignatieff's book Blood and Belonging: Journeys into the New Nationalism (1993), explores a distinction between two fundamentally different forms of nationalism: "ethnic" nationalism, in which loyalty is based primarily on inherited factors such as race and mother tongue; and "civic" nationalism, in which loyalty is focused on an open political community.

Ignatieff was born in Canada in 1947; he is the son of George Ignatieff, a distinguished Canadian diplomat. After a short academic career in the field of history, Michael Ignatieff has become a well-known and much-travelled journalist and broadcaster. He currently resides in London, England.

• • • • • • • •

As a political doctrine, nationalism is the belief that the world's peoples are divided into nations, and that each of these nations has the right of self-determination, either as self-governing units within existing nation states or as nation states of their own.

As a cultural ideal, nationalism is the claim that while men and woman have many identities, it is the nation which provides them with their primary form of belonging.

As a moral ideal, nationalism is an ethic of heroic sacrifice, justifying the use of violence in the defence of one's nation against enemies, internal or external.

These claims—political, moral and cultural—underwrite each other. The moral claim that nations are entitled to be defended by force or violence depends on the cultural claim that the needs they satisfy for security and belonging are uniquely important. The political idea that all peoples should struggle for nationhood depends on the cultural claim that only nations can satisfy these needs. The cultural idea in turn underwrites the political claim that these needs cannot be satisfied without self-determination.

Each one of these claims is contestable and none is intuitively obvious. Many of the world's tribal peoples and ethnic minorities do not think of themselves as nations; many do not seek or require a state of their own. It is not obvious, furthermore, why national identify should be a more important element of personal identify than any other; nor is it obvious why defence of the nation justifies the use of violence.

But for the moment what matters is that nationalism is centrally concerned to define the conditions under which force or violence is justified in a people's defence, when their right of self-determination is threatened or denied. Self-determination here may mean either democratic self-rule or the exercise of cultural autonomy, depending on whether the national group in question believes it can achieve its goals within the framework of an existing state or seeks a state of its own.

All forms of nationalism vest political sovereignty in 'the people'—indeed the word 'nation' is often a synonym for 'the people'—but not all nationalist movements create democratic regimes, because not all nationalisms include all of the people in their definition of who constitutes the nation.

One type, civic nationalism, maintains that the nation should be composed of all those—regardless of race, colour, creed, gender, language or ethnicity—who subscribe to the nation's political creed. This nationalism is called civic because it envisages the nation as a community of equal, rights-bearing citizens, united in patriotic attachment to a shared set of political practices and values. This nationalism is necessarily democratic since it vests sovereignty in all of the people. Some elements of this ideal were first achieved in Great Britain. By the mid-eighteenth century, Britain was already a nation state composed of four nations—the Irish, the Scots, the Welsh and the English—united by a civic rather than an ethnic definition of belonging, i.e. by shared attachment to certain institutions: the Crown, Parliament and the rule of law. But it was not until the French and American revolutions, and the creation of the French and American republics, that civic nationalism set out to conquer the world.

Such an ideal was made easier to realize in practice because the societies of the Enlightenment were ethnically homogeneous or behaved as if they were. Those who did not belong to the enfranchised political class of white, propertied males—workers, women, black slaves, aboriginal peoples—found themselves excluded from citizenship and thus from the nation. Throughout the nineteenth and early twentieth century, these groups fought for civic inclusion. As a result of their struggle, most Western nation states now define their nationhood in terms of common citizenship and not by common ethnicity. One prominent exception is Germany.

Napolean's invasion and occupation of the German principalities in 1806 unleashed a wave of German patriotic anger and Romantic polemic against the French ideal of the nation state. The German Romantics argued that it was not the state which created the nation, as the Enlightenment believed, but the nation, its people, which created the state. What gave unity to the nation, what made it a home, a place of passionate attachment, was not the cold contrivance of shared rights, but the people's pre-existing ethnic characteristics: their language, religion, customs and traditions. The nation as Volk had begun its long and troubling career in European thought. All of the peoples of nineteenth-century Europe under imperial subjection—the Poles and Baltic peoples under the Russian yoke, the Serbs under Turkish rule, the Croats under the Habsburgs—looked to the German ideal of ethnic nationalism when articulating their right to self-determination. When Germany achieved unification in 1871 and rose to world-power status, her achievement was a demonstration of the success of ethnic nationalism to all the captive nations of imperial Europe.

Of these two types of nationalism, the civic has a greater claim to sociological realism. Most societies are not mono-ethnic; and even when they are, common ethnicity does not of itself obliterate division, because ethnicity is only one of the many claims on an individual's loyalty. According to the civic nationalist creed, what holds a society together is not common roots but law. By subscribing to a set of democratic procedures and values, individuals can reconcile their right to shape their own lives with their need to belong to a community. This in turn assumes that national belonging can be a form of rational attachment.

Ethnic nationalism claims, by contract, that an individual's deepest attachments are inherited, not chosen. It is the national community which defines the individual, not the individuals who define the national community. This psychology of belonging may have greater depth than civic nationalism's, but the sociology that accompanies it is a good deal less realistic. The fact, for example, that two Serbs share Serbian ethnic identity may unite them against Croats, but it will do nothing to stop them fighting each other over jobs, spouses, scarce resources and so on. Common ethnicity, by itself, does not create social cohesion or community, and when it fails to do so, as it must, nationalist regimes are necessarily impelled towards maintaining unity by force rather than by consent. This is one reason why ethnic nationalist regimes are more authoritarian than democratic.

They may also prove authoritarian because they are, in essence, a form of democracy conducted in the interests of the ethnic majority. Most of the new post-Cold War nation states give lip-service to the idea of a society of civic equals, and provide safeguards for minority rights. In reality, new nations like Serbia and Croatia, the Baltic states, the new Asian republics, have instituted ethnic-majority domination. Ethnic nationalism is a particular temptation for those ethnic majorities—like the Baltic peoples and the Ukrainians—formerly ruled by the imperially backed Russian minority.

It is sometimes argued that authoritarian ethnic nationalism only takes root where civic nationalism has never established itself. On this account, ethnic nationalism is flourishing in Eastern Europe because forty years of communist single-party rule effectively destroyed whatever civic or democratic culture there once had been in the region. If so, it ought to be true that ethnic nationalism does not sink deep roots in societies with extensive democratic traditions. Unfortunately this is not the case. European racism is a form of white ethnic nationalism—indeed it is a revolt against nationalism itself, against the very idea of a nation based in citizenship rather than ethnicity. This revolt is gaining ground in states like Britain, Italy, France, Germany and Spain with ample, if varying degrees of democratic experience.

There is also a host of examples—Northern Ireland, India and Canada, to name three—where ethnic nationalism flourishes within states formally committed to civic democracy. In Northern Ireland, between 1920 and 1972, the Loyalist Protestant majority used the British parliamentary system to maintain a comprehensive form of majoritarian tyranny against the Catholic minority. Being steeped in the British democratic and legal tradition did nothing to stop Loyalists from bending democracy to nationalist ends. In India, forty-five years of civic democracy have barely contained the ethnic and religious nationalisms which are currently tearing the country's system apart. In Canada, the picture is more optimistic, but the analytical point is the same. Full inclusion within a federal democratic system has not abated the force of Quebecois nationalism.

In all of these places, the fundamental appeal of ethnic nationalism is as a rationale for ethnic majority rule, for keeping one's enemies in their place or for overturning some legacy of cultural subordination. In the nations of Eastern Europe, ethnic nationalism offers something more. For when the Soviet empire and its satellite regimes collapsed, the nation state structures of the region also collapsed, leaving hundreds of ethnic groups at the mercy of each other. Since none of these groups had the slightest experience of conciliating their disagreements by democratic discussion, violence or force became their arbiter. Nationalist rhetoric swept through these regions like wildfire because it provided warlords and gunmen with a vocabulary of opportunistic self-justification. In the fear and panic which swept the ruins of the communist states people began to ask: so who will protect me now? Faced with a situation of political and economic chaos, people wanted to know who to trust, and who to call their own. Ethnic nationalism provided an answer that was intuitively obvious: only trust those of your own blood.

But if nationalism legitimizes an appeal to blood loyalty, and in turn blood sacrifice, it can only do so persuasively if it seems to appeal to people's better natures, and not just to their worst instincts. Since killing is not a business to be taken lightly, it must be done for a reason which makes its perpetrator think well of himself. If violence is to be legitimated, it must be in the name of all that is best in a people, and what is better than their love of home?

Nationalists are supremely sentimental. Kitsch is the natural aesthetic of an ethnic 'cleanser.' There is no killer on either side of the checkpoints who will not pause, between firing at his enemies, to sing a nostalgic song or even recite a few lines of some ethnic epic. The latent purpose of such sentimentality is to imply that one is in the grip of a love greater than reason, stronger than the will, a love akin to fate and destiny. Such a love assists the belief that it is fate, however tragic, which obliges you to kill.

Stripped of such sentimentality, what then is this belonging, and the need for it, which nationalism seems to satisfy so successfully? When nationalists claim that national belonging is the overridingly important form of all belonging, they mean that there is no other form of belonging—to your family, work or friends—which is secure if you do not have a nation to protect you. This is what warrants sacrifice on the nation's behalf. Without a nation's protection, everything that an individual values can be rendered worthless. Belonging, on this account, is first and foremost protection from violence. Where you belong is where you are safe; and where you are safe is where you belong. If nationalism is persuasive because it warrants violence, it is also persuasive because it offers protection from violence. The warlord is his people's protector; if he kills he does so in defence of the noblest cause: the protection of the innocent.

But belonging also means being recognized and being understood. As Isaiah Berlin has written in *Two Concepts of Liberty*, when I am among my own people, 'they understand me, as I understand them; and this understanding creates within me a sense of being somebody in the world.' To belong is to understand the tacit codes of the people you live with; it is to know that you will be understood without having to explain yourself. People, in short, 'speak your language.' This is why, incidentally, the protection and defence of a nation's language is such a deeply emotional nationalist cause, for it is language, more than land and history, which provides the essential form of belonging, which is to be understood. One can, of course, be understood in languages and in countries other than one's own; one can find belonging even in exile. But the nationalist claim is that full belonging, the warm sensation that people understand not merely what you say but what you mean, can only come when you are among your own people in your native land.

Anyone whose father was born in Russia, whose mother was born in England, whose education was in America, and whose working life has been spent in Canada, Great Britain and France, cannot be expected to be much of an ethnic nationalist. If anyone has a claim to being a cosmopolitan, it must be me. I wish I spoke more languages than I do, I wish I had lived in more nations than I have, and wish that more people understood that expatriation is not exile: it is merely the belonging of those who choose their home rather than inherit it.

For many years, I believed that the tide was running in favour of cosmopolitans like me. There seemed so many of us, for one thing. There were at least a dozen world cities—gigantic, multi-ethnic melting pots which provided a home for expatriates, exiles, migrants and transients of all kinds. For the urban professional populations of these major cities, a post-national state of mind was simply taken for granted. People in these places did not bother about the passports of the people they worked or lived with; did not care about the country-of-origin label on the goods they bought; they simply assumed that in constructing their own way of life they would borrow from the customs of every nation they happened to admire. Cosmopolitans made a positive ethic out of cultural borrowing: in culture, exogamy was better than endogamy, and promiscuity was better than provincialism.

There was nothing new in itself about this cosmopolitan ethic. We have lived with a global economy since 1700, and many of the world's major cities have been global entrepôts for centuries. A global market has been limiting the sovereignty and freedom of manoeuvre of nation states at least since Adam Smith first constructed a theory of the phenomenon at the outset of the age of nationalism in 1776. A global market in ideas and cultural forms has existed at least since the Enlightenment republic of letters. Rootless cosmopolitans have existed as a social type in the big imperial cities for centuries.

Two features, however, distinguish the big city cosmopolitanism of our era from what has gone before. First of all is its social and racial diffusion. Twentieth-century democracy and unprecedented post-war prosperity have extended the privileges of cosmopolitanism from a small white moneyed male elite to a substantial minority of the population of the nation states of the developed world. Suddenly, there are a lot of us about, and our sense of sharing a post-nationalist consciousness has been mightily reinforced by cheap air travel and telecommunications.

The second obvious change is that the global market we live in is no longer ordered by a stable imperial system. For two hundred years, the global expansion of capitalism was shaped by the territorial ambitions and policing authority of a succession of imperial powers, the British, French, German, Austro-Hungarian and Russian empires of the nineteenth and early twentieth centuries; and the Soviet and American joint imperium after the Second World War. Since 1989, we have entered the first era of global cosmopolitanism in which there is no framework of imperial order.

There have been three great re-orderings of the nation-states of Europe in this century: at Versailles in 1918, when the new nations of Eastern Europe were created from the ruins of the Austro-Hungarian, Turkish and Russian empires; at Yalta in 1945, when Roosevelt, Stalin and Churchill allocated the nation states of Western and Eastern Europe to two spheres of influence; and between 1989 and 1991, when the Soviet empire and the communist regimes of Eastern Europe collapsed. What distinguishes the third of these is that it has occurred without any imperial settlement whatever. No treaty exists to regulate the conflict between the territorial integrity of nation states in Eastern Europe and the right to self-determination of the peoples within them. For every resolution of this conflict by civilized divorce, Czech-style, there have been a dozen armed conflicts. The basic reason is obvious enough: the imperial police have departed.

The Americans may be the last remaining superpower, but they are not an imperial power: their authority is exercised in the defence of exclusively national interests, not in the maintenance of an imperial system of global order. As a result, large sections of Africa, Eastern Europe, Soviet Asia, Latin America and the Near East no longer come within any clearly defined sphere of imperial or great power influence. This means that huge sections of the world's population have won the 'right of self-determination' on the cruellest possible terms: they have been simply left to fend for themselves. Not surprisingly, their nation states are collapsing, as in Somalia and in many other nations of Africa. In crucial zones of the world, once heavily policed by empire—notably the Balkans—populations find themselves without an imperial arbiter to appeal to. Small wonder then, that unrestrained by stronger hands, they have set upon each other for that final settling of scores so long deferred by the presence of empire.

Globalism in a post-imperial age only permits a post-nationalist consciousness for those cosmopolitans who are lucky enough to live in the wealthy West. It has brought chaos and violence for the many small peoples too weak to establish defensible states of their own. The Bosnian Muslims are perhaps the most dramatic example of a people who turned in vain to more powerful neighbours to protect them. The people of Sarajevo were true cosmopolitans, fierce believers in ethnic heterogeneity. But they lacked either a reliable protector or a state of their own to guarantee peace among contending ethnicities.

What has happened in Bosnia must give pause to anyone who believes in the virtues of cosmopolitanism. It is only too apparent that cosmopolitanism is the privilege of those who can take a secure nation state for granted. Though we have passed into a post-imperial age, we are not in a post-nationalist age, and I cannot see how we will ever do so. The cosmopolitan order of the great cities—London, Los Angeles, New York, Paris—depends critically on the rule-enforcing capacities of the nation state. When this order breaks down, as it did during the Los Angeles riots of 1992, it becomes apparent that civilized, cosmopolitan multiethnic cities have as great a propensity for ethnic warfare as any Eastern European country.

In this sense, therefore, cosmopolitans like myself are not beyond the nation; and a cosmopolitan, post-nationalist spirit will always depend, in the end, on the capacity of nation states to provide security and civility for their citizens. In that sense alone, I am a civic nationalist, someone who believes in the necessity of nations and in the duty of citizens to defend the capacity of nations to provide the security and the rights we all need in order to live cosmopolitan lives. At the very least, cosmopolitan disdain and astonishment at the ferocity with which people will fight to win a nation state of their own is misplaced. They are, after all, only fighting for a privilege cosmopolitans have long taken for granted ....

15

FASCISM

*A*ll *varieties of liberalism, conservatism, and socialism have one thing in common: they are primarily concerned with the proper role of government in the political community. Nationalism, however, is more concerned with the boundaries of the political community: Who should be included and who should be excluded? There are as many varieties of nationalist ideology as there are communities because each nation generates its own mythology about the origin, history, and destiny of its people. This diversity means that nationalism is extraordinarily hard to character-ize, and any single example is seriously misleading if taken as typical of all nation-alist thought.*

Reading 15 is Benito Mussolini's summary of the ideology of fascism, which we consider to be an exaggerated form of nationalism. In Mussolini's doctrine, nation and state are fused into one totalitarian entity. He goes so far as to say that "the nation is created by the State," and further asserts that warfare of nation against nation is essential to fascism. Such militarism takes to an extreme the general nationalistic tendency to think of the nation as the community to which we owe our highest allegiance.

Benito Mussolini (1883–1945) was the founder of Italian fascism. He assumed leadership of the Italian government in 1922 through the famous "march on Rome." He had been a socialist until World War I brought his nationalism to the fore, and as a result his fascist ideology is a combination of nationalism and socialism with traditional conservative themes of order and hierarchy. The reading which follows is a translation of Mussolini's article on fascism from volume 14 of the Enciclopedia

Italiana *and appears in* Through Fascism to World Power: A History of the Revolution in Italy.

• • • • • • • • •

FUNDAMENTAL IDEAS

Philosophic Conception

1. Like every concrete political conception, Fascism is thought and action. It is action with an inherent doctrine which, arising out of a given system of historic forces, is inserted in it and works on it from within. It has therefore a form co-related to the contingencies of time and place; but it has at the same time an ideal content which elevates it into a formula of truth in the higher region of the history of thought.

There is no way of exercising a spiritual influence on the things of the world by means of a human will-power commanding the wills of others, without first having a clear conception of the particular and transient reality on which the will-power must act, and without also having a clear conception of the universal and permanent reality in which the particular and transient reality has its life and being. To know men we must have a knowledge of man; and to have a knowledge of man we must know the reality of things and their laws.

There can be no conception of a State which is not fundamentally a conception of Life. It is a philosophy or intuition, a system of ideas which evolves itself into a system of logical construction, or which concentrates itself in a vision or in a faith, but which is always, at least virtually, an organic conception of the world.

Spiritualised Conception

2. Fascism would therefore not be understood in many of its manifestations (as, for example, in its organisations of the Party, its system of education, its discipline) were it not considered in the light of its general view of life. A spiritualised view.

To Fascism the world is not this material world which appears on the surface, in which man is an individual separated from all other men, standing by himself and subject to a natural law which instinctively impels him to lead a life of momentary and egoistic pleasure. In Fascism man is an individual who is the nation and the country. He is this by a moral law which embraces and binds together individuals and generations in an established tradition and mission, a moral law which suppresses the instinct to lead a life confined to a brief cycle of pleasure in order, instead, to replace it within the orbit of duty in a superior conception of life, free from the limits of time and space; a life in which the individual by self-abnegation and by the sacrifice of his particular interests, even by death, realises the entirely spiritual existence in which his value as a man consists.

Positive Conception of Life as a Struggle

3. It is therefore a spiritualised conception, itself also a result of the general reaction of the Century against the languid and materialistic positivism of the Eighteenth Century. Anti-positivist, but positive: neither sceptical nor agnostic, neither pessimistic nor passively optimistic, as are in general the doctrines (all of them negative) which place the centre of life outside of man, who by his free will can and should create his own world for himself.

Fascism wants a man to be active and to be absorbed in action with all his energies: it wants him to have a manly consciousness of the difficulties that exist and to be ready to face them. It conceives life as a struggle, thinking that it is the duty of man to conquer that life which is really worthy of him: creating in the first place within himself the (physical, moral, intellectual) instrument with which to build it.

As for the individual, so for the nation, so for mankind. Hence the high value of culture in all its forms (art, religion, science) and the supreme importance of education. Hence also the essential value of labour, with which man conquers nature and creates the human world (economic, political, moral, intellectual).

Ethical Conception

4. This positive conception of life is evidently an ethical conception. And it comprises the whole reality as well as the human activity which domineers it. No action is to be removed from the moral sense; nothing is to be in the world that is divested of the importance which belongs to it in respect of moral aims. Life, therefore, as the Fascist conceives it, is serious, austere, religious; entirely balanced in a world sustained by the moral and responsible forces of the spirit. The Fascist disdains the "easy" life.

Religious Conception

5. Fascism is a religious conception in which man is considered to be in the powerful grip of a superior law, with an objective Will which transcends the particular individual and elevates him into a fully conscious member of a spiritual society. Anyone who has stopped short at the mere consideration of opportunism in the religious policy of the

Fascist regime, has failed to understand that Fascism, besides being a system of government, is also a system of thought.

Historical and Realist Conception

6. Fascism is an historic conception in which man could not be what he is without being a factor in the spiritual process to which he contributes, either in the family sphere or in the social sphere, in the nation or in history in general to which all nations contribute. Hence is derived the great importance of tradition in the records, language, customs, and rules of human society. Man without a part in history is nothing.

For this reason Fascism is opposed to all the abstractions of an individualist character based upon materialism typical of the Eighteenth Century; and it is opposed to all the Jacobin innovations and utopias. It does not believe in the possibility of "happiness" on earth as conceived by the literature of the economists of the Seventeenth Century; it therefore spurns all the teleological conceptions of final causes through which, at a given period of history, a final systematisation of the human race would take place. Such theories only mean placing oneself outside real history and life, which is a continual ebb and flow and process of realisations.

Politically speaking, Fascism aims at being a realistic doctrine; in its practice it aspires to solve only the problems which present themselves of their own accord in the process of history, and which of themselves find or suggest their own solution. To have the effect of action among men, it is necessary to enter into the process of reality and to master the forces actually at work.

The Individual and Liberty

7. Anti-individualistic, the Fascist conception is for the State; it is for the individual only in so far as he coincides with the State, universal consciousness and will of man in his historic existence. It is opposed to the classic Liberalism which arose out of the need of reaction against absolutism, and which had accomplished its mission in history when the State itself had become transformed in the popular will and consciousness.

Liberalism denied the State in the interests of the particular individual; Fascism reaffirms the State as the only true expression of the individual.

And if liberty is to be the attribute of the real man, and not of the scarecrow invented by individualistic Liberalism, then Fascism is for liberty. It is for the only kind of liberty that is serious—the liberty of the State and of the individual in the State. Because, for the Fascist, all is comprised in the State and nothing spiritual or human exists—much less has any value—outside the State. In this respect Fascism is a totalizing concept, and the Fascist State—the unification and synthesis of every value—interprets, develops and potentiates the whole life of the people.

Conception of a Corporative State

8. No individuals nor groups (political parties, associations, labour unions, classes) outside the State. For this reason Fascism is opposed to Socialism, which clings rigidly to class war in the historic evolution and ignores the unity of the State which moulds the classes into a single, moral and economic reality. In the same way Fascism is opposed to the union of the labouring classes. But within the orbit of the State with ordinative functions, the real needs, which gave rise to the Socialist movement and to the forming of labour unions, are emphatically recognized by Fascism and are given their full expression in the Corporative System, which conciliates every interest in the unity of the State.

Democracy

9. Individuals form classes according to categories of interests. They are associated according to differentiated economical activities which have a common interest; but first and foremost they form the State. The State is not merely either the numbers or the sum of individuals forming the majority of a people. Fascism for this reason is opposed to the democracy which identifies peoples with the greatest number of individuals and reduces them to a majority level. But if people are conceived, as they should be, qualitatively and not quantitatively, then Fascism is democracy in its purest form. The qualitative conception is the most coherent and truest form and is therefore the most moral, because it sees a people realised in the consciousness and will of the few or even of one only; an ideal which moves to its realisation in the consciousness and will of all. By "all" is meant all who derive their justification as a nation, ethnically speaking, from their nature and history, and who follow the same line of spiritual formation and development as one single will and consciousness—not as a race nor as a geographically determined region, but as a progeny that is rather the outcome of a history which perpetuates itself; a multitude unified by an idea embodied in the will to have power and to exist, conscious of itself and of its personality.

Conception of the State

10. This higher personality is truly the nation, inasmuch as it is the State. The nation does not beget the State, according to the decrepit nationalistic concept which was used as a basis for the publicists of the national States in the Nineteenth Century. On the contrary, the nation is

created by the State, which gives the people, conscious of their own moral unity, the will, and thereby an effective existence. The right of a nation to its independence is derived not from a literary and ideal consciousness of its own existence, much less from a *de facto* situation more or less inert and unconscious, but from an active consciousness, from an active political will disposed to demonstrate in its right; that is to say, a kind of State already in its pride *(in fieri)*. The State, in fact, as a universal ethical will, is the creator of right.

Dynamic Reality

11. The nation as a State is an ethical reality which exists and lives in measure as it develops. A standstill is its death. Therefore the State is not only the authority which governs and which gives the forms of law and the worth of the spiritual life to the individual wills, but it is also the power which gives effect to its will in foreign matters, causing it to be recognised and respected by demonstrating through facts the universality of all the manifestations necessary for its development. Hence it is organisation as well as expansion, and it may be thereby considered, at least virtually, equal to the very nature of the human will, which in its evolution recognises no barriers, and which realises itself by proving its infinity.

The Role of the State

12. The Fascist State, the highest and the most powerful form of personality, is a force, but a spiritual one. It re-assumes all the forms of the moral and intellectual life of man. It cannot, therefore, be limited to a simple function of order and of safeguarding, as was contended by Liberalism. It is not a simple mechanism which limits the sphere of the presumed individual liberties. It is an internal form and rule, a discipline of the entire person: it penetrates the will as well as the intelligence. Its principle, a central inspiration of the living human personality in the civil community, descends into the depths and settles in the heart of the man of action as well as of the thinker, of the artist as well as of the scientist; the soul of our soul.

Discipline and Authority

13. Fascism, in short, is not only a lawgiver and the founder of institutions, but an educator and a promoter of the spiritual life. It aims to rebuild not the forms of human life, but its content, the man, the character, the faith. And for this end it exacts discipline and an authority which descends into and dominates the interior of the spirit without opposition. Its emblem, therefore, is the lictorian *fasces,* symbol of unity, of force and of justice.

16

CONSERVATISM, LIBERALISM, AND SOCIALISM IN CANADA

*A*lthough liberalism, conservatism, socialism, and nationalism are recogniz-
ably similar around the world, these ideologies interact with each other under the
influence of political culture to form distinctive configurations within national
boundaries. Reading 16 addresses this phenomenon. In showing how the unique
factors of Canadian history have influenced political thought in this country, Gad
Horowitz demonstrates that ideologies are not just abstract intellectual systems but
rather are the ideas of living people in a specific setting. His interpretation is built
on the "fragment theory" of the American writer Louis Hartz, who argued that the
"new societies" of the modern age—Canada, the United States, Australia, South
Africa—are ideological fragments of the more complex European matrix from which
they arose. The founders of these colonial fragments carried with them a certain
ideology that was important in its European mother country at the time of the founding—royal absolutism in the case of New France, Lockean liberalism in the case of
the United States—but not dominant in Europe as a whole. Thus the key to understanding the political thought of a colonial new society is to understand the ideology
that prevailed at the time of the founding. This is particularly challenging in the
Canadian case, since there were several "foundings" widely separated in space and
time. Horowitz attempts to unpack these complexities to produce a portrait of the
abiding characteristics of Canadian political thought. His major conclusion is that in
comparison to the United States, where liberalism has clearly dominated political
thought for two centuries, Canada is more like Europe in its ideological variety.

Reading 16 is an abridged version of Gad Horowitz's article, "Conservatism, Liberalism and Socialism in Canada: An Interpretation," which appeared in Volume 32 of the Canadian Journal of Economics and Political Science. The author is a professor of political science at the University of Toronto. Since it was published a quarter century ago, Horowitz's interpretation has been much debated and criticized, but it remains the starting point for the study of ideology in Canada.

• • • • • • • • •

INTRODUCTION: THE HARTZIAN APPROACH

In the United States, organized socialism is dead; in Canada socialism, though far from national power, is a significant force. Why this striking difference in the fortunes of socialism in two very similar societies?

Any attempt to account for the difference must be grounded in a general comparative study of the English-Canadian and American societies. It will be shown that the relative strength of socialism in Canada is related to the strength of toryism, and to the different position and character of liberalism in the two countries.

In North America, Canada is unique. Yet there is a tendency in Canadian historical and political studies to explain Canadian phenomena not by contrasting them with American phenomena but by identifying them as variations on a basic North American theme. I grant that Canada and the United States are similar, and that the similarities should be pointed out. But the pan-North American approach, since it searches out and concentrates on similarities, cannot help us to understand Canadian uniqueness. When this approach is applied to the study of English-Canadian socialism, it discovers, first, that like the American variety it is weak, and second, that it is weak for much the same reasons. These discoveries perhaps explain why Canadian socialism is weak in comparison to European socialism; they do not explain why Canadian socialism is so much stronger than American socialism.

The explanatory technique used in this study is that developed by Louis Hartz in *The Liberal Tradition in America* and *The Founding of New Societies*. It is applied to Canada in a mildly pan-North American way by Kenneth McRae in "The Structure of Canadian History," a contribution to the latter book.

The Hartzian approach is to study the new societies founded by Europeans (the United States, English Canada, French Canada, Latin America, Dutch South Africa, Australia) as "fragments" thrown off from

Europe. The key to the understanding of ideological development in a new society is its "point of departure" from Europe: the ideologies borne by the founders of the new society are not representative of the historic ideological spectrum of the mother country. The settlers represent only a fragment of that spectrum. The complete ideological spectrum ranges—in chronological order, and from right to left—from feudal or tory through liberal whig to liberal democrat to socialist. French Canada and Latin America are "feudal fragments." They were founded by bearers of the feudal or tory values of the organic, corporate, hierarchical community; their point of departure from Europe is before the liberal revolution. The United States, English Canada, and Dutch South Africa are "bourgeois fragments," founded by bearers of liberal individualism who have left the tory end of the spectrum behind them. Australia is the one "radical fragment," founded by bearers of the working class ideologies of mid-nineteenth-century Britain.

The significance of the fragmentation process is that the new society, having been thrown off from Europe, "loses the stimulus to change that the whole provides." The full ideological spectrum of Europe develops only out of the continued confrontation and interaction of its four elements; they are related to one another, not only as enemies, but as parents and children. A new society which leaves part of the past behind it cannot develop the future ideologies which need the continued presence of the past in order to come into being. In escaping the past, the fragment escapes the future, for "the very seeds of the later ideas are contained in the parts of the old world that have been left behind." The ideology of the founders is thus frozen, congealed at the point of origin.

Socialism is an ideology which combines the corporate-organic-collectivist ideas of toryism with the rationalist-egalitarian ideas of liberalism. Both the feudal and the bourgeois fragments escape socialism, but in different ways. A feudal fragment such as French Canada develops no whig (undemocratic) liberalism; therefore it does not develop the democratic liberalism which arises out of and as a reaction against whiggery; therefore it does not develop the socialism which arises out of and as a reaction against liberal democracy. The corporate-organic-collectivist component of socialism is present in the feudal fragment—it is part of the feudal ethos—but the radical rationalist-egalitarian component of socialism is missing. It can be provided only by whiggery and liberal democracy, and these have not come into being.

In the bourgeois fragment, the situation is the reverse: the radical rationalist-egalitarian component of socialism is present, but the corporate-organic-collectivist component is missing, because toryism has been left behind. In the bourgeois fragments "Marx dies because there is no sense of class, no yearning for the corporate past." The absence of socialism is related to the absence of toryism.

It is *because* socialists have a conception of society as more than an agglomeration of competing individuals—a conception close to the tory view of society as an organic community—that they find the liberal idea of equality (equality of opportunity) inadequate. Socialists disagree with liberals about the essential meaning of equality because socialists have a tory conception of society.

In a liberal bourgeois society which has never known toryism the demand for equality will express itself as left-wing or democratic liberalism as opposed to whiggery. The left will point out that all are not equal in the competitive pursuit of individual happiness. The government will be required to assure greater equality of opportunity—in the nineteenth century, by destroying monopolistic privileges; in the twentieth century by providing a welfare "floor" so that no one will fall out of the race for success, and by regulating the economy so that the race can continue without periodic crises.

In a society which thinks of itself as a community of classes rather than an aggregation of individuals, the demand for equality will take socialist form: for equality of condition rather than mere equality of opportunity; for co-operation rather than competition; for a community that does more than provide a context within which individuals can pursue happiness in a purely self-regarding way. At its most "extreme," socialism is a demand for the *abolition* of classes so that the good of the community can truly be realized. This is a demand which cannot be made by people who can hardly see class and community: the individual fills their eyes.

THE APPLICATION TO CANADA

It is a simple matter to apply the Hartzian approach to English Canada in a pan-North American way. English Canada can be viewed as a fragment of the American liberal society, lacking a feudal or tory heritage and therefore lacking the socialist ideology which grows out of it. Canadian domestic struggles, from this point of view, are a northern version of the American struggle between big-propertied liberals on the right and the *petit bourgeois* and working-class liberals on the left; the struggle goes on within a broad liberal consensus, and the voice of the tory or the socialist is not heard in the land. This pan-North American approach, with important qualifications, is adopted by Hartz and McRae in *The Founding of New Societies*. English Canada, like the United States, is a bourgeois fragment. No toryism in the past; therefore no socialism in the present.

But Hartz notes that the liberal society of English Canada has a "tory touch," that it is "etched with a tory streak coming out of the American revolution" ....

The most important un-American characteristics of English Canada, all related to the presence of toryism, are: (a) the presence of tory ideology in the founding of English Canada by the Loyalists, and its continuing influence on English-Canadian political culture; (b) the persistent power of whiggery or right-wing liberalism in Canada (the Family Compacts) as contrasted with the rapid and easy victory of liberal democracy (Jefferson, Jackson) in the United States; (c) the ambivalent centrist character of left-wing liberalism in Canada as contrasted with the unambiguously leftist position of left-wing liberalism in the United States; (d) the presence of an influential and legitimate socialist movement in English Canada as contrasted with the illegitimacy and early death of American socialism; (e) the failure of English-Canadian liberalism to develop into the one true myth, the nationalist cult, and the parallel failure to exclude toryism and socialism as "un-Canadian"; in other words, the legitimacy of ideological diversity in English Canada.

From a world perspective, these imperfections in English Canada's bourgeois character may appear insignificant. From the point of view of one who is interested in understanding English Canada not merely as a bourgeois fragment, but as a unique bourgeois fragment, the imperfections are significant.

THE PRESENCE OF TORYISM AND ITS CONSEQUENCES

Many students have noted that English-Canadian society has been powerfully shaped by tory values that are "alien" to the American mind. The latest of these is Seymour Martin Lipset, who stresses the relative strength in Canada of the tory values of "ascription" and "elitism" (the tendency to defer to authority), and the relative weakness of the liberal values of "achievement" and "egalitarianism." He points to such well-known features of Canadian history as the absence of a lawless, individualistic-egalitarian American frontier, the preference for Britain rather than the United States as a social model, and generally, the weaker emphasis on social equality, the greater acceptance by individuals of the facts of economic inequality, social stratification, and hierarchy. One tory touch in English Canada which is not noted by Lipset, but has been noted by many others (including McRae), is the far greater willingness of English-Canadian political and business elites to use the power of the state for the purpose of developing and controlling the economy ....

... Let us put it this way: pre-revolutionary America was a liberal fragment with insignificant traces of toryism, extremely weak feudal survivals. But they were insignificant in the *American* setting; they were far over-shadowed by the liberalism of that setting. The Revolution did not have to struggle against them; it swept them away easily and painlessly, leaving no trace of them in the American memory. But these traces of toryism were expelled into a *new* setting, and in this setting they were no longer insignificant. In this new setting, where there was no preestablished overpowering liberalism to force them into insignificance, they played a large part in shaping a new political culture, significantly different from the American. As Nelson wrote in *The American Tory*, "the Tories' organic conservatism represented a current of thought that failed to reappear in America after the revolution. A substantial part of the whole spectrum of European ... philosophy seemed to slip outside the American perspective." But it *reappeared* in Canada. Here the sway of liberalism has proved to be not total, but considerably mitigated by a tory presence initially and a socialist presence subsequently ....

The next step in tracing the development of the English-Canadian political culture must be to take account of the tremendous waves of British immigration which soon engulfed the original American Loyalist fragment. ... The political culture of a new nation is not necessarily fixed at the point of origin or departure; the founding of a new nation can go on for generations. If the later waves of immigration arrived before the *point of congealment* of the political culture, they must have participated actively in the process of culture formation. If this be so, the picture of English Canada as an almost exactly American liberal society becomes very difficult to defend. For *even if* it can be granted that the Loyalists were (almost exactly) American liberals, it is clear that later participants in the formation of the culture were not.

Between 1815 and 1850 almost one million Britons emigrated to Canada. The population of English Canada doubled in twenty years and quadrupled in forty. The population of Ontario increased tenfold in the same period—from about 95,000 in 1814 to about 950,000 in 1851 ....

The difficulty in applying the Hartzian approach to English Canada is that although the point of departure is reasonably clear, it is difficult to put one's finger on the point of congealment. Perhaps it was the Loyalist period; perhaps it was close to the mid-century mark; there are grounds for arguing that it was in the more recent past. But the important point is this: no matter where the point of congealment is located in time, the tory streak is present before the solidification of the political culture, and it is strong *enough* to produce *significant* "imperfections," or non-liberal, un-American attributes to English-Canadian society.

My own opinion is that the point of congealment came later than the Loyalists. The United States broke from Britain early, and the break was complete. Adam Smith and Tom Paine were among the last Britons who were spiritual founding fathers of the United States. Anything British, if it is of later than eighteenth century vintage, is un-American. The American mind long ago cut its ties with Britain and began to develop on its own. When did Canada break from Britain? When did the Canadian mind begin to develop on its own? Not very long ago most Canadians described themselves as followers of the "British way of life," and many railed against egalitarian ideas from south of the border as "alien." Nineteenth-century British ideologists are among the spiritual founding fathers of Canada. In the United States they are alien, though we may make an exception for Herbert Spencer.

The indeterminate location of the point of congealment makes it difficult to account in any *precise* way for the presence of socialism in the English-Canadian political cultural mix, though the presence is indisputable. If the point of congealment came *before* the arrival of the first radical or socialist-minded immigrants, the presence of socialism must be ascribed primarily to the earlier presence of toryism. Since toryism is a significant part of the political culture, at least part of the leftist reaction against it will sooner or later be expressed in its own terms, that is, in terms of *class* interests and the good of the community as a corporate entity (socialism) rather than in terms of the individual and his vicissitudes in the competitive pursuit of happiness (liberalism). If the point of congealment is very early, socialism appears at a later point not primarily because it is imported by British immigrants, but because it is contained as a potential in the original political culture. The immigrants then find that they do not have to give it up—that it is not un-Canadian—because it "fits" to a certain extent with the tory ideas already present. If the point of congealment is very late, the presence of socialism must be explained as a result of *both* the presence of toryism and the introduction of socialism into the cultural mix before congealment. The immigrant retains his socialism not only because it "fits" but also because nothing really *has* to fit. He finds that his socialism is not un-Canadian partly because "Canadian" has not yet been defined.

Canadian liberals cannot be expected to wax enthusiastic about the non-liberal traits of their country. They are likely to condemn the tory touch as anachronistic, stifling, undemocratic, out of tune with the essentially American ("free," "classless") spirit of English Canada. They dismiss the socialist touch as an "old-fashioned" protest, no longer necessary (if it ever was) in this best (liberal) of all possible worlds in which the "end of ideology" has been achieved. The secret dream of the Canadian liberal is the removal of English Canada's "imperfections"—in other words, the total assimilation of English Canada into the larger North American culture. But there is a flaw in this dream which might give pause even to the liberal. Hartz places special emphasis on one very unappetizing characteristic of the new societies—intolerance—which is strikingly absent in English Canada. Because the new societies other than Canada are unfamiliar with legitimate ideological diversity, they are unable to accept it and deal with it in a rational manner, either internally or on the level of international relations.

The European nation has an "identity which transcends any ideologist and a mechanism in which each plays only a part." Neither the tory, nor the liberal, nor the socialist, has a monopoly of the expression of the "spirit" of the nation. But the new societies, the fragments, contain only one of the ideologies of Europe; they are one-myth cultures. In the new setting, freed from its historic enemies past and future, ideology transforms itself into nationalism. It claims to be a moral absolute, "the great spirit of a nation." In the United States, liberalism becomes "Americanism"; a political philosophy becomes a civil religion, a nationalist cult. The American attachment to Locke is "absolute and irrational." Democratic capitalism is the American way of life; to oppose it is to be un-American.

To be an American is to be a bourgeois liberal. To be a French Canadian is to be a pre-Enlightenment Catholic; to be an Australian is to be a prisoner of the radical myth of "mateship"; to be a boer is to be a pre-Enlightened bourgeois Calvinist. The fragments escape the need for philosophy, for thought about values, for "where perspectives shrink to a single value, and that value becomes the universe, how can value itself be considered?" The fragment demands solidarity. Ideologies which diverge from the national myth make no impact; they are not understood, and their proponents are not granted legitimacy. They are denounced as aliens, and treated as aliens, because they *are* aliens. The fragments cannot understand or deal with the fact that *all* men are *not* bourgeois Americans, or radical Australians, or Catholic French Canadians, or Calvinist South Africans. They cannot make peace with the loss of ideological certainty.

The specific weakness of the United States is its "inability to understand the appeal of socialism" to the third world. Because the United States has "buried" the memory of the organic medieval community "beneath new liberal absolutism and nationalisms" it cannot understand that the appeal of socialism to nations with a predominantly non-liberal past (including French Canada) consists precisely in the promise of "continuing the corporate ethos in the very process" of modernization. The American reacts with isolationism, messianism, and hysteria.

English Canada, because it is the most "imperfect" of the fragments, is not a one-myth culture. In English Canada ideological diversity has not been buried beneath an absolutist liberal nationalism. Here Locke is not the one true god; he must tolerate lesser tory and socialist deities at his side. The result is that English Canada does not direct an uncomprehending intolerance at heterodoxy, either within its borders or beyond them. (What a "backlash" Parti-Pris or PSQ-type separatists would be getting if Quebec were in the United States!) In English Canada it has been possible to consider values without arousing the all-silencing cry of treason. Hartz observes that "if history had chosen English Canada for the American role" of directing the Western response to the world revolution, "the international scene would probably have witnessed less McCarthyite hysteria, less Wilsonian messianism."

Americanizing liberals might consider that the Pearsonian rationality and calmness which Canada displays on the world stage—the "mediating" and "peace-keeping" role of which Canadians are so proud—is related to the un-American (tory and socialist) characteristics which they consider to be unnecessary imperfections in English-Canadian wholeness. The tolerance of English-Canadian domestic politics is also linked with the presence of these imperfections. If the price of Americanization is the surrender of legitimate ideological diversity, even the liberal might think twice before paying it.

... My argument is essentially that non-liberal British elements have entered into English-Canadian society *together* with American liberal elements at the foundations. The fact is that Canada has been greatly influenced by both the United States and Britain. This is not to deny that liberalism is the dominant element in the English-Canadian political culture; it is to stress that it is not the sole element, that it is accompanied by vital and legitimate streams of toryism and socialism which have as close a relation to English Canada's "essence" or foundations" as does liberalism. English Canada's "essence" is both liberal and non-liberal. Neither the British nor the American elements can be explained away as "superstructural" excrescences.

UN-AMERICAN ASPECTS OF CANADIAN CONSERVATISM

So far, I have been discussing the presence of toryism in Canada without referring to the Conservative party. This party can be seen as a party of right-wing or business liberalism, but such an interpretation would be far from the whole truth; the Canadian Conservative party, like the British Conservative party and unlike the Republican party, is not monolithically liberal. If there is a touch of toryism in English Canada, its primary carrier has been the Conservative party. It would not be correct to say that toryism is *the* ideology of the party, or even that some Conservatives are tories. These statements would not be true even of the British Conservative party. The primary component of the ideology of business-oriented parties is liberalism; but there are powerful traces of the old pre-liberal outlook in the British Conservative party, and less powerful but still perceptible traces of it in the Canadian party. A Republican is always a liberal. A Conservative may be at one moment a liberal, at the next moment a tory, and is usually something of both.

If it is true that the Canadian Conservatives can be seen from some angles as right-wing liberals, it is also true that figures such as R.B. Bennett, Arthur Meighen, and George Drew cannot be understood simply as Canadian versions of William McKinley, Herbert Hoover, and Robert Taft. Canadian Conservatives have something British about them that American Republicans do not. It is not simply their emphasis on loyalty to the crown and to the British connection, but a touch of the authentic tory aura—traditionalism, elitism, the strong state, and so on. The Canadian Conservatives lack the American aura of rugged individualism. Theirs is not the characteristically American conservatism which conserves only *liberal* values.

It is possible to perceive in Canadian conservatism not only the elements of business liberalism and orthodox toryism, but also an element of "tory democracy"—the paternalistic concern for the "condition of the people," and the emphasis on the tory party as their champion—which, in Britain, was expressed by such figures as Disraeli and Lord Randolph Churchill. John A. Macdonald's approach to the emergent Canadian working class was in some respects similar to that of Disraeli. Later Conservatives acquired the image of arch reactionaries and arch enemies of the workers, but let us not forget that "Iron Heel" Bennett was also the Bennett of the Canadian New Deal.

The question arises: why is it that in Canada the *Conservative* leader proposes a New Deal? Why is it that the Canadian counterpart of Hoover apes *Roosevelt*? This phenomenon is usually interpreted as sheer historical accident, a product of Bennett's desperation and opportunism. But the answer may be that Bennett was not Hoover. Even in his "orthodox" days Bennett's views on the state's role in the economy were far from similar to Hoover's; Bennett's attitude was that of Canadian, not American, conservatism. Once this is recognized, it is possible to entertain the suggestion that Bennett's sudden radicalism, his sudden concern for the people, may not have been mere opportunism. It may have been a manifestation, a sudden activation under pressure, of a latent tory-democratic streak. Let it be noted also that the depression produced two Conservative splinter parties, both with "radical" welfare state programmes and both led by former subordinates of Bennett: H.H. Stevens' Reconstruction party and W.D. Herridge's New Democracy.

The Bennett New Deal is only the most extreme instance of what is usually considered to be an accident or an aberration—the occasional manifestation of "radicalism" or "leftism" by otherwise orthodox Conservative leaders in the face of opposition from their "followers" in the business community. Meighen, for example, was constantly embroiled with the "Montreal interests" who objected to his railway policies. On one occasion he received a note of congratulation from William Irvine: "The man who dares to offend the Montreal interests is the sort of man that the people are going to vote for." This same Meighen expressed on certain occasions, particularly after his retirement, an antagonism to big government and creeping socialism that would have warmed the heart of Robert Taft; but he combined his business liberalism with gloomy musings about the evil of universal suffrage—musings which Taft would have rejected as un-American. Meighen is far easier to understand from a British than from an American perspective, for he combined, in different proportions at different times, attitudes deriving from all three Conservative ideological streams: right-wing liberalism, orthodox toryism, and tory democracy.

The Western or agrarian Conservatives of the contemporary period, John Diefenbaker and Alvin Hamilton, who are usually dismissed as "prairie radicals" of the American type, might represent not only anti-Bay Street agrarianism but *also* the same type of tory democracy which was expressed before their time by orthodox business-sponsored Conservatives like Meighen and Bennett. The populism (anti-elitism) of Diefenbaker and Hamilton is a genuinely foreign element in Canadian conservatism, but their stress on the Tory party as champion of the people and their advocacy of welfare state policies are in the tory democratic tradition. Their attitudes to the monarchy, the British connection, and the danger of American domination are entirely orthodox Conservative attitudes. Diefenbaker Conservatism is therefore to be understood not simply as a Western populist phenomenon, but as an odd *combination* of traditional Conservative views with attitudes absorbed from the Western Progressive tradition.

Another aberration which may be worthy of investigation is the Canadian phenomenon of the red tory. At the simplest level, he is a Conservative who prefers the CCF-NDP to the Liberals, or a socialist who prefers the Conservatives to the Liberals, without really knowing why. At a higher level, he is a conscious ideological Conservative with some "odd" socialist notions (W.L. Morton) or a conscious ideological socialist with some "odd" tory notions (Eugene Forsey). The very suggestion that such affinities might exist between Republican and Socialists in the United States is ludicrous enough to make some kind of a point.

Red toryism is, of course, one of the results of the relationship between toryism and socialism which has already been elucidated. The tory and socialist minds have some crucial assumptions, orientations, and values in common, so that from certain angles they may appear not as enemies, but as two different expressions of the same basic ideological outlook. Thus, at the very highest level, the red tory is a philosopher who combines elements of socialism and toryism so thoroughly in a single integrated *Weltanschauung* that it is impossible to say that he is a proponent of either one as *against* the other. Such a red tory is George Grant, who has associations with both the Conservative party and the NDP, and who has recently published a book which defends Diefenbaker, laments the death of "true" British conservatism in Canada, attacks the Liberals as individualists and Americanizers, and defines socialism as a variant of conservatism (each "protects the public good against private freedom").

THE CHARACTER OF CANADIAN SOCIALISM

Canadian socialism is un-American in two distinct ways. It is un-American in the sense that it is a significant and legitimate political force in Canada, insignificant and alien in the United States. But Canadian socialism is also un-American in the sense that it does not speak the same language as American socialism. In Canada, socialism is British, non-Marxist, and worldly; in the United States it is German, Marxist, and other-worldly.

I have argued that the socialist ideas of British immigrants to Canada were not sloughed off because they "fit" with a political culture which already contained non-liberal components, and probably also because they were introduced into the political culture mix before the point of congealment. Thus socialism was not alien here. But it was not alien in yet another way; it was not borne by foreigners. The personnel and the ideology of the Canadian labour and socialist movements have been primarily British. Many of those who built these movements were British immigrants with past experience in the British labour movement; many others were Canadian-born children of such immigrants. And in British North America, Britons could not be treated as foreigners.

When socialism was brought to the United States, it found itself in an ideological environment in which it could not survive because Lockean individualism had long since achieved the status of a national religion; the political culture had already congealed, and socialism did not fit. American socialism was alien not only in this ideological sense, but in the ethnic sense as well; it was borne by foreigners from Germany and other continental European countries. These foreigners sloughed off their socialist ideas not simply because such ideas did not "fit" ideologically, but because as foreigners they were going through a general process of Americanization; socialism was only one of the many ethnically alien characteristics which had to be abandoned. The immigrant's ideological change was only one incident among many others in the general process of changing his entire way of life. According to David Saposs, "the factor that contributed most tellingly to the decline of the socialist movement was that its chief following, the immigrant workers, ... had become Americanized."

A British socialist immigrant to Canada had a far different experience. The British immigrant was not an "alien" in British North America. The English-Canadian culture not only granted legitimacy to his political ideas and absorbed them into its wholeness; it absorbed him as a person into the English-Canadian community, with relatively little strain, without demanding that he change his entire way of life before being granted full citizenship. He was acceptable to begin with, by virtue of being British. It is impossible to understand the differences between American and Canadian socialism without taking into account this immense difference between the ethnic contexts of socialism in the two countries.

The ethnic handicap of American socialism consisted not only in the fact that its personnel was heavily European. Equally important was the fact that it was a *brand* of socialism—Marxism—which found survival difficult not only in the United States but in all English-speaking countries. Marx has not found the going easy in the United States; but neither has he found the going easy in Britain, Canada, Australia, or New Zealand. The socialism of the United States, the socialism of De Leon, Berger, Hillquit, and Debs, is predominantly Marxist and doctrinaire, because it is European. The socialism of English Canada, the socialism of Simpsons, Woodsworth, and Coldwell, is predominantly Protestant, labourist, and Fabian, because it is British ....

The CCF has not been without its otherworldly tendencies; there have been doctrinal disagreements, and the party has always had a left wing interested more in "socialist education" than in practical political work. But this left wing has been a constantly declining minority. The party has expelled individuals and small groups—mostly Communists and Trotskyites—but it has never split. Its life has never been threatened by disagreement over doctrinal matters. It is no more preoccupied with theory than the British Labour party. It sees itself, and is seen by the public, not as a coterie of ideologists but as a party like the others, second to none in its avidity for office. If it has been attacked from the right for socialist "utopianism" and "impracticality," it has also been attacked from the right for abandoning the "true" socialist faith in an unprincipled drive for power ....

CANADIAN LIBERALISM: THE TRIUMPHANT CENTRE

Canadian Conservatives are not American Republicans; Canadian socialists are not American socialists; Canadian liberals are not American liberal Democrats.

The un-American elements in English Canada's political culture are most evident in Canadian conservatism and socialism. But Canadian liberalism has a British colour too. The liberalism of Canada's Liberal party should not be identified with the liberalism of the American Democratic party. In many respects they stand in sharp contrast to one another.

The three components of the English-Canadian political culture have not developed in isolation from one another; each has developed in interaction with the others. Our toryism and our socialism have been moderated by liberalism. But by the same token, our liberalism has been rendered "impure," in American terms, through its contacts with toryism and socialism. If English-Canadian liberalism is less individualistic, less ardently populistic-democratic, more inclined to state intervention in the economy, and more tolerant of "feudal survivals" such as monarchy, this is due to the uninterrupted influence of toryism upon liberalism, an influence wielded in and through the conflict between the two. If English-Canadian liberalism has tended since the depression to merge at its leftist edge with the democratic socialism of the CCF-NDP, this is due to the influence which socialism has exerted upon liberalism, in and through the conflict between them. The key to understanding the Liberal party in Canada is to see it as a *centre* party, with *influential* enemies on both right and left ....

King had to face the socialist challenge. He did so in the manner of European Liberal Reform. No need to worry about abandoning individualism; Locke was not Canada's national god; like European liberalism, Canadian liberalism had been revised. The similarity of socialism and Liberal Reform could be acknowledged; indeed it could be emphasized and used to attract the socialist vote. At the same time, King had to answer the arguments of socialism, and in doing so he had to spell out his liberalism. He had to stop short of socialism openly. Social reform, yes; extension of public ownership, yes; the welfare state, yes; increased state control of the economy, yes; but not too much. Not socialism. The result was that King, like the European liberals, could not go as far as Roosevelt ....

"In America, instead of being a champion of property, Roosevelt became the big antagonist of it; his liberalism was blocked by his radicalism." In Canada, since King had to worry not only about Bennett and Meighen and Drew, but also about Woodsworth and Coldwell and

Douglas, King had to embark upon a defence of private property. *He* was no traitor to his class. Instead of becoming the antagonist of property, he became its champion; his radicalism was blocked by his liberalism.

An emphasis on the solidarity of the nation as against divisive "class parties" of right and left was "of the very essence of the Reformist Liberal position in Europe." "Who," asks Hartz, "would think of Roosevelt as a philosopher of class solidarity?" Yet that is precisely what Roosevelt would have been if he had had to respond to a socialist presence in the American political culture. And that is precisely what King was in fact in Canada. His party was "the party of national unity." One of the most repeated charges against the CCF was that it was a divisive "class party"; the purpose of the Liberal party, on the other hand, was to preserve the solidarity of the Canadian people—the solidarity of its classes as well as the solidarity of French and English.

Hartz sums up Roosevelt in these words: "What emerges then ... is a liberal self that is lost from sight: a faith in property, a belief in class unity, a suspicion of too much state power, a hostility to the utopian mood, all of which were blacked out by the weakness of the socialist challenge." King's liberal self was not lost from sight, for the socialist challenge was stronger in Canada than in the United States.

The Liberal party has continued to speak the language of King: ambiguous and ambivalent, presenting first its radical face and then its conservative face, urging reform and warning against hasty, ill-considered change, calling for increased state responsibility but stopping short of socialism openly, speaking for the common people but preaching the solidarity of classes.

In the United States, the liberal Democrats are on the left. There is no doubt about that. In Canada, the Liberals are a party of the centre, appearing at times leftist and at times rightist. As such, they are much closer to European, especially British, Liberal Reform than to the American New Deal type of liberalism.

In the United States, the liberal Democrats are the party of organized labour. The new men of power, the labour leaders, have arrived politically; their vehicle is the Democratic party. In English Canada, if the labour leaders have arrived politically, they have done so in the CCF-NDP. They are nowhere to be found in the Liberal party. The rank and file, in the United States, are predominantly Democrats; in Canada at least a quarter are New Democrats, and the remainder show only a relatively slight, and by no means consistent, preference for the Liberals as against the Conservatives.

In the United States, left-wing "liberalism," as opposed to right-wing "liberalism," has always meant opposition to the domination of American life by big business, and has expressed itself in and through the Democratic party; the party of business is the Republican party. In Canada, business is close to both the Conservatives and the Liberals. The business community donates to the campaign funds of both and is represented in the leadership circles of both ....

The Liberal party in Canada does not represent the opposition of society to domination by organized business. It claims to be based on no particular groups, but on *all*. It is not against any particular group; it is for *all*. The idea that there is any real conflict between groups is dismissed, and the very terms "right" and "left" are rejected: "The terms 'right' and 'left' belong to those who regard politics as a class struggle .... The Liberal view is that true political progress is marked by ... the reconciliation of classes, and the promotion of the general interest above all particular interests."

17

NEW POLITICS

To a considerable degree, the traditional ideologies of liberalism, conservatism, and socialism are preoccupied with the creation and distribution of wealth. Although they have differing views of the role of government in that process, they all address the same issues. According to Ronald Inglehart, a political scientist at the University of Michigan, there has been a decisive shift since World War II in the politics of industrial societies. The direction of change is toward what he calls "post-materialism"—heightened concern with individual expression and quality of life. Post-materialism gives rise to new issue complexes, such as multiculturalism, feminism, and environmentalism, that cut across the old lines of ideological division.

Reading 17, written by Neil Nevitte for this volume, applies Inglehart's thesis to Canada, using Canadian public opinion data in a comparative context. Readers looking for a more detailed and rigorous treatment of the same topic can consult "The Ideological Contours of 'New Politics' in Canada: Policy, Mobilization and Partisan Support" by Neil Nevitte, Herman Bakvis, and Roger Gibbins, in volume 17 of the Canadian Journal of Political Science.

• • • • • • • •

Important changes seem to be sweeping across the western world. Citizens are more cynical about politics; trust in politicians has declined; confidence in government has eroded; and publics are less animated by the battles between the old left and the old right, the age-old conflicts between the haves and the have-nots. Traditional representative institutions are under stress and publics are harder to govern. These changes, some observers argue, are not haphazard. Rather, they signify the retreat of old politics and the emergence of new politics.

The central elements of the new politics thesis can be summarized fairly easily. The massive body of evidence pointing to the "decline of political parties," namely, the decomposition of longstanding electoral alignments, the weakening of citizen attachments to traditional political parties, and the increased electoral volatility among mass publics, indicate fundamental shifts in the value systems of the populations of modern states. The rise of new politics, it is suggested, has produced problems of governability for a combination of reasons. First, associated with the rise of new politics is the emergence of a new political agenda. That agenda gives prominence not to the class conflict that shaped political debate in the old industrial states, but to concerns about women, minorities, the environment, animal rights, gay rights, nuclear power, and peace. Central to the new agenda are those issues which are broadly defined as relevant to quality of life. Second, a substantial body of cross-national evidence shows that support for the new politics agenda is disproportionately concentrated within particular segments of the citizenry of advanced industrial states—a new class. That new class is younger, better educated, better informed about, and more interested in politics than its counterparts of preceding generations. New politics theorists argue that the emergence of this new class is a result of the structural changes associated with the late stages of industrialism, or post-industrialism. Members of the new class, mostly those born since the Second World War, are increasingly influential as they are now moving into the command posts of society. Because this new-class generation is only gradually displacing those generations that still cleave to old politics concerns, representative institutions are confronted with a dilemma, namely, how to satisfy a divided public, of which one part makes political demands based on a traditional agenda and the other part is driven by a new agenda.

Third, and perhaps of greatest significance, the rise of new politics is producing new patterns of political participation. Cross-national evidence drawn from a large number of advanced industrial states indicates that citizens holding new politics values are not just younger and better educated: they are also more knowledgeable about politics, more demanding of politicians and governments, and more "issue driven." In some ways, supporters of new politics exhibit precisely the qualities that make up the ideal citizen of the democratic polity: they are well-informed, articulate, sophisticated, and participatory. But they are also less deferential, more elite challenging, more critical of the status quo, and more dissatisfied with conventional hierarchically organized, representative institutions. The longstanding gap between the political skills of leaders and followers has narrowed. It is the combination of a new agenda and the redistribution of political skills that poses challenges to political parties, especially to those wedded to old assumptions about political leadership and representation. Thus, in West European countries in particular, the rise of new politics has not only reoriented and divided old political parties, it has also produced new ones and swelled the ranks of issue-driven social movements promoting the goals of the new agenda. New politics, in short, is boisterous politics.

THE SHAPE OF NEW POLITICS

Most perspectives on new politics start with the observation that there are important qualitative differences between the early and late industrial experiences. First, advanced industrial, or post-industrial, states have crossed a number of thresholds. Typically, all have experienced sustained and increasing levels of affluence, their economies are driven by the service sector, the education level of their publics has risen, all have confronted the "information revolution" and a corresponding growth in communications-related technologies, all have extensive social welfare networks in place, and their populations have been subject to dramatic increases in social, geographic, and occupational mobility. Furthermore, these developments have taken place in a relatively short time span, in about the last twenty-five years.

Second, although new politics theorists argue that these structural transformations are linked to value change, they differ in the precise descriptions of the value changes. Some see the shift primarily in terms of the increased salience of inner-directedness. Others focus on the changing meaning attached to the idea of "success." Still others identify new attitudes towards authority, conformity, religiosity, and the work ethic as central. Regardless of differences in focus, there is substantial agreement that the traditional "old politics" goals which emphasized economic growth, public order, national security, and traditional lifestyles have been replaced by such new politics goals as individual freedom, social equality, participation, and the quality of life.

Third, there is also broad consensus about the consequences of structural and value change for political participation. We have already noted that the rise of a new agenda and the erosion of traditional patterns of political participation provide two indications of how conventional forms of political behaviour have been reshaped. New politics, however, is also related to vigorous new forms of unconventional political behaviour—direct action politics. Political protest is not new. Most western liberal democracies have had some historical experience with peasant revolts, food riots, and, later, with industrial strife and protests from the disenfranchised and other marginalized groups. Working from traditional assumptions about the politics of industrialized societies, it would be reasonable to suppose that with an expanded franchise, with greater affluence, and with redistributive policies providing support for the vast majority of citizens, the incidence of protest would wane. The evidence, however, contradicts that expectation. Protest behaviour has increased in advanced industrial states. Furthermore, direct action politics is most frequently found in those societies that are most affluent. New politics protest differs from traditional forms of direct action in two significant respects. First, it is not the desperate weapon of last resort on the part of the disenfranchised; it is the strategy of choice from the politically astute middle class. Nor are new politics protests spontaneous; rather, they are a deliberate, planned tactic backed by both resources and sophisticated techniques—public-awareness campaigns, organized demonstrations, and media opportunities—aimed at mobilizing public opinion and influencing policy makers.

EXPLAINING NEW POLITICS

There is general agreement about the essential elements of new politics and its consequences, but there are significant differences in the explanations of why new politics has emerged. One line of argument is that new politics is the result of inherent weaknesses in welfare states. Welfare states, it is suggested, have buckled under the structural stresses induced by late industrialism. Another line of reasoning is that new politics is nothing more or less than the politics of the new class. Some point out that new politics has simply filled an ideological vacuum caused by the erosion of sharp class conflicts. New politics has emerged, as it were, in the wake of receding traditional ideological polarities. Yet others argue that there has been no change in the ideological temperature; the polarities organizing debate and political life have simply shifted to work along different axes. Within this latter school of thought, Ronald Inglehart's post-materialism theory, elaborated in great detail in *The Silent Revolution*, provides one of the most comprehensive accounts of the origins, nature, and consequences of new politics value change. Inglehart identifies the rift between materialists and post-materialists as the primary value cleavage dividing publics in advanced industrial states. Like others, he links the origins of this value divide to the structural changes of late industrialism, and proceeds to demonstrate, with a vast body of cross-national evidence, how post-materialism has produced political changes.

The essential elements of post-materialist theory hinge on the combined effects of two hypotheses—the scarcity hypothesis and the socialization hypothesis. The scarcity hypothesis suggests, like the economic theory of diminishing returns, that individuals place value on those things that are in short supply. The socialization hypothesis stipulates that the basic values acquired by individuals are fundamentally shaped by the conditions that prevailed during their pre-adult years. Thus, those generations that experienced such first-hand traumas as the Second World War or the depression will give priority to materialist goals—economic security and safety needs—while those without direct experience of such traumas, those born for example since 1945 and who have been raised in an era of relative prosperity, will tend to take such goals as economic security for granted. Instead, they will give priority to "higher-order" aesthetic, intellectual, and participatory needs for belonging and participating. Inglehart's post-materialist theory is elegant; it relies on only a few well-tested assumptions, and has been verified repeatedly in more than twenty countries over nearly two decades. The theory has attracted a great deal of interest as well as critical scrutiny, but its central findings and basic thesis remain intact.

NEW POLITICS IN CANADA

Given the vast accumulation of data indicating that new politics is now a feature of political life in most advanced industrial states, there is good reason to believe that it will also have an impact on Canadian politics. Indeed, it would be remarkable if that were not the case. By most standard measures, Canada certainly qualifies as a post-industrial state. It has enjoyed substantial increases in wealth in the course of the last twenty-five years, the service sector of the economy has grown, there has been a dramatic increase in educational opportunities, and the middle class has expanded. There is also qualitative evidence indicating that confidence in political institutions has declined while the political agenda now includes a host of new politics concerns— women's issues, environmentalism, minority rights—along with a wide range of other quality of life issues. But is there direct evidence of new politics value change? The short answer is yes. National attitudinal surveys conducted in 1981 and 1990 indicate that post-materialism, Inglehart's measure of new politics values, is on the rise. By 1990, one in four Canadians counted as post-materialists, up from one in six in 1981.

Detecting the presence of post-materialist values in Canada is one thing, but is the distribution of post-materialism in Canada typical of the distributions of new politics values in other advanced industrial states? The details of that story remain to be told, but available evidence suggests that they are. Figure 17.1, for example, illustrates the distribution of materialist/post-materialist values across various age groups in Canada and in four other advanced industrial states.

FIGURE 17.1 *Age Differences in Value Priorities*

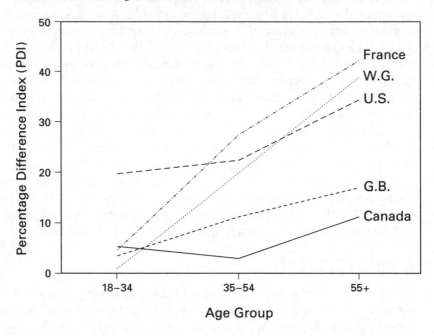

The percentage difference index (PDI) is simply the percentage of materialists minus the percentage of post-materialists. Figure 17.1 illustrates two basic points. First it shows that compared to the other countries under consideration, the level of post-materialism in Canada is relatively high. Those Canadians in the 18–34 age group exhibit levels of post-materialism that clearly are typical of those found in other states, and those in the older age groups exhibit levels that are somewhat higher than those found in comparable age groups elsewhere.

New politics theorists, Inglehart included, predict that post-materialist values are most likely concentrated among those with higher levels of formal education. Figure 17.2 provides unequivocal support for that prediction. Furthermore, these data show once more that the Canadian evidence conforms to patterns found elsewhere. With increased levels of education, there is a sharp decline in concern for materialist goals—economic growth and strong defense. With respect to both of these sociostructural indicators then, the Canadian evidence of the distribution of post-materialist/materialist values is consistent with evidence drawn from other post-industrial settings.

We have emphasized that a variety of theorists speculate that the rise of new politics is linked to a redistribution of political skills and that one aspect of these skills is political interest. Consequently, we would expect to find relatively low levels of political interest on the part of

FIGURE 17.2 *Education Differences in Value Priorities*

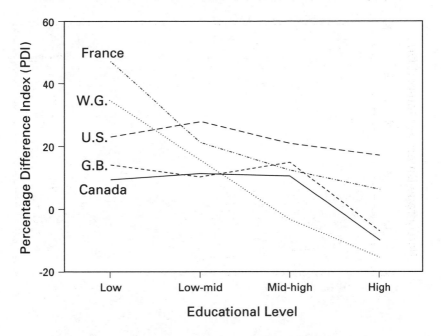

materialists and relatively high levels among post-materialists. Figure 17.3 tracks the distribution of political interest among materialists, those respondents with a mix of materialist and post-materialist values, and those who qualify as pure post-materialists. Once again, these data show that Canadian respondents are entirely typical of the broader cross-national trend. Only American and French respondents are more interested in politics. But more important than the particular levels of political interest displayed in these data is the trend. Post-materialists, regardless of national setting, always report higher levels of political interests than do their materialist co-nationals.

Political interest, arguably, is a precondition for political action. We have indicated that new politics theorists expect post-materialists to be more likely than materialists to engage in unconventional forms of political participation. That, in the final analysis, is one main reason why countries with high levels of post-materialism are harder to govern. Canadians, traditionally, have been depicted as deferential, counter-revolutionary, and supporters of "law and order." If that perspective has any contemporary validity, we would expect Canadians to be much less likely than their counterparts elsewhere, perhaps particularly their American counterparts, to engage in protest behaviour. Respondents surveyed in Britain, Canada, France, the United States, and West Germany were presented with an identical list of six "protest activities"

FIGURE 17.3 *Political Interest by Value Priorities*

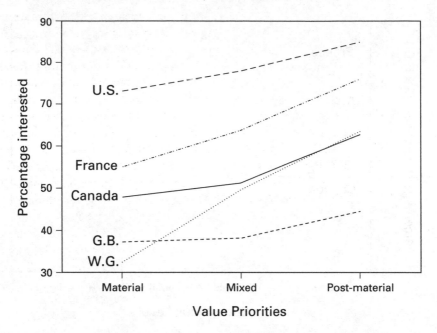

ranging from "signing a petition" and "participating in a boycott" to "occupying a factory" and engaging in "physical violence." All were asked to report, "Which have you done?" The results of that rough measure of protest participation are presented in Figure 17.4 and the results are striking.

They show first that post-materialists are far more likely to have engaged in protest behaviour than are materialists. Second, they also show some dramatic cross-national differences and clustering across the post-materialist value types. French post-materialists, clearly, are far more likely to have participated in protest behaviour, a legacy perhaps of France's tradition of "hot politics." On the other hand, the similarities across the post-materialist value types in the other four countries are equally striking. There is no evidence, according to these data, of any historic residuals of the American Revolution or for that matter of Canada's counter-revolution. Indeed the differences between the American and Canadian data are so slight as to be insignificant.

CONCLUSIONS

We started this overview with the point that important changes seem to be sweeping across advanced industrial states. These changes, it was argued, have far-reaching implications for the distribution of political

FIGURE 17.4 *Protest Participation by Value Priorities*

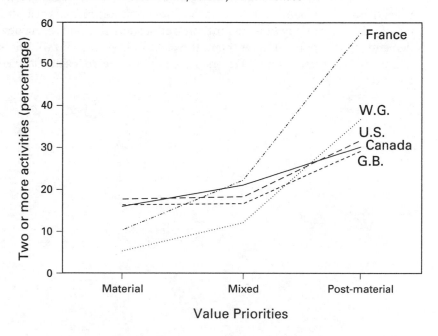

skills, the emergence of a new agenda, political participation, and for the kinds of demands that are placed upon political institutions. The speculation was that the forces that structured political debate and political conflict for a large part of the late nineteenth century and for about two thirds of the twentieth century seem to have run their course.

The new politics theories provide one perspective on the transformations that are taking place, and they offer a plausible account for why pressure groups promoting direct action strategies aimed at changing the status quo appear to have multiplied. By the same token, they may also help explain why institutions, political parties, and political leaders that are geared to conventional expectations about apathetic publics are surprised and under siege. According to the sketchy evidence presented here, there is no reason to suppose that Canada has escaped the winds of new politics. Indeed, Canadian politics appears to be buffeted by precisely the same forces that have reshaped political debate, political conflict, and political institutions in other states. The continued advance of new politics, however, is not guaranteed. With a sudden and deep economic downturn, for example, Inglehart predicts that the growth of post-materialism would halt or even temporarily reverse. But if economies in the western world continue to grow and if the political skills of citizens continue to expand, then the prospects for further advances of new politics and of even greater demands for citizen participation appear to be good. Precisely how the forces unleashed by new politics are played out, however, depends upon a variety of factors including how institutions and leaders respond to the new demands that are placed upon them, the electoral system, and the effectiveness of interest groups, factors that are unique to each national context.

P A R T

3

**Forms of
Government**

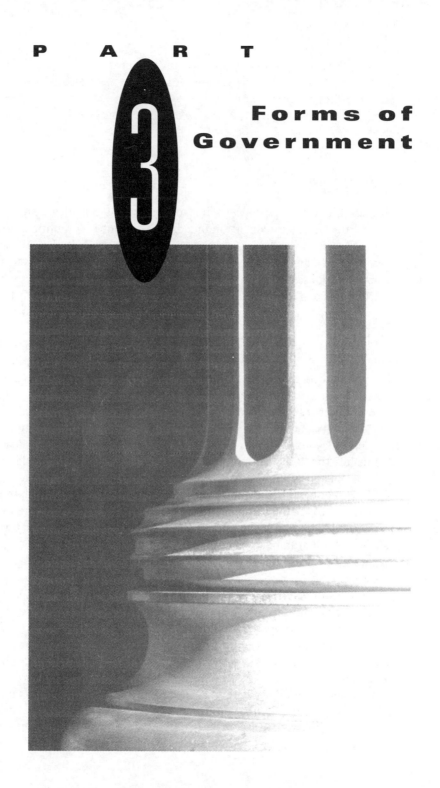

INTRODUCTION

Political ideologies provide useful summaries of the ideals shared in society; they also contain recommendations about how political power should be distributed. Government, it has been said, is the art of the possible, and one of the most fundamental challenges facing all societies is how to organize political authority so that governments can be both effective and can generate at least a minimal level of public support. The seven readings presented in Part III explore that theme from a variety of perspectives.

It begins with James Madison's Federalist No. 10 (Reading 18), which remains a classic statement of the basic principles of pluralism—the view that society should drive the state and that governments should play only a minimal role in citizens' affairs. But how can citizens signify their preferences? The next two readings provide other perspectives on that question. Richard Rose (Reading 19) outlines the central role that elections play in the democratic process. And Patrick Boyer (Reading 20) makes the case that referendums are useful vehicles for citizens to indicate their preferences more directly.

Few regimes operate according to the pure pluralist principle that the society drives the state. There are even fewer instances of the totalitarian model in which the state drives society. As Juan Linz argues in Reading 21, a number of examples correspond to a third model, the authoritarian variant, in which state-society relations co-exist in an uneasy equilibrium.

Institutional arrangements also play a decisive role in mediating state-society relations and the remaining readings canvas a number of prevailing alternatives. Douglas Verney (Reading 22) examines the sharing and coordination of political power in parliamentary and presidential systems. Garth Stevenson addresses the same broad issues from the standpoint of federalism in Reading 23. Social conditions place very real constraints upon the effective organization of political power and in Reading 24, Arend Lijphart outlines how consociational institutional arrangements can promote stable, effective and legitimate government in societies that are deeply divided along linguistic and religious lines.

18 PLURALISM

In this reading, James Madison (1751–1836), one of the principal framers of the Constitution of 1787 and the fourth president of the United States (1807–17), presents one of the most influential early statements of pluralism, or as he called it, "the factious spirit." The term pluralism has become an important part of social science vocabulary expressing the idea of diversity. Cultural pluralism refers to the diversity of cultures, social pluralism, the diversity of society. In political science, pluralism has come to mean the diversity of interests. Madison, like other liberals who assume that individuals are the best judge of their own interests, recognized that liberty feeds faction, and that the free play of faction could undermine the stability of government. Rather than sacrificing liberty to achieve stable government, a cure worse than the disease, Madison searched for ways to structure government so as to control the worst effects of faction. The following reading, drawn from the famous Federalist No. 10, is an attempt by Madison to counter the arguments made by a landed minority which believed that a democratic republic would result in the oppression of that minority by the majority.

• • • • • • • • •

Among the numerous advantages promised by a well-constructed Union, none deserves to be more accurately developed than its tendency to break and control the violence of faction. The friend of popular governments never finds himself so much alarmed for their character and fate as when he contemplates their propensity to this dangerous vice. He will not fail, therefore, to set a due value on any plan which, without violating the principles to which he is attached, provides a proper cure for it. The instability, injustice, and confusion introduced into the public councils have, in truth, been the mortal diseases under which popular governments have everywhere perished, as they continue to be the favorite and fruitful topics from which the adversaries to liberty derive their most specious declamations. The valuable improvements made by the American constitutions on the popular models, both ancient and modern, cannot certainly be too much admired; but it would be an unwarranted partiality to contend that they have as effectually obviated the danger on this side, as was wished and expected. Complaints are everywhere heard from our most considerate and virtuous citizens, equally the friends of public and private faith and of public and personal liberty, that our governments are too unstable, that the public good is disregarded in the conflicts of rival parties, and that measures are too often decided, not according to the rules of justice and the rights of the minor party, but by the superior force of an interested and overbearing majority. However anxiously we may wish that these complaints had no foundation, the evidence of known facts will not permit us to deny that they are in some degree true. It will be found, indeed, on a candid review of our situation, that some of the distresses under which we labor have been erroneously charged on the operation of our governments; but it will be found, at the same time, that other causes will not alone account for many of our heaviest misfortunes; and, particularly, for that prevailing and increasing distrust of public engagements and alarm for private rights which are echoed from one end of the continent to the other. These must be chiefly, if not wholly, effects of the unsteadiness and injustice with which a factious spirit has tainted our public administration.

By a faction I understand a number of citizens, whether amounting to a majority or minority of the whole, who are united and actuated by some common impulse of passion, or of interest, adverse to the rights of other citizens, or to the permanent and aggregate interests of the community.

There are two methods of curing the mischiefs of faction: the one, by removing its causes; the other, by controlling its effects.

There are again two methods of removing the causes of faction: the one, by destroying the liberty which is essential to its existence; the other, by giving to every citizen the same opinions, the same passions, and the same interests.

It could never be more truly said than of the first remedy that it was worse than the disease. Liberty is to faction what air is to fire, and aliment without which it instantly expires. But it could not be a less folly to abolish liberty, which is essential to political life, because it nourishes faction than it would be to wish the annihilation of air, which is essential to animal life, because it imparts to fire its destructive agency.

The second expedient is as impracticable as the first would be unwise. As long as the reason of man continues fallible, and he is at liberty to exercise it, different opinions will be formed. As long as the connection subsists between his reason and his self-love, his opinions and his passions will have a reciprocal influence on each other; and the former will be objects to which the latter will attach themselves. The diversity in the faculties of men, from which the rights of property originate, is not less an insuperable obstacle to a uniformity of interests. The protection of these faculties is the first object of government. From the protection of different and unequal faculties of acquiring property, the possession of different degrees and kinds of property immediately results; and from the influence of these on the sentiments and views of the respective proprietors ensues a division of the society into different interests and parties.

The latent causes of faction are thus sown in the nature of man; and we see them everywhere brought into different degrees of activity, according to the different circumstances of civil society. A zeal for different opinions concerning religion, concerning government, and many other points, as well of speculation as of practice; an attachment to different leaders ambitiously contending for pre-eminence and power; or to persons of other descriptions whose fortunes have been interesting to the human passions, have, in turn, divided mankind into parties, inflamed them with mutual animosity, and rendered them much more disposed to vex and oppress each other than to co-operate for their common good. So strong is this propensity of mankind to fall into mutual animosities that where no substantial occasion presents itself the most frivolous and fanciful distinctions have been sufficient to kindle their unfriendly passions and excite their most violent conflicts. But the most common and durable source of factions has been the various and unequal distribution of property. Those who hold and those who are without property have ever formed distinct interests in society. Those who are creditors, and those who are debtors, fall under a like discrimination. A landed interest, a manufacturing interest, a mercantile interest, a moneyed interest, with many lesser interests, grow up of necessity in civilized nations, and divide them into different classes, actuated by different sentiments and views. The regulation of these various and interfering interests forms the principal task of modern legislation and involves the spirit of party and faction in the necessary and ordinary operations of government.

No man is allowed to be a judge in his own cause, because his interest would certainly bias his judgment, and, not improbably, corrupt his integrity. With equal, nay with greater reason, a body of men are unfit to be both judges and parties at the same time; yet what are many of the most important acts of legislation but so many judicial determinations, not indeed concerning the rights of single persons, but concerning the rights of large bodies of citizens? And what are the different classes of legislators but advocates and parties to the causes which they determine? Is a law proposed concerning private debts? It is a question to which the creditors are parties on one side and the debtors on the other. Justice ought to hold the balance between them. Yet the parties are, and must be, themselves the judges; and the most numerous party, or in other words, the most powerful faction must be expected to prevail. Shall domestic manufacturers be encouraged, and in what degree, by restrictions on foreign manufacturers? are questions which would be differently decided by the landed and the manufacturing classes, and probably by neither with a sole regard to justice and the public good. The apportionment of taxes on the various descriptions of property is an act which seems to require the most exact impartiality; yet there is, perhaps, no legislative act in which greater opportunity and temptation are given to a predominant party to trample on the rules of justice. Every shilling with which they overburden the inferior number is a shilling saved to their own pockets.

It is in vain to say that enlightened statesmen will be able to adjust these clashing interests and render them all subservient to the public good. Enlightened statesmen will not always be at the helm. Nor, in many cases, can such an adjustment be made at all without taking into view indirect and remote considerations, which will rarely prevail over the immediate interest which one party may find in disregarding the rights of another or the good of the whole.

The inference to which we are brought is that the *causes* of faction cannot be removed and that relief is only to be sought in the means of controlling its *effects*.

If a faction consists of less than a majority, relief is supplied by the republican principle, which enables the majority to defeat its sinister views by regular vote. It may clog the administration, it may convulse the society; but it will be unable to execute and mask its violence under the forms of the Constitution. When a majority is included in a faction, the form of popular government, on the other hand, enables it to sacrifice to its ruling passion or interest both the public good and the rights of other citizens. To secure the public good and private rights against the danger of such a faction, and at the same time to preserve the spirit and the form of popular government, is then the great object to which our inquiries are directed. Let me add that it is the great desideratum by which alone this form of government can be rescued from the opprobrium under which it has so long labored and be recommended to the esteem and adoption of mankind.

By what means is this object attainable? Evidently by one of two only. Either the existence of the same passion or interest in a majority at the same time must be prevented, or the majority, having such coexistent passion or interest, must be rendered, by their number and local situation, unable to concert and carry into effect schemes of oppression. If the impulse and the opportunity be suffered to coincide, we well know that neither moral nor religious motives can be relied on as an adequate control. They are not found to be such on the injustice and violence of individuals, and lose their efficacy in proportion to the number combined together, that is, in proportion as their efficacy becomes needful.

From this view of the subject it may be concluded that a pure democracy, by which I mean a society consisting of a small number of citizens, who assemble and administer the government in person, can admit of no cure for the mischiefs of faction. A common passion or interest will, in almost every case, be felt by a majority of the whole; a communication and concert results from the form of government itself; and there is nothing to check the inducements to sacrifice the weaker party or an obnoxious individual. Hence it is that such democracies have ever been spectacles of turbulence and contention; have ever been found incompatible with personal security or the rights of property; and have in general been as short in their lives as they have been violent in their deaths. Theoretic politicians, who have patronized this species of government, have erroneously supposed that by reducing mankind to a perfect equality in their political rights, they would at the same time be perfectly equalized and assimilated in their possessions, their opinions, and their passions.

A republic, by which I mean a government in which the scheme of representation takes place, opens a different prospect and promises the cure for which we are seeking. Let us examine the points in which it varies from pure democracy, and we shall comprehend both the nature of the cure and the efficacy which it must derive from the Union.

The two great points of difference between a democracy and a republic are: first, the delegation of the government, in the latter, to a small number of citizens elected by the rest; secondly, the greater number of citizens and greater sphere of country over which the latter may be extended.

The effect of the first difference is, on the one hand, to refine and enlarge the public views by passing them through the medium of a chosen body of citizens, whose wisdom may best discern the true interest of their country and whose patriotism and love of justice will be least likely to sacrifice it to temporary or partial considerations. Under such a regulation it may well happen that the public voice, pronounced by the representatives of the people, will be more consonant to the public good than if pronounced by the people themselves, convened for the purpose. On the other hand, the effect may be inverted. Men of factious tempers, of local prejudices, or of sinister designs, may, by intrigue, by corruption, or by other means, first obtain the suffrages, and then betray the interests of the people. The question resulting is, whether small or extensive republics are most favorable to the election of proper guardians of the public weal; and it is clearly decided in favor of the latter by two obvious considerations.

In the first place it is to be remarked that however small the republic may be the representatives must be raised to a certain number in order to guard against the cabals of a few; and that however large it may be they must be limited to a certain number in order to guard against the confusion of a multitude. Hence, the number of representatives in the two cases not being in proportion to that of the constituents, and being proportionally greatest in the small republic, it follows that if the proportion of fit characters be not less in the large than in the small republic, the former will present a greater option, and consequently a greater probability of a fit choice.

In the next place, as each representative will be chosen by a greater number of citizens in the large than in the small republic, it will be more difficult for unworthy candidates to practise with success the vicious arts by which elections are too often carried; and the suffrages of the people being more free, will be more likely to center on men who possess the most attractive merit and the most diffusive and established characters.

It must be confessed that in this, as in most other cases, there is a mean, on both sides of which inconveniences will be found to lie. By enlarging too much the number of electors, you render the representative too little acquainted with all their local circumstances and lesser interests; as by reducing it too much, you render him unduly attached to these, and too little fit to comprehend and pursue great and national objects. The federal Constitution forms a happy combination in this respect; the great and aggregate interests being referred to the national, the local and particular to the State legislatures.

The other point of difference is the greater number of citizens and extent of territory which may be brought within the compass of republican than of democratic government; and it is this circumstance principally which renders factious combinations less to be dreaded in the former than in the latter. The smaller the society, the fewer probably will be the distinct parties and interests composing it; the fewer the distinct parties and interests, the more frequently will a majority be found of the same party; and the smaller the number of individuals composing a majority, and the smaller the compass within which they are placed, the more easily will they concert and execute their plans of oppression. Extend the sphere and you take in a greater variety of parties and interests; you make it less probable that a majority of the whole will have a common motive to invade the rights of other citizens; or if such a common motive exists, it will be more difficult for all who feel it to discover their own strength and to act in unison with each other. Besides other impediments, it may be remarked that, where there is a consciousness of unjust or dishonorable purposed, communication is always checked by distrust in proportion to the number whose concurrence is necessary.

Hence, it clearly appears that the same advantage which a republic has over a democracy in controlling the effects of faction is enjoyed by a large over a small republic—is enjoyed by the Union over the States composing it. Does this advantage consist in the substitution of representatives whose enlightened views and virtuous sentiments render them superior to local prejudices and to schemes of injustice? It will not be denied that the representation of the Union will be most likely to possess these requisite endowments. Does it consist in the greater security afforded by a greater variety of parties, against the event of any one party being able to outnumber and oppress the rest? In an equal degree does the increased variety of parties comprised within the Union increase this security? Does it, in fine, consist in the greater obstacles opposed to the concert and accomplishment of the secret wishes of an unjust and interested majority? Here again the extent of the Union gives it the most palpable advantage.

The influence of factious leaders may kindle a flame within their particular States but will be unable to spread a general conflagration through the other States. A religious sect may degenerate into a political faction in a part of the Confederacy; but the variety of sects dispersed over the entire face of it must secure the national councils against any danger from that source. A rage for paper money, for an abolition of debts, for an equal division of property, or for any other improper or wicked project, will be less apt to pervade the whole body of the Union than a particular member of it, in the same proportion as such a malady is more likely to taint a particular county or district than an entire State.

In the extent and proper structure of the Union, therefore, we behold a republican remedy for the diseases most incident to republican government. And according to the degree of pleasure and pride we feel in being republicans ought to be our zeal in cherishing the spirit and supporting the character of federalists.

19

INDIRECT DEMOCRACY: ELECTIONS

*E*lections are still the cornerstone of liberal democracies. Even though we take them for granted, and many individuals choose not to vote, elections remain the crucial institution in our governmental process. It is trite but true that elections legitimize governmental powers. The fact that citizens of a polity can, on a regular basis, choose who will govern remains one basic reason for our consent in the process. The fact that we go to the polls to vote people into office, or to throw them out, reinforces the limited character of our government.

In Reading 19, Richard Rose points out the significance of elections for individual voters as well as for the political system as a whole. He then briefly examines some of the ways in which we have tried to explain the act of voting. While voting studies may be a science, precise reasons for exercising individual volition are almost inexplicable.

The fact remains that at election time the people are sovereign. Yet, as Rose notes, beyond elections that sovereignty is "limited and short lived." A government's mandate is secure as long as it maintains confidence in the House. But elections constitute only one means by which individuals in a polity can participate in the political process. Between elections interest groups, political parties, and individual actions may place a great deal of pressure on governments. If governors want to be re-elected, they must heed at least some of the pressure. That elections always loom on the horizon is highly consequential for the system as whole.

Richard Rose is a professor and director of the Centre for the Study of Public Policy at the University of Strathclyde, Scotland. He has extensive publications in

British and American politics, and political parties and voting studies. This selection is from his book The Problem of Party Government.

• • • • • • • • •

The liberal philosophy of politics pervasive in Britain assigns a particularly important role to elections. The demands of individuals are meant to cause the governing party to respond by producing benefits satisfying the majority of the electorate: individuals will then modify their demands and party preferences in a continuing feedback of views, in which the voters are the prime movers of the system. Alternatively, the prime mover in politics can be seen as the governing party, making demands upon the individual to pay taxes, obey laws, provide military service, etc. Citizens immediately respond by complying with or ignoring government injunctions (cf. Rose, 1973, p. 467). In Britain, they can also respond with their votes; in countries without free competitive elections, their only form of protest may be subversive action ....

THE POSSIBLE CONSEQUENCES

The literature of politics contains many assertions about the possible significance of elections for individual voters and for the political system generally. The two perspectives are related, but it is useful to distinguish between a citizen's view, and the much wider perspective of the political scientist.

The potential significance of an election for individual voters may include the following factors:

First, voting involves individual *choice* of governors or major governmental policies. Joseph Schumpeter (1952, chapters 21–3) and Robert T. McKenzie (1963, chapter 11) emphasize the voter's task as nothing more and nothing less than that of choosing between teams of competing leaders at general elections. In America, the use of primary elections to choose candidates gives a much greater measure of choice than is present in duopolistic competition, or in simple-plurality general election contests. Referenda and balloting on constitutional amendments afford voters the opportunity to choose or reject specific policies, but this device is now everywhere of limited political importance. A number of writers have argued that voters also choose between policy alternatives in national elections. But few academic analysts would go so far as to assert that voters can mandate their representatives at an election, although the word "mandate" is still prevalent in the discourse of politicians.

Second, voting permits individuals to participate in a reciprocal and continuing exchange of influence with office-holders and candidates.

The need for election or re-election may lead incumbents and candidates to alter their policies in order to retain or gain office. This approach is dynamic, because it considers how alternatives for choice are derived, and what the elected do. Carl Friedrich (1937, p. 203ff.) has described the exchange of influence between elections as arising from "a law of anticipated reactions" in which politicians continuously adjust policy decisions on the basis of assumptions about future as well as past voter preferences. Voters can also influence the selection of candidates, even in the absence of primary elections, if party leaders are sensitive to popular preferences. For example, the anticipated electoral unpopularity of Sir Alec Douglas-Home led to his resignation as leader of the Conservative party in 1965.

Third, voting can encourage or help maintain individual allegiance to the existing constitutional régime. A voter may feel that he owes voluntary acceptance of the authority of a popularly elected régime whether or not his preferred party wins, or even in the absence of a choice of parties. The government of the elect gains a populist rather than a Calvinist meaning; *vox populi* replaces *vox dei*. In an essay on the politics of Afro-Asian nations, Edward Shils (1962, p. 38) has gone so far as to argue:

> The granting of universal suffrage without property or literacy quali-
> fications is perhaps the single factor leading to the formation of a
> political society .... The drawing of the whole adult population peri-
> odically into contact with the symbols of the center of national polit-
> ical life must, in the course of time, have immeasurable consequences
> by stirring people up and giving them a sense of their own potential
> significance, and attaching their sentiments to symbols which
> comprehend the entire nation. The importance of electoral participa-
> tion as a means of reinforcing allegiance can be seen in arguments for
> compulsory voting. In the late nineteenth century, these arguments
> had liberal connotations. In the past four decades, compulsory voting
> has often been associated with Communist and Fascist regimes.

Fourth, voting can contribute to an individual's disaffection from the existing constitutional régime. Disaffection may be induced by the result of a specific election, or it may have non-electoral antecedents and simply be reinforced by an election in which an individual does not wish to endorse any of the alternatives. A modicum of involuntary non-voting is always to be expected on grounds of health and travel. Organized boycotts of ballots are infrequent and difficult to organize. The tactic is sometimes invoked in Ireland. Sinn Fein campaigned in the 1973 Northern Ireland Assembly elections with the slogan, "Vote early and spoil your ballot early." Their efforts met with little success. The fear of disaffection arising from an election result with many spoiled ballots or votes for extremist parties has led some authors to produce arguments "In Defence of Apathy."

Fifth, voting has emotional significance for individuals …. W.J.M MacKenzie (1954; 1957) suggests that the ritual function of voting may, at its highest, be comparable to a coronation service. The frequent use of sporting or military metaphors to describe elections suggests that for some persons election contests provide emotional satisfaction akin to watching athletic events or old war films, with the behaviour of individual contestants more important than the result. At a low level of intensity, the emotional significance of voting may be compared to that derived from "being done good to" by listening to a sermon, or fulfilling a minor social duty.

Sixth, voting may be functionless, devoid of any emotional or politically significant consequences for individuals. This extreme form of apathy is not likely to be found among many people who personally record their votes. But very high turnout figures for non-competitive elections suggest that substantial numbers of subjects may have had votes recorded in their name, while they had no personal awareness of voting.

The potential significance of elections for the political system as a whole can be described as follows:

First, elections are a recognized means of providing succession in leadership. The problem of political succession is common to all systems, for even a lifetime dictator will eventually need replacement. At a minimum, an election, even if a plebiscite with only one individual seeking endorsement, provides a legal means for validating a claim to govern. In the Western world, elections are expected to involve competition between two or more possible claimants to succeed to office, and the presence or absence of competition is a basic characteristic distinguishing "free" elections. In Britain, elections are said to decide who governs. This is not an inevitable consequence, for the electoral system does no more than provide Members of Parliament. It is the party system that converts the results of a parliamentary election into a government. Only five of the fifteen men who have become Prime Minister in this century first entered Downing Street as the immediate consequence of a general election victory.

Second, elections can be used to control the policy decisions of government. Nowhere in England are voters allowed to determine by referendum what policies shall prevail. In Scotland and Wales citizens are allowed to vote on laws licensing the sale of drink, and in Northern Ireland a referendum was held in 1973 on the maintenance of Ulster as part of the United Kingdom. American states have shown much greater enthusiasm for balloting on legislation, whether to enact or repeal it. In many states, Americans can also vote on tax rates or the issuance of local authority bonds to finance capital expenditure.

Third, elections can influence the policy decisions of government. In post-war Britain, the electoral calendar has a significant influence upon the government's economic policy. In the months preceding a general election, the governing party will seek to manipulate economic conditions to maximize a sense of prosperity. Often, the post-election consequence is the adoption of deflationary policies to compensate for the artificially induced boom created in a pre-election period.

Fourth, elections can help to legitimate a régime or to maintain its legitimacy. In countries where constitutional authority is relatively recent, citizen allegiance cannot be taken for granted. Moreover, the Constitution itself may vest ultimate authority in the people. In such circumstances, only by popular election (whether competitive or not) can governors claim formal legitimacy for their actions. In Britain, authority is derived from the Crown. In the nineteenth century, the gradual expansion of the franchise allowed a slowly increasing portion of subjects to participate as citizens in choosing men who would advise and exercise this authority. Today, elections provide a justification for the authority of governors who must take decisions with which many will disagree. The ultimate argument for obeying a law is that it is made by people elected to be law-makers.

Fifth, in extreme cases, elections may lead to the repudiation of a régime because of the intensity of conflict among groups competing for office. Repudiation may take the form of a refusal of a government to leave office following its apparent defeat, the revolt of losers (e.g. the response of Southern states in America to the election of Abraham Lincoln in 1860) or the abolition of the existing régime by a newly elected government. For example, the election of an African government in Northern Rhodesia made maintenance of a Federation in Central Africa impossible; in the blunt words of Kenneth Kaunda to his opponents, "My friend has lost—and lost forever" (Mulford, 1964, p. 186). The only occasion on which a British election led to the repudiation of authority occurred in Ireland. In 1918 Sinn Fein, the pro-independence party, won an overwhelming majority of seats in twenty-six counties of Southern Ireland. While the contingency may be very remote, it is interesting to speculate what the reaction would be at Westminster if Scotland or Wales returned a majority of Nationalists at a British general Election.

Sixth, to describe an election as functionless is to state that it has no observable, verifiable consequences for the political system. It would be possible to hypothesize that in many new nations where elections are unfamiliar, communications poor and administration primitive, elections may tend toward this. But an election which has no observable impact upon control of office is not necessarily functionless, for an uncontested election can be a slack resource which citizens invoke in case of political controversy. In urban and rural districts councillors may be returned year after year without contest until an issue, such as a motorway or a new housing estate, causes controversy and a contested election within a previously undivided community.

While elections have nearly the same mechanical features everywhere, they do not have the same functions. *The World Handbook of Political and Social Indicators* (Taylor and Hudson, 1972, Table 2.9) reports that among 136 nations, 112 regularly have events meeting conventional definitions of elections. Insufficient evidence is available for another sixteen countries, primarily in Africa. Only eight nations (of which Spain is the only European example) do not regularly hold elections.

Elections usually involve the participation of a majority of a country's adult population. The average turnout for elections in a hundred countries for which this could be calculated is 79.5 per cent. As of 1970, Britain ranks seventy-sixth for voter participation—but still ahead of the United States, where the 1972 Presidential election turnout of 55.7 per cent was ninety-second. While the statistics from some countries reporting high voter turnout are suspect, Britain also lags far behind most Western nations in voting participation. Of the nine member nations in the European Economic Community, Britain, along with Ireland, consistently ranks lowest in the proportion participating in national elections.

The significance of an election for a political system can be crudely indicated by noting whether countries have free, competitive elections, and whether the majority of the electorate is literate. As these two conditions vary, the potential significance of an election is likely to vary. According to *World Handbook* figures, thirty-eight countries have free elections and at least half their electorate is literate. In these countries elections can provide for the peaceful succession of office-holders, and also influence policy. Several nations have competitive elections, but a predominantly illiterate electorate; India is the only one to have had free elections endure for any significant period of time. It is doubtful whether the electorate can consciously affect policy, because of the limitations upon the feedback of political information imposed by illiteracy.

In societies without free competitive elections, the chief significance of a ballot is likely to be legitimating a régime or encouraging disaffection if results go wrong. This is most likely in those sixteen societies, mostly communist, which have a majority of literate adults, while lacking competitive elections. The act of voting for an approved state is likely to have meaning whether it signifies identification with governors, passive acceptance of the powers that be, or the indignities of coerced "choice." In the thirty-six primarily Afro-Asian nations that lack competitive elections and have a majority of illiterate voters, elections are most likely to be functionless, an act undertaken in conformity to alien custom, lacking even the significance of native rites ....

THE USES OF ELECTIONS

Voting has a much greater significance for the political scientist or the candidate than it has for the voter. For individuals, a chief function of voting is emotional or allegiance-maintaining. Englishmen regard it as their duty to vote, and this view is supported by strong social pressures. When an election is held, from 60 to 80 per cent of persons will vote, even if they can see no difference between the parties, think the election result will have no effect on themselves, do not care who will win the election, and do not identify with any of the parties (Butler and Stokes, 1964; see also Campbell et al., 1960, 97–105).

Theories that describe elections as occasions of choice or political influence usually include assumptions about the presumed rationality of voters. The term rationality is one for which there is no standardized meaning. Rationality in voting might require individuals to have a high degree of political information and powers of logical reasoning. Yet Anthony Downs (1957) has shown that logically it is irrational for a voter to meet the criteria of rationality outlined above. The authors of *The American Voter* have estimated that only about one-seventh of the electorate can give a reasonably detailed and consistent explanation of their party preferences (Campbell *et al.*, 1960, chapter 10). A similar proportion would hold true for Britain. That fraction of the electorate positively concerned about the election outcome is not making a choice between Conservative, Labour and Liberal candidates, but rather, affirming an identification with one of these parties. An election is not only an occasion for a voter to confirm his allegiance to government, but also to confirm loyalty to a party with which he has long identified, on social and psychological motives, or, as in February 1974, to reject an identification.

The full significance of the formally political act of voting is best understood if one allows through the full implications of the social psychologist's dictum, "Our approach is in the main dependent on the point of view of the actor" (Campbell *et al.*, 1960, pp. 27ff.) The language of political science unfortunately leads us to narrow our attention from the multiplicity of roles that an individual has, by defining him in terms of one relatively minor and intermittent role, that of voter. The word voter refers to an abstraction, just as much as does the term economic man. The chief social roles of an individual are those of spouse, parent, relative, wage earner, friend, etc. For most individuals the role of citizen or subject is likely to be of little significance; the act of voting exhausts his commitment to political activity. It would thus be much more accurate and only a little cumbersome if, instead of writing about voting behaviour, we wrote about the behaviour of ordinary individuals in electoral situations.

This argument does not mean that politics is relatively less important for an individual than participation in other more or less voluntary social organizations. Only a minority of Englishmen are regularly active in trade unions, churches or other major institutions of English life. The level of participation is not different in kind when one compares party politics, trade unions and organized religion. In religion and in trade unionism, the great majority of individuals have a group identification, as is the case in politics; yet there, too, only a small minority go beyond identification and regularly participate in activities of the groups with which they identify. The great bulk of individuals are much more concerned with primary group relationships among family and friends than they are with the goals of relatively remote national institutions.

The failure of the literature of voting behaviour to cope properly with this phenomenon is partly methodological. In a situation in which each adult is eligible to vote, studying voters by means of a national cross-section sample is logical, even though the great majority interviewed will be answering questions of far more interest to the interviewers than to the surveyed. Confronted by an interviewer asking questions about politics, a substantial number of individuals may give a long series of don't know answers or answers of low intensity, consistency or durability ....

Any judgement about the meaning of elections is determined by the standards adopted for evaluation. Understandably, politicians and students of politics tend to forget that most citizens do not have the time or inclination to follow political events as closely as they do. Reciprocally, politicians may know less about gardening, sports, industry or trade union work than those who specialize in non-political affairs. Approaching an election from the point of view of the voter leads one to consider what it is reasonable for him to do. An inability to show great knowledge of politics is not proof that an individual votes unreasonably.

John Plamenatz (1958, p. 9) has argued, "A choice is reasonable, not because the chooser, when challenged, can give a satisfactory explanation of why he made it, but because if he could give an explanation, it would be satisfactory." Studies of voting behaviour find that the great majority of voters cannot give a satisfactory explanation of their own volition. Yet a careful reading of any set of life-history interviews makes it clear that intellectually satisfactory justifications of choice can be elucidated for many inarticulate voters, whether elderly spinsters, embittered miners, or bus conductors, prosperous young married couples, or middle-aged shopkeepers. Instead of discussing politics in terms of explicit ideologies and relating these to issues in Parliament, such individuals usually view politics in terms of simpler, more persisting distinctions concerning group interests, or the nature of the times, voting for the government in good times and against it in bad. If such criteria are accepted as reasonable for the ordinary individual to apply, then, instead of one-seventh of the electorate being considered reasonable, that is, having, a detailed, coherent political outlook, more than three-quarters of the British electorate can be classified as reasonable voters (cf. Campbell *et al.,* 1960, chapter 10).

The functions of elections cannot be seen in isolation from other elements of the political process. Collectively, voters are sovereign one day in every four or five years. This sovereignty is limited and short-lived. Voters can choose who governs, but not how they are governed. An individual gains a very small amount of influence by the act of voting. Yet without the familiar mechanisms of elections, Britain could not be governed as we know it today. Inheritance, co-option, a *coup d'état* or violence—devices used elsewhere to constitute governments—would be invoked.

If an individual wishes to be more than a mere voter, he must seek additional means to express his views. He can act through the market place, voting with his feet about economic policies by changing jobs, altering his consumer spending, increasing his effort at work, or emigrating. The extreme sensitivity of British government to fluctuations in economic conditions makes such actions prompt and important constraints upon the government of any party. A person wishing to go beyond the minimal influence of a voter can also join a political party, using organization to strengthen his individual voice in the politics of collective choice.

REFERENCES

(The place of publication is London unless otherwise stated.)

Butler, D.E., and Stokes, Donald (1964), Nationwide survey data analysed by the present author from a magnetic tape available through the Inter-University Consortium for Political Research, Ann Arbor, Michigan.

Campbell, Angus, Converse, Philip E., Miller, Warren E., and Stokes, Donald (1960), *The American Voter*, New York, Wiley.
Downs, Anthony (1957), *An Economic Theory of Democracy*, New York, Harper.
Friedrich, Carl J. (1937), *Constitutional Government and Democracy*, New York, Harper.
McKenzie, R.T. (1955: 2nd ed., 1963), *British Political Parties*, Heinemann.
Mackenzie, W.J.M. (1954), 'Representation in Plural Societies', *Political Studies*, vol. II, no. 2.
Mackenzie, W.J.M. (1957), 'The Export of Electoral Systems', *Political Studies*, vol. V, no. 3.
Mulford, D.C. (1964), *The Northern Rhodesia General Election, 1962*, Nairobi, Oxford University Press.
Plamenatz, John (1958), 'Electoral Studies and Democratic Theory: a British View', *Political Studies*, vol. VI, no. 1.
Schumpeter, Joseph (1952), *Capitalism, Socialism and Democracy*, 4th ed., Allen and Unwin.
Shils, Edward A. (1963), *Political Development in the New States*, The Hague, Mouton.
Taylor, C.L., and Hudson, M.C. (1972), *World Handbook of Political and Social Indicators*, 2nd ed., New Haven, Yale.

20 DIRECT DEMOCRACY: REFERENDUMS

Although modern democracy in practice is usually indirect or representative democracy, it is also possible for people to make decisions directly through casting a ballot on a proposition. Most functioning democracies resort to referendums at least occasionally, as Canada did in the 1992 referendum on the Charlottetown Accord.

In this selection from The People's Mandate: Referendums and a More Democratic Canada *(1992), Patrick Boyer argues in favour of Canada adopting a referendum procedure that could be used for ordinary legislation, not just for constitutional amendments. Boyer, who was a Progressive Conservative Member of Parliament when he published this book, is one of Canada's foremost authorities on direct democracy. He has also written several books on various aspects of electoral law in Canada.*

• • • • • • • •

The present turmoil in Canada, while distressing to many, is actually a positive symptom of the necessary transmutation through which our country must now go. The Canadian story is essentially a tale of evolution and adaptation, and we are again moving to a new stage, into a reality far different from what we have known ....

The collective wisdom of a large body of well-informed people most reliably produces the best decisions. Therefore, the consensus deliberately reached by a large, diverse group ought to be trusted more than the conclusions or commands of a small, homogeneous group or a single individual. Pooled information and variety in experience can blend to produce not only a sound course of action, but also and as important, the underlying consensus necessary to implement it. We must find the courage to fully accept this truth and its consequences. It means trusting in democratic methods that enable collective wisdom to be accurately expressed ....

Canada has remained a timid democracy. The establishment that has run our country has proceeded comfortably—not always in the interests of the people, nor indeed of the country itself—supported by Canadians' deference to authority and a strange willingness to be passive spectators in our own land. We have become what anthropologists call "participant observers." When describing Canadians' attributes or practices, our historians, commentators, and politicians frequently refer to a disembodied third person "they" rather than an inclusive "we." This linguistic distancing is a specious objectivity that has contributed over time to the eerie notion that nobody really lives here. We refer to "the system" or "the government" as if it were some autonomous entity, separate and far away, rather than part of us, something over which we do have power ....

Isn't the new image of democracy in Canada one in which greater popular participation is understood as being vital to our national well-being? Does personal involvement not become necessary in a country where the duties and responsibilities, as well as the "rights," of each citizen are being emphasized?

The role of direct voting by Canadian citizens on issues of transcendent national importance can be positive and constructive. We have already accumulated a rich, if little-known, Canadian experience on this subject of referendums. This story has had a poor chance of taking hold of the Canadian imagination, however, because the political élites who benefit from the present arrangements have largely played their part in suppressing and discrediting the relevance of direct democracy to our Canadian situation.

Wider use of referendums and plebiscites could help cure some of the present ailments in the Canadian body politic. At the same time, they are not magic elixirs or cure-alls: the role of referendums, while precise, is limited. There is the risk of overdosing on this medicine. Nonetheless, intelligent use of this instrument of direct popular participation is worthy of more than the usual out-of-hand dismissal given it by those individuals who conveniently and sometimes maliciously misinterpret our Canadian experience with referendums and plebiscites. Some of these people dress up their excuses with lofty principles about parliamentary democracy, while their objective is really that of maintaining the status quo.

Again, not every issue has to be "put to the people." The main work of enacting laws, resolving issues, and debating public concerns must continue in our elected and deliberative legislative bodies. Many Canadians seem at present to feel that elected representatives, of whatever party, cannot be counted on to make decisions and that constituent assemblies are needed—a return in a sense to the amphitheatre of Athens where direct democracy was born. As a member of Parliament, I obviously believe in the institutions of "representative democracy." But, on the basis of seven years' experience in Parliament and for reasons given in this book, I must conclude that serious imbalances created by rigid party discipline must be corrected if we are to keep on calling MPs elected "representatives." Even with their faults, our legislatures are still vital to our system of government.

Perhaps every decade, or maybe once in the life of each Parliament, one or two topics of overriding national importance should be subjected to the fullest expression of popular opinion. Certainly major constitutional amendments ought to be submitted for ratification by a direct vote of the people in a referendum .... Direct voting might also be especially appropriate where the government of the day lacks a "mandate" for a fundamental policy change that could significantly alter the nature or operation of our country. This approach of using the instrument of direct democracy for special purposes would neither threaten nor displace our institutions of representative democracy but could complement and actually enhance their role ....

Our Canadian identity, further, could be strengthened through the use of plebiscites because we would be forced, in very specific terms, to speak out and debate with one another about the kind of country we want. To move beyond the vague generalities that too often pass for public discourse in our land would be refreshing. The plebiscite process could thus help us to define ourselves and supplement the "weary mixture-as-before" approach that is preventing the required interest in our national life. Instead of passively letting elected representatives in Parliament make all the decisions for us, or relying on editorial page writers and CBC commentators to do our thinking, it would be far more stimulating and productive to have everyone coming to terms with his or her own view about a public issue. That is what happened in Prince Edward Island in 1988, as the heritage and future of the Island were debated in relation to the question of building a fixed-link crossing to the mainland. It happened in Quebec in 1980 when the referendum forced every Quebecker to consider his or her individual future, as a resident in a province that either would become a separate entity or would remain within a greater Canada. It also happened in 1982 in the Northwest Territories as northerners came to grips with the plebiscite question on whether to divide the region into two territories.

A larger dose of direct democracy could also counteract a number of other developments that have caused political life and the governing process in Canada to suffer in the past decade. Examples of such developments include the ascendant and unchecked role of opinion polling and pollsters, the increasing dominance of single-issue groups, the growing power and influence of professional lobbyists, the hardening partisanship and rigidity of party lines in Parliament, and the hijacking of decision making from the legislatures by what has been called "executive federalism."

In these days when we suffer a plague of opinion polls, it is worth recognizing the several ways that plebiscites are a superior method of divining the public mind. First, instead of the "representative sample" of an opinion poll, each citizen has his or her own say in a plebiscite. Second, plebiscites give the possibility of a well-considered opinion that polls do not. A person may be watching a hockey game, cooking a meal, working in the garden, or otherwise distracted, when a pollster phones and asks, out of the blue, for an on-the-spot opinion on some issue of the day. In a plebiscite everyone discusses and deliberates over the issue several weeks before expressing his or her verdict. We do not elect our representatives on the first day of a multi-week election campaign, but on the last. For the same good reason people ought also to have the chance to obtain information, to debate and to reflect, before "electing" one of several choices on important public issues.

A plebiscite, it is important to realize, is more than a large-scale, formalized opinion poll. With opinion polls, there can and will always be doubt about the wording of the pollster's question, quibbling as to the representativeness of the sample, and a feeling that it is "nothing more than an opinion poll" to be contradicted by someone else's poll tomorrow. Nothing, on the other hand, speaks with the same eloquence as a counting of ballots, deliberately cast on a question by the voting citizens of a province or the entire country, after a cathartic debate.

Single-issue groups and special interest organizations are a second concern. While they have long played a role in our political system, their recent emergence on centre stage has tended to distort the broader political agenda that pluralistic and industrialized countries like Canada must constantly address. Lobbyists have always been present wherever power is exercised, and in our system of government they do perform an important role. Yet, as they have come to much greater prominence during the 1980s, their role is one that many observers, quite rightly, are finding increasingly awkward. The sensation is something like seeing a football player appear on the ice at a hockey match. He may be a superb athlete, dressed in a colourfully handsome uniform, and capable of deftly executing complicated plays with great strength and aplomb, but his blocking and tackling is not part of hockey. His discordant performance is unsettling to the spectators. In the past decade, the emergence in Ottawa of the new breed of paid professional lobbyists (responded to, so far, by the Lobbyist Registration Act, in force since September 30, 1988) marks, in practical terms, a serious interference in the operation of government or, to put it in moral terms, a corruption of Canadian democracy.

The third phenomenon we should be wary of is excessive partisanship. In the Senate and the House of Commons, simple matters are blown out of proportion by political grandstanding for perceived partisan advantage. Major issues have sometimes been trivialized, again by the same destructiveness that substitutes party lines and a phoney adversarial stance for honest debate and intelligent analysis.

The fourth phenomenon, that of our legislatures being reduced to "rubber stamps" for decisions already taken by cabinet, has to be troubling to anyone concerned about maintaining the dynamic counterbalances essential to a parliamentary democracy. The firm control of government by the prime minister, and at the provincial level by the premiers, has been solidified in the emergence of "executive federalism" and includes cabinet and a committee system that gives contemporary Canada a tableau of governance where dissent is perceived as disloyalty, and even reasonable accommodation of differences becomes a struggle of the first order.

... [w]e will benefit from making Canada a more democratic country where people participate in and have greater responsibility for decisions that affect them; direct voting to obtain a mandate from the people, is, therefore, its central focus. It is a rising theme in current political discussion in Canada, but the lack of information about Canadian experience with referendums and plebiscites has hobbled intelligent assessment of this important democratic instrument.

Like a general election, this specialized electoral procedure of direct popular voting is certainly not a neutral or antiseptic device for registering voter opinion. The controversial nature of referendum issues is almost a guarantee that the troops in the trenches will wage battle with all available weapons, ... It has been observed that frequently referendums, "even in the most democratic countries, have to some degree been engineered to produce a popular endorsement for what those in power happen to want." Yet precisely because of this, it is important to have in place a realistic and comprehensive statute to govern the holding of direct votes in Canada, just as we long ago enacted the Canada Elections Act to govern the general voting to elect our representatives and thus ensure the fairness of that process. The problems of conducting elections (people were killed in a number of nineteenth-century election riots) did not dissuade us from democratic elections but led to our embracing them more firmly and working to eliminate the abuses that threatened them. The risks (more perceived perhaps than real) of direct voting on issues should not now find us more timid than our forbears in creating an appropriate legal structure and procedure, and getting on with it ....

21

AUTHORITARIANISM

*W*hile *pluralism is often characterized as the domination of the state by society, totalitarianism can be viewed as the reverse—the domination of society by the state. In the following reading, Juan Linz, a professor of political sociology at Yale University, argues that the political experiences of many countries do not fit easily into either of these categories. In these countries, which Linz classifies as authoritarian, the state penetrates society but does not dominate it. Drawing upon the example of Spanish politics during the era of Francisco Franco's dictatorship, Linz outlines the distinctive characteristics of authoritarian regimes and explores the balance of forces that can make authoritarian systems stable. Typically, authoritarian regimes exercise limited control over society; some interests are shaped by the state, but others enjoy a measure of autonomy. Mass participation is discouraged because it is viewed as a potential threat to order, yet the power of authoritarian leaders is constrained by, and exercised through, an often uneasy coalition of elites representing military, economic, clerical, and other traditional as well as civilian bureaucratic interests. In the absence of a single ideal or coherent ideology justifying the legitimacy of the state, authoritarian regimes claim the role of guarantors of traditional values. Linz's article, "An Authoritarian Regime: Spain," appears in* Mass Politics: Studies in Political Sociology.

●　●　●　●　●　●　●　●　●

TYPES OF POLITICAL SYSTEMS

This paper attempts to conceptualize some differences between political systems, taking the present Spanish regime as example and point of departure. In the decades since World War II, the distinction elaborated by political scientists between democratic governments and totalitarian societies has proven useful scientifically and even more polemically. The terms democratic and totalitarian have come to be used as dichotomous or at least as a continuum. An effort is made to fit various regimes into one or the other type, often basing the decision on nonscientific criteria. While the classification has been useful, it is increasingly necessary to go beyond it. From the beginning social scientists have felt uneasy about placing countries like Spain, and even Fascist Italy or pre-1945 Japan, into the totalitarian category. The uneasiness has grown as they came to deal with the "progressive" one-party regimes of the underdeveloped areas and the "modernizing" military dictatorships. So for example A, Inkeles remarks on

> ... a mode of analysis which can encompass totalitarian systems as divergent in their concrete institutional structure as the Communist and Nazi systems, which most closely approximate the ideal type; Fascist Italy, which only imperfectly approximated it; and Franco Spain which only imperfectly fits the model in a few crucial respects.

Even a correspondent like Herbert Matthews, far from friendly to the Spanish regime, writes:

> The power [of Franco] is almost unlimited. This does not make Spain a totalitarian country in either the Communist or the Fascist sense. It is an authoritarian country. The authority is exercised by keeping all parts of the regime weak or in conflict with each other. Order is kept essentially because the Spanish people want it, and through the Army and police. This makes Franco's power supreme when he wants to exercise it. Since, like all modern dictators, he does not allow any single man or group to become strong and threaten his power, there is no alternative to Francisco Franco, at least no visible alternative. As long as his position is not attacked and the nation's affairs function smoothly, he keeps hands off.

Raymond Aron faced the same problem after characterizing the constitutional pluralist regimes and the regimes *de parti monopoliste,* when he wrote about a "third class of regime where is no single party nor multiple parties, not based on electoral legitimacy nor on revolutionary legitimacy," giving as examples Portugal, Spain and the first phase of Vichy.

Gabriel Almond, in his important article on comparative political systems, has formulated most clearly some main characteristics of this type of regime which we shall call authoritarian; the term is used by many in this connection, even by spokesmen of such regimes. Almond writes:

> [The totalitarian political structure] is anti-pluralistic in intent and method if not in accomplishment .... Recent developments in the Soviet Union seem to be directed toward providing some explicit structural bases for policy discussion and conflict .... But what has so far been attained ... is far from the structural pluralism which is so typical for authoritarian regimes. If one takes such a system as that of Spain it is evident that religious bodies, organized interests, status groups, bureaucratic agencies, as well as the Falange party are "acknowledged" elements in a pluralistic political structure. Interest conflict is built into the system, and is not merely latent and spasmodic as in the totalitarian pattern.
>
> The structures of the two systems differ in a second significant respect. The totalitarian system tends to be highly mobilized, tense and expansive internally and externally. The authoritarian tends to be more stable, more relaxed, although these are differences in degree.

It could be argued that there is no need for a new type—the authoritarian—since regimes so described are really imperfect forms of either totalitarian or democratic polities, tending ultimately in one or the other direction and close, at least in their ideals, to one or the other pole. Failure to reach the totalitarian stage might be due to administrative inefficiency, economic underdevelopment, or external influences and pressures. In regimes approving in principle a Western "progressive" conception of democracy—like the Mexican or Turkish leadership after their national revolutions—failure might be attributed to economic backwardness and religious traditionalism. To formulate it as sociologists, we might say that when certain functional prerequisites for a stable democracy are absent, some form of authoritarianism is established, in order—presumably—to prepare the country for it; or in other cases a premature transition to democracy leads to a setback in the form of an authoritarian regime. From another angle, we might say that certain characteristics of the social structure make it impossible for those in power to move toward true totalitarianism without endangering their own position. This hypothesis assumes that those in power are deliberately pursuing a totalitarian social order, which strictly speaking may not be the case even for some stages in a transition which actually results in a totalitarian society.

We prefer for purposes of analysis to reject the idea of a continuum from democracy to totalitarianism and to stress the distinctive nature of authoritarian regimes. Unless we examine the features unique to them, the conditions under which they emerge, the conceptions of power held by those who shape them, regimes which are not clearly either democratic or totalitarian will be treated merely as deviations from these ideal types and will not be studied systematically and comparatively.

Like any ideal type, the notion of the authoritarian regime is an abstraction which underlines certain characteristics and ignores, at least for the time being, the fluidity of reality, differences in degree, and contradictory tendencies present in the real world. In any of the European regimes of the inter-war years that we would call authoritarian, Fascist elements played a role and significant minorities were striving for a totalitarian state; the Hungary of Horthy, the colonels' regime in Poland, the Rumanian and Yugoslav royal dictatorships, the Portuguese Estado Novo, the Austrian corporative Dollfuss regime, Vichy, are examples. Today the model of the Soviet Union operates similarly in many underdeveloped areas. Such regimes exist under many formal garments and their lack of an elaborate and consistent ideology makes them particularly susceptible to mimicry.

The external forms of the thirties and forties, the uniforms and ceremonies and terminology, and the appeals of today to democratic or socialist values, are more easily assimilated than the institutional realities they represent. We may be seriously misled if we study such regimes through constitutions, laws, speeches, the writing of unknown and unrewarded "ideologists," without inquiring how these are actually translated into social reality. The laws may say, for example, that everyone has to be a member of certain organizations, but later almost nobody is; the law gives the corporative system a monopoly of interest representation, but a study of businessmen shows that they belong to literally hundreds of autonomous interest groups which existed before the regime came to power; a political indoctrination course is provided for in the universities but it turns out to be a course in labour and welfare institutions, and everyone is allowed to pass.

The utility of treating authoritarian regimes as a distinct type will lie in helping us understand the distinctive ways in which they resolve problems common to all political systems: maintaining control and gaining legitimacy, recruiting elites, articulating interests and aggregating them, making decisions, and relating to various institutional spheres like the armed forces, religious bodies, the intelligentsia, the economy, etc. If we can find that they handle such problems differently from both democratic and totalitarian regimes, and furthermore if quite different regimes, classified as authoritarian, handle them in ways that turn out to be similar, the distinction will have been justified. Later we will explore in some detail a few examples along these lines ....

DEFINITION OF AN AUTHORITARIAN REGIME

Authoritarian regimes are political systems with limited, not responsible, political pluralism: without elaborate and guiding ideology (but with distinctive mentalities); without intensive nor extensive political mobilization (except at some points in their development); and in which a leader (or occasionally a small group) exercises power within formally ill-defined limits but actually quite predictable ones.

To avoid any confusion we want to make it clear that personal leadership is a frequent characteristic but not a necessary one, since a junta arrangement can exist and the leader's personality might not be the decisive factor. Furthermore, the leader does not need to have charismatic qualities, at least not for large segments of the population nor at all stages of development of the system. In fact he may combine elements of charismatic, legal and traditional authority in varying degrees, often at different points in time—though the charismatic element often tends to be more important than the legal authority, at least for some sectors of the population.

PLURALISM

We speak of regime, rather than government, to indicate the relatively low specificity of the political institutions: they often penetrate the life of the society, preventing, even forcibly, the political expression of certain group interests (as religion in Turkey and Mexico, labor in Spain), or shaping them by interventionist economic policies. But in contrast to some of the analysts of totalitarianism, such as Inkeles, we speak of regimes rather than societies because the distinction between state and society is not obliterated. The pluralistic element is the most distinctive feature of these regimes, but let us emphasize that in contrast to democracies with their almost unlimited pluralism, we deal here with *limited* pluralism. The limitation may be legal or de facto, serious or less so, confined to strictly political groups or extended to interest groups, as long as there remain groups not created by nor dependent on the state which influence the political process one way or another. Some regimes even institutionalize the political participation of a limited number of independently existing groups or institutions, and actually encourage their emergence. To take an example, when Primo de Rivera created his National Assembly he provided for the representation of the church, cultural institutions, the nobility, the army and the business community, as well as the newly created party; at the same time he encouraged the creation of economic interest groups that have been the pressure groups of Spanish business ever since. Another example is the institutionalization of a complex pluralism in the officially dominant Partido Revolucionario Institucional of Mexico, that prompts V. Padgett to write: "An 'official' party need not necessarily be an instrument of imposition. It may be a device for bridging the gap between authoritarianism and representative democracy." With such a limited but relatively autonomous pluralism, there is likely to be some competition for power, more or less informal, despite open declarations of monopoly. It is quite characteristic in this respect that the Falange, after entering the Franco coalition, dropped Point 27, which read:

> We shall work to triumph in the struggle with only the forces subject to our discipline. We shall make very few pacts. Only in the final push for the conquest of the state will the command arrange for the necessary collaborations, always provided that our predominance be assured.

This pluralism contrasts with the strong domination, if not the monopoly, imposed by the totalitarian party after conquering power; its penetration, through the process the Nazis called Gleichschaltung (synchronization), of all kinds of groups and organizations; the creation of functional organizations serving as transmission belts and auxiliaries for the party, politicizing even areas remote from politics, like sports and leisure.

Serrano Suñer, the once powerful brother-in-law of Franco, head of the Junta Politica, minister of interior and foreign affairs and master engineer of the decree founding the unified party, writes quite accurately and with awareness of the alternatives, as follows:

> In truth, be it an advantage or disadvantage, it is time to say that in Spain there has never been anything that would really look like a totalitarian state, since for this it seems to be a necessary condition that the single party should exist in strength and be really the sole basis of support for the regime—the only instrument and in a sense the only holder of power ... the complex of forces participating in the Uprising—the army, traditional elements, parties, etc.—has never disappeared, thanks to a policy of equilibrium and through the persistence of the unified elements without ever fusing and without deciding in favor of a total pre-eminence of the official party.
>
> To give each his due: this regime has not been totalitarian as it has not been democratic or liberal. What it would have been without the world war only God knows. What it will finally be is still to be seen.

The difference between authoritarian and democratic pluralism is that the latter is in principle almost unlimited; it is not only tolerated but legitimate; and its open participation in the competition for power, through political parties, is institutionalized. In a democracy political forces not only reflect social forces, but represent them and to some extent commit them to the support of government policies once these are arrived at; political forces are dependent on the support of constituencies. The "iron law of oligarchy" may make this relative, but the formal principle is upheld.

In authoritarian regimes the men who come to power reflecting the views of various groups and institutions do not derive their position from the support of these groups alone, but from the trust placed in them by the leader, monarchy or "junta," who certainly takes into account their prestige and influence. They have a kind of constituency, we might call it a potential constituency, but this is not solely or even principally the source of their power.

The co-optation of leaders is a constant process by which different sectors or institutions become participants in the system. In the consolidated totalitarian system this process takes place between bureaucracies or organizations that are part of the political structure created by the system, generally dependent on the party or an outgrowth of it; in the authoritarian regime pre-existent or newly emergent elements of the society can be represented by this means. The authoritarian regime may go very far toward suppressing existing groups or institutions inimical to the social order; this process of control may affect others, and the threat of control is always present; but due to a number of circumstances the control process is arrested. The strength of ideological commitments; the size, integration, quality of the group wishing a monopoly of power; the strength and legitimacy of existing institutions, and their international ties; the degree of economic autarchy possible; all are factors which may limit maximum suppression of dissidence. Ultimately the conception of power held by the authoritarian leader may make the decisive difference.

MENTALITY VERSUS IDEOLOGY

Styles of leadership, and different ways of conceiving the relation between state power and society, must be examined if we are to analyze the authoritarian regime in its various forms.

We will purposely use the term mentality rather than "ideology." The German sociologist Theodor Geiger has formulated a useful distinction between *ideologies*, which are systems of thought more or less intellectually elaborated and organized, often in written form, by intellectuals, pseudo-intellectuals, or with their assistance; and *mentalities*, which are ways of thinking and feeling, more emotional than rational, that provide noncodified ways of reacting to situations. Ideologies have a strong utopian element; mentalities are closer to the present or the past. Totalitarian systems have ideologies, a point emphasized by all students of such systems, while authoritarian regimes are based more on distinctive mentalities which are difficult to define. The more traditional an authoritarian regime is, the greater the role of the military and civil servants, the more important "mentalities" become in understanding the system, and the more a focus on ideologies, even those loudly proclaimed by the regime, may be misleading ....

APATHY VERSUS MOBILIZATION

Stabilized authoritarian regimes are characterized by lack of extensive and intensive political mobilization of the population. Membership participation is low in political and para-political organizations and participation in the single party or similar bodies, whether coerced, manipulated or voluntary, is infrequent and limited. The common citizen expresses little enthusiastic support for the regime in elections, referenda, and rallies. Rather than enthusiasm or support, the regime often expects—even from office holders and civil servants—passive acceptance, or at least they refrain from public anti-government activity. Let us stress this depoliticization is characteristic of stabilized authoritarian regimes, but would not be necessarily true for their formative stages, particularly since their emergence in a crisis would involve considerable and often very intensive popular participation. We would like to argue that this participation is not likely to be maintained over a long period of time, unless the regime moves into a totalitarian or a more formally democratic direction. However, the degrees of mobilization might be the most useful criteria on which to distinguish subtypes of authoritarian regimes.

On the one side we have those that Raymond Aron has characterized as "regimes without parties" which "require a kind of depoliticization of the governed," and others we could call "populistic" in which there is a more continuous effort of mobilization, without reaching the pervasiveness and intensity of the totalitarian model. Recognizing the importance of such a distinction, we would like to suggest that often the difference might be more that of stages in the development of non-democratic regimes than a substantive difference. It would be to misunderstand contemporary Spain to ignore the high level of participation in party activities, youth groups, politically oriented welfare activities—not to mention rallies, parades, etc.—during the years of the Civil War in Nationalistic Spain; and the intensity of involvement, ideological and emotional, of people in all sectors of the population must be stressed. No one can deny that this disappeared during the years after the victory. This was not only because, first, the leadership lacked interest in maintaining it, but also because the social structure of a semideveloped country, and the social, institutional and ideological pluralism, made such levels of participation untenable without either channeling them through organized parties or substituting that pluralism with a hierarchical, disciplined and ideologically committed single party. In the contest of the early forties, the first possibility was excluded and the will to impose a truly totalitarian system, destructive of the coalition character of the forces Franco led to victory, was absent from an army (including its leaders) which had no single well-defined ideology. I would like to leave the question open if in the future some of the more "populistic" one-party regimes in Africa and the Moslem countries will not undergo a similar process, transforming the parties and connected organizations into adjuncts of the state apparatus (the bureaucracy) and/or patronage organizations, with little genuine participation, even of a manipulative type ....

It would take too long to analyze here all the causes of low mobilization or our doubts about the capacity of such regimes to sustain a significant degree of mobilization for any length of time (without considerable changes in other respects—limitation of pluralism and emphasis on an ideology—in a totalitarian direction), but we may list at least some factors. In the absence of a modern revolutionary ideology, reformism, particularly bureaucratic and technocratic reformism, does not provide a chiliastic vision for action, and the structure of underdeveloped countries does not motivate sustained, regular day-to-day activity .... With social and economic change come the growth of private interests and the struggle to improve one's living standards. Only in a society where the government is the principal employer, or controls the economy as through co-operatives, can it offer financial rewards to the citizens who participate, but this does not insure that participation will be political; it may come to resemble participation in interest groups like those characterizing democratic society. Economic development and industrialization seem to be a precondition for a lively associational life under any system. Limited literacy and low incomes are such obstacles that only the diversion of considerable resources can assure participation for any length of time.

Undoubtedly such social and structural factors may be overcome if the leadership is really committed to the idea of a mobilized society, as the Communist and, even to a minor extent, the Italian Fascist experiences show. The very different attitude of one typical authoritarian leader is well described in these comments of Macartney writing about a Hungarian political leader in the 20's:

He did not mean opposition ever to be in a position to seriously challenge his own will. But he did not think it any part of the duty of government to pry into and regiment each detail of the subject's conduct, much less his thoughts. For this he was too large-minded, or too cynical, too little a perfectionist ....

In authoritarian regimes, intermediate systems are frequent: membership may be obligatory but involve nothing more than paying dues, or strictly voluntary without creating any advantages. Presumably political goals take primacy in totalitarian organizations while specific interests predominate in democratic organizations ....

The depoliticization of officially created associations has certainly not been unique to Spain; with the "end of ideology," the politicization of interest and leisure groups characteristic of European democratic parties from the turn of the century to World War II has also receded. In fact it could be argued that authoritarianism provided a welcome relief from overpoliticization in democratic societies which had not developed apolitical voluntary associations in proportion to the number of fiercely conflicting political groups. An Italian metal worker in his fifties expressed this when he said of his working class neighborhood in Genoa:

I was born here. Then everyone used to know each other, we used to get together, loved each other. After the war came politics. Now we all hate each other. You are a Communist, I am a Socialist, he is a Demo-Christian. And so we avoid each other as much as possible ....

THE AUTHORITARIAN PARTY

According to the legal texts of many authoritarian regimes, their single parties occupy a similarly dominant position: to the totalitarian party monopolizing power, recruiting the elite, transmitting both the aspirations of the people and the directives of the leadership. In fact, however, some regimes that in reality approach the totalitarian model legally have multiparty systems, while in others which are legally single party monopolies, the party plays a comparatively limited role. Therefore it is imperative to examine the authoritarian party in its sociological reality.

First and foremost, the authoritarian party is not a well-organized ideological organization which monopolizes all access to power. As we will see later, a considerable part of the elite has no connection with the party and does not identify with it. Party membership creates few visible advantages and imposes few, if any, duties. Ideological indoctrination is often minimal, the conformity and loyalty required may be slight, and expulsions and purges are not frequent and do not represent an important mechanism of social control. The party is often ideologically and socially heterogeneous. Far from branching out into many functional organizations, in an effort to control the state apparatus and penetrate other spheres of life as the Nazi party did, it is a skeleton organization of second-rate bureaucrats. The party becomes only one more element in the power pluralism; one more group pressing for particular interests; one more channel through which divergent interests try to find access to power; one more recruiting ground for elite members. Since tight discipline lacks widespread ideological legitimacy, various functional groups that might have been transmission belts for the leadership's directives, become apolitical interest groups, or autonomous nuclei where a few activists, even those emerging from the grass roots, may follow independent policies.

The importance of the party has many indicators: the number of high officials that were active in the party before entering the elite; the membership figures; the degree of activity indicated by the party budget; agitprop activity; the prestige of power accorded to party officials; the presence of party cells or representatives in other institutions; the importance of training centers; the attention paid to party organs and publications; the vigor of ideological polemics within the party factions. By all these criteria the Spanish party has never been too strong and today is obviously weak. A look at the party's provincial headquarters, in contrast to other government offices of the Sindicatos (a functional organization theoretically dependent on the party) should convince anyone of the party's second-rate role in Spain.

The different roles of the authoritarian and totalitarian parties may be explained by differences in their origin. Most single parties in authoritarian countries have been created after accession to power rather than before. They have been created by fusing a variety of groups with different ideological traditions and varying social bases, not by completely subordinating some elements to one dominant force. Where politicians of other groupings, including the minor Fascist parties, have been co-opted, no disciplined, integrated organization emerged. In other cases, when the military dictator has tried to create a patriotic national unity organization, the effort was carried out by officers and bureaucrats, who typically do not have the demagogic skills needed to create a lively organization. They are further hampered because they continue devoting most of their attention to government or army offices, where real power, and not merely the promise of it, lies. The old politicians, rallying to organizations like the Imperial Rule Assistance Association or the ex-CEDA (conservative-demochristian deputies in the Republic) leaders in the Falange, are not able to adopt the new style that a totalitarian party requires. Since the party is not tested in a struggle for power, it attracts more than its share of office seekers and opportunists, few idealists, true believers, real revolutionaries. Since its ideology is not defined, indoctrination of the numerous newcomers, entering en masse, is likely to be scanty, and the facts of life soon disillusion the more utopian. Since the primary staff need is to staff the state apparatus, the premium will be on recruiting professionals and bureaucrats, and not the armed intellectuals or bohemians, the marginal men that give the totalitarian movement its peculiar style.

The prominence of the army or civil service in the regime before the party was created, and the solidarity of these groups against newcomers when it comes to making key appointments, makes the rewards of party activity less appealing than membership in the NSDAP or, later, the SS. In underdeveloped countries the army is particularly important, since it does not like the rise of rivals and will seek to prevent the creation of anything like party militias or workers' guards. Any attempt to build up the party beyond a certain point, particularly after the German experience, is likely to encounter the open opposition of the army, as Perón soon discovered …. A comment by Serrano Suñer, former chairman of the Junta Politica of the party, describes the relation between army and political groups in many such regimes: "In the last analysis the center of gravity, the true support of the regime (despite all the appearances which we foolishly try to exaggerate) was and would continue to be the army; the nationalist army—an army that was not politically defined." …

FORMS OF SOCIAL CONTROL

Similarities between authoritarian regimes and the totalitarians can perhaps go furthest in the control of mass media, particularly in countries in the process of modernization where the technological and capital requirements for setting up the media make such control very easy. Media may vary greatly in autonomy, even under the same regime, but limited pluralism readily creates some islands of exemption; in Spain, for example, church publications are free from government censorship.

The small size of the elite and the persistence within the regime of ties created prior to it, allow for considerable free communication, unless the regime is willing to use a good deal of coercion. The same may be said of contacts with other countries, particularly by the elite. While the monopoly of mass media may be as great as that in totalitarian societies, the impact of this monopoly is less because it is not enhanced by intensive personal propagandizing through agitators and other informal leaders. Even when the freedom of the press is curtailed, truly totalitarian control is not present if there is freedom of travel and, at least, freedom of conversation. (As long as one does not make more than five copies of one's opinions, one cannot be prosecuted for illegal propaganda in Spain.) It may well be that the excesses of control to which a Stalin or Hitler went are really unnecessary ....

THE POSITION OF THE MILITARY

All political systems face the problem of subordinating the military to political authority, and once military dictators start devoting their energies to political problems, they face the same issue. Methods of controlling the military differ in democracies, totalitarian systems, and authoritarian regimes; the equilibrium established between political and military authority will differ as well. In most authoritarian regimes the limited popular consensus, which made such forms of rule necessary or possible in the first place, means there is more need for potential force; this gives the army a privileged position. Normally military affairs are left to military men and not to civilians. The absence of a mass party, and in some countries of a trustworthy and specialized bureaucracy, often leads to the use of military men in political appointments, patronage positions and the administration. The technical branches provide experts for public service or nationalized industries. Nationalism as a simple ideology, easily shared by all classes, makes for an emphasis on the army as a bearer of national prestige. If the break with the past was made by a military coup, the position of the army is likely to be even more enhanced ....

In such regimes emerging from a military action, the army may enjoy a privileged position and hold on to key positions, but it soon co-opts politicians, civil servants and technicians who increasingly make most decisions. The more a regime becomes consolidated, the fewer purely military men staff the government, except when there are no alternative sources of elites. In this sense it may be misleading to speak of a military dictatorship, even when the head of state is an army man. In fact he is likely to carry out a careful policy of depoliticization and professionalization of the army, while he maintains close ties with the officer corps to hold its loyalty.

The military background of key men in authoritarian regimes, and their usual lack of ideological sophistication, make it particularly important to understand the military mentality in relation to internal politics, to styles of political life, conceptions of authority, ideas about cost versus results, legitimate forms for expressing grievances, and so on. The few studies on the role of the military in politics have only raised the issue; real data are still to be assembled.

AUTHORITARIAN REGIMES AND WEBER'S TYPES OF LEGITIMACY

Due to the prominent role of the leader in authoritarian regimes, there is some temptation to identify them with charismatic rule. However we would like to argue that Max Weber's categories can and should be used independently of the distinction between democracy, authoritarianism, and totalitarianism. Within each of these systems the legitimacy of the ruler, for the population or his staff, can be based on one or another of these types of belief.

Undoubtedly charisma has played an important role for masses and staff under Hitler and Lenin; totalitarian regimes have also made demands on their civil service, based on legal authority; and democratic prime ministers have enjoyed charisma. Authoritarian regimes may also have a charismatic element, since they often come into being during serious crisis situations, and control of the mass media facilitates the creation of an "image" of the unique leader. Genuine belief in charisma is likely to be limited, however, since the man assuming leadership was often unknown before, and to his fellow officers is often a primus inter pares, who owes his position often simply to rank. With notable exceptions—Perón or Nasser—the modern army as a rational institution does not breed the irrational leadership type, full of passion, demagogic, convinced of his mission. He is not likely to have, at least for his fellow officers and collaborators, the same appeal that a Lenin or a Hitler could have for those who initiated with him, as marginal men, the long hard struggle for power.

At the same time limited pluralism and the lack of ideological self-righteousness allow more room for the development of general rules institutionalizing the exercise of power, and there is thus a trend toward the secularization of whatever charisma was acquired during crisis. This transition to legal authority has been emphasized in the case of the Spanish regime by one of its leading political theorists, and is even reflected in legal texts. Staffing the system with officers and civil servants, rather than the "old shirts" of street fighting days, contributes to the growth of legalism.

Authoritarian regimes may come to power as de facto authorities with little legitimacy, and develop some charismatic appeal; but they end in a mixture of legal, charismatic and traditional authority. The low level of mobilization may often mean that large parts of the population remain in the position of subjects, recognizing agents of power without questioning their legitimacy; for them habit and self-interest may be more important, and belief unnecessary for effective control.

TRADITIONAL AND AUTHORITARIAN REGIMES

One question some of our readers may raise is: Aren't many such regimes really only a form of autocratic and conservative rule like we find in preconstitutional and traditional monarchies? It would be foolish to deny that the distinctions are fluid, that a number of authoritarian regimes have emerged out of such political forms, and that the formal constitutional framework may still be a monarchical one. However, we want to stress that we would not want to include in our concept any political system which would strictly fit under the concept of traditional authority in Weber's sense and where rule is based on historical continuity, impersonal familial or institutionalized charisma or various mixtures of patrimonial or feudal rule ... using these terms in a somewhat technical sense. To make it clear, neither Abyssinia, nor Yemen before the recent revolution, nor Tibet, Afghanistan, nor some of the other political entities along the Himalayan border fit our concept, to mention contemporary systems. Nor would the prerevolutionary European absolute monarchies of the past. Authoritarian regimes are a likely outcome of the breakdown of such traditional forms of legitimacy. This results from a partial social and political mobilization and a questioning of the traditional principles of legitimacy (largely due to their secularization) by significant segments of the society. Authoritarian systems—even those we might call reactionary—are modernizing in the sense that they represent a discontinuity with tradition, introducing criteria of efficiency and rationality, personal achievement and populistic appeals .... The attempts of the present Spanish regime to find its constitutional and legitimacy form as a traditional monarchy certainly suggest the difficulties encountered when moving from an authoritarian regime to a traditional one. There can be no doubt that many of those who are willing to recognize the claims to legitimate rule of Franco would not transfer their allegiance to a traditional monarchy. In our times authoritarian rule almost inevitably leads to questioning traditional authority, if for no other reason than by making the people aware of the importance of the effective head of the government and its secular character. Authoritarian rule might be an intermediate stage in or after the breakdown of traditional authority, but not the route toward its restoration. To specify further the differences would take us at this time too far from the Spanish case.

This might be the place to stress a very important characteristic of many, if not most, authoritarian regimes: the coexistence in them of different legitimizing formulae. The actual pluralism of such regimes and the lack of effective legitimate institutionalization of that pluralism within a single legitimate political formula allowing competition of the pluralistic elements for power, almost inevitably lead to the coexistence of competing legitimacy formulae. So in the case of Spain the traditionalist monarchy desired by the Carlists, a restoration of the pre-1931 monarchy, some form of Catholic corporativism like the present regime under monarchical (or even republican) form, a more dynamic totalitarian vision along fascist lines, even a transition to a democratic republic under christian democratic leadership, are all different formulas open to the supporters of the regime. These supporters give their support in the hope that the regime will satisfy their aspirations and they withdraw their support in so far as they realize that the regime is not doing so, or unable to do so. If we had more space we could develop some of the parallels with Binder's description of the Iranian situation.

Fortunately for many such systems, the great mass of the population in semi- or underdeveloped societies is not concerned with the legitimizing formulae. Instead the population obeys out of a mixture of habit and self-interest, either characterizing the political culture of passive subjects or the parochial (to use the terminology of Almond and Verba). The confusion concerning the sources of legitimacy inherent in many such regimes contributes much of the confusion and pessimism of those most likely to be politically involved. Because of this often the more privileged and those close to the centers of power may appear more alienated from the regime than they really are (at least for all practical purposes). This can help to explain the relative stability of many such systems despite the freedom with which criticism is expressed. The identification with such regimes may not be found in their political formulas, but in the identification with the basic values of the society, its stratification system, and many nonpolitical institutions, which are their infra-structure.

22

PARLIAMENTARY AND PRESIDENTIAL SYSTEMS OF GOVERNMENT

State-society relations indicate a great deal about the performance of political systems. But a more complete picture emerges when we understand how political authority is institutionally organized. The vast majority of contemporary political systems work from parliamentary or presidential principles of the distribution of power. In this reading. Douglas Verney, a professor of political science at York University, Toronto, sets out the main features of parliamentary and presidential government. In tracing the historical origins of both types of government, Verney identifies important common ground: both aim to limit abuses of power. In comparing these systems, it is tempting to resort to such catch phrases as "separation of powers," "checks and balances," and "balance of powers" to capture the differences. Verney, however, provides an important antidote to this formalistic perspective. He shows that, in parliamentary systems, the possible abuse of power can be checked without separating institutions and that, in presidential systems, effective government can only be achieved through the coordination of separate executive, legislative, and judicial functions. This historical perspective also underscores the important fluctuations in the relative balance of power between the executive, the legislative, and the judiciary in presidential systems and the shifting locus of influence within parliamentary systems. The reading was excerpted from Douglas Verney's book Analysis of Political Systems.

• • • • • • • • •

PARLIAMENTARY GOVERNMENT

Parliamentarism is the most widely adopted system of government, and it seems appropriate to refer to British parliamentary experience in particular because it is the British system which has provided an example for a great many other countries. Nowadays when it is fashionable to speak of political systems and theories as "not for export" it is worth bearing in mind the success with which a system adopted piecemeal to suit British constitutional developments has proved feasible in different situations abroad. This is not to imply that the British parliamentary system should be taken as the model and that others are, as it were, deviations from the norm, although generations of Englishmen have been tempted to make this assumption ....

Indeed an examination of parliamentarism in various countries indicates that there are two main types of parliamentary procedure, the British and the Continental. In British parliamentary procedure, as adopted in the Commonwealth and Ireland, legislation is initiated in the full Assembly and not in committees. Private members speak only from their places, not from a tribune. Continental procedure is sometimes called "French" but seems to have parallel origins in Sweden and Norway. Moreover according to Hawgood in practice "it was Belgium, and not Britain, France, Sweden or Norway, that became the pattern and prototype for constitutional monarchies everywhere during the century following 1831"—the year in which the Belgian Constitution came into force.

This analysis of parliamentarism is concerned less with distinguishing the various forms of parliamentarism than with establishing the highest common factors in different parliamentary systems. It is not therefore necessary to account for all the political institutions existing in parliamentary countries, still less to describe devices such as federalism which are common to all three types of government, presidential and conventional as well as parliamentary. It may surprise those who have tended to regard British government as the model as well as the Mother of Parliaments to know that the United Kingdom could abolish the Monarchy, adopt a single code of constitutional laws on the pattern of the French or American Constitutions, transform the House of Lords into a Senate (or even do away with it), introduce a multi-party system based on proportional representation, institute a number of parliamentary committees to deal with specific topics such as finance and foreign affairs, and still possess a parliamentary system.

There would seem to be a number of basic principles applicable to both of the chief varieties of parliamentary government. These can be analysed and later used for purposes of comparison with presidential and convention government.

The Assembly Becomes a Parliament

Where parliamentary government has evolved rather than been the product of revolution there have often been three phases, though the transition from one to the other has not always been perceptible at the time. First there has been government by a Monarch who has been responsible for the whole political system. Then there has arisen an Assembly of members who have challenged the hegemony of the King. Finally the Assembly has taken over responsibility for government, acting as a Parliament, the Monarch being deprived of most of his traditional powers.

This has certainly been the pattern in Britain. As late as the seventeenth century King James I could still preach the doctrine of the Divine Right of Kings. Addressing the Houses of Parliament in 1609 he said, "For Kings are not only God's Lieutenants upon earth, and sit upon God's throne, but even by God Himself they are called Gods." In France the Charter of 1814, framed on the restoration of the French Monarchy during Napoleon's exile to Elba, assumed the divine right of the Bourbons to the throne. During this first phase, if such it may be called, the "Government" consisted of Secretaries who helped the King in his administration. If there was a "Parliament" it was partly because a high court of justice was necessary and partly because the Monarch wanted a sounding-board of public opinion and needed support, especially of a financial nature, for his foreign policies. Between 1302 and 1614 the French States-General met as a whole in less than forty-two years. Even in England the Houses of Parliament met in only 198 of the years between 1295 and 1614—though whereas the English Parliament was about to assert its real authority by the end of the period the States-General was to meet for the last time until 1789. The foundations of the English Parliament's strength were maintained and strengthened in the Tudor period and it required considerable finesse on the part of the Monarch to manage the two Houses. But there was as yet no question of challenging the supreme position of the Monarch as Executive ....

However, by establishing their power over the purse, Assemblies were ultimately able to claim their own area of jurisdiction. Henceforth the Monarch's role was increasingly that of an Executive dependent ultimately on the goodwill of the Legislature. Constitutional development entered a second phase in which the term "legislative power" was given to Assemblies to distinguish them from the "executive power" of the King. The English Civil War and the 1688 Revolution did not establish parliamentarism in England but made explicit this division of executive and legislative power between the King and the two Houses. No doubt, as we can now see, the ultimate supremacy of the Houses of Parliament could never be challenged again, but John Locke was quite right to say, as he did in his *Second Treatise of Civil Government*, that both authorities could in a sense claim to be supreme. During the eighteenth century division of responsibility became generally acknowledged and thanks to the writings of Montesquieu and Blackstone this device of government became widely celebrated as the "separation of powers." Whereas on the Continent of Europe despotic governments were the rule there was in Britain a division of power between the King and the Houses of Parliament which Englishmen considered to be the "guardian of their liberties and a bulwark against tyranny." ...

But even as the theory of the separation of powers was coming into vogue the transition to the third and present phase was under way in Britain. In the eighteenth century the King was already losing his executive power to Ministers who came to regard the Assembly, not the Monarch, as the sovereign to whom they were really responsible. Ministers were increasingly chosen from among members of the Assembly and resigned when the Assembly withdrew its confidence from them. The change was slow and it was not until the reign of Queen Victoria that parliamentary government as we know it today was fully established. As late as 1867 Bagehot could still feel it necessary to deny that the executive and legislative powers were separated in Britain, and to argue that in the British political system there was a "fusion of powers." By this time parliamentary government was already formalized in the Belgian Constitution. In Sweden, where the separation of powers had only recently been established, the introduction of parliamentarism had to wait until the formation of Liberal Governments in the first two decades of the twentieth century.

In parliamentary monarchies such as Britain, Belgium and Sweden, the Monarch has ceased in practice (though not in form) to exercise even the executive power. Government has passed to "his" Ministers who are responsible to the Legislature. Parliamentary government implies a certain fusion of the executive and legislative functions, the body which has been merely an Assembly of representative being transformed into a Parliament.

In short, the first phase ended in Britain about the time of the death of Elizabeth I, the last of the Tudors. The following century (1603–1714), known as the Stuart period, saw the rise of Parliament and the recognition of its distinct sphere of influence and power. But the gradual transition to the third and present phase of parliamentary government, which began with the appointment of Walpole as First Minister in 1721, was not completed until the reign of Victoria (1837–1901) since when parliamentary government has been in operation.

It is somewhat confusing, however, to find the term "Parliament" commonly used to describe the Assembly throughout all three phases.

Clearly the English Parliament of the sixteenth century was a very different body from the British Parliament of today. For the sake of clarity, the term "Assembly" or "Houses of Parliament" is used in this study to describe the British Parliament as it was before the introduction of parliamentary government, that is to say before the Government came to consist of members of Parliament responsible to that body rather than to the Monarch.

Equally confusing is the use of the term "Parliament" at the present time in two different senses. The statement "Parliament is supreme" refers to Parliament as a whole, members of the Government included, and is correct usage. On the other hand the phrase "The Government is responsible to Parliament" presumably means that the Government is dependent upon the support of *other* members of the Legislature, the Government excluded. In the one instance "Parliament" is used broadly, to include both members of the Government and "private members" as they are often called in Britain, and in the other it connotes these private members only. Unfortunately there is no generic term to describe the private members, either in Britain or abroad. (The term "private member"—and still less "back-bencher"—hardly does justice to the eminent office of Her Majesty's Leader of the Opposition, or even to his colleagues on the Opposition Front Bench.) This fact alone demonstrates the fusion of powers which has taken place, and for all practical purposes the Assembly as such has ceased to exist. Indeed, it is arguable that to insist upon the drawing of a distinction is to encourage a misunderstanding of the nature of parliamentary government, which has so successfully obliterated it.

It is true that for the most part the use of the term "Parliament" at one time to include the Government and at others to exclude it seems to cause little difficulty; provided some knowledge of the parliamentary system is assumed. In a comparative study of political systems, however, such ambiguity presents certain problems if like is to be compared with like. It therefore becomes necessary to insist on a more precise usage. "Parliament" will at all times signify a body which includes the Government. When it is necessary to refer to the Legislature excluding members of the Government the term "Assembly" will be used ....

Not all parliamentary systems are monarchical, and in those countries which are republics another personage, usually called the President, takes the place of the constitutional monarch as Head of State. A noteworthy feature of several republics is that at one time they too were monarchies, but during revolutions the monarchy was swept away. The process of constitutional development was often crowded into a very short period, some republics passing straight from a state of monarchical despotism to a form of parliamentarism ....

The first characteristic of parliamentarism may now be summarized. It is a political system where the Executive, once separate, has been challenged by the Assembly which is then transformed into a Parliament comprising both Government and Assembly.

The Executive Is Divided into Two Parts

One important consequence of the transformation of the Assembly into a Parliament is that the Executive is now split in two, a Prime Minister or Chancellor becoming head of the Government and the Monarch or President acting as Head of State. Usually the Monarch occupies his throne by hereditary title (though elected monarchies, e.g. in Malaya, are not unknown), while a President is elected by Parliament. It does not follow that the Head of State fills a purely formal or decorative office. Constitutional monarchs still have important prerogatives and even if those which they do not (or dare not) use are left out of consideration there remains a considerable field in which their powers are politically significant.

In principle there should be no objection to, and perhaps much to be said for, a clear statement of the respective functions of Head of State and Government. But the British view appears to be that the relationship of the two parts of the Executive is better left to the operation of flexible convention than written into the law of the Constitution. In several European monarchies there has been a similar transfer of power from Monarch to Ministry, but without a re-statement of their respective functions. Thus Article 4 of the Swedish Constitution still reads: "The King alone shall govern the realm." Part of Article 30 of the Norwegian Constitution reads:

> Everyone who holds a seat in the Council is in duty bound to express fearlessly his opinions, to which the King is bound to listen. But it remains with the King to take a resolution according to his own judgment.

The Governments of these countries are thus shielded by the Constitution when they claim freedom of action on the part of the Crown whose powers they wield.

Where the Head of State is a President there is less reticence about making the duties of the divided Executive explicit, presumably because the President is elected by Parliament. In constitutional monarchies experience has shown that if the Monarch does not have his duties constitutionally defined and protected greater flexibility is possible. (In other words, the King can be deprived of more and more of his prerogative powers.) There is an important exception to this rule in Japan. Fear that the Emperor might not accept the role of a constitutional Monarch has led to the explicit withdrawal of all governmental functions from him in the new constitution. Executive power is vested expressly in the Cabinet. In parliamentary republics there is a fairly general apprehension lest the President engross the powers which pertain to the Government. The Constitution of the French Fourth Republic accordingly stated what powers the President of the Republic (Articles 29–44) and the President of the Council of Ministers (45–54) might wield.

On the other hand Presidents are sometimes allowed a greater authority than Monarchs because their status is achieved, not ascribed as a result of inherited title. The French President, for example, had a temporary veto over legislation which Monarchs might possess in theory but certainly do not exercise in practice. But where, as in the Fifth Republic and in Finland, the President has special rights comparable with or superior to those of the Ministry, the system ceases at this point to be truly parliamentary.

It is a characteristic of hereditary monarchies that the King cannot be held personally responsible and so his Ministers must bear responsibility for him. No such inhibition seems to affect republics, where the President is elected. Consequently when the President oversteps his position he is subject to impeachment, for high treason in France, for unconstitutional activity in the Federal German Republic, and for both in Italy.

The second characteristic of parliamentarism may now be summarized. The Executive is divided into a Head of State and a Government whose relationship with the Head of State may or may not be precisely formulated.

The Head of State Appoints the Head of Government

The value of a divided Executive in constitutional monarchies is fairly obvious. For one thing, the proper business of State can be carried on by a government responsible to the Legislature while the mystique of Monarchy is preserved. There seems no apparent reason, at first glance, for dividing it in Republics. Admittedly it is useful to have someone above the day-to-day political warfare to receive ambassadors and to decorate ceremonial occasions, but this hardly seems to justify the expense of such an office. After all, the President of the United States, who as head of the American government bears the greatest responsibilities of any statesman in the world, manages to combine with his high and lonely eminence the even higher office of Head of State.

However, it is in the very nature of the parliamentary system that there shall be two distinct offices, and that the head of the Government shall be appointed by the Head of State. Were the electorate itself to perform this task, directly or through a special College of electors as in the United States or Finland, the system would become, in this respect at least, presidential in character. For Parliament to elect the head of the Government would be to adopt the procedure which is characteristic of the convention system. The different methods of selecting the head of the Government distinguish as clearly as anything else the three theories of governmental organization.

Nor is the duty of appointing the head of the Government a mere formality. It is true that the Head of State is bound by the results of parliamentary elections and must appoint the head of the party which is clearly the victor. But this is the situation only where one party or stable coalition has obtained an absolute majority of seats, which is called appropriately in Scandinavia "Majority-parliamentarism." But in many parliamentary systems, especially multi-party systems, no party has an absolute majority and "minority-parliamentarism" prevails. In selecting the Prime Minister who can best obtain a working majority the Head of State may have to use his personal discretion. The last occasion on which such a situation arose in Britain was in 1931, and the role of the Monarch during this crisis is still disputed. Even where there is majority-parliamentarism problems may occur. The Prime Minister may resign for personal reasons, as Sir Anthony Eden did in 1957, without leaving an obvious successor, and then the Monarch has to make a very important personal decision. The Conservative Party was criticised on this occasion for not appointing a leader before this situation arose, and no doubt the Queen's selection would have been merely a formality had this been done. But it is quite possible that on some future occasion, for example when a party is divided about a new leader, the Head of State may once again be compelled to use his or her discretion. It may be desirable that where the Head of State is a Monarch the selection of the head of the Government shall be a formality but this can by no means be guaranteed in a parliamentary system.

Some parliamentary republics, notably Western Germany and the French Fourth Republic, have escaped from this dilemma by the introduction of an element of convention theory whereby selection of a Prime Minister has three stages. The President nominates a candidate, the Assembly shows its approval by electing him (in Germany) or by giving him a vote of confidence (in France) and then the president appoints him as Prime Minister.

Parliamentarism, therefore, implies some balance of power even though the separation of institutions still characteristic of presidential government has given way to fusion. Unlike convention government it is not government by Assembly, nor is it the absorption of the Executive by the Assembly. It is the creation of a completely new institution in the political system, a Parliament, in which the Assembly and the Government are somehow miraculously blended. The duty of the Head of State to appoint the head of the Government—the third characteristic of parliamentarism—is as necessary to preserve that balance as the popular election of both President and Assembly is to preserving the balance in presidential systems.

The Head of the Government Appoints the Ministry

An interesting feature of parliamentarism is the distinction made between the Prime Minister and other Ministers. The former is appointed by the Head of State; the latter are nominated by the Prime Minister after his appointment. Usually the selection of various Ministers allows a certain amount of personal choice to a head of Government, which cannot usually be said of the appointment of a Prime Minister by the Head of State. Ministers are formally appointed by the Head of State, who may often no doubt exert an informal influence upon appointments—but so may the state on party alignments and factions in the Assembly. It remains a cardinal principle that the Prime Minister alone is responsible for the composition of the Ministry. Where, as in Australia, Ministers are sometimes elected by their party this is a departure from the parliamentary principle in the direction of convention government.

The Ministry (or Government) is a Collective Body

The transfer from the monarchical Executive to a Council of Ministers has meant that a single person has been replaced by a collective body. Whereas under *anciens régimes* it was the King's pleasure (*le Roi le veult*), under parliamentarism the Prime Minister is merely first among equals (*primus inter pares*), though no doubt some Prime Ministers are more forceful than others …. In the United States, of course, the President is sole Executive, but it is a hallmark of the parliamentary system that the Government shall be collective.

Ministers Are Usually Members of Parliament

Members of the Government have a double role to play in the parliamentary system. They are not only Ministers but are at the same time members of Parliament, elected (unless they are members of the British House of Lords) like the members of the Assembly and equally dependent upon the goodwill of their constituents. The problem of distinguishing between Parliament and Assembly is most acute when this role is analysed. In Britain there is no law that Ministers must be members of one of the Houses of Parliament (though it is required that at least three members of the Cabinet must be drawn from the House of Lords) but there is a convention that they are in fact always members of one or other. Thus when Mr. Bevin became Minister of Labour in 1940 a seat was found for him in the House of Commons. When Sir Percy Mills joined Mr. Macmillan's Government in 1957 he was made a peer. The Constitution of the French Fourth Republic specifically stated that Ministers are collectively and individually responsible to the National Assembly and there is an implication that they should be members of that body.

Since, according to the usage adopted in this chapter, Parliament comprises both Government and Assembly, a member of the Government is *ipso facto* a member of Parliament, but by definition he cannot be a member of the Assembly. In full parliamentary countries such as the United Kingdom where Ministers are members of Parliament it is difficult to make the distinction between Government, Parliament, and Assembly clear. Indeed the attempt to make one seems artificial.

However, not all parliamentary countries have accepted the necessity for Ministers to be members of one of the Houses of Parliament. In Sweden up to a third of the Ministry of fifteen members have on occasion in recent years not been Members of Parliament. In the Netherlands, Norway and Luxembourg, Ministers are actually forbidden to be Members of Parliament after their appointment. Here there is a relic of the old doctrine of the separation of powers when Ministers were responsible to the Monarch. (Traces of the doctrine may be found elsewhere, for example, in the traditional French rule that Ministers may not be members of parliamentary committees.)

Generally speaking, nevertheless, it is usual for most if not all Ministers to be Members of Parliament. Where they are not, the system may still be said to be of the parliamentary type if they can take part in parliamentary debates and are truly responsible to the Assembly for the conduct of the Executive. In Norway, Sweden, the Netherlands and Luxembourg, all parliamentary monarchies, these conditions are fulfilled. In the French Fifth Republic, where the government is not responsible to Parliament for the conduct of the President, they are not.

The Government Is Politically Responsible to the Assembly

In parliamentary systems the Government is responsible to the Assembly which may, if it thinks that the Government is acting unwisely or unconstitutionally, refuse to give it support. By a formal vote of censure or by simply not assenting to an important Government proposal the Assembly can force the Government to resign and cause the Head of State to appoint a new Government.

In the *anciens régimes* of Europe Ministers were responsible not to the Assembly but to the King, as in Nepal today. They were truly

Ministers of the Crown. The question "To whom is the Monarch responsible?" was not one which a constitutional lawyer or a political scientist would care to answer, though a moral philosopher would probably say that he was governed by the moral law or the spirit of the constitution. There was no institution charged with the enforcement of his responsibility and no definition of what constituted responsible and irresponsible action. Legally as "God's Lieutenant," though not morally, the King could do no wrong. Hobbes went so far as to assert in the mid-seventeenth century that there should be no limits to the Sovereign's power and that in practice an absolute sovereign power was better than the alternative—anarchy. To this day Monarchs as a rule cannot be held constitutionally responsible for their actions.

An escape from this dilemma was first provided by the introduction of a rule that Ministers could be held responsible by the Assembly for the advice which they rendered. Thus although Article 30 of the Norwegian Constitution stressed the right of the King to act according to his own judgment, Article 5 stated: "The King's person shall be sacred; he cannot be blamed or accused. The responsibility shall rest upon his Council." During the period of what may be termed "limited monarchy" or the "separation of powers" before parliamentarism was established the Assembly was supposed to hold Ministers responsible by this device.

In comparison with the present-day procedure of an adverse vote the method adopted was complicated and not altogether successful. Ministers were required to countersign all documents issued by the King-in-Council before they became law. A committee of the Assembly examined these documents and held the countersigning Minister responsible for their contents. In certain countries, such as Sweden, a distinction was drawn between advice which was unwise and proposals which were unconstitutional. Where the committee of the Assembly decided that due regard had not been paid to the welfare of the State it could advise the Assembly to request the monarch to dismiss the offending Minister. But no action could be taken to ensure that this request was acceded to. Where Ministers were deemed to have acted unconstitutionally they could be impeached before a special court. Neither means of checking the Government proved effective in Sweden in the nineteenth century and today these provisions of the Constitution are a dead letter. Yet some Swedish authorities have been reluctant to accept the notion that day-to-day political pressure in the Assembly has replaced them, partly, no doubt, because Sweden has only recently (1917) emerged from a century of limited monarchy. It is particularly difficult for constitutional lawyers to recognize conventions which run counter to the letter of the Constitution.

Countersignature still has its uses in republics as a last resort to prevent the Head of State from acting unconstitutionally. A President elected by the Assembly is more likely in a time of crisis to claim to represent the real public interest. Unless he can obtain a countersignature for his actions he leaves himself open to criticism and can, if necessary, be impeached. Although a dead letter in the constitutions of parliamentary monarchies, the requirement of a countersignature has been written into several recent constitutions in parliamentary republics.

The Head of Government May Advise the Head of State to Dissolve Parliament

In the pre-parliamentary monarchies of Europe the Monarch could, if dissatisfied with his Assembly, dissolve one or more Houses in the hope of securing a more amenable selection of representatives after a new election. Today, when the Executive is divided, it is still the Head of State who dissolves Parliament, but he does so on the request, and only on the request, of the head of Government. In Denmark the Constitution actually states that either the King or the Prime Minister may dissolve Parliament. But where the Head of State acts independently, as President Macmahon did in France in 1877, parliamentarism is not being practised.

For parliamentary dissolution is very different from the earlier form of dissolution. In the old days a challenge by the Assembly to the Executive did not lead to a change of Executive but to a change (or attempted change) of the Assembly. Nowadays a defeat of the Government by the Assembly causes the Prime Minister either to resign or to request a dissolution. But the dissolution is not of the Assembly but of Parliament, that is to say of the Government as well—although the Government (in Britain at least) stays in power until the new Parliament assembles. The conflict between the two parts of Parliament is left to the electorate to resolve.

The power of the Government to request a dissolution is a distinctive characteristic of parliamentarism. Some British writers consider that the threat of dissolution is essential in order that the Ministry may secure the loyal support of its party, but other parliamentary systems survive without Whips who whisper hints of dissolution to recalcitrant back-benchers.

Nevertheless, dissolution must remain the ultimate sanction ....

Certain states generally regarded as parliamentary severely restrict the right of the Executive to dissolve the Assembly. In Norway the *Storting* dissolves itself, the Head of State being allowed to dissolve only special sessions, but this is a departure from parliamentarism inspired by the convention theory of the French Revolution. In France, where the right of the Government of the Fourth Republic to request a dissolution of Parliament was restricted by the Constitution, the political system also exhibited certain convention characteristics.

Parliament as a Whole Is Supreme Over Its Constituent Parts, Government and Assembly, Neither of Which May Dominate the Other

The notion of the supremacy of Parliament as a whole over its parts is a distinctive characteristic of parliamentary systems. This may seem a glimpse of the obvious to those accustomed to parliamentary government, but it is in fact an important principle, all too often forgotten, that neither of the constituent elements of Parliament may completely dominate the other. The Government depends upon the support of the Assembly if it is to continue in office, but the Assembly is not supreme because the Government can, if it chooses, dissolve Parliament and appeal to the electorate at the polls. Many parliamentary systems have failed because one or other of them has claimed supremacy, and Parliament as a whole has not been supreme over both Government and Assembly.

In practice the nature of parliamentary supremacy varies from country to country. In the United Kingdom and Scandinavia the emphasis is on the Government's role in Parliament and in Britain the system is actually called "Cabinet Government." In others, notably the French Third and Fourth Republics, the dominant role in Parliament was played by the Assembly. Generally speaking, where there is majority-parliamentarism the Government has a sense of security, subject only to the sudden onset of a crisis. No Government has been defeated on a motion of confidence in the House of Commons for about thirty years, though it took merely a drop in his customarily large majority to cause Mr. Chamberlain to resign as Prime Minister in 1940. Governments lacking the support of an absolute majority of members are in a much more exposed position, and in France for example, changes of Government following loss of confidence by the Chamber of Deputies or National Assembly were fairly frequent.

Many countries appear in practice to depart from the parliamentary ideal of a balance between the Government and the Assembly. On the one hand there are states like France where the capacity of the Assembly to change Governments at will has been an indication not, as is sometimes thought, of an interesting variation of the parliamentary principle, but of a departure from it in the direction of Assembly government. On the other there are countries like the United Kingdom where the increasing tendency for the Government to dominate parliamentary business may be a departure from the parliamentary principle in the opposite direction ....

It would be more in keeping with parliamentarism as it is defined in this study to deny the right of either Government or Assembly such absolute authority. Parliamentarism implies cooperation between the executive and legislative branches, neither dominating the other and both recognizing the supremacy of the larger institution, Parliament as a whole.

The notion of parliamentary supremacy described in this section is not to be confused with the legal notion of parliamentary sovereignty. Whereas the former explains the relation of Parliament to its component parts, the latter is concerned with its external relations. All Parliaments are supreme over the Governments and Assemblies which compose them. But not all are sovereign, that is to say legally unrestricted in their powers. In Britain Parliament is sovereign in the sense that the Queen-in-Parliament is not limited legally by the Constitution. In other parliamentary states, however, the power of Parliament and the Head of State is limited by the terms of written constitutions. It need hardly be emphasized therefore that parliamentary sovereignty, which plays so large a part in British politics, is by no means a characteristic of parliamentary systems generally.

And of course parliamentary supremacy or sovereignty is strictly a governmental notion affecting relations between the branches of government. It is compatible with the belief that in a very real sense it is the electorate which is ultimately supreme: hence the notion of popular sovereignty, taken for granted in the United States and assumed in the United Kingdom by those who believe that government should act in accordance with a mandate from the people.

The Government as a Whole Is Only Indirectly Responsible to the Electorate

A parliamentary Government, though directly responsible to the Assembly, is only indirectly responsible to the electorate. The Government as a whole is not directly elected by the voters but is appointed indirectly from amongst the representatives whom they elect to the Assembly. The earlier direct relationship of Monarch and people whereby persons could petition their Sovereign disappeared as parliamentarism was introduced. Today the route to the Government lies through elected representatives though in Britain, for example, one may still formally petition the Monarch. It is true that members of the Government, like other members of Parliament, must (unless they are peers) stand before their constituents for election. However, they do so not as members of the Government but as candidates for the Assembly in the ordinary way. The responsibility for transforming them, once elected, into Ministers rests with the Prime Minister alone (and of course with the Monarch in the case of the Prime Minister).

As late as the nineteenth century in Britain it was thought to be bad form for a member of the Government, including the Prime Minister, to appeal to the electorate in general as well as to his constituents during an election. Not until after the second Reform Bill of 1867 was there a departure from this tradition. Today elections are fought on a national basis, Government and Opposition appealing as national parties to a national electorate. There has also grown up an important channel of direct communication between Ministries and the public, and even Prime Ministers have their public relations advisers. Nevertheless, this growth in direct communication has not been accompanied by a feeling of direct responsibility to the electorate. A Prime Minister returning from an important international conference does not usually address the public either by Press or television until he has first reported to Parliament.

It may still be argued that in reality, if not in constitutional theory, there is an exception to this principle of indirect responsibility, at least in two-party states. Are not, it may be asked, the people at election time presented in fact with two alternative Governments for one of which they vote? In a broad sense this is no doubt true, but there is a world of difference between, say, the election of the American President by the American people and the appointment of a British Government. The individual British voter, unlike his American counterpart, elects only a member of the Assembly. He may even, if he is a Liberal, Independent or Communist, vote for a particular candidate or party with full knowledge that he cannot have anything to do with the formation of a Government, at least in the immediate future. Should the voter elect a Labour Member of Parliament and then discover that the Labour Party is to form the new Government, his responsibility is indirect, as is that of all Labour voters. The people have not directly elected a Government: what they have done is to elect a party whose leader is called upon by the Monarch to form a Government of *his* own choosing.

This point is not always well taken. In a recent book, *The British Political System*, a French writer, André Mathiot, describes the British Cabinet under the heading "A government Chosen by the People." He rightly points to the plebiscitary element in British elections as a result of the two-party system. It is true that "The electorate actually votes for members of Parliament, but they are really choosing the government by deciding which party is to have a majority in the House of Commons." But Mathiot slurs over the fact that *members* of the Government are selected neither by the people nor by the victorious party. It is a misleading oversimplification to state that "the Prime Minister and the Cabinet are appointed by the Queen but really chosen by the people." Ministers are in fact chosen by the Prime Minister, and as for the premiership itself this has been transferred on many occasions without any consultation of the people. There were no general elections preceding the appointments of Lloyd George in 1916, Stanley Baldwin in 1923, Winston Churchill in 1940 or Harold Macmillan in 1957.

Where there is a multi-party system in which no party has a majority the relation of Government and voters is much more indirect. Of course nobody knows which parties will increase their representation, but even if this can be guessed the nature of the coalition Government may be unknown. The task of forming a Government falls to party leaders and the Head of State after the results are announced, and is hardly the direct result of the election. In such circumstances the electors clearly are responsible directly only for candidates and parties, the Government being the responsibility of those leaders who are successful in the election.

Parliament Is the Focus of Power in the Political System

The fusion of the executive and legislative powers in Parliament is responsible for the overriding ascendancy of Parliament in the political order. It is the stage on which the drama of politics is played out; it is the forum of the nation's ideas; and it is the school where future political leaders are trained. For parliamentarism to succeed, the Government must not fret at the constant challenge which the Assembly offers to its programme, nor wince at the criticism made of its administration. The Assembly in turn must resist the temptation to usurp the functions of Government. Here is a delicate balance of powers which check each other without the benefit of separate institutions.

Above all, politicians, party militants and voters have to accept the parliamentary spirit of give and take. They must be loyal to Parliament as well as to their party, not doubting the good faith of those with whom they disagree. Where this confidence is lacking or is betrayed, parliamentarism falls into disrepute and the system may become unworkable. The weakness of parliamentarism in France has been due in large measure to the unwillingness of large numbers of Frenchmen to give their Parliament this trust and loyalty. Many party militants on the Right have wanted to abolish Parliament and replace it with a separated Executive and Assembly as in presidential theory. Many on the Left would have preferred to see power transferred to the Assembly as in the brief days of the Convention and the Commune. In all parties, within and without the National Assembly, there were those who could not be true parliamentarians because they doubted the suitability of parliamentary government for France. In such circumstances parliamentarism cannot flourish. It must be, if it is to succeed, the focal point of the nation's political interest, the centre of the political system ....

PRESIDENTIAL GOVERNMENT

Presidential government is often associated with the theory of the separation of powers which was popular in the eighteenth century when the American constitution was framed. Two writers in particular drew attention to this notion. John Locke, writing at the end of the seventeenth century, suggested that the long conflict between the British Monarch and the Houses of Parliament would best be resolved by the separation of the King as Executive from the two Houses as Legislature, each body having its own sphere. In the mid-eighteenth century a French observer of the British political scene, Montesquieu, pronounced himself in favour of the British system of government as one which embodied, in contrast to the despotism of the Bourbons, the separation of the executive, legislative and judicial powers. Historically the theory as expounded by Locke and more especially Montesquieu is important for an understanding of the climate of opinion in which the American Constitution was framed.

However, it is one thing to study this celebrated theory for historical purposes but quite another to trace its contemporary significance for an understanding of presidential government. It was, after all, based on the assumption that a Monarch would act as Executive and an Assembly as Legislature. The theory was considered to be an improvement on the absolute monarchies of the Continent, which it undoubtedly was, and was praised with them in mind. There was as yet no experience of parliamentarism. Today such constitutional monarchies as still survive are based on the parliamentary principle.

Another offspring and successor of the theory is presidential government, but the substitution of an elected President for a hereditary Monarch has, as we have seen, created a system hardly comparable with pre-parliamentary limited monarchies. If presidential government is regarded simply as a direct form of expression of the eighteenth century doctrine of the separation of powers then (as indeed many people have thought) the Americans may, by adopting their rigid Constitution, have artificially prevented their political system from developing into parliamentarism. But if, as it is argued here, the system is a successor to that doctrine then it is not like limited monarchy, the precursor of parliamentary government, but one of its two offsprings, the other being parliamentarism.

Indeed the use of the term "separation of powers" to describe the presidential system is something of a misnomer, as is its counterpart the "fusion of powers" of parliamentarism. In theory it is possible to conceive of complete separation of the executive, legislative and judicial functions, but there is no evidence of its practical feasibility. If government is to be carried on the powers must be co-ordinated and must overlap. Thus in the United States the President (the Executive) wields legislative power when he signs or vetoes bills sent to him by Congress. Congress (the legislative branch) shares in the Executive's authority when it ratifies treaties and confirms appointments. The Supreme Court (the Judiciary) may use its powers to interpret the Constitution so as to encroach on both the executive and legislative spheres. In parliamentary theory, despite the fusion of powers implied by parliamentary supremacy, an important distinction is drawn between the three branches, and textbooks on constitutional law begin with an account of the separation of powers. It is still considered everywhere to be one of the bulwarks against tyranny and dictatorship—except perhaps in the Vatican. (Article I of the Fundamental Law of the City of the Vatican states: "The Sovereign Pontiff, sovereign of the city of the Vatican, has full legislative, executive and judicial powers.") If the powers are not really separated in presidential systems, neither are they altogether fused in parliamentary states.

Where presidential and parliamentary government *do* differ is over the separation not of powers but of institutions and persons. In the parliamentary system there is a single institution called Parliament which combines two other institutions and their personnel—the Government and the Assembly. It may, as in the United Kingdom, combine part of the judiciary as well (the House of Lords being the highest court of appeal) and thus Parliament may seem to wield executive, legislative and judicial power. There is no such combination of functions in presidential systems, the Executive being quite separate from the Assembly as an institution. Moreover the personnel of the two institutions, and of the Judiciary, are different.

The term "separation of powers" is therefore an inadequate and misleading description of the theory underlying presidential government. It is inadequate because as stated by Montesquieu and Blackstone it applied to a monarchical Executive which has since been generally replaced by parliamentarism, and because it does not explain the theory of presidential government. It is misleading because the powers are separated in both presidential and parliamentary theory. These are distinguished partly by the degree of separation of powers but more particularly by the separation of institutions and persons which is so marked a characteristic of presidential but not parliamentary theory.

In parliamentary government, where the legislative and executive powers have to a marked degree been fused, it is sometimes difficult to draw a distinction between the Government and the Assembly which together form Parliament. In presidential government, on the other hand, a clear distinction *is* drawn between these two branches of the political system. The President is the Executive, being both Head of State and head of Government, and is quite separate from the Assembly. Indeed the use of the terms "Government" and "Ministry" employed in parliamentarism to distinguish the repository of real political power from the Head of State is inappropriate in the presidential context. Americans tend to use the expression "Administration" to describe the President and his aides. The term "Parliament" is never used because in presidential systems there is no place for an institution which combines the executive and legislative powers.

The term *presidential* has been chosen because in this system the offices of head of Government and Head of State are combined in a President. The term is as expressive as *parliamentary* was to describe the system where the Government and Assembly are fused in a Parliament.

It seemed appropriate to begin an analysis of parliamentary government by reference to British political institutions. It is equally valuable to study presidentialism by first examining the American political system. The United States was the first important country to break with the European monarchical tradition and to shake off colonial rule. The break occurred in the eighteenth century when Britain was still a limited monarchy and the theory of the separation of powers was in vogue. The American Constitution bears witness to these influences and to the colonial government of Governor and Legislature, an elected President replacing the King or Governor as the Executive power. A number of countries—all twenty American republics, Liberia, the Philippines, South Korea and South Vietnam—have followed the example of the United States, though rarely with comparable success. The American political system is therefore the model and prototype of presidential government. Yet the United States, like the United Kingdom, could abolish or transform many of its institutions and remain based on the same theory of government. For example, the framers of the 1787 Constitution could have proposed an elective Monarch instead of a President, a House of Lords rather than a Senate, and a unitary political system instead of a federal union of states without destroying the presidential principle—though the name "presidential" would hardly be suitable for a system where the Executive was an elective Monarch. Presidential, like parliamentary, theory has certain basic characteristics irrespective of any particular political system.

The nature of presidential theory can best be understood by restating the eleven propositions of Chapter II [of *Analysis of Political Systems* ....] as they apply to presidential government.

The Assembly Remains an Assembly Only

Parliamentary theory implies that the second phase of constitutional development, in which the Assembly and Judiciary claim their own areas of jurisdiction alongside the Executive, shall give way to a third in which Assembly and Government are fused in a Parliament. Presidential theory on the other hand requires the Assembly to remain separate as in the second phase. The American Revolution led to a transfer from colonial rule to the second stage of separate jurisdiction, and there have been some observers who have thought that the rigid Constitution has prevented the "natural" development of the American political system towards parliamentarism. This is not so. By abolishing the Monarchy and substituting a President for the King and his Government, the Americans showed themselves to be truly revolutionary in outlook. The presidential system as established in the U.S.A. made parliamentarism both unnecessary and impracticable in that country. The Assembly (Congress in the United States) remains an Assembly.

The Executive Is Not Divided but Is a President Elected by the People for a Definite Term at the Time of Assembly Elections

The retention of a separate Executive in the United States was made feasible because the Executive remained undivided. It was not, of course, the same institution as the pre-parliamentary monarchical Executive. Such a Monarch governed by virtue of an ancient tradition into which he was born, and with all the strength and potential weaknesses that this implied. The presidential Executive is elected by the people. In an era when Governments have had to rely not on some mystique but on popular support the Americans have found a solution which has enabled their separate single Executive to withstand criticism. The suggestions that the United States should adopt parliamentarism have proved abortive largely because it cannot be said of the Presidency, as it could of hereditary Monarchy, that the institution lacked democratic roots.

An undivided Executive obviously requires no delineation of the respective functions of Head of state and the Government. The powers of the Executive are defined vis-à-vis the Assembly and the Judiciary and each checks the others to ensure that the balance of power is not unduly disturbed. Yet this has not prevented a change in their status and role. In the United States as late as 1884 Woodrow Wilson (then a professor of political science, not President of the United States) could regard the Senate and House of Representatives as the pivot of the system and could call his book on American politics *Congressional Government*. Today, ... the influence of the President has appreciably extended. In other presidential systems the President usually wields very considerable powers. If there is any trend it is away from parliamentarism, not towards it.

The President is elected for a definite term of office. This prevents the Assembly from forcing his resignation (except by impeachment for a serious misdemeanour) and at the same time requires the President to stand for re-election if he wishes to continue in office. It seems desirable that the chief Executive's tenure should be limited to a certain number of terms. For a long time there was a convention in the United States that no President should run for a third term …. President Roosevelt swept the convention aside in 1940—but some of his most loyal friends refused to support his candidacy. After his re-election for the fourth time in 1944 there was a movement to make it unconstitutional to run more than twice. An amendment to the Constitution to this effect was passed by Congress in 1947 and adopted by the necessary three-quarters of the States by 1951.

Equally important for the proper operation of the presidential system is the election of the President at the time of the Assembly elections. This associates the two branches of government, encourages party unity and clarifies the issues. Admittedly in the United States simultaneous elections do not prevent the return of a Republican President and a Democratic Congress, but the tensions would be even greater if the President was elected for a seven-year term as in France. General de Gaulle was elected as President in 1958 about the time of the Assembly elections, but the opportunity to make this coincidence permanent was not seized. However, since the de Gaulle constitution allows for dissolution of Parliament as well as the resignation of the Government (but not the President) serious difficulty may be avoided.

The Head of the Government Is Head of State

Whereas in pre-parliamentary Monarchies the Head of State was also the head of the Government, in the presidential system it is the head of the Government who becomes at the same time Head of State. This is an important distinction because it draws attention to the limited pomp and circumstance surrounding the presidential office. The President is of little consequence until he is elected as political head by the electorate and he ceases to have any powers once his term of office has expired. The ceremonial aspect of his position is but a reflection of his political prestige.

Presidential theory, if it is to be successfully applied, demands a certain sophistication of the electorate. In parliamentary states, as Sir Winston Churchill once noted, war victories are celebrated by a cheer for the Head of State; defeats by a change of Government. In presidential systems a voter who may oppose the President as head of the

Government has nevertheless to be loyal to the President as Head of State.

In the appointment of a political Executive it is a characteristic of parliamentary systems that the head of Government shall be appointed by the Head of State. The absence of any distinction between the two offices in presidential systems makes such an appointment unnecessary. Nor is the Executive elected by the Assembly since this would be contrary to the doctrine of the separation of powers. It is the mark of presidential government that both Executive and Assembly should be selected by the electorate.

The President Appoints Heads of Departments Who Are His Subordinates

In parliamentarism the Prime Minister appoints his colleagues who together with him form the Government. In presidential systems the President appoints Secretaries (sometimes called Ministers) who are heads of his Executive Departments. Formally, owing to the rule whereby appointments are subject to the confirmation of the Assembly or one of its organs (in the United States the Senate, in the Philippines the commission on appointments) his choice may be restricted to persons of whom that body approves. In practice the President has a very wide choice. Whereas in parliamentary systems Ministers are usually selected from those who have served a political apprenticeship in the Assembly, it is by no means customary in presidential systems for heads of Departments (or for that matter the President himself) to have had experience in the legislative branch of government.

The President Is Sole Executive

In contrast to parliamentary government, which is collective, the Prime Minister being first among equals, presidential government tends to be individual. Admittedly the term "Cabinet" is used in the United States to describe the meetings of the President with his Secretaries, but it is not a Cabinet or Ministry in the parliamentary sense. There is a famous story of Abraham Lincoln meeting with his Cabinet. He put a proposal to them and then took a vote in which he alone supported his suggestion. He then remarked: "Noes 7, Ayes 1. The Ayes have it." In this respect the "loneliest office in the world" bears some resemblance to pre-parliamentary Monarchies where the King alone wielded executive power. President Truman made the point even more succinctly as President by placing a notice on his desk: *The buck stops here*. Such being the nature of the presidential Executive it would seem inappropriate to use the term "Cabinet" at all ....

Members of the Assembly Are Not Eligible for Office in the Administration and Vice-Versa

Instead of the parliamentary convention or law whereby the same persons may be part of both the executive and legislative branches of government, it is customary in presidential states for the personnel to be separate. Neither the President nor his aides may sit in the U.S. Congress. Few of the other American republics have copied the complete separation practised in the United States. While Ministers may not be members of the Assembly (except in Cuba and Peru) they are usually entitled to attend and take part in debates. This appears to accord with the practice of some pre-parliamentary Monarchies where, despite a strict rule that the Monarch should not attend debates, Ministers were often allowed to be present whether members or not. In a few countries (Costa Rica, Bolivia, El Salvador and Panama) Ministers give up their seats to alternates (*suplente*) for the period they hold office.

The Executive is Responsible to the Constitution

The President is not, like parliamentary Governments, responsible to the Assembly. Instead he is, like pre-parliamentary Monarchs, responsible to the Constitution. But whereas in the *anciens régimes* this was but a vague notion, in presidential systems it is usually laid down with some precision in a constitutional document. Acts of the President may, as in the United States, be declared unconstitutional by the Supreme Court, though as Chief Justice Marshall discovered when attempting to protect the rights of the Cherokee Indians, it is one thing to hand down a decision and another to enforce it. However, should a President persist in acting unconstitutionally the Assembly can take action itself and impeach him or his aides. (The term "civil officer" is used to describe them in the United States.)

Impeachment in pre-parliamentary Monarchies was confined to Ministers who were held responsible for the King's actions through an elaborate system of counter-signature. The Monarch himself could only be dealt with by drastic action for which there was no constitutional procedure. He could be forced to abdicate without any right of self-defence, as happened to James II of England, Gustav IV of Sweden, Kaiser Wilhelm II of Germany, and Napoleon I, Charles X, Louis Philippe and Napoleon III of France. If he appeared to stand in the way of important political and social changes he might even be executed like Charles I of England or Louis XVI of France. In presidential systems, however, both Ministers and Presidents may be impeached. Where, as in Honduras and Paraguay, there is no provision for impeachment the system is not, in this important respect, presidential. In several South American Constitutions there are provisions which compel the

President to dismiss his Ministers through political pressure as well as after impeachment. Thus in Peru ministers must resign after a vote of no-confidence.

It is usually the Assembly which holds the President ultimately responsible to the Constitution by the impeachment process. This does not imply that he is responsible to that body in the parliamentary sense of depending on its confidence in any political capacity. Impeachment enforces *juridical* compliance with the (constitutional) letter of the law and is quite different from the exercise of political control over the President's ordinary conduct of his office. Political responsibility implies a day-to-day relationship between Government and Assembly; impeachment is the grave and ultimate penalty (only one American President, Andrew Johnson was impeached, unsuccessfully) necessary where ordinarily the Executive and Assembly are not mutually dependent.

The President may not be dependent on the Assembly for his political survival but he is very dependent on its goodwill for the furtherance of his policies. The Budget, foreign programmes, senior appointments all require its acquiescence. If there is no agreement the Assembly may decide to take no action. It cannot however replace the President.

The President Cannot Dissolve or Coerce the Assembly

The Assembly, as we have just seen, cannot dismiss the President. Likewise the President may not dissolve the Assembly. Neither, therefore, is in a position to coerce the other, and it is not surprising that this system is, par excellence, one of checks and balances. In countless ways almost incomprehensible to those accustomed to parliamentarism the presidential system exhibits this mutual independence of the executive and legislative branches of government. In the United States, President Eisenhower declined for some time to take issue in 1954 with Senator McCarthy on the grounds that a Senator's conduct was primarily the responsibility of the U.S. Senate, not the Executive. In 1957, after the suicide of the Canadian Ambassador to Egypt, the President was unable to assure the Canadian people that congressional committees would in future exercise more discretion since he was not responsible for the behaviour of the Senate. Conversely, the Senate, whose Southern members had blocked civil rights legislation for over half a century, did nothing in 1948 when President Truman abolished racial segregation in the armed forces—even in the South. For as President Mr. Truman was Commander-in-Chief and could act without reference to Congress.

The position of a President is very different from that of a pre-parliamentary Monarch who could dissolve his Assembly if he felt that this was desirable. A President may call a special session of the Assembly if he fails to obtain his demands at the ordinary session and he may, if the Houses disagree, adjourn their meetings (though no American President has attempted the latter). But he may not appeal to the electorate to think again about its choice of a legislative branch of government by dissolving the Assembly. Where the President does have the constitutional authority of dissolution, as in Haiti and Paraguay, the system does not conform to the presidential pattern.

The Assembly Is Ultimately Supreme Over the Other Branches of Government and There Is No Fusion of the Executive and Legislative Branches as in a Parliament

It was remarked of parliamentary systems that neither the Government nor the Assembly is supreme because both are subordinate parts of the parliamentary institution. In presidential systems such fusion of the executive and legislative powers is replaced by separation, each having its own sphere. As we have just observed, constitutionally the Executive cannot interfere in the proceedings of the Assembly, still less dissolve it, and the Assembly for its part cannot invade the province of the Executive.

In practice the relation of the two, at least in the United States, is much more subtle than the theory of the separation of powers and checks and balances would indicate. The President is head of the Government and leader of his party. He controls an immense amount of patronage. He is responsible for the preparation of major legislation (even if technically it is introduced by members of the Assembly) and for securing its successful passage through the Assembly. Certainly Franklin D. Roosevelt effectively dominated the United States Congress in the famous "Hundred Days" of 1933. Conversely, to say that Congress cannot invade the province of the Executive does not mean that it cannot obstruct his policies, or, if it so chooses, refuse the appropriations which are usually necessary for their implementation. If the United States Congress refused to grant the President the funds he required he would have to go without. In practice a compromise is nearly always reached, and the President is left to mind his own Executive business. In certain Latin American countries the President can automatically decree the budget if the Legislature fails to vote it. There is also a provision to this effect in the constitution of the French Fifth Republic.

Since there is no Parliament there can be no parliamentary supremacy. Where, then, does supreme power lie in the event of a serious controversy? It has been demonstrated that the Assembly cannot force the resignation of the President any more than he can dissolve the Assembly. Moreover, both branches of government may find that their actions are declared unconstitutional by yet a third power, the Judiciary. In a sense the Constitution is supreme. The short answer is that it is intended in presidential government that the different branches shall check and balance one another and that none shall predominate.

Yet in a very real sense it is the Assembly which is ultimately supreme. The President may have considerable authority allocated to him in the Constitution but he may be powerless unless the Assembly grants him the necessary appropriations. If he acts unconstitutionally the Assembly may impeach him. In the event of a serious conflict even the Judiciary must bow to the will of the Assembly because this body has the right to amend the Constitution. The American Constitution is not, as is sometimes asserted, simply "what the judges say it is."

It may be suggested that the position does not appear to be altogether different from that in parliamentary states where ultimately the legislature may amend the Constitution. This is not so. In parliamentary states the Constitution has to be amended by both Government and Assembly acting as Parliament, whereas in presidential systems the Assembly may amend the Constitution without regard to the President. For example, the American Congress has limited the presidential tenure of office to two terms.

It is true that this authority of the Assembly is sometimes qualified. In the United States three-quarters of the State legislatures or conventions must ratify amendments to the constitution. In states which possess unitary constitutions it is often thought desirable that amendments shall be passed only if there is a two-thirds majority in favour or if, following a general election, a new Assembly gives further approval. The "sovereign people" themselves are thus consulted. But in each instance it is an Assembly, not the Executive or Judiciary, which has the power to change the constitution: it is the legislative branch which is supreme.

The Executive Is Directly Responsible to the Electorate

Governments in parliamentary countries are appointed by the Head of State; they are not elected. By contrast the presidential Executive is dependent on a popular vote and the President alone (and Vice-President if there is one), of all the persons in the political system, is elected by the whole body of electors. Whereas the pre-parliamentary Monarchies could not in the end withstand the pressure of the people's representatives upon their control of government a President can say to members of the Assembly: "You represent your constituency: I represent the whole people." There is no reply to this argument, and it is perhaps not surprising that in many South American countries and in France at various times the President has been able to go one step further and to assert that he *alone* represented the people.

Admittedly in form the President of the United States is still indirectly elected by an Electoral College, but so long as there are two main parties and one candidate who obtains at least fifty per cent of the vote in the College the result is a foregone conclusion after the national elections. The growth of political parties and the realities of political life have in practice placed the nomination of candidates for the Presidency in the hands of the parties, and elections in those of the electorate. If one of the various proposals to abolish the College were adopted, it might alter the balance of power among the States but it would make no difference to the fundamentally direct relationship of President and people. In other presidential countries, without exception, election is direct.

It is a distinctive feature of the system that the President should owe his position not, as in parliamentary government, to appointment, nor, as in convention theory, to selection by the Assembly, but to the electorate at election time. Between elections the President speaks to the voters directly, not indirectly through an Assembly. He cannot, except on special occasions, deliver a speech to the Assembly and unlike Prime Ministers in parliamentary states he may not use it as a forum. Hence in the United States there has grown up the fireside chat, the television appearance, and above all the weekly press conference where the President is the host.

The electorate in presidential countries therefore bears a double burden. The voters elect representatives from their own district to the Assembly, but instead of leaving the selection of the Government to the Assembly and Head of State they also elect a President as Executive. In their wisdom they may prefer a President who belongs to a party which has only minority status in the Assembly. They will, nevertheless, at least in the United States, expect the two branches of government to reach a workable compromise.

There Is No Focus of Power in the Political System

The political activities of parliamentary systems have their focal point in Parliament. Heads of State, Governments, elected representatives, political parties, interest groups and electorates all acknowledge its supremacy.

It is tempting to assume that there must be a similar focal point in presidential systems. This is not so. Instead of concentration there is division; instead of unity, fragmentation. In the design of Washington, D.C., the President's home, the White House, is at the opposite end of Pennsylvania Ave. to the capital where Congress meets. Geographical dispersion symbolizes their political separation.

Nor is it accurate to say that the difference is simply one of degree of fusion: that instead of one focus there are several. It would hardly be less apposite to say that the difference between a political system in which there is only one political party and others in which there are two or more lies simply in the number of parties. In both instances there is a difference in kind more fundamental than the obvious one of degree.

In parliamentary systems, for example, there cannot for long be profound differences of opinion between Government and Assembly. Where a division appears it is in the nature of parliamentarism either for the Government to resign or for an election to take place. The differences must be resolved in order that mutual confidence between Government and Assembly, essential to the operation of the system, be restored. Differences are confined to political parties, which exist to express the various opinions in the matter.

In presidential systems there are also differences between parties and where there is federalism there may be important differences between regions as well. But in addition there is a gulf between the President and the Assembly (to say nothing of possible differences between members of his Administration, bound together by no ties of collective responsibility). Moreover, these differences, especially those between the President and Assembly, are part of the system, friction and discord being an indication not of imminent chaos but of its proper operation. In the late spring of every year the *New York Times* remarks on the unwillingness of Congress to enact the President's programme and tries to forecast the probability of his most important measures passing into Law. Later in the summer as Congress recesses it lists those which have been successful. In 1957 they amounted to barely half of President Eisenhower's 155 bills.

Parliamentarians often find it incredible that the Executive in a presidential system should at times have so little control over legislation. "What is the use," they ask, "of a Government which does not govern?" But of course in a presidential system there is no Government. There is no recognized centre of the political system on which people and politicians focus their interests and aspirations. Unlike parliamentarism, which ensures the co-ordination of the various branches of the political system, the presidential system assumes that the executive and legislative branches shall be constantly checking and balancing each other's activities. It may therefore prevent action from being taken unless there is wide agreement and considerable pressure (hence the role of pressure groups in the United States).

Those who admire efficient government may be inclined towards the Cabinet government form of parliamentarism. Those who prefer more limited government may turn towards presidentialism. It should not be assumed, however, that the presidential form, because it is divided, is necessarily one of weak government. Admittedly, where presidential leadership is lacking the system may even appear to be on the verge of breaking down. But where there is a vigorous Executive he may in fact dominate the Assembly, as several American Presidents (notably Franklin D. Roosevelt) have succeeded in doing.

Miraculously, in the United States this domination has never gone too far. In much of Central and South America, where there is the form of presidential government but not the substance, the presidential system has been distorted by dictatorship.

It is difficult to explain the failure of presidential government in so many parts of South America and it is perilous to confine such explanation to purely political factors. Historically and culturally South and Central America are utterly different from the United States. However, there are a number of particular political features of these countries' systems which deserve note, not least of which is the multi-party system which characterises several of them. Where a President is elected by what is in effect a minority vote instead of by the clear majority customary in the United States he lacks that sense of being the people's representative which is so marked a feature of the American presidency. At the very least it adds a complicating factor to the relations of President, Assembly and people, and in all probability contributes to political instability.

Where there is a multi-party system there is the temptation to add to the President's status and independence by giving him a longer term of office than the Assembly. Not surprisingly the French Fifth Republic's constitution gives the President a term of seven years compared to the Assembly's four. Such a long term, while of small moment in a parliamentary system, may make a President in a non-parliamentary system a powerful figure.

23

FEDERALISM

Political systems can also be examined from the perspective of how political power is spatially distributed. The spatial dimension, typically, is understood as a continuum. At one pole, in unitary systems, political power is formally concentrated in the hands of central government. In practice, most unitary political systems allow local governments to exercise some authority, but that authority, in the final analysis, is only exercised at the will of central governments. In federal systems, powers are shared by central and constituent governments, which each have a share of sovereignty. At the other pole, in confederal systems, constituent governments retain sovereignty except when they specifically delegate functions to the central government.

In the following reading, Garth Stevenson, a professor of political science at Brock University, traces the roots of federal and confederal political systems and contrasts both with unitary systems. He argues that traditional legal definitions of federalism are not quite sufficient because they obscure the dynamic qualities of federalism. Stevenson suggests that because federalism rests on the division of jurisdictions between at least two levels of government, and because no one level of government can abolish the jurisdiction of the other, federalism entails a continual process of bargaining. In exploring a variety of cross-national examples of the origins and workings of federal systems, Stevenson places Canadian federalism in a larger context. The reading is drawn from Stevenson's book Unfulfilled Union: Canadian Federalism and National Unity.

• • • • • • • •

During Canada's centennial celebrations in 1967, a national magazine invited its readers to participate in selecting the most typically Canadian joke. The winning entry proved to be a local version of the ancient elephant joke, which recounts how persons of various nationalities responded in different ways to the task of writing an essay on some aspect of the elephant. While the German wrote on the elephant as a military weapon, the Frenchman on the elephant's love life, and so forth, the Canadian essayist's title was "The elephant: Does it fall under federal or provincial jurisdiction?"

Not only the outcome but the occasion of this contest testifies to the pervasiveness of federalism in Canadian life. The centennial which we celebrated in 1967, after all, was not really the centennial of Canada, not even the centennial of the Canadian state (which was founded in 1841), but only the centennial of Canadian federalism. In geo-political terms it was also the centennial of the date at which New Brunswick and Nova Scotia became part of Canada, but that event was not the first, the last, nor even the most important step in Canada's territorial expansion, although it may have paved the way for the greater expansion that followed.

Federalism, clearly, is for most Canadians inseparable from their image of their country, and this has probably never been more true than it is at present. Except among separatists, belief in the desirability of some kind of federalism, however defined, seems to be virtually universal. Indeed even some separatists in western Canada favour a federation, although one that would be confined to the four western provinces. If political science students observed by the author over several years are in any way representative, it appears that Canadians are completely unable to imagine their country as being other than federal, or as having any existence apart from federalism. If pressed to consider alternatives, they invariably assume that this must mean the dissolution of the federal tie and independence for each of the ten provinces.

While unusual and perhaps even unique by world standards, this obsession with federalism is by no means misguided. Federalism is undoubtedly, for better or for worse, a fundamental attribute of the way in which Canada conducts its public business. Interest groups and political parties are structured along federal lines, corresponding with the structures of government itself, as are educational institutions, the professions, and even the private sector of the economy. Statistical data are collected and organized in such a way as to highlight the boundaries between the provinces. Intergovernmental conferences have become a basic part of the political process, arguably more important than Parliament or the provincial legislatures.

These facts are not in dispute, nor can they be explained away, even by those who agree with John Porter that the obsession with federalism is an obstacle to creative politics and who dismiss the reputed sociocultural differences between the various provinces as "hallowed nonsense." Porter's point, however, is well taken when he argues that the attention given to federalism distracts attention from other issues, and may even be deliberately designed to do so. If politics is about who gets what, when, and how, Canadians are subtly but constantly encouraged to view these fundamental questions in jurisdictional or interprovincial terms. What does Quebec want? What does Alberta stand to lose? What is "Ottawa" taking from "the provinces" and what will they seek in return? Are we becoming more centralized or more decentralized?

A few lonely critics, like Porter, have argued that these are completely meaningless questions, designed only to mystify the masses. In contrast, politicians, the media, and an increasing number of academics often go to the other extreme and give the impression that these are the only significant questions in Canadian political life. The reality lies somewhere between the two extremes. Questions about federalism are real and important, even if they may sometimes be posed in mystifying language, but they are not the only questions in our political life. So pervasive is federalism to Canadians, however, that the more fundamental questions to which Porter and others have drawn attention cannot easily be considered or resolved outside of the federal context in which they occur.

DEFINING FEDERALISM

Despite their constant use by Canadians, and their frequent use in other countries, the word "federal" and its various derivatives are not lacking in ambiguity. Their history has been long and complex, and their polemical use is neither a recent nor a uniquely Canadian phenomenon. Even those who are professionally concerned with the study of federalism have failed to agree on what it means, what is included, and what should be excluded. As we shall see, almost any possible definition presents problems.

Certain works used in political discourse, like "legislature," "bureaucracy," or "election" are quite easily defined, for the fairly narrow and concrete phenomena to which they refer are easily recognized. Other words, such as "democracy," "liberalism" or "socialism" pose greater problems because they are broader in scope and too intimately associated with past and present ideological controversies to be defined in a manner that satisfies everyone. Some would go so far as to argue that these words are no more than ideological symbols, devoid of real content and substance. Certainly their repeated use as ideological symbols has left them vulnerable to such accusations.

Only a few political thinkers—Pierre Elliott Trudeau would probably be one of them—have endowed the concept of federalism with this heavy load of symbolic attributes. It has thus seemed plausible to treat federalism as a concrete, easily defined, and value-free concept. Yet somehow the effort to treat it thus never entirely succeeds. The concept of federalism seems to be a hybrid with some qualities from both categories of political concept.

In searching for definitions, the reader of the *Oxford English Dictionary* will find "federal" to mean "of or pertaining to a convenant, compact or treaty" but with the cautionary note that this definition is obsolete. Persevering, one finds a further definition: "of or pertaining to or of the nature of that form of government in which two or more states constitute a political unity while remaining more or less independent with regard to their internal affairs." Apart from the question-begging "more or less," which neatly evades the essence of the problem, this definition is notable chiefly for the fact that it establishes federalism as a form of *decentralized* government.

Even this apparent precision, however, vanishes when one seeks in the same dictionary the meaning of "federation," for this is said to mean "the formation of a political unity out of a number of separate states, provinces or colonies, so that each retains the management of its internal affairs." In this definition a new and different basis of distinction appears, for it is explicitly stated that the components of the federation, whether states, provinces, or colonies, previously enjoyed a separate existence.

Defining federalism in this way would seem to have the advantage that federal countries could be easily identified, but there are ambiguities here as well. The three Prairie provinces in Canada and a majority of the fifty states in the United States had no separate existence prior to the federal union; they were formed subsequently out of territories which the central government had acquired by purchase or conquest. Since it would be absurd to exclude Canada or the United States from any definition of federalism, the definition must be modified to specify that only some of the subnational units need to have enjoyed a previously separate existence.

So far we have been preoccupied mainly with distinguishing a federation from a non-federal or unitary state. However, a definition of federalism must also serve the purpose, which is even more essential in Canada's present circumstances, of distinguishing federalism from other forms of *decentralized* government. The European Community, for example, is not a federation because the powers of the Commission at Brussels and of the other community institutions are too insignificant in relation to the governments of the member countries. As was noted earlier the use of the term "federal" with reference to a "covenant, compact or treaty" is now considered obsolete, although at one time the word was so used. The "sovereignty-association" proposed by the Parti Québécois, as well as other hypothetical arrangements that would drastically reduce the powers of the central government in Canada, must be excluded from any useful definition of federalism, not because they are undesirable (although the author happens to be of this opinion) but because to include them in a category that also includes the United States and the Federal Republic of Germany would make the category too heterogeneous to have any analytic usefulness.

This brings us to another problem of semantics, namely the distinction between a *federation* and a *confederation*. These closely related words were not at first clearly distinguished, and in Canada are still not, but in the rest of the world they have gradually acquired distinct meanings. Outside of Canada, "confederation" is a word used mainly by historians, most often in reference to various arrangements among sovereign states (usually for the purposes of mutual defence) that fall short of establishing a new state or a central government with meaningful power and authority. Perhaps the European Community, the North Atlantic Treaty Organization (NATO), and other such institutions are the closest contemporary equivalents of these early "confederations."

The earliest confederation in the English-speaking world was the New England Confederation, which lasted from 1643 to 1648, a period for much of which England was too distracted by its own bourgeois revolution to provide much protection for its North American colonies. Threatened by the Indian tribes and the nearby colonies of other European powers, the New Englanders formed an alliance and established a commission of eight delegates, four from each colonial government, to decide collectively on questions of defence and external relations. Since these delegates had no authority apart from that of the colonial governments that appointed them, and since in practice it soon appeared that any one government could veto a decision by the commissioners, this confederation was more like a modern international organizational organization than a modern federal state.

In 1778, two years after the Declaration of Independence, the thirteen colonies formed a military alliance with rudimentary common institutions somewhat similar to those of the earlier New England Confederation. The agreement which brought this new arrangement into force was known as the Articles of Confederation, an appellation that would lead subsequent generations of Americans to associate the word "confederation" with loose alliances of this type, while reserving the word "federal" for their present, more centralized constitution. However, the Americans of the eighteenth century had not yet made this distinction. Instead, the word "federal" seems to have been used in the sense in which the *Oxford English Dictionary* now regards as obsolete, to refer to the Articles of Confederation themselves. At the Philadelphia Convention of 1787, where the present constitution of the United States was drafted, supporters of the Virginia Plan, on which that constitution is based, used the term "federal" in that same sense, and argued that a "merely federal" union, such as then existed, was inadequate to secure the objectives of "common defence, security of liberty, and general welfare." In its place they proposed to establish what they called a "national" government, which would have authority to impose its will on the states.

A delegate from New York, where opposition to the latter idea seems to have been exceptionally strong, protested that the Virginia Plan was unacceptable:

> He was decidedly of the opinion that the power of the Convention was restrained to amendments of a Federal nature, and having for their basis the confederacy in being .... New York would never have concurred in sending Deputies to the Convention, if she had supposed the deliberations were to turn on a consolidation of the states, and a National Government.

In response to such sentiments, the nationalists who wanted "a consolidation of the States" began to use the reassuring and familiar word "federal" with reference to their own plans, although they did not abandon its use with reference to the Articles of Confederation.

This deliberate attempt to blur what was in fact a fundamental distinction can best be seen in the series of anonymous essays by which Alexander Hamilton, John Jay, and James Madison attempted to persuade the voters of New York to ratify the proposed new constitution. These essays, which still rank among the classics of political science, are themselves known as the Federalist Papers, although their purpose was to argue the inadequacy of "federalism" in its original sense. Once the union was achieved, the word "Federalist" was adopted as the name of the political party representing the mercantile and financial interests who wanted a strong central government and subordinate states. In fact Hamilton, the first leader of the Federalist Party, had presented at the Philadelphia Convention a plan for a constitution even more centralized than the one that was finally adopted. Some of Hamilton's ideas, although rejected by his own countrymen, were later to be incorporated in the British North America Act of 1867.

As a result of these developments, the word "federal" and its derivatives became associated with a considerable degree of centralization, at least in the United States. The Swiss Confederation, which until 1848 was little more than a loose alliance of sovereign states, and the German Confederation, an even more nebulous organization established by the Congress of Vienna in 1815, helped to perpetuate the view that "confederation" referred to a compact that fell short of establishing a new central government. The Swiss, however, somewhat confused the issue by continuing to use the word "confederation" even after they had adopted a constitution that was "federal" in the new American sense.

As far as Canada is concerned, one constitutional historian has speculated that the use of the term "confederation" to describe the proposed union of the British North American colonies had exactly the same purpose as the adoption of the word "federal" by proponents of the Virginia Plan after 1787. In both cases, according to this view, a word normally associated with the absence of a strong central government was deliberately misused by those who in fact intended to create one in an effort to confuse those who might find such a project alarming. John A. Macdonald was certainly using an idiosyncratic definition in 1861 when he stated that "the true principle of a Confederation" means a system in which all the powers not specifically assigned to the provinces were given to the central government, unlike the American constitution whose tenth amendment, adopted in 1791, said precisely the reverse. A.A. Dorion, the leading French Canadian opponent of Macdonald's "Confederation," was more correct, or at least more conventional, a few years later when he defined "a real confederation" as "giving the largest powers to the local governments and merely a delegated authority to the general government." However, Macdonald won and Dorion lost, so that Macdonald's usage of the term has acquired semiofficial status in Canada, however bizarre it may seem to Americans. Dorion's definition may be historically justified but has become somewhat irrelevant, since none of the "confederations" that Dorion had in mind are still in existence, nor have any new ones under that name been established. Both Canada and Switzerland, however, use the word "confederation" for what is actually a federal union in the modern American sense.

Although it is relatively easy to determine what federalism is not, the many writers on the subject have failed to agree on a satisfactory definition of what it is, even though almost every one of them has attempted to produce a definition. The most frequently used definitions, such as those used by K.C. Wheare, Danial Elazar, W.H. Riker, and Geoffrey Sawer, emphasize institutional and legal criteria: two levels of government, each independent of the other; a written constitution specifying the jurisdiction of each; judicial review of legislation as a means of maintaining the jurisdictional boundaries; the requirement that each level of government have a direct relationship with the people; and so forth. Political scientists like Elazar and Riker tend to interpret these criteria rather broadly, while lawyers like Wheare and Sawer are most inclined to exclude doubtful cases. Wheare, although born in Australia and teaching in England, included as federal constitutions only those which closely resembled the constitution of the United States, with the result that only Australia and Switzerland passed the test. He admitted, however, that Canada was a federal state in practice, even though certain features of the British North America Act departed from the federal norm.

Apart from the fact that they tell us little about how political systems really operate, these formal criteria are so restrictive that their applicability to even those considered the most federal of states can be questioned. Federal legislation in Switzerland is not subject to judicial review; provincial statutes in Canada can be disallowed; and the West German federal government is not completely independent of the *land* governments since the *länder* control the upper house of the federal parliament. One political scientist, Michael Reagan, has even questioned whether the United States qualifies as a federation by these criteria, since he considers that in practice there is no field reserved to the states in which Congress is unable to legislate.

In reaction against the rigidity and formality of these traditional criteria, writers on federalism began in the 1950s to explore alternative approaches to its definition. W.S. Livingston abandoned institutional criteria almost entirely and developed the concept of a "federal society," which he defined as any society in which economic, religious, racial, or historical diversities are territorially grouped. A formally unitary state in which political practices and conventions protected such diversities, such as the United Kingdom, should be considered to have some federal characteristics. Rufus Davis went a step further, questioning whether any "federal principle" could really be developed to distinguish federal from nonfederal states; the difference was merely one of degree. Carl Friedrich defined federalism not as a static situation but as a process by which a number of separate political communities were gradually integrated.

While political scientists shifted their attention from formal institutions to political processes and behaviour, economists took an entirely different approach to defining federalism. Wallace Oates, in his book entitled *Fiscal Federalism*, wrote that federalism existed in any state where the public sector was decentralized, so that some decisions about taxing and spending were made by smaller territorial subdivisions in response to demands originating within themselves. From an economist's perspective it matters little whether such decentralization is protected by constitutional guarantees or whether it can be unilaterally revoked by the central government. At least in the short term, the economic consequences are the same in either case. While useful for its purpose, this definition is so broad that hardly any state, at least in the industrialized world, could avoid being classified as federal.

It is probably rash to attempt yet another definition of federalism when so many authorities have failed to agree on one that is totally satisfactory. Possibly no single definition of so elusive and controversial a concept could be satisfactory for all purposes. Nonetheless, the following definition is offered in the belief that it meets three essential criteria for a definition of federalism: (1) the definition should not be unduly restrictive; (2) it should serve to distinguish a federal state both from a unitary state and from looser forms of association; and (3) it should emphasize the political aspects of federalism.

With these criteria in mind, federalism will be defined as follows. It is a political system in which most or all of the structural elements of the state (executive, legislative, bureaucratic, judiciary, army or police, and machinery for levying taxation) are duplicated at two levels, with both sets of structures exercising effective control over the same territory and population. Furthermore, neither set of structures (or level of government) should be able to abolish the other's jurisdiction over this territory or population. As a corollary of this, relations between the two levels of government will tend to be characterized by bargaining, since neither level can fully impose its will on the other.

The condition that neither level of government should be able to abolish the other's jurisdiction effectively distinguishes federalism both from a unitary state and from looser forms of association. In a unitary state there may be some decentralization for administrative and even legislative purposes, but the central government can take back the power it has delegated to the lower levels of government or can even abolish them, as the British Parliament abolished the Parliament of Northern Ireland. In an alliance, league, or common market, on the other hand, the member states can withdraw or secede, an action which clearly prevents the central institutions from exercising any jurisdiction over their territories or populations. If the definition is a valid one, it follows that in a true federation the provinces or states have no right to secede. If such a right existed before, they surrendered it when they entered the federal union.

A somewhat legalistic way of expressing these characteristics of federalism is to say that the provinces or states are not sovereign entities, but at the same time the central government does not possess full and complete sovereignty either, since it lacks the power to abolish the other level of government. These facts may be represented symbolically by a written constitution, judicial review, elaborate procedures for amendment, and statements to the effect that sovereignty resides in "the people" (as in the United States) or "the Crown" (as in Canada). These symbolic aspects of federalism are not unimportant, but their importance exists only because they metaphorically represent, and may provide ideological justification for, real facts concerning the distribution of political power.

As to which countries are federal by this (or any other) definition, opinions will vary. Any effort to classify a particular country should be based on observation of how its political institutions actually operate. In some countries military coups and other changes of regime have occurred so frequently that one cannot say what is their "normal" or usual pattern of political activity. Others have simply not been studied enough for reliable data to be available. There is no doubt, however, that the few countries which are invariably included on any list of federations—and Canada is unquestionably one of these—would qualify as federations under this definition. On the other hand, countries such as the United Kingdom, which may have characteristics in common with at least some of the federations, would not.

FEDERALISM ON OTHER CONTINENTS

The origins of American federalism have been discussed already, while those of Canadian federalism will be considered in more detail ... It would be unduly parochial, however, not to make a few comments about the origins of Swiss and German federalism.

Although they differ in many respects, an important similarity is the fact that in both cases a looser, non-federal association between sovereign states was transformed into a true federation as a result of war. In Switzerland the conservative Catholic cantons launched the Sonderbund War of 1847 to protect themselves against the emerging threat of bourgeois liberalism. Their defeat enabled the more progressive cantons to impose a federal constitution following the American model and establish a modern liberal state in place of the outmoded "confederation." In the German case, the defeat of Austria by Prussia in the war of 1866 led to the dissolution of the loose "confederation" which had been established in 1815 as the successor to the old Holy Roman Empire. With Austria now excluded from further involvement in German affairs, a Prussian-dominated federation was established in northern Germany in 1867. The southern states entered it voluntarily in 1870, at the end of which year it adopted the title of "German Empire." Some form of German federalism has existed ever since, except during Hitler's dictatorship and for a few years after his defeat.

In the twentieth century federal unions have been formed in Australia (1901), the USSR (1924), Malaya (1948), Rhodesia and

Nyasaland (1953), the West Indies (1958), and Cameroun (1961). In four of these six cases the federating units were colonies of the British Empire, although in the Australian case the initiative for federation was taken entirely by the Australians themselves. Soviet federalism permitted the new Russian republic to reunite with most of the outlying territories of the old empire, which had been temporarily detached from Russia during its civil war. The Federal Republic of Cameroun united two territories which had been held under United Nations trusteeship by Britain and France, respectively. In the early 1960s Malaya changed its name to Malaysia when it absorbed a number of other British colonies. The Rhodesia and Nyasaland and West Indian federations disintegrated at about the same time, with some of their components becoming independent and others remaining under British rule.

A number of other countries are frequently referred to as federations, although it cannot be said, at least without serious qualification, that they resulted from a union of previously separate entities. Argentina, Brazil, Mexico, and Venezuela all adopted "federal" constitutions in the nineteenth century, possibly in imitation of the United States. Most external observers, however, are sceptical about Latin American federalism, on the grounds that the component states do not retain any meaningful degree of autonomy.

Outside of North America and central Europe, federalism has had its greatest influence on the Indian sub-continent, where one-fifth of the world's population lives. The British ruled most of India, including the present Pakistan and Bangladesh, as a unitary colony from 1857 until 1935. In the latter year the Government of India Act established provincial legislatures, and thus a sort of quasi-federalism similar to what John A. Macdonald intended for Canada. In 1947 the British handed over their authority to two new states, India and Pakistan, which between them soon absorbed the various princely states that had never been under direct British rule. Both successor states have adopted constitutions that divide legislative powers between two levels of government, and the subnational governments, at least in India, enjoy considerable autonomy. However, the central government in India was able to "reorganize" the boundaries of the component states soon after independence, an event that would surely be unthinkable in such genuinely federal countries as Canada, Switzerland, or the United States. It is also interesting that the Supreme Court of India, in an important case upholding the central government's power to expropriate mineral resources belonging to the states, declared flatly that India was a decentralized unitary state rather than a federal one.

The case of Nigeria is very similar. Although they had previously ruled it as a unitary state, the British endowed it with the dubious blessing of a federal constitution in 1954. It remained a federation after gaining its independence in 1960, but the federal constitution was suspended by the military regime during the ultimately successful civil war against the separatists in the southeastern province, who attempted with some foreign assistance to establish an independent "Biafra." Postwar Nigeria, however, has re-established subnational state governments, even though the boundaries of the new states bear no relation to the old.

EXPLANATIONS FOR FEDERALISM

An explanation for federalism which is particularly relevant to the central and eastern European experience was offered by Rudolf Schlesinger in a book published in 1945. Schlesinger suggested that federalism arose in situations where national consciousness was focussed on a collectivity which did not coincide with the traditional boundaries of dynastic states. In Germany the national community included a number of dynastic states, while in the Austrian and Russian empires the dynastic state included a number of national communities. In either case federalism developed, with one level of government corresponding to the rising forces of nationalism, industrialism, and the bourgeoisie. In Western Europe, where the new communities and the old units tended to coincide, there was no need for federalism, and unitary states have been the general rule.

Many students of federalism, however, refuse to recognize as a federation any state that did not result from a union of previously separate entities which retained their identities after union. As a result, efforts to generalize about the reasons why federations come into existence tend to ignore the ambiguous cases or those in which the subnational governments were established by devolutions of power from the centre. K.C. Wheare lists the conditions leading to federal union as follows: the need for common defence, desire for independence from foreign powers, desire to gain economic benefits, some previous political association, similar political institutions, geographical closeness, similar social conditions, and the existence of political elites interested in unification. No previous or subsequent writer on federalism has really added anything to this list.

Despite its completeness, or perhaps because of it, Wheare's list of conditions is not very informative. The first two conditions are almost indistinguishable, the last would seem to be present by definition, and several of the others are so vague as to be almost useless. Wheare does not present anything that can be called a theory of federal unification.

The most interesting theoretical question about the origins of federal unions is whether military insecurity or anticipated economic benefits is the more important motive, or whether in fact both must be present. It is also conceivable that a security motive might be more important in some cases and an economic motive in others.

The case for the pre-eminence of economic motives was made most memorably by Charles Beard in his classic study, *An Economic Interpretation of the Constitution of the United States*. Beard suggested that the move of the Americans to adopt their present constitution was led by merchant capitalists and that the constitution itself was carefully drafted to protect their economic interests. For Beard, American politics after the Revolutionary War were dominated by the conflict between his class and the more numerous but less influential farmers who, in his view, mainly opposed the constitution. The merchants wanted a strong central government to repress further revolutionary outbreaks by agrarian radicals (such as Massachusetts had experienced in 1786–87), to prevent the repudiation of debts and the printing of paper money, and to protect their commerce on the high seas. The adoption of the constitution marked the swing of the revolutionary pendulum back to the right and the restoration of "order."

Not all economic interpretations of federalism emphasize class conflict, as Beard's does. The kind of economic motives that Wheare seems to have had in mind are those emphasized by more conventional American historians and their Canadian and Australian counterparts: larger markets, the removal of tariff barriers, penetration of the western hinterlands, and so forth. Marxist historians, of course, would view even these types of motives as reflecting the interests of ruling classes, and perhaps as leading to conflict with other classes that opposed them. Even where there was such opposition, however, the establishment of a federal state might not be necessary to achieve these objectives. Western European capitalists seem to be achieving quite similar objectives through the very limited integrative arrangements represented by the European Community, which falls far short of establishing federalism.

Security motives for federal union are emphasized by William H. Riker, who views federalism as a "bargain" by which political elites in the states or provinces agree to sacrifice some, but not all, of their autonomy in return for protection against an external threat or, more rarely, a share in the benefits of military expansion and conquest. The bargain is usually initiated by a relatively large and powerful entity (Virginia, the Province of Canada, or Bismarck's Prussia) and accepted by smaller states or provinces, which have both more to lose (because they will have relatively little influence within a larger union) and more to gain (because they could not hope to attain security, let alone expansion, by themselves).

Obvious external threats to security were certainly present at the time of union in some federations, such as Switzerland, Bismarck's Germany, the USSR, and Pakistan .... Security motives are somewhat harder to discern, though not entirely absent, in other cases, such as those of Australia, postwar West Germany, and Cameroun.

It may be that no single factor can explain every instance of the formation of a federal union, and even in a particular case a variety of factors may contribute. The author of a recent book on federalism, R.D. Dikshit, adopts both of these assumptions. Dikshit's purpose is to explain not only why federal unions evolve, but also why they differ in the extent of the powers conferred on the central government, and why some federal unions are more durable and successful than others. Dikshit distinguishes factors leading to union from factors leading to the retention of some degree of regional autonomy. A preponderance of the first will lead to the formation of a unitary state, while a preponderance of the second will prevent any union from taking place. Only a balance between the two will lead to federalism, and only if the balance is maintained will federalism survive.

Dikshit's factors leading to union are essentially the same as K.C. Wheare's, although he differs from Wheare in including a common language, culture, and religion as one of his conditions. His factors conducive to the maintenance of regional autonomy are essentially the reverse of the factors leading to union, for example, regionally grouped cultural diversity rather than cultural homogeneity, competitive economies with conflicting interests rather than the expectation of economic benefits from union, and so forth. Federal union does not demand that all of the factors in either category be present, for there are several possible combinations that will bring it about, although the precise nature of the new federal state will vary accordingly. West Germany is a very centralized federation, according to Dikshit, because most of the factors leading to union were present in 1949, while the factors conducive to maintaining regional autonomy were virtually absent. Only the absence of a military threat (since the country was effectively protected by the United States) prevented a centralized unitary state from emerging instead of a federation. On the other hand, Pakistan at the time of its formation had practically all of the conditions which lead to the maintenance of regional autonomy, while the military threat from India was the only factor that contributed to union. The result was a weak federation that could not prevent the secession of its largest unit in the civil war of 1971.

EVALUATING FEDERALISM

For a Canadian audience it is perhaps necessary to explain that evaluating federalism means evaluating the consequences of having two distinct levels of government, rather than a national government only. Since most Canadians find it impossible to imagine Canada as a unitary state, few have considered it worthwhile to discuss and evaluate the relative merits of federal and unitary institutions. Some such discussion took place prior to 1867, but since then the vast majority of Canadians outside of Quebec have simply taken federalism for granted. In Quebec, admittedly, there has been controversy over federalism, but what is really being debated there is whether or not Quebec should be independent, not the advantages and disadvantages of federal institutions as such. No one in Quebec contemplates abolishing the provincial level of government.

In other parts of the world, by contrast, the respective merits of federal and unitary government have been lengthily, although inconclusively, debated. Among the more strikingly unfavourable assessments was that of former Nigerian Prime Minister Sir Abubaker Balewa, who at his last meeting with Harold Wilson said to him: "You are fortunate. One thing only I wish for you, that you never have to become Prime Minister of a federal and divided country."

Since he was assassinated four days after making this remark, and since his death proved to be the opening of the Nigerian civil war, Balewa's pessimism was probably justified. Others have expressed, although in less memorable circumstances, his view that federations are characterized by disorder, conflict, and political bickering, which may be the less attractive side of the intergovernmental bargaining that is, by our definition, an almost inevitable aspect of federal politics. Defenders of federalism, on the other hand, would argue that regional and cultural conflicts are obviously not caused by federalism, since they exist in unitary states like Ethiopia, Spain, or the United Kingdom.

A classic argument against federalism was presented by A.V. Dicey, a late nineteenth-century writer on British constitutional law, who maintained that federalism produced weak and ineffective government, conservatism, and legalism. Dicey's views, and especially his assertion that "federal government means weak government," may have some relevance for Canada today, almost a century after they were expressed. Federalism was weak, according to Dicey, because energy was wasted in conflicts between the two levels of government, because the central government had to respond to regional demands, or appear to do so, at the expense of efficiency and effectiveness, and because the power of either level to act was constrained by a rigid constitution. It was conservative because the existence of a rigid written constitution produced a "superstitious reverence" for existing principles and institutions. It was legalistic because lawyers and judges were inevitably called upon to interpret the constitution and define the respective powers of the two levels of government.

While much of Dicey's analysis is plausible, it is far from evident, with hindsight, that the unitary British system of government which he so admired avoided any of the defects which he associated with federalism. Nor is the untrammeled authority of the legislature invariably a blessing, as Dicey complacently assumed in the salad days of Victorian liberalism. Finally, the connection asserted between conservatism and legalism may be questioned. Particularly in the United States, the judiciary has often been more liberal and enlightened than either the executive or legislative branches of government.

In Dicey's defence it may be argued that the United States, Canada, and Australia, all of which are federations, have lagged behind the unitary states of northern and western Europe in their provisions for social welfare, income security, full employment, and public ownership and control of the economy. Possibly the inefficacy of federalism, and the restrictions which it places on the power of the central government, are partly to blame.

The admirers of federalism have not lacked arguments of their own since the middle of the eighteenth century, when Montesquieu published his *De l'esprit des lois*. It is not entirely clear what Montesquieu meant by federalism, and no state that we would call federal existed in his lifetime, but his views greatly influenced the creators of the American constitution. As well as having originated the notion of "the separation of powers," Montesquieu argued that a federal republic was a means of combining the freedom possible in a small state with the security against external threats that was only possible in a large one.

Since in the thermonuclear era it is doubtful whether any state can guarantee security, a modern variation on Montesquieu's view might be that federalism combines the economic advantages of large size with the possibilities for self-government that exist in a smaller political community. A non-federalist could argue that neither part of this proposition is fully supported by experience. The prosperity of Norway, Switzerland, Singapore, and Kuwait suggests that size is not a prerequisite to economic success. On the other hand, the reputed benefits of grass-roots democracy and freedom in a "small" subnational political system may really exist in the Swiss canton of Appenzell-Inner-Rhodes but bear no discernible relation to the facts of political life in Quebec, Ontario, New York, or California, all of which are larger than many nation-states.

Another argument sometimes heard in support of federalism is really the converse of Dicey's argument against it. According to this view, a "weak" state whose power is divided between two sets of authorities and restrained by legal restrictions is safer than a "strong" and vigorous state, because it is less likely to be oppressive. Dispersed and divided power is less dangerous than concentrated power, and the cumbersome decision-making procedures in a federal state make it less likely that unpredictable eruptions of popular sentiment will be reflected in public policy. Even if government at one level tries to be oppressive, government at the other level, as well as the judiciary, will prevent it from doing too much harm. This is essentially Madison's argument in the celebrated number ten of the Federalist Papers, and it recurs in several of the other papers as well. It was also a favourite argument of American conservatives during Franklin Roosevelt's New Deal and of Australian conservatives during the Labor Government of Gough Whitlam. When subjected to critical examination, this argument for federalism looks remarkably like an ideological facade for vested economic interests.

A somewhat different but related argument for federalism is that it protects minorities and enables cultural, linguistic, religious, and ideological diversity to flourish. A prominent supporter of this perspective is Pierre Elliott Trudeau, whose well-known but often misunderstood hostility to "nationalism" is really no more than the view that the state should not be intolerant of diversity and should not be identified with any ethnic or cultural group. In a federal state, he would argue, this is less likely to happen.

Several examples can be cited of diversities protected by federalism. Multilingualism in Switzerland provides an obvious example. West German states and Canadian provinces have adopted a variety of solutions to the difficult problem of the relationship between Roman Catholic and public education. Socialists in prewar Vienna and the CCF-NDP in Saskatchewan achieved important reforms that would not have been possible at the national level. The more progressive American and Australian states extended the vote to women and abolished capital punishment long before there was nation-wide support for these innovations.

Nonetheless, in certain respects this optimistic view of federalism is not fully supported by experience. Federalism may protect those minorities which happen to make up a majority within one of the provinces or states, but it protects them precisely by allowing them to act as majorities, which means that they in turn can oppress the sub-minorities under their jurisdiction. Federalism has ensured the survival of the French language in Canada, but it has been of no benefit to Chinese in British Columbia, Hutterites in Alberta, or Jehovah's Witnesses in Quebec. All of these groups were unpopular at various times, and the provincial governments were more responsive to the hostile sentiments directed against these minorities than was the more remote central government. Had Canada been a unitary state, these groups might have benefited. The history of blacks in the American South and of Australian aborigines in the state of Queensland supports a similar conclusion.

One is tempted to conclude that both the arguments against federalism and the arguments in its favour can be as easily refuted as supported. Franz Neumann, in his essay "On the Theory of the Federal State," concluded that federalism might be good, bad, or indifferent, depending on the circumstances, and that it was impossible to evaluate federalism in general. W.H. Riker, in his book on federalism, stated that each particular case of federalism had to be examined separately to determine the balance sheet of costs and benefits. Attempting to perform this exercise himself, although in a rather superficial manner, he decided that federalism had benefited francophones in Canada, white racists in the United States, and business interests in Australia. In a later essay, however, he concluded rather inconsistently that federalism really made no difference in terms of policy outcomes, a statement which he attempted to support by arguing that federal Australia was little different from unitary New Zealand. From this he reached the further conclusion, which readers of this volume may be unhappy to hear, that the study of federalism was a waste of time! While it is hoped that Riker was incorrect in this conclusion, his earlier view that each case of federalism should be examined individually on its own merits is one with which the present writer would concur ....

24

CONSOCIATIONALISM

A difficult challenge in modern democracies is the problem of reconciling powerful minority interests. Consociationalism is one way of organizing liberal democracies fragmented and deeply divided along linguistic, regional, ethnic, or religious lines. Arend Lijphart argues that these societies are not impossible to order; on the contrary there are specific things that can be done to blunt the lines of cleavage. He suggests consociationalism as a way of structuring the democratic process of government to overcome some of the divisive forces in society, and outlines four characteristics that distinguish this form of government. The heart of his argument is based upon "proportionality," i.e., representation based upon the size of the group, or its proportion of the total society. The concept of consociationalism is applied more often in Europe than it is in Anglo-American countries. Arend Lijphart is a Dutch political scientist now teaching at the University of California, San Diego. The following reading is excerpted from his book Democracy in Plural Societies: A Comparative Exploration, *Yale University Press, 1977.*

• • • • • • • • •

Consociational democracy can be defined in terms of four characteristics. The first and most important element is government by a grand coalition of the political leaders of all significant segments of the plural society. This can take several different forms, such as a grand coalition cabinet in a parliamentary system, a "grand" council or committee with important advisory functions, or a grand coalition of a president and other top officeholders in a presidential system. The other three basic elements of consociational democracy are (1) the mutual veto or "concurrent majority" rule, which serves as an additional protection of vital minority interests; (2) proportionality as the principal standard of political representation, civil service appointments, and allocation of public funds; and (3) a high degree of autonomy for each segment to run its own internal affairs.

GRAND COALITION

The primary characteristic of consociational democracy is that the political leaders of all significant segments of the plural society cooperate in a grand coalition to govern the country. It may be contrasted with the type of democracy in which the leaders are divided into a government with bare majority support and a large opposition. British democracy is the clearest example of the latter type; the government-versus-opposition model will therefore also be referred to as the British model. The style of leadership in the consociational model is coalescent; in the British model it is competitive or, as Martin O. Heisler suggests, "adversarial."[1]

Grand coalitions violate the rule that in parliamentary systems cabinets should have, and normally do have, majority support, but not the support of an overwhelming majority. A small coalition not only allows the existence of an effective democratic opposition, but it is also formed more easily because there are fewer different viewpoints and interests to reconcile ....

The function of a grand coalition can also be clarified by placing it in the context of the competing principles of consensus and majority rule in normative democratic theory. On the one hand, broad agreement among all citizens seems more democratic than simple majority rule, but, on the other hand, the only real alternative to majority rule is minority rule—or at least a minority veto. Most democratic constitutions try to resolve the dilemma by prescribing majority rule for the normal transaction of business when the stakes are presumably not too high, and extraordinary majorities or several majorities over a period of time for the most vital decisions, such as for adopting or amending constitutions. They thus follow Jean Jacques Rousseau's advice that "the more grave and important the questions discussed, the nearer should be the opinion that is to prevail approach unanimity."[2] In practice, majority rule works well when opinions are distributed unimodally and with relatively little spread—in other words, when there is considerable consensus and the majority and minority are in fact not very far apart. When the people are "fundamentally at one," Lord Balfour once said, they "can safely afford to bicker."[3] But, in a political system with clearly separate and potentially hostile population segments, virtually all decisions are perceived as entailing high stakes, and strict majority rule places a strain on the unity and peace of the system ....

It is true—in fact, almost tautological—that a moderate attitude and a willingness to compromise are prerequisites for the formation of a grand coalition. On the other hand, the prospect of participating in the government is a powerful stimulus to moderation and compromise, because it minimizes the risk of being deceived by the other parties or by one's own undue optimism concerning *their* willingness to be accommodating. By being in the government together, parties that do not quite trust each other have an important guarantee of political security. For this it is necessary, of course, to be in the coalition at the same time rather than in a diachronic grand coalition ....

MUTUAL VETO

The most important method of consociational government—the grand coalition in one form or another—is complemented by three secondary instruments: mutual veto, proportionality, and segmental autonomy. All four are closely related to each other, and they all entail deviations from pure majority rule. The mutual veto, to be discussed first, represents negative minority rule.

Participation in a grand coalition offers important political protection for minority segments, but no absolute and foolproof protection. Decisions have to be made in grand coalitions, and when these are reached by majority vote, though the minority's presence in the coalition does give it a chance to present its case as forcefully as possible to its coalition partners, it may nevertheless be outvoted by the majority. When such decisions affect the vital interests of a minority segment, such a defeat will be regarded as unacceptable and will endanger inter-segmental elite cooperation. A minority veto must therefore be added to the grand-coalition principle; only such a veto can give each segment a complete guarantee of political protection. The minority veto is synonymous with John C. Calhoun's concurrent majority, which also had the protection of minority interests as its principal goal: it invests each segment with "the power of protecting itself, and places the rights and safety of each where only they can be securely placed, under its own guardianship. Without this there can be no systematic, peaceful, or effective resistance to the natural tendency of each to come into conflict with the others."[4]

The great danger of the minority veto is that it will lead to minority tyranny, which may strain the cooperation in a grand coalition as much as the outvoting of minorities. There are three reasons why this danger is not as serious as it appears. First, the veto is a *mutual* veto that all minority segments possess and can use; Calhoun uses the term "mutual negative" as an equivalent of concurrent majority. The too frequent use of the veto by a minority is not very likely because it can be turned against its own interests, too. Second, the very fact that the veto is available as a potential weapon gives a feeling of security which makes the actual use of it improbable: "By giving to each interest, or portion, the power of self-protection, all strife and struggle between them for ascendancy is prevented, and thereby ... every feeling calculated to weaken the attachment to the whole is suppressed." Accordingly, Calhoun argues, each segment "sees and feels that it can best promote its own prosperity by conciliating the good will and promoting the prosperity of the others." Finally, each segment will recognize the danger of deadlock and immobilism that is likely to result from an unrestrained use of the veto: "Impelled by the imperious necessity of preventing the suspension of the action of government ..., each portion would regard the sacrifice it might have to make by yielding its peculiar interest to secure the common interest and safety of all, including its own, as nothing compared to the evils that would be inflicted on all, including its own, by pertinaciously adhering to a different line of action.[5]

The mutual veto can be an informal and unwritten understanding or a rule that is formally agreed on and possibly anchored in the constitution. The Netherlands and Switzerland are examples of the informal application of the veto. In Austria, it was formally affirmed by the leaders of the Socialist and Catholic parties before each coalition government was formed: in the Coalition Committee, all decisions had to be made unanimously. In Belgium, the mutual veto has never been more than an informal principle in the relations among the Catholic, Socialist, and Liberal *familles spirituelles,* but it has received constitutional recognition with regard to questions involving the linguistic groups. Lode Claes wrote in the early 1960s: "Increasingly, in parliament and other gatherings, a majority decision is not regarded as sufficiently representative when a tabulation of votes for and against shows them not to be equally divided between the two parts of the country."[6] In 1970, this view was translated into a constitutional amendment: laws affecting the cultural and educational interests of the language groups can be passed only if majorities of both the Dutch-speaking and French-speaking parliamentary representatives give their approval. This entails a formal veto power for both linguistic segments.

PROPORTIONALITY

The principle of proportionality also represents a significant deviation from majority rule and, like the mutual veto, is closely interconnected with the grand coalition principle. Proportionality serves two important functions. First, it is a method of allocating civil service appointments and scarce financial resources in the form of government subsidies among the different segments. It can be contrasted with the winner-take-all principle of unrestrained majority rule. Because one of the motivations behind the formation of a minimum winning coalition is that the "spoils" of government can be divided among as small a number of participants as possible, the proportional allocation rule makes a minimum winning coalition less profitable and therefore less probable.

Proportionality, as a neutral and impartial standard of allocation, removes a large number of potentially divisive problems from the decision-making process and thus lightens the burdens of consociational government. An even more important function of proportionality relates to the decision-making process itself. Jürg Steiner defines the proportional model as one in which "all groups influence a decision in proportion to their numerical strength." In this respect, too, the proportionality and grand coalition rules are linked: "A roughly proportional distribution of influence in policy problems can usually only be assured if the decision is bargained over with the participation of all groups."[7] But proportionality adds a refinement to the grand coalition concept: not only should all significant segments be represented in decision-making organs, but they should also be represented proportionally. For instance, the Swiss "magic formula" for the composition of the Federal Council is a proportional formula. And in Austria the grand coalition cabinets were constituted in such a way as to reflect the electoral strengths of the two coalition partners as faithfully as possible.

The proportional composition of cabinets and other decision-making bodies does not solve the problem of how to achieve proportional influence when the nature of the decision is basically dichotomous: for instance, should a certain action be taken, yes or no? Unless there is a spontaneous unanimity, there will be winners and losers in such a situation: ultimately, the use of either majority rule or minority veto cannot be avoided. There is no solution to this dilemma, but there are two methods that can alleviate it and can be regarded as partial solutions. One is to link several issues and to solve them simultaneously by reciprocal concessions: the usual terms applied to this method are logrolling, package deal, and, in Austria, *Junktim*.[8]

The other method is to delegate the most difficult and fateful decisions to the top leaders of the segments. The proportionality principle is a vital instrument in this process. In the ideal-type British model, majority rule applies both to the decisions of the voters and to the composition of the cabinet. The voters in each constituency select one candidate together with, ideally speaking, a clear set of policies. The cabinet, supported by the majority of these winning candidates, then executes the winning program. In this model, the basic decision is made by majority rule at the electoral level. The proportional model, in sharp contrast, *postpones* the decision by majority rule (or minority veto) as long as possible. As an electoral system, it merely translates voting strength into parliamentary seats as faithfully as possible, without requiring a set of policy decisions. Decisions are postponed again by the formation of a proportionally constituted grand coalition cabinet, and possibly of a still higher organ such as the Koalitionsausschuss and the Petka. This method of postponing the decisions to the highest levels entails the concentration of decision-making in the hands of a small group of top leaders. The advantage of this arrangement is that in intimate and secret negotiations the likelihood of achieving a package deal is maximized and that of the imposition of a veto minimized.

Strictly speaking, the polar opposite of the proportional method of postponing and delegating decisions is not British-type majority rule but majority rule without the intervention of elected representatives, such as in a referendum, especially when it is coupled with the initiative. Switzerland therefore exhibits a curious mixture of proportional delegation of decisions to the level of the national executive with occasional lapses into the polar opposite, direct democracy and majority rule—only slightly tempered by the fact that on constitutional questions both popular and cantonal majorities are required for passage.

There are two variations of the principle of proportionality that entail even greater deviations from majority rule: the deliberate overrepresentation of small segments, and parity of representation. The latter can also be regarded as the maximum extension of the former: the minority or minorities are overrepresented to such an extent that they reach a level of equality with the majority or the largest group. The practical effect of majority rule in the British model is to exaggerate the representation and influence of the majority. Parity and minority overrepresentation have the opposite effect. Both are devices for providing added protection and security to small segments. Parity is an especially useful alternative to proportionality when a plural society is divided into two segments of unequal size. In such a case, proportionality does not eliminate a majority-minority confrontation in decision-making bodies because it merely reflects segmental strengths. An example of a paritarian body is the Belgian cabinet which, according to the new constitutional provisions of 1970, must consist of equal numbers of Dutch-speaking and French-speaking ministers (not counting the premier) and in which the francophone minority is thus overrepresented.

SEGMENTAL AUTONOMY AND FEDERALISM

The final deviation from majority rule is segmental autonomy, which entails minority rule: rule by the minority over itself in the area of the minority's exclusive concern. It is the logical corollary to the grand coalition principle. On all matters of common interest, decisions should be made by all of the segments together with roughly proportional degrees of influence. On all other matters, however, the decisions and their execution can be left to the separate segments.

The delegation of rule-making and rule-application powers to the segments, together with the proportional allocation of government funds to each segment, is a powerful stimulus to the various segmental organizations. One aspect of the definition of a plural society is that the representative organizations of the society follow segmental cleavages. This means that segmental autonomy increases the plural nature of an already plural society …. It is in the nature of consociational democracy, at least initially, to make plural societies more thoroughly plural. Its approach is not to abolish or weaken segmental cleavages but to recognize them explicitly and to turn the segments into constructive elements of stable democracy.

A special form of segmental autonomy is federalism, although federalism can also be applied in nonplural societies, of course. As a theory, federalism has a few significant parallels with consociational theory: not only the granting of autonomy to constituent parts of the state, which is its most important feature, but also the overrepresentation of the smaller subdivisions in the "federal" chamber. Federal theory can therefore be regarded as a limited and special type of consociational theory. Similarly, federalism can be used as a consociational method when the plural society is a "federal society": a society in which each segment is territorially concentrated and separated from the other segments, or, to put it differently, a society in which the segmental cleavages coincide with regional cleavages.[9] Because government at the subnational level is in practice always organized along territorial lines, federalism offers an especially attractive way of implementing the idea of segmental autonomy.

Conversely, segmental autonomy may also be regarded as a generalization of the federal idea. An attempt was actually made to develop such a system of nonterritorial federalism by Otto Bauer and Karl Renner as a solution to the nationalities problem of the Austro-Hungarian Empire. They referred to their proposal as federalism on the basis of the "personality principle" in contrast to the usual territorial principle. Each individual should be able to declare to which nationality he wished to belong, and these nationalities would become autonomous *Kulturgemeinschafte*. Bauer explicitly drew a parallel between these proposed cultural communities and the frequently coexisting religious communities of Catholics, Protestants, and Jews, who independently take care of their own religious affairs.[10]

In the European consociational democracies, both territorial and nonterritorial federalism have played a significant role. The former type has been particularly important in Switzerland ... and, increasingly since 1970, in Belgium. Where the segments are geographically too interspersed, segmental autonomy has been established on the personality principle: in the Netherlands, Austria, and, as far as the religious-ideological subcultures rather than the linguistic communities are concerned, in Belgium. Austria is formally a federal republic, but its system of segmental autonomy is mainly of the nonterritorial form. It should be noted that, although it is easier to delegate governmental and administrative responsibilities to territorially concentrated than to nonterritorial segments, autonomy has proved to be compatible with both approaches. Especially in the realm of cultural affairs—education and communication—segmental autonomy in the Netherlands, Austria, and Belgium has become very extensive.

SECESSION AND PARTITION

One of the reasons why Eric A. Nordlinger excludes federalism, as well as segmental autonomy in general, from his set of conflict-regulating practices in plural societies is that it may encourage the breakup of the state: "The combination of territorially distinctive segments and federalism's grant of partial autonomy sometimes provides additional impetus to demands for greater autonomy," and, when these demands are refused, "secession and civil war may follow.[11] One answer to this argument is that the same objection could be raised to other elements of consociational democracy. For instance, the mutual veto or the threat of it can be invoked too frequently and insistently by one segment in order to wrest extraordinary concessions from the others, and such an abuse of the veto may provoke violent conflict. Another danger is a segment's insistence on changing proportionality to overrepresentation in its own favor, even when the objective conditions do not warrant it. In short, all of the consociational methods must be applied with caution and restraint. Second, it is hard to imagine that the imposition of a unitary and centralized democratic system would be able to prevent secession if the basic ingredient of separatist sentiment were strong.

A more fundamental rejoinder to Nordlinger's objection is that secession should not be regarded as an undesirable result of the tensions in a plural society under all circumstances. There are three types of solutions to deal with the political problems of a plural society while maintaining its democratic nature. One is to eliminate or substantially reduce the plural character of the society through assimilation—a method with a low probability of success, especially in the short run. The second is the consociational solution which accepts the plural divisions as the basic building blocks for a stable democratic regime. Especially if the second solution should be very unlikely to succeed or if it was tried and failed, the remaining logical alternative is to reduce the pluralism by dividing the state into two or more separate and more homogeneous states.

The consociational model is an intermediate model that stands between the unitary British model and the model of international diplomacy; it resembles the latter particularly as far as the mutual veto and the freedom of action of its units are concerned. Secession into sovereign statehood goes a significant step beyond segmental autonomy, of course, but it is not incompatible with the basic assumptions underlying the consociational model. The model supports J. S. Furnivall's comment that a geographically intermingled plural society does not have the advantage of a federation, to which "the *remedy* [of secession] is open ... if the yoke of common union should become intolerable."[12] Instead of being viewed negatively as a source of problems, the geographical concentration of segments in a plural society can be viewed as having the positive advantage of allowing the application of either federalism as a consociational device or partition as an ultimate solution. The real problem occurs when the segments are geographically intermingled. Such a situation excludes the possibility of territorial federalism as a form of segmental autonomy and limits the choice to less far-reaching forms of autonomy. And partition results in homogeneously constituted separate states only if it is accompanied by the resettlement of minority populations.

There are authors who advocate partition even under these unfavorable circumstances. A striking instance is the recommendation made at the end of the Second World War by Louis Wirth: "It will be wise in the forthcoming peace settlements to recognize the importance in the drawing of national boundaries of the distribution of ethnic groups and to be prepared for the transference of people to more congenial states in case ethnic boundaries must be violated." In order to strengthen his argument, he pointed to the "valuable precedent" of the "fairly satisfactory exchange of Turkish, Bulgar, and Greek populations after the Graeco-Turkish war of 1919–23," and he concluded as follows: "In the light of these events, the minority question can no longer be considered insoluble."[13] A more recent example in Norman Pounds's discussion of partition, in which he recognizes the thorny problem of population exchanges, as well as the undesirability of multiplying the number of small states in the world, but nevertheless maintains that "partition and its consequences may be a small price to pay for [avoiding] internal strife and even civil war.[14]

The question of the costs of partition and resettlement—in terms of not only the necessary physical resources but also and particularly the human suffering involved—is a relative one and should be measured against the benefits; but it is clear that these costs should not be underestimated. On the other hand, partition is worthy of consideration as a serious possibility and deserves at least a fair hearing—which it is unlikely to receive in the contemporary antipartition mood among statesmen and scholars. As Samuel P. Huntington remarks: "The twentieth century bias against political divorce, that is, secession, is just about as strong as the nineteenth century bias against marital divorce. Where secession is possible, contemporary statesmen might do well to view it with greater tolerance."[15] Among scholars, the bias against political divorce is supported by the traditional notion in international relations theory that the root cause of conflict among states is the absence of a common government. Hedley Bull is one of the few theorists who have explicitly stated their disagreement with this pervasive assumption: "Formidable though the classic dangers are of a plurality of sovereign states, these have to be reckoned against those inherent in the attempt to contain disparate communities within the framework of a single government."[16] In the field of peace research, there is a similar tendency to frown on peace which is achieved by separating the potential enemies—significantly labeled "negative" peace—and to strive for peace based on fraternal feeling within a single integrated and just society: "positive" peace.[17]

DISADVANTAGES OF CONSOCIATIONAL DEMOCRACY

Because the consociational model serves not only as an empirical explanation of the political stability of a set of small European democracies but also as a normative example to plural societies elsewhere in the world, it is necessary to evaluate its real and alleged weaknesses. These are of two kinds: consociational democracy may be criticized for not being democratic enough and also for being insufficiently capable of achieving a stable and efficient government.

If one regards the presence of a strong opposition as an essential ingredient of democracy, consociational democracy is by definition less democratic than the British government-versus-opposition pattern; grand coalition government necessarily entails either a relatively small and weak opposition or the absence of any formal opposition in the legislature. This objection is not an entirely fair one: the ideal of a vigorous political opposition, which can be realized to a large extent in homogeneous societies, cannot be used as a standard for evaluating the political performance of plural societies. Under the unfavorable circumstances of segmental cleavages, consociational democracy, though far from the abstract ideal, is the best kind of democracy that can realistically be expected. The objection is also mistaken: it presupposes that parties alternate in government and opposition. As discussed earlier, segmental cleavages tend to be inflexible and do not allow much movement of votes between parties. It cannot be considered very democratic to exclude the minority segment or segments permanently from participation in the government. It should also be pointed out that a grand coalition does not rule out opposition completely. As long as there is a parliament or other body to which a grand coalition is responsible, criticism may be directed not only against the entire coalition but even more so against individual members of the coalition by supporters of the other parties. This is what the Austrians called *Bereichsopposition* ("opposition to what is happening under the agreed-upon jurisdiction of the other party") during the era of Catholic-Socialist grand coalitions.[18]

Another set of criticisms of the democratic quality of the consociational model is that it falls short of the democratic trinity of liberty, equality, and fraternity. The segment to which an individual belongs stands between him and the national society and government, and the segment may be oppressively homogeneous. The consociational model resembles the "communal society" of William Kornhauser's typology, in which the intermediate groups are "inclusive" in the sense that they tend to "encompass all aspects of their members' lives.[19] A highly homogeneous and conformist society may have the same dampening effect on individual liberty. This is not paradoxical: consociational democracy results in the division of a plural society into more homogeneous and self-contained elements.

The separation of the different segments and the autonomy they have to run their own affairs also affects the ideal of equality in at least two ways. First, consociational democracy is more concerned with the equal or proportional treatment of groups than with individual equality. Second, segmental isolation and autonomy may be obstacles to the achievement of societywide equality. Regional inequalities tend to be greater in federally organized democracies than in unitary ones, and among sovereign states than within federal states.[20] In this respect, too, the consociational model stands in between the British model and the model of international politics. On the other hand, segmental separateness is not at all incompatible with segmental equality. As a matter of fact, the Catholic, Calvinist, and Socialist subcultures and their organizations in the Netherlands are often described as emancipation movements, and they have by and large achieved their goals of a full and equal role in Dutch national life within the framework of consociational democracy. Separation may tend toward, but does not inherently lead to, inequality ....

A final objection to the democratic quality of consociational democracy is that it requires what Nordinger calls "structured elite predominance" and, conversely, a passive and deferential role of all nonelite groups. Segmental leaders have the difficult task of, on the one hand, reaching political accommodations with and making concessions to the leaders of other segments and, on the other hand, maintaining the confidence of their own rank and file. It is therefore helpful if they possess considerable independent power and a secure position of leadership. But this does not entail a semidictatorial position. Nordinger points out that structured elite predominance does not "necessarily or even usually involve the subjugation of nonelites. [It] is usually tempered with a good measure of responsiveness to nonelite wishes and demands. In open regimes nonelites generally set distinct outer limits to their leaders' demands and control."[21] Nor is consociational democracy incompatible with a considerable degree of participation in segmental organizations by nonelite members of the segment. In fact, Lorwin writes that the segmented pluralism of the five small European democracies he analyzes "has, on the whole, made for more, rather than for less, participation in voluntary associations." One of the obvious reasons is that, "all other things being equal, the more pluralism in an area of socioeconomic association, the larger number of posts to fill at all levels."[22] Moreover, the elitism of consociational democracy should not be compared with a theoretical—and naive—ideal of equal power and participation by all citizens but with the degree of elite predominance that is the norm in democratic regimes of all kinds. This may still reveal a difference but not a glaring contrast.

Perhaps the most serious and fundamental criticism of consociational democracy concerns not its undemocratic character but its potential failure to bring about and maintain political stability. Several of its characteristics may lead to indecisiveness and inefficiency: (1) Government by grand coalition means that decision-making will be slow. It is much easier to reach agreements in a small coalition with a narrower range of policy outlooks than in a large coalition spanning the entire range of a plural society; this is one of the reasons why, *ceteris paribus,* minimum winning coalitions are more likely to form than grand coalitions in the first place. (2) The mutual veto involves the further danger that decision-making may be completely immobilized. It may therefore produce the very stagnation and instability that consociational democracy is designed to avoid. (3) Proportionality as a standard of recruitment to the civil service entails a higher priority to membership in a certain segment than to individual merit, and may thus be at the expense of administrative efficiency. (4) Segmental autonomy has a price in the literal sense of the word: to the extent that it requires the multiplication of the number of governmental and administrative units as well as the establishment of a large number of separate facilities for the different segments, it makes consociational democracy an expensive type of government.

The gravest problem is that of immobilism; by comparison the problems of administrative inefficiency and cost are relatively minor. It should be pointed out, however, that the characteristics of consociationalism responsible for these minor disadvantages may have positive functions with regard to the pace and effectiveness of decision-making. For instance, Steiner argues that in Switzerland "by virtue of the federal structure demands are split up among different political levels," which contributes to a "relatively small input of demands" at the national level and, consequently, to the alleviation of the burdens of decision-making at that level and a lower probability of immobilism.[23] Similarly, the principle of proportionality is a convenient and time-saving method for allocating resources and appointments .... The experience of the European consociational democracies shows that deadlock and immobilism are not at all inevitable.

A final criticism involves the question of both democratic quality and democratic stability. The government-versus-opposition pattern has the advantage that dissatisfied citizens can cast their vote against the government without voting against the regime. In the consociational model, government and regime coincide. Dissatisfaction with governmental performance therefore quickly turns into disaffection from the regime. Although this is indeed a serious weakness, it does not have to be fatal. If voter disaffection is mobilized by new political parties, these may be antisystem or antiregime parties but they are not necessarily antidemocratic. And because the typical electoral system of consociational democracy is proportional representation, it is easy for new parties to gain a voice in the political process. This is what happened when consociational democracy began to break down in the Netherlands in the late 1960s. The relative ease with which consociationalism can be discarded makes the persistence of a democratic regime more likely. This argument can also serve as a final reply to the various charges of the insufficiently democratic character of consociational democracy: when these weaknesses are felt to be increasingly onerous, and particularly when they are regarded as less and less necessary because a society has become less plural, it is not difficult to move from a consociational to a more competitive democratic regime.

NOTES

1. Martin O. Heisler, ed., *Politics in Europe: Structures and Processes in Some Postindustrial Democracies* (New York: McKay, 1974), p. 52.
2. Jean Jacques Rousseau, *The Social Contract*, trans, G.D.H. Cole (New York: Dutton, 1950), p. 107.

3. Quoted in Carl J. Friedrich, *Constitutional Government and Democracy: Theory and Practice in Europe and America*, rev. ed. (Waltham, Mass.: Blaisdell, 1950), p. 422.
4. John C. Calhoun, *A Disquisition on Government*, ed. C. Gordon Post (New York: Liberal Arts Press, 1953), p. 28.
5. Ibid., pp. 37–38, 52. See also George Kateb, "The Majority Principle: Calhoun and His Antecedents," *Political Science Quarterly* 84, no. 4 (December 1969): 583–605; and Giuseppe Di Palma, *The Study of Conflict in Western Society: A Critique of the End of Ideology* (Morristown, N.J.: General Learning Press, 1973), pp. 10–13.
6. Lode Claes, "The Process of Federalization in Belgium." *Delta* 6, no. 4 (winter 1963–64): 45.
7. Jürg Steiner, "The Principles of Majority and Proportionality," *British Journal of Political Science* 1, no. 1 (January 1971): 63.
8. Gerhard Lehmbrudh, *Proporzdemokratie: Politisches System und politische Kultur in der Schweiz und in Österreich* (Tübingen: Mohr, 1967), pp. 26–29.
9. See Michael B. Stein, "Federal Political Systems and Federal Societies," *World Politics* 20, no. 4 (July 1968): 721–47.
10. Otto Bauer, *Die Nationalitätenfrage und die Sozialdemokratie* (Vienna: Wiener Volksbuchhandlung, 1907), pp. 353–63. See also Karl Renner, *Das Selbstbestimmungsrecht der Nationen in besonderer Anwendung auf Österreich* (Leipzig: Deuticke, 1918); Carl J. Friedrich, "Corporate Federalism and Linguistic Politics," paper presented at the Ninth World Congress of the International Political Science Association, Montreal, 1973; and Karl Aun, "Cultural Autonomy of Ethnic Minorities in Estonia: A Model for Multicultural Society?" paper presented at the Third Conference of Baltic Studies in Scandinavia, Stockholm, 1975.
11. Eric A. Nordlinger, *Conflict Regulation in Divided Societies*, Occasional Papers in International Affairs, no. 29 (Cambridge, Mass: Center for International Affairs, Harvard University, 1972), p. 32. See also Charles D. Tarlton, "Symmetry and Asymmetry as Elements of Federalism: A Theoretical Speculation," *Journal of Politics* 27, no. 4 (November 1965): 861–74.
12. J.S. Furnivall, *Netherlands India: A Study of Plural Economy* (Cambridge: Cambridge University Press, 1939), p. 447 (italics added).
13. Louis Wirth, "The Problem of Minority Groups," in *The Science of Man in the World Crisis*, ed. Ralph Linton (New York: Columbia University Press, 1945), p. 372.
14. Norman J.G. Pounds, "History and Geography: A Perspective on Partition," *Journal of International Affairs* 18, no. 2 (1964): 172.
15. Samuel P. Huntington, "Foreword" to Nordinger, *Conflict Regulation*, p. vii. Moreover, the disadvantages frequently attributed to small size should not be exaggerated. Robert A. Dahl and Edward R. Tufte conclude that "a country's chances of survival do not depend significantly on its size"; see their *Size and Democracy* (Stanford: University Press, 1973), p. 122. And a factor analysis of 236 variables for 82 nations found that

size (in terms of population) and wealth (GNP per capital) were *virtually unrelated* factors; see Jack Sawyer, "Dimensions of Nations: Size, Wealth, and Politics," *American Journal of Sociology* 73, no. 2 (September 1967): 145–72.

16. Hedley Bull, "Society and Anarchy in International Relations," in *Diplomatic Investigations: Essays in the Theory of International Politics*, Herbert Butterworth and Martin Wight, eds., (London: Allen and Unwin, 1966), p. 50. See also Arend Lijphart, "The Structure of the Theoretical Revolution in International Relations," *International Studies Quarterly* 18, no. 1 (March 1974): 41–74.

17. See Johan Galtung, "Violence, Peace, and Peace Research," *Journal of Peace Research* 6, no. 3 (1969): 183–86.

18. Otto Kirchheimer, "The Waning of Opposition in Parliamentary Regimes," *Social Research* 24, no. 2 (summer 1957): 127–56.

19. William Kornhauser, *The Politics of Mass Society* (New York: Free Press of Glencoe, 1959), pp. 83–84.

20. See David R. Cameron and Richard I. Hofferbert, "The Impact of Federalism on Education Finance: A Comparative Analysis," *European Journal of Political Research* 2, no. 3 (September 1974): 225–58.

21. Nordlinger, *Conflict Regulation*, pp. 73–74.

22. Val R. Lorwin, "Segmented Pluralism: Ideological Cleavages and Political Cohesion in the Smaller European Democracies," *Comparative Politics* 3, no. 2 (January 1971): 157–58.

23. Steiner, "Principles of Majority and Proportionality, " p. 69.

P A R T

4

The
Political
Process

INTRODUCTION

In Part III we suggested that one of the more difficult problems facing all societies is organizing political authority. In Part IV we take another step in analyzing government and politics by examining the process that goes on within those structures. The readings in this section discuss the various aspects of the dynamic interaction that occurs among the individuals, institutions, and agencies that are involved in public decision-making for societies.

Politics is a systematic process in which political inputs (demands and supports) are converted into political outputs (laws and policies). The process is influenced by a variety of factors: political culture, interest groups, political parties, the communications media, elections, an executive, a bureaucracy, the legislature, and the courts. The interaction of all these components produces public decisions for society. In practical terms, politics becomes the means for hammering out public policies on issues such as defence, health care, the environment, regional disparities, energy shortages, unemployment, welfare, and capital punishment. G. Bruce Doern and Peter Aucoin have described this policy-making process as

> a plurality of processes which are closely interlocked. More particularly, one might visualize a series of interlocking circles of activity, each encompassing different but usually related values, instruments of governing, and forms of contact between the executive-bureaucratic arena and the other arenas of Canadian politics.

The process of politics has cultural as well as structural dimensions. The structural dimension is obvious; it involves interest groups, legislatures, the courts, and so on. The cultural dimension is less obvious; it involves attitudes, beliefs, and values that provide an orientation to politics and the political process. Political culture is an important component because it is assumed to influence how individuals behave in politics. In Reading 25, Walter A. Rosenbaum delineates the various meanings of the concept of political culture. He also outlines some of the problems involved in researching political culture.

In the past, interest groups such as those of business, labour unions, farmers, and teachers have been prominent components in the political process. Currently, however, a host of new social movements are taking a more active role in politics, as described in Reading 26. For example, in most communities, provinces, and at the national level, feminists and environmentalists lobby hard to achieve their goals in the political arena. In effect, today one finds a much broader spectrum of political interests actively pressuring governments in the public policy-making process.

Political parties also are significant structures in the political process, and they are the subject of Reading 27. As most Western nation-states moved to universal adult suffrage, the political party emerged as a key instrument for organizing mass participation in politics. Theoretically, political parties provided a vital link between the rules and the ruled, individuals with a means for contacting political leaders, and political leaders with a means for keeping their finger on the pulse of society. In practice, however, not all analysts feel political parties have lived up to their democratic expectations. The parties have come under fire for not fulfilling their roles as the link between the people and their governors. John Meisel, in an interesting assessment of this problem, notes some of the primary reasons for the declining role of political parties.

The way in which members of an elected assembly handle their job of representing constituents is the subject of Edmund Burke's essay, Reading 28. While the selection is dated (some 200 years old), the three models of representation are as significant today as they were then. One needs to understand the alternatives that can be used in the process of representing many different interests.

The interaction of institutions in politics involves not only the informal activities of interest groups, political parties, and the communications media but also the formal, constitutional activities of legislatures, executives, the bureaucracy, and the courts. It is impossible at this point to delve into all the different arguments about these institutions and their activities. The following selection, however, highlight significant positions found in the literature today.

Many analysts now agree that the prime minister and the cabinet do indeed hold a position of dominance in the legislative process. The argument is based on the fact that cabinets, utilizing the extensive resources of the bureaucracy, initiate most legislative proposals, and apply party discipline in herding proposals past formidable barriers in a session of Parliament. Through this command of the process, the cabinet is in a position to manage the vast household of government. The cabinet, then, becomes the focus of power for the legislative machinery.

It is rare indeed that an insider would discuss the role of minister, prime minister, or cabinet, in the policy-making process. But this is exactly what Richard Crossman does in Reading 29. The selection is a candid insider's view of the relationships between the prime minister, other ministers, and the civil service. Crossman offers a personal interpretation of the role of cabinet committees in initiating policy proposals, the predominant role of the prime minister in the cabinet process, and the complex relationship between the minister and the department for which he is responsible.

Invariably, bureaucracies pose a problem in modern democracies. Even though they are supposed to be "professional" organizations, standing above politics and administering without favour, they are one of the most powerful institutions in the political process. They have an agenda of their own, and without a strong elected minister to control their actions, they can become the dominant force in the political process. In Reading 30, Max Weber offers a classic analysis of the nature of bureaucracies in modern governments, indicating problems inherent in that organization.

The final selection, Reading 31, discusses the role of the courts in the political process in Canada after the adoption of the Charter of Rights and Freedoms. Before the Charter, Canadian courts were not considered "activist," i.e., they did not take an active role in challenging the law-making function of Parliament. In the past, the position of the courts was dictated by the principle of parliamentary supremacy and by the fact that no *written* charter limited the powers of Parliament. Once the Charter was passed, many critics and analysts speculated that the powers of Parliament would be trimmed, and that we were in for a period of judicial supremacy. Using court decisions since 1982, F.L. Morton assesses the impact of the Charter on the roles of the courts and Parliament. He suggests that compared with pre-Charter numbers, the courts are now exercising judicial review more frequently.

25 POLITICAL CULTURE

*T*he study of government and politics consists of two dimensions: the cultural and the structural. Familiar examples of political structures are interest groups and political parties, or the executive, legislature, and judiciary. Political culture is the "psychological" dimension of politics, reflecting an individual's orientation to the political world.

Political culture consists of the attitudes, beliefs, and values one holds regarding the political process and one's place in that process. Political culture can influence individual political behaviour by affecting one's choice of a candidate or political party in an election. Political culture can also influence the interaction of institutions in the political process. For example, the way freedom is valued in a society may well influence the relationship between interest groups and the executive or the administration.

Another important aspect of political culture is how it is transmitted to individuals in society. Political socialization is the process whereby political attitudes and values are transmitted from generation to generation. A number of institutions in society serve as the vehicles for the transmission process: the family, schools, peer groups, the work place, and government itself.

This section by Professor Walter A. Rosenbaum from the University of Florida provides a good description of the concept of political culture. He outlines numerous facets of the concept, and suggests some of the difficulties in researching political cultures. It is an abridged version of "The Meaning of Political Culture," which appears in his book Political Culture.

• • • • • • • •

A fragmentation grenade explodes inside a crowded Catholic pub in Northern Ireland, shredding the air with shrapnel, killing four people, and adding another vicious episode to a civil war between Protestants and Catholics that has already claimed more than a thousand victims in that violence-racked land. Far away, a Montreal housewife removes from a supermarket shelf a ketchup bottle with a unique label, a modest symbol of crisis averted. Found only in Canada, the label bears French and English wording of equal size proclaiming "ketchup" and "ketchup aux tomates"; repealing the law requiring such bilingual labels would produce a parliamentary crisis. To Canada's south, an opinion poll declares that the American public, apparently shaken by continuing revelations of scandal within the executive branch, is losing confidence in the Presidency—a scant 19 per cent of the public express strong faith in that institution. Still, the American people do not seem moved to demand any radical alterations in their political system.

Such provocative items, chosen from one day's news, are likely to prompt the question "Why?" Why cannot Catholics and Protestants in Northern Ireland reach a political accommodation without civil war? Why is language a politically explosive issue in Canada? Why do Americans express low confidence in their Chief Executive yet remain curiously undemonstrative in the sort of situation that has provoked political violence in other nations? Here—in our effort to understand both the commonplace and the extraordinary in political life—the study of *political culture* properly begins. The concept of political culture offers a potentially powerful, and almost always useful, approach to daily political events by identifying the underlying psychological forces that shape much of civic life.

Political culture can be defined in two ways, depending upon the level at which we want to study political life. If we concentrate on the individual, political culture has a basically psychological focus. It entails all the important ways in which a person is subjectively oriented toward the essential elements in his political system. We want to know what he feels and thinks about the symbols, institutions, and rules that consti- tute the fundamental political order of his society and how he responds to them. In effect, we are probing the psychological dimension of a person's civic life; we ask what bonds exist between him and the essen- tials of his political system and how these affect his behavior.

The second definition of political cultures refers to the collective orientation of people toward the basic elements in their political system. This is a "system level" approach. We are interested in how large masses of citizens evaluate their political institutions and officials. To say, for example, that a nation's political culture is largely "integrated" means that most people within the system have similar, or compatible, political culture orientations which are congenial to the political institutions within which they live. When political culture is discussed, it usually refers to these mass political orientations across the whole political system.

Before sharpening this definition, I can briefly illustrate how an awareness of political culture enhances our understanding of the political events we described above. Northern Ireland's violence, for example, flows in part from the widespread conviction among the Catholic minority that the government is illegitimate and in part from the profound distrust of each other's religious communities that permeates the Catholic and Protestant factions alike, frustrating political accommodation and moderation. In short, one must know something about public attitudes toward government and toward other political factions before explaining the civil war. In a similar vein, Canada's official bilingualism is comprehensible only when we note the importance that the large French minority attaches to its language and culture; its conviction that it is struggling for cultural survival against the English majority, and its determination, forces official governmental recognition of its cultural demands, even to the level of ketchup bottles. Finally, Americans have traditionally held their Constitution in high esteem, believing that the government it designed is legitimate and proper; moreover, there is broad public conviction that political change should be orderly and peaceful, following the customary means ordained by the Constitution. Undoubtedly, this sentiment keeps most citizens loyal to their basic governmental system and wary of radical or violent change. They may have been disillusioned with President Nixon but not disposed to demand major refashioning of the Presidency; they may criticize Congress or the Court, but they are not yet prepared to redesign either institution. There are, to be sure, no simple, all-inclusive explanations for complex political events; political culture never explains all. Still, a sensitivity to the perspective it provides on political life adds depth and richness to our appreciation of political events.

THE ESSENTIALS OF POLITICAL CULTURE

To say that political culture involves the important ways in which people are subjectively oriented toward the basic elements of their political system is an accurate but not yet satisfactory definition. One needs a firmer notion of what "subjective orientations" this involves and, consequently, we need to spell out, clearly and concretely, the distinctive elements of thought, feeling, and behavior that concern us. At this point a nettlesome issue arises. Scholars themselves have never reached a consensus on the proper components of political culture; so many different formulations have been offered (twenty-five by one count) that one might think he was grappling with the riddle of the Sphinx. At one extreme, some analysts include in political culture "all politically relevant orientations either of a cognitive, evaluative or expressive sort"— so unbounded a definition that an investigator would have to spend an interminable time compiling an elephantine list of orientations to be sure nothing *politically relevant* escaped notice. At the other extreme, certain analysts attempt to make the list manageable by limiting political culture to orientations toward national political institutions, a good beginning except that it may omit other dimensions of political life very instrumental in shaping the fundamental political order of a society. Fortunately, this profusion of definitions need not mean intellectual anarchy, for one can distill from them a set of common items most scholars would agree belong among the essentials; we shall call these the "core components" of political culture.

The Core Components

What the core elements appear to share is a fundamental importance in shaping a nation's political order. Whenever analysts offer such a list they are, in effect, using a rule of thumb: Those dimensions of an individual's thoughts, feelings, or behaviors that are linked to the creation and maintenance of a society's fundamental political order belong under the label "political culture." Thus, insists one observer, political culture must be limited to the "attitudes, beliefs and sentiments that give order and meaning to the political process and provide the underlying assumptions and rules that govern behavior."

It is helpful to think of these core components as orientations toward different elements in the political order. Such a list commonly includes the following particulars:

1. *Orientations Toward Governmental Structures*
   a. *Regime Orientation*—How an individual evaluates and responds to the basic governmental institutions of his society, its symbols, officials, and norms (collectively, the "regime"); this may include a more detailed investigation of orientations toward specific institutions and offices or an investigation of preferences for alternative governmental structures.
   b. *Orientations Toward Governmental Inputs and Outputs*—How individuals feel and respond toward various demands for public policy ("inputs"); and policy decisions made by government ("outputs"); this may include an inventory of a person's knowledge concerning how these processes operate, what demands he may make upon government, and how effective he believes governmental policy to be.

2. *Orientations Toward Others in the Political System*
   a. *Political Identifications*—The political unit (nation, state, town, region), geographic areas, and groups to which one feels he belongs, that are in some significant subjective sense a part of his own social identity; in particular, these include those units and groups to which he feels a strong loyalty, obligation, or duty.
   b. *Political Trust*—The extent to which one feels an open, cooperative, or tolerant attitude in working with others in civic life; essentially, political trust expresses the intensity of a person's conviction that other individuals or groups mean him well (or ill) in political life.
   c. *"Rules of the Game"*—An individual's conception of what rules should be followed in civic life; these subjective preferences may or may not be consistent with prevailing law and other norms supposed to govern civic conduct.

3. *Orientations Toward One's Own Political Activity*
   a. *Political Competence*—How often, and in what manner, a person participates in civil life, the frequency with which he uses the political resources available to him in civic affairs; this may include some evaluation of his knowledge of his political resources.
   b. *Political Efficacy*—"The feeling that individual political action does have, or can have, an impact on the political process"; this includes a belief that political change is possible and that one can accomplish change through civic action—individuals are customarily ranked on a scale according to whether their "sense of political efficacy" is "high" or "low."

When an investigator turns his attention to the political culture of any society, he is likely to concentrate upon those political culture orientations that are *widely shared*, on the assumption that they are most likely to influence the political process because they affect the behavior of large masses. For instance, if an examination of American political culture concentrates upon political trust and reveals that a very small portion of the population exhibits a political paranoia toward Catholics, an investigator would probably consider this sentiment less important for the operation of the political system than a finding that most Americans are generally trustful, or at least tolerant, toward the political motives of other religious groups. (Of course it would be important to examine the political orientations of the anti-Catholic minority in order to understand their own political behavior.) Moreover, many of these political-culture orientations are *implicit, and often unconscious,* in an *individual's life*—so basic that he hardly reflects upon them. In this sense, many are "primitive" orientations because they are "so implicit and taken for granted that each individual holds them and believes that all others hold them"; they become "unstated assumptions, or postulates, about politics." Though held unconsciously, these beliefs and attitudes govern civic behavior, help shape the governmental order, and, for many people, define political reality. We should also note (because emphasizing a concept often seems to make it larger than life) that there is nothing metaphysical or otherwise superhuman about the operation of political culture. Political culture *expresses itself in the daily thinking and activity of people* going about the business of civic life just as their other beliefs and feelings are expressed in other aspects of the social world. Many beliefs and feelings embraced in the term "political culture" can be considered normal, commonplace, even dull—but extremely important precisely because they are so frequently commonplace; they define what is often the basic political order, the "given' in civic behavior for a society. To study political culture is, in many respects, to hold up a mirror to ourselves. We (individually and collectively) are the carriers of the culture, who not only observe it in others but also express it in our own behavior. In short, "political culture" is a conceptual shorthand for feelings, thoughts, and behaviors we note, or infer, from watching men living out their civic daily lives ....

TABLE 25.1
Some Operational Definitions of Political Culture Orientations

Orientation	*Operational Definition*
Political Identification	Nation of citizenship Political units and groups toward which one feels positively or negatively Political units and groups with which one is most often involved
Political Trust	Willingness to collaborate with various groups in different types of social action Group memberships Rating of groups in terms of trustworthiness, political motives, type of membership, etc.
Regime Orientations	Belief in the legitimacy of the regime Feelings toward, and evaluation of, major political offices and regime symbols Involvement in political activity supporting or opposing the regime

Orientation	Operational Definition
"Rules of the Game"	How one feels political opinions should be expressed Concepts of political obligations for oneself and others Concepts of how political decisions should be made by government Attitudes toward political deviation and dissent
Political Efficacy	Belief that government is responsive to one's opinions Belief in importance of civic activism and participation Belief in possibilities of political change
Political Competence	Frequency of voting and other types of political activity Knowledge of political events and their influence on oneself Interest in political affairs
Input-output Orientation	Satisfaction with governmental policy Knowledge of how political demands are made on government Belief in effectiveness of policy inputs and outputs

A Growing Interest

Long before modern scholars minted the term "political culture" much of what it now includes was studied under such names as political ideology, national character, and political psychology; still, in the past several decades, political analysts have approached the topic with a greater sense of urgency and greater investments of time and resources than ever before, so that the study has reached an unprecedented intensity within the last decade. Behind this surge of interest lie several explanations. More than anything else, the pervasive political violence in the modern world, the problems of nation building in the postcolonial countries, and the recent availability of survey research methods that offer an especially useful device for enlarging our understanding of the field have stimulated a renewed interest in political culture.

Political instability is now a global commonplace. Since 1945, there have been successful coups in eighteen of twenty Latin American countries, in seven Central African nations, and in six Middle Eastern and West African nations. Even the older Western European and North American nations have endured political upheavals; the boundaries and regimes of European countries have been redesigned with sometimes startling rapidity, and internal turmoil is chronic in many countries. Since World War II the Greeks, for instance, have experienced five years of civil war, several general elections involving fifty political parties, three dozen governments, three successful coups, the fall of a constitutional monarchy, three referenda, and assorted bloody political riots. In addition, the post-World War II period has spawned a host of new African and Asian nations struggling, and often failing, to create and maintain national governments in the aftermath of their colonial experience. These struggles, in particular, have forcefully raised the problems of nation building in a major concern among both scholars and statesmen involved in the quest for global peace.

These developments were especially congenial to renewed interest in political culture, for it became apparent that explanations of political stability and nation growth, if they could be found, must go beyond an examination of different governmental forms or constitutions, or other formalities; rather, some deep probing seemed imperative to understand how emotional and attitudinal linkages are formed between members of a political community and their government and to describe how different patterns of linkage encouraged or inhibited national development and order. Moreover, such issues could not be resolved without some cross-national comparisons of political cultures; the study of political culture had to be global in its sweep. At this point, an additional incentive appeared in the development of survey research methodology, which seemed to make the empirical study of political culture especially practical by providing scholars with a technique for interviewing large numbers of individuals and obtaining detailed information about their political culture. Although the survey research technique is only one method for studying political culture (we shall shortly examine many others) it has been widely used and has undoubtedly contributed to the growing interest in the field.

The *survey research* methodology used in political culture study is an adaptation of public-opinion study techniques that have already been tested and proven in the United States and most other Western countries. Survey research enables scholars to carefully probe the civic orientations of many individuals in a multitude of national settings, to collect and process the data with great rapidity, and to apply very sophisticated techniques of interpreting the results. This means, among other things, that scholars can now go "into the field" to study national populations directly, can obtain wholly new types of information, and can tabulate results with new versatility and precision. With such new methods, not only could new questions be asked and new data collected, but there appeared the promise that for the first time a truly solid, diversified, empirical base could be provided for generalizing about patterns of political culture and their consequences.

Beyond this, interest in political culture has been stimulated by the problem of bridging the gap between the "macro" and "micro" levels of political life. As survey research and other techniques provide a growing abundance of information about how individuals feel and respond to civic life, the problem arises of relating these "micro" studies of individual political behavior to the performance of whole political systems or major subunits—the "macro" level of analysis. The concept of political culture seems to offer an intellectual link between individual behavior and the survival and performance of political systems, because it relates the general to the particular. Many analysts reason that the essential components of political culture, that is, the individual orientations, must ultimately have a powerful influence upon the performance of whole political systems, so that these individual attitudes can be related to the political order in which they evolve.

The bond between system performances and mass political orientations is not a fact but, rather, a working hypothesis that spurs investigators to test its validity; the incentive is that the results, should they show a strong link between political culture and political system performance, would provide an enormous "pay-off" in the form of a greater understanding of the foundations of political order and chaos.

VARIATION AND CHANGE IN POLITICAL CULTURE

One essential, and intriguing, question about political culture is, How does it develop and change? This issue arises in different ways. Looking at a nation which has experienced more than a century of general political order and great continuity in its political institutions, a researcher suspects that there must be considerable stability within its political culture and seeks to discover how this is maintained. Another researcher, observing a once stable system degenerating into political violence, wonders if one explanation may be a sudden disruption in the traditional political culture and looks for the source. Yet another researcher, studying a newly developing nation, traces many of its difficulties in reaching a consensus on the form of its government to different patterns of political culture within the system; he wants to know why differing cultural patterns persist. In such ways, it becomes apparent that any understanding of political culture must, at some point, explain the origin, development, and change of the particular system under consideration. Let us examine several formative influences upon political culture generally believed to be important.

Political Socialization

To many analysts, the study of political culture begins with the maxim "political behavior is learned behavior." They assert that a person's political orientations are powerfully shaped by the individuals and institutions that influence him early in life, particularly by home, school, and friends. In general, political socialization refers to the "process whereby the individual learns his political values, attitudes, beliefs and behaviors." In the perspective of political socialization, an individual is born, psychologically, the citizen of no land; he does not know what government is "his," is ignorant of the officials, symbols, rituals, and values he is supposed to honor or despise, and must be taught his political identity. In his earliest years, therefore, a person is likely to be taught the most fundamental political orientations he is expected to have—that is, he first acquires the rudiments of political culture under the powerful molding force of institutions to which he is deeply attached and from which he is especially open to influence. Of course, individuals "learn" about politics throughout their lives and, in varying degrees, alter political perspectives; virtually no one enters adulthood with an immutable political orientation. In many political systems, apparently, persons who become members of the political elite are socialized into the values, behaviors, and attitudes considered appropriate to their position at a much later time in life than they acquire their basic orientations toward the political order. Generally, it appears that the nature and extent of one's political socialization in a society may depend upon the population group to which one belongs and what political role one will play in it. Still, analysts place great emphasis upon early learning because they believe it is particularly influential and resistant to later change. In fact, one scholar asserts that the major point of early socialization is "induction into the political culture."

When study moves to political socialization, attention centers upon two questions: (1) which institutions are most active in socializing individuals into a political system? and (2) what is the content of the political information communicated to individuals? As one compares political systems, it is apparent that the political socialization of the young will often be the responsibility of very different institutions, and that the nature of the material taught will vary enormously. In the United States, most Western European nations, and Great Britain, most early socialization is handled by family and school; in Communist countries, however, a child may be exposed early and continually to socialization through organizations representing the Communist Party and may, indeed, be taken out of the family for long periods of time and given intensive experience in Party-inspired work and recreation programs. In some nations, religious denominations attempt to shape the political perceptions of growing children. It is impossible to list all the religious, political, ethnic, or vocational groups that might play a part in socializing children into political life, for it is always a matter to be determined on a country-by-country basis.

In the same manner, the content of political socialization varies enormously between nations. In the United States, for example, the schools largely confine socialization to teaching "good citizenship," which usually means inculcating a respect for government and community, teaching the basic rituals of the political system (voting, for example), and instilling interest and pride in civic history. In other systems, by way of contrast, children may be taught early to have strong attachments to particular leaders, ideologies, and parties, and to have equally strong hostility to current enemies of the state or party; the spectacle of kindergarten children in the People's Republic of China playing games involving guerilla wars against "capitalist aggressors" is a graphic illustration of how far ideological war can be carried into the basic socialization scheme of a nation. Again, it is less important at this point to identify national patterns of socialization than to develop a sensitivity to the range and variety of socializing agents and the political messages they convey.

In political systems with considerable continuity of governmental institutions and stable civic processes, political socialization is most likely to be a conservative process, initiating new generations into the political values and behaviors of the ongoing system or inducing relatively modest change. Indeed, many analysts assert that the continuing stability of a political system depends, in good measure, upon the ability of the socialization process to perform this conservative function. It is understandable, then, why newly established regimes advocating changed ideologies and governmental structures are likely to place such enormous emphasis upon controlling the education system and on managing other institutions which educate the young. New modes of socialization are used to bring coming generations under the banner of the new movement.

Despite the plausibility of these assertions about the impact of political socialization on political culture, most of them have yet to be proven. It is known that there is some carry-over of political values, attitudes, and behaviors from childhood education into adulthood—in most European nations and the United States, for example, adult party preference and attitudes toward major policy problems seem to be moderately correlated with childhood learning. At the same time, there are: no conclusive evidence that most adults largely reproduce political orientations learned in childhood, no firm evidence about which institutions are likely to be most effective in childhood political learning, and few empirical studies closely following changes in political orientation through the lifetime of a sample of individuals. In many respects, this lack of information arises from the difficulty of obtaining reliable information about childhood socialization from adults and from obstacles to isolating a set of individuals for study through the life cycle. But an important additional problem is the inability of researchers to get access to populations in non-Western societies (particularly Communist systems) and the consequent poverty of data available for making generalizations on a truly cross-cultural basis. Thus, the most reasonable conclusion seems to be that far more empirical studies are needed before the role of political socialization in political culture development can be accurately assessed.

Historical Experience

Another very broad category of factors that affect individual orientations toward political systems are those events and experiences encountered through the life cycle after childhood socialization is past. Because political learning is a lifelong process and political orientations are, to some degree, susceptible to change in most people, we naturally expect an adult's political views and behaviors to respond, in some manner, to the historical events that form part of his own life ….

The events most likely to affect a nation's political culture are those affecting great masses of people directly, profoundly, and tangibly—wars, depressions, and other crises. Such events throw the capacities of government into sharp relief, causing people to become deeply involved in political life and, often, testing and examining their basic feelings, beliefs, and assumptions about it. Major social crises often leave profound impressions upon mass political orientations. In Germany and Japan, the disastrous management of World War II, leading to the desolation of both nations, left the existing regimes and their ideologies badly discredited among large segments of the population; this situation made the task of reconstructing the governments of West Germany and Japan along more democratic lines considerably easier. Deep aversion to the prewar forms of government has remained in both nations. The United States Government's role in Vietnam, together with the administrations' failure to maintain public support for continued involvement, left large masses of Americans, especially the young, alienated from the system (at least temporarily). The civil wars in Northern Ireland, the Congo, and Algeria made establishment of national governments by consensus extremely difficult, since the violence spawned deep political distrust among major religions and social factions in those nations. It is not only dramatic events, however, which cause mass political orientations to develop and change significantly; like water on the rock a slow but steady succession of occurrences may gradually wear away old values and replace them with new ones. It is important to recognize that political learning is lifelong and that basic political orientations often alter with the passage of time and circumstance.

Socio-economic Variables

A common discovery in political culture studies is that political orientations are often strongly associated with the socio-economic characteristics of populations. This means that variations among socio-economic groups within a polity tend to include significantly different patterns of political culture. This is one reason for the well-known fact that in virtually no society is there a political culture pattern typical of almost all individuals or social groups; group political orientations strongly deviant from the predominant one in a society are called "sub-cultures." Evidence of socioeconomic influence in political orientations abounds. In the United States, studies reveal that trust in government and confidence in the effectiveness of political action through traditional forms is diminished among blacks, Indians, and other minorities who feel the force of discrimination; in African nations, where regional and tribal loyalties are often very strong, the political groups or governmental units to which an individual feels most strongly attached may depend upon his tribal lineage, place of residence, or family background. One of the major tasks in political culture research is to identify these socio-economic variations in a society and to describe them. Almost any socio-economic characteristics may be associated with variations in political orientation within a society; the ones most frequently noted are race, occupation, family or caste, education, and income.

There are several reasons why social factors are so often associated with variations in political orientation. Frequently, political status within a society is determined by social status; since political rights, obligations, and benefits may be tied to social position, it is quite likely that individuals with different social backgrounds will have quite divergent views of political life. Social groups privileged with easy access to government, considerable material rewards from the system, and other indulgences may understandably feel more attached to the dominant institutions and values of civic life than those who are, in various ways, deprived or discriminated against. Moreover, it often happens that social status within societies is tied to education; those within the middle and upper levels of the social hierarchy, having received better education than those in lower social classes, may feel more confident of their political skills, better informed about civic life, and more aware and interested in political life, and may demonstrate many other political orientations that differ from those of less educated individuals. Finally, differing social characteristics may lead to very different expectations about what government should do: Landowners and laborers, creditors and debtors, professionals and nonprofessionals are not likely to seek the same ends from civic life nor receive the same satisfactions; social cleavages within societies are almost always rich in potential clashes of political interest and in varying assessments of how well the system operates or should operate.

Political Variables

Any list of the factors shaping and modifying political culture would be incomplete without attention to government itself and to political parties. No group has a greater stake in the development and change of political culture than does a nation's governmental elite, for their continued existence and effectiveness may depend, in the long run, upon how the mass of people are oriented toward them and toward the political institutions they manage. All governments place heavy emphasis upon controlling the major institutions of political socialization (especially the education system) and on prescribing, in varying degrees, what shall be taught; the intent is to produce a mass political culture compatible with the regime and, once this is achieved, to preserve it. In cases where a major change in regime may occur within a society—a "modernizing" elite taking the reins of government from a traditional one or a Communist regime succeeding a non-Communist one—the new government often places a high priority upon the reshaping of the political culture through the re-education of children and adults into the new allegiances and values they are expected to have with the change of political order. In these instances, no longer rare, the regime becomes the most powerful agent in remolding a political culture.

In many polities, political parties play a major role in shaping mass political orientations. This may be in collaboration with, or opposition to, the dominant regime. In totalitarian countries, it is common for the single dominant party to be an organ of the regime and to penetrate all major social, occupational, cultural, and political aspects of life, taking the lead in teaching and rewarding whatever political orientations are desired by the regime. In many societies, however, political parties are part of the regime's opposition (and, in some cases, may be prohibited from overt activity); they may submit members to intensive indoctrination with political values, loyalties, and attitudes quite hostile to the dominant regime or some of the other political parties—the common situation, for instance, when Marxist parties operate in non-Marxist systems. The impact of party indoctrination will vary, of course, among political systems. In the United States, Great Britain, and most other Western European countries the dominant parties share a basic agreement on the nature of the constitutional order and the proper political processes for the nation; pronounced differences in party programs show up with respect to policy rather than regime norms. Thus, as a rule, party members are not likely to possess sharply different political-culture attributes by virtue of belonging to different parties. By contrast, parties which represent regional, social, religious, or other interests sharply at variance with the dominant regime may well be socializing members into a very different cultural orientation from those found in other parties.

This by no means exhausts the number of factors which may be important in shaping or transforming a political culture. Nor should one treat what has been said about the shaping of political culture as some unalterable truth. In reality, all the factors we have suggested as important in shaping political culture, and all the ways in which they seem to affect that culture, should be considered as working hypotheses—the best approximation to the truth we can make with the information now available to us. Our view of political culture is largely shaped by the methods and data at hand; as new methods of inquiry become available and new sources of information open up, our understanding of the forces shaping political culture is bound to change. In one sense, this is frustrating to both researcher and reader. It is far more satisfying to be told "the truth" about political culture than to be told what "seems" to be the truth. In another sense, however, the tentativeness of our conclusions leaves us open to new information and new arguments. This keeps the imagination flexible and guards against dogmatism. Moreover, it underscores how dependent we are on our techniques of study for the conclusions we reach. Indeed, it is not possible to judge the adequacy of our understanding of political culture unless we know how the information is gathered and what strengths or weaknesses lie in our methods.

26

NEW SOCIAL MOVEMENTS

New Social movements have become increasingly prominent actors in the political lives of most advanced industrial states. The goals of these movements range widely—from environmentalism, peace, and animal rights, to feminism and the quality of life. Even so, they have a number of features in common: all question the traditional priorities of industrial society, they call for new forms of political representation, they attract support from the new middle class, and they rely upon unconventional styles of political participation. In this reading, Karl-Werner Brand draws attention to the predecessors of these new movements as he searches for historical cycles. In doing so, Brand accentuates the continuities rather than the novelty of these movements.

Karl-Werner Brand is Lecturer in Political Theory and Political Sociology at the Technical University of Munich, Germany.

This reading is an excerpt from his "Cyclical Aspects of New Social Movements: Waves of Cultural Criticism and Mobilization Cycles of New Middle-Class Radicalism" in Challenging The Political Order, *edited by Russell J. Dalton and Manfred Kuechler (Oxford University Press Inc.).*

• • • • • • • •

Since the beginning of the 1960s, various and sequential waves of new movements have changed social and political life in Western democracies. Among those which sprang up in the 1960s were public interest and citizen-action groups, community action, neighborhood and self-help groups, civil rights, anti-Vietnam war, and student movements. They were followed in the 1970s and early 1980s by women's, regional, environmental, anti-nuclear power, and peace movements. New left-libertarian and green political parties evolved, and a variety of subcultural life-styles and new "alternative" urban milieus grew rapidly. This development undercut the post-war consensus which had suggested the "end of ideology," based on advancing economic growth and industrial modernization.

In the 1950s and early 1960s empirical findings of a relatively high degree of political apathy were still functionally interpreted as a prerequisite to stability in Western democracies. Then, analysts were confronted by widespread social mobilization which appeared not only to overload existing institutions of political participation but also questioned established structures of governance and legitimacy. In the view of conservative observers—or those who had become conservative vis-à-vis the new confrontation—a "crisis of governability" was threatening Western democracies.

Only twenty years later, in the mid-1980s, almost all observers agree that the wave of political participation and movement mobilization has ebbed. The utopian visions of the 1960s and 1970s have faded away. The movements' impulses have diffused into cultural and social life. Their themes (environmental protection, disarmament, women's equality, self-help, decentralization) have won a permanent slot on political agendas. Their organizations and the new forms of politics they created are becoming institutionalized. A new normalcy is apparently emerging (for West Germany, see Brand, Büsser, and Rucht, 1986) ....

NEW SOCIAL MOVEMENTS: SKETCH OF A NEW MOVEMENT TYPE

Discussing the specifics of "new social movements," most observers agree on the following points (see Klandermans, 1986):

- new social movements are not concerned with questions of distribution, economic power, or political power; rather, they stress questions of the way and the quality of life in modern, industrial societies;
- these movements recruit primarily from the well-educated post-war generation of the new middle class, in changing coalitions with marginalized social groups;
- they do not evolve a new consistent ideological system. Instead, new movements emphasize the "right to uniqueness" within the context of a secular, pluralistic culture and on the basis of postmaterialist values;
- they emphasize principles of autonomous, decentralized organization;
- they have conferred a new acceptability on "unconventional" forms of political participation.

Is this shift in themes, social actors, organizations, and action forms *vis-à-vis* the "old" class and status movements permanent? Are there indicators that new stable cleavages are developing, or at least a new and permanent conflict constellation? Any answers to these questions will be more or less speculative. Nevertheless, existing empirical research on new movements, as well as the visible features of ongoing socio-structural transformation, provide some indications of their social and political perspectives.

My thesis is that this openness to and dependence upon changing social moods has substantially influenced the development and the public resonance of the new movements, their rise in the 1960s, their thematic shifts in the 1970s, and their decline in the 1980s. This will be seen in more detail in the next section.

FROM THE 1950s TO THE 1960s: CHANGING SOCIAL MOODS AND THE MOBILIZATION CYCLE OF NEW SOCIAL MOVEMENTS

Looking back over three decades, it seems evident that the changing social climate of these times had a persistent influence on the development of new social movements, on changes in their thematic emphases, standards of criticism, utopian models, and mobilization opportunities. At the same time, then, it is surprising that the role of social moods has until now hardly been studied systematically within the context of social movement research.

What I call the *Zeitgeist*, "social mood," or "cultural climate" of a given period means the specific configuration of world-views, thoughts and emotions, fears and hopes, beliefs and utopias, feelings of crisis or security, of pessimism or optimism, which prevail in this period. This *Zeitgeist* creates a specific sensitivity for problems; it narrows or broadens the horizon of what seems socially and politically feasible; it directs patterns of political behavior and life-styles; it channels psycho-social energies outward into the public or inward into the private sphere. Thus it provides or deprives social movements of essential public response.

Some recent publications by American authors point to the cyclical appearance of a cultural climate which promotes an overall social and political mobilization. Hirschman (1982) conceptualizes these cycles as a periodic alternation between times of "private interest" and "public action." Schlesinger (1986) reconstructs these continuing shifts in 30-year cycles of American history. Huntington (1981) proposes a 60-year cycle of "creedal passion periods." Namenwirth and Weber (1987) postulate a long-term cycle of value change of about 150 years and a short-term cycle of about 50 years on the basis of a quantitative content analysis of American party platforms and British "Speeches From the Throne." It still remains questionable, however, whether there exists a general cultural climate which is equally supportive or inhibitive to all kinds of social movement. The mobilization waves of labor movement and middle-class radicalism by no means always converge. Thus the assumption that for different kinds of social movements there are also differing favorable or unfavorable conditions within the cultural context seems more tenable. The following discussion focuses on a special variation of such social moods—the spread of cultural criticism or modernization critique—which provide new social movements as well as their predecessors with an especially favorable sounding-board.

Before turning to empirical evidence for this thesis, however, I want to introduce the concept of cultural criticism as it is used here more systematically. What I call "cultural criticism" or "modernization critique" means a heterogeneous pattern of critique of fundamental aspects of modern life, such as commercialization, industrialization, political centralization, bureaucratization and democratization, cultural rationalization and pluralization. I refer to this concept in a threefold sense.

First, critique of modernization can feed on pre-modern, agrarian, religion-based world-views. This kind of anti-modernism develops during the stages of transition from traditional to modern societies. It can take the form of criticism "from below" referring to popular traditions, and the form of criticism "from the top" referring to old patterns of legitimacy and social order.

Second, critique of modernization can appear in a form that is best described with the German term *Zivilisationskritik*. This form of cultural criticism is no longer embedded in an agrarian, pre-modern way of life. Rather, it springs from an already, at least to some extent, modernized society which experiences a rapid change in social structures and what Nietzsche termed a "re-evaluation of all values." Anti-modern attitudes of this kind have a pessimistic touch. They get their special characteristics by a general feeling of a loss of sense and orientation and by fears of status deprivation, moral decay, and social decline. Compensatorily, a sentimental attachment to pastoral traditions, to rural life with its simple virtues, spreads; an idealized nature becomes the source of moral and physical recovery. Moralistic and puritanic traits also become stronger.

Third, critique of modernization can take the form of an artistic and intellectual criticism of alienation, which appears in two variations: one that is primarily aesthetical, and another that is primarily moral-idealistic. The latter is aroused by the discrepancy between universal, humanistic values and the harsh reality of economic exploitation, political oppression, and social misery; or in a more general sense, by the contrast between moral principles and the functional imperatives of capitalist, industrial, and bureaucratic development. The aesthetic-countercultural variant takes classical form in the European Romanticism of the early nineteenth century. Initially a revolt against the Enlightenment, against obsolete rules and conventions, utilitarianism, and the mechanistic belief in progress, romanticism is the expression of a new subjective sensibility. In addition, it is deeply impressed by the cataclysmic events of the French Revolution and the dissolution of the old order. Thus it displays a tension between cultural avantgardism (an aesthetic cult of individuality) and a feeling of homelessness, a yearning for "real community," for a reconciliation of the world through love, "poetization of life," or religious feeling. Seen structurally, the appearance of this kind of cultural criticism is connected with the rise of a new class of autonomous artists and "intellectuals."

These patterns of modernization critique usually appear together, in various mixtures, in times of widespread cultural criticism. In Western countries, however, the pre-modern variant of anti-modernism has progressively lost ground from the middle of the nineteenth century onward.

Coming back to the cultural context of the mobilization cycle of new social movements, a typical sequence of basic social moods can be determined from the 1950s to the 1980s in virtually all Western democracies: from the conservative 1950s with their emphases on private and material values, to the technocratic reform enthusiasm, the optimistic cultural-revolutionary thrust and moral radicalism of the 1960s, changing to the sobering 1970s which saw a growing crisis-consciousness and the spread of pessimistic anti-modern moods, finally giving way to the neo-conservative, "postmodern" *Zeitgeist* of the 1980s. It is the social mood of cultural criticism of the 1960s and 1970s—a mix of moral-idealistic and aesthetic-countercultural critique of modernization, on the one hand, and a more pessimistic pattern of *Zivilisationskritik*, on the other hand — which gives the new movements, as part of a comprehensive social-mobilization process, their stimulus. Both decades, however, create differing sensibilities to problems of capitalist democracies and the industrial way of life which open up differing perspectives for social action.

In each country, of course, this general sequence of prevailing social moods is modified by the specifics of national politics, economic development, and political culture. In particular, there are very different historical burdens and starting points for post-war development in countries such as the Federal Republic and the United States. These national variations are also dependent on the differing ability of the new movements to gain public acceptance for their definition of problems and reality. In this chapter, however, only the general trends are at issue. Focusing on the question of how these changing cultural opportunity structures influence the development of new social movements, these general shifts in the cultural climate will now be discussed in more detail.

The 1950s and early 1960s were times of generally stable economic growth which parallel a previously unknown increase in material standards of living. Standardized, durable mass consumer goods (televisions, refrigerators, washing machines, automobiles) became available to almost everyone. Supermarkets and self-service stores expanded; advertising became omnipresent and a prime growth sector. Structural economic changes increased the proportion of white-collar jobs. Science and technology became socially dominant forces, also in the public's consciousness. Old class contrasts appeared to erode. The rise of the "affluent society" heralded the "end of ideology." Functional thinking, belief in technical progress, privatized-material orientations, and a moral conventionality moulded the world of the 1950s. Anti-communism and the cold war reinforced this domestic political complacency. That applies to the America of Eisenhower no less than to the West Germany of Adenauer or Britain's "Butskellism," supported by a new social welfare state consensus.

The 1960s saw a dramatic shift of personal attention and energies to the public sphere. The consensus about the prevailing *petit-bourgeoisie*, privatistic values broke down. The complacency of the 1950s gave way to a critical view of and moral outrage about the shadowy side of the "affluent society." The still-existing and considerable sector of poverty, continuing race and minority-group discrimination, and decay of metropolitan areas appeared as scandals against the background of a continually improving standard of living and a basic, unbroken belief in modern progress. Measured against the universally propagated ideals of Western democracies—freedom, self-determination, equal opportunities—established structures of power and inequality appeared unbearable. So did idealistically embellished military inventions in foreign countries. This criticism which began to divide younger and older generations was intensified still further by the growing importance of consumption and leisure time, which stimulated the rise of a new hedonism and lifestyle oriented toward self-fulfilment, sexual freedom, and spontaneity. Measured against modernism's promises of happiness, the successor generation found life boring, empty, and alienating in a society focused on acquisition and functionality. The break in values taking place in this generation since the beginning of the 1960s—gradually at first and then increasingly confrontational—was indeed a cultural revolution penetrating all spheres of daily life.

The social movements of these years took the idealistic and utopian promises of the "affluent society" at their word, measured them against (inferior) reality, and emphatically demanded the promise as reality. But the still unbroken, optimistic belief in progress also nourished trust in technocratic solutions to existing problems "from the top" or the fundamental changeability of existing structures "from below". This tension between, on the one hand, various facets of emerging critique concerning the dark sides and deficits of advanced capitalism, and, on the other hand, the firm belief in the fundamental possibility of realizing its humanistic ideals, motivated the political reform phase of the 1960s (and in Europe also that of the early 1970s). This tension also underlay the exuberance of the cultural revolutionary uprising and the impetus for various emancipatory, consumption-critical, and romantic anti-capitalist movements of this period. Moreover, political reform programs and the pressure of social movements mutually strengthened one another.

In the 1970s the mood darkened. General optimism about progress and belief in the rapid changeability of political and social structures disappeared. Failure of utopian-anarchist expectations for revolutionary change furthered dogmatic tendencies and the development of many cadre-political sects within the New Left, and induced some to terrorist strategies. A more broadly effective reaction, however, involved the diversion of interest in social macro-structures to the closer proximity of everyday life. This subjective turn took on many different forms. It led to increasing interest in self-experiences and therapies of all sorts. Individual psychic and physical well-being moved to the center of attention, and a new health cult developed. A growing need for transcendental experiences and spirituality stimulated broad interest in Eastern religions and meditational techniques.

Apart from this subjective turn, there were also clearer articulations of interests related to encroachments on the quality of life, such as continuing environmental pollution and threats to health through noise, toxic substances, or nuclear radiation. Citizen initiatives and local self-help groups sprang up. Industrial conflicts became militant. Regional movements, rebelling against "internal colonialism," demanded cultural and political autonomy. Thus the "turn inward" also had a politically offensive impact. It created new conflicts around daily needs, questions of individual identity, and subjective concern about the burdens of economic, political, and cultural modernization. The low responsiveness of established political institutions to these new problems caused a rapid loss of legitimacy for political parties and government (in the American case accelerated by the Vietnam war and Watergate). That loss was paralleled by a higher evaluation of autonomous forms of interest representation.

These tendencies received a dramatic touch through a series of crisis experiences which fundamentally shattered the belief in technical progress and the trust in technological reform efforts. First, and most fundamentally, the limits of industrial growth burst into public consciousness in the early 1970s (at the latest with the 1973 oil crisis), mirrored in discussions about population explosion, exhaustion of natural resources, and threatening ecological catastrophes. Second, there was the additional experience of world-wide economic recession, paralleled by increasing unemployment and inflation which could not be effectively countered through the panacea of the 1960s, the touted Keynesian instrument. Third, the growing mood of crisis and loss of perspective was strengthened by disappointment with the low effectiveness and non-intentional counter-productive effects of the implemented policy reforms. All of that initiated a pessimistically tinged, anti-modern mood which has determined general sentiments since the mid-1970s. By this time, a general critique of technology, bureaucracy, and rationalism found broad public resonance. The urban middle class was caught up in a new longing for a simple, healthy, and natural way of life. There was also greater nostalgia for pre-modern ways of life and fascination with mystical, holistic, non-scientific ways of experiencing.

The mood-change toward anti-modern *Zivilisationskritik* produced ambivalent political results. On the one side, it substantially contributed to a conservative trend and a new moralism and traditionalism. On the other side, it strengthened ecological crisis-consciousness and interest in alternative life-styles. The ecological and anti-nuclear power movement focused the new uneasiness into mass protests. The anti-modern-tinged ecological protest, however, did not link up everywhere with the existing countercultural and emancipatory currents of protest. In only a few countries a new political polarization emerged as comprehensive as that in the Federal Republic of Germany (see Brand, 1985). In Germany, the anti-modernist mood of the 1970s was still aggravated by a deepening economic crisis and East-West tensions in the early 1980s; it solidified itself into a general catastrophism, giving impetus to a struggle against the deployment of middle-range missiles and to the new party of the Greens.

A further change in the *Zeitgeist* is obvious in the 1980s—a "postmodern" mood spreads. In it the fundamental critique of modernization loses much of its impetus. Concerns of the new social movements are taken up by parties and partially institutionalized. Alternative milieus lose their clear-cut oppositional identity. A new realism and pragmatism spreads. The historicism of postmodern architecture couples with the pluralism of life-styles: "anything goes." Yuppiedom, the unconcealed hunt after money and status symbols, stands unconnected next to poverty and mass unemployment. Neo-conservatism holds sway over the intellectual political climate. The Left, already deprived of its attraction by the prevailing anti-modernism of the 1970s, loses still more ground. Trade unions' negotiating power is persistently weakened by permanently high unemployment, forced economic and technological structural changes, and by massive governmental strategies of confrontation. Patriotism, orchestrated with new conservative self-confidence, unites with a nostalgic renaissance of the 1950s ....

RECURRING WAVES OF MODERNIZATION CRITIQUE AND THE PRECURSORS OF NEW SOCIAL MOVEMENTS

Figure 26.1 shows—for descriptive purposes—the periods marked by the upsurge of widespread cultural criticism (modernization critique), as well as the mobilizing phases of some of the precursors of the new social movements in the nineteenth and twentieth centuries for three countries (Germany, Great Britain and the United States). The figure includes the women's movement, the peace movement, and the environmental movement, as well as the broad spectrum of "alternative

FIGURE 26.1 *Periods of cultural criticism, phases of high movement mobilization, and long-term economic waves in Britain, Germany, and the United States, 1800–1990*

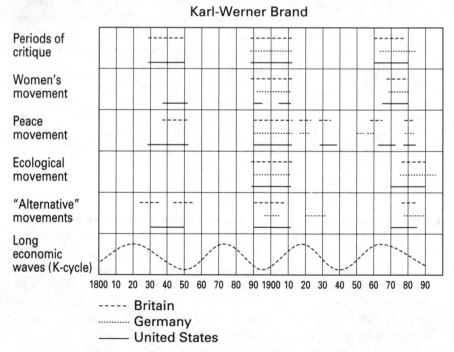

Source: Compiled by the author. Long-term economic waves are from Gordon et al., 1982.

movements." Although radical-democratic movements of young middle-class intellectuals or humanitarian crusades (such as the anti-slavery crusade) in the nineteenth century could also be regarded as predecessors of the new social movements, the selected movements appear to be typical of the specific mixture of emancipative, moral, and romantic-idealistic motives that inspired the movements of the 1960s and 1970s. Finally, the figure shows, for possibilities of comparison, the development of long-term economic waves that have become known as Kondratieff cycles (Gordon et al., 1982). Assuming that the industrial development of Western, capitalist societies follows long up-swing and down-swing phases which last some 40 to 60 years is still controversial (see Freeman, 1983). It seems to be, however, sufficiently supported for use as a heuristic model.[1] The question is whether or not these long economic waves coincide with the periodical appearance of widespread cultural criticism and new middle-class radicalism, thus suggesting some kind of causal linkage.

The mobilization phases of the selected movements cannot always be dated precisely to the exact year. Only occasionally is the beginning or the end of a phase of increased mobilization indicated by clear-cut events. The development of the movement organizations, for example, does not always coincide with the development of the movement's following and public resonance. Most historical studies agree, however, in the dating of their ups and downs.[2] Certainly, the exact timing of the spread of anti-modern or modernization-critical moods is more difficult. The degree to which such currents influence the way of thinking and feeling of a given period has to be reconstructed from contemporary documents, from *feuilleton* and public speeches, literary and artistic trends, the development of new scientific (and anti-scientific) schools and last, but not least, from the anxieties and utopias underlying the various social reactions to the problems of their times. For the purpose of this discussion, however, I date these phases by means of a secondary analysis of relevant cultural and socio-historical studies.

MOBILIZATION WAVES OF THE PRECURSORS OF NEW SOCIAL MOVEMENTS

Whereas the *women's movement* in England and Germany did not take organizational shape before the middle of the nineteenth century, eliciting only gradually broader responses, the women's movement in the United States experienced a first peak in its formative years in the 1840s, initially in close association with the anti-slavery crusade. In all three countries, however, feminism developed into a true mass movement only during the two decades surrounding the turn of the century (Banks, 1981; Evans, 1977; Flexner, 1975; Rendall, 1984; Rowbotham, 1973; Schenk, 1981).

Organized pacifism begins with the end of the Napoleonic wars, when peace societies were founded almost simultaneously in England (1816) and the United States (1815). In these two countries the peace movement showed a first broad mobilizing phase in the 1830s and 1840s. But pacifism, too, became a mass movement only around the turn of the century, and in Germany as well. The years after World World I brought a widespread revival of anti-military feeling and pacifist movements in Europe. Whereas in Germany they flourished only up to the mid-1920s, there was a new upsurge of pacifism in Britain at the end of the 1920s, which lasted till the confrontation with Fascism began to absorb the intellectuals' political commitment. In the United States, a new wave of pacifism spread in the 1930s, combining with the struggle against economic exploitation, and coming to an end before World War II. The Cold War atmosphere of the post-war era proved uncongenial to the expansion of pacifist ideas, in both Britain and the United States. Only in West Germany did the moral burdens of the Nazi regime and the still fresh remembrance of the catastrophic war destructions cause an upsurge of protest against rearmament and the deployment of nuclear weapons in the 1950s. The British CND, however, starting at the end of the 1950s, heralded the subsequent mobilization cycle of the new social movements (Brock, 1968, 1970, 1972; Riesenberger, 1985).

Environmentalism as an organized movement can be traced back to the early Victorian campaign against cruelty to animals and for bird protection, to the spread of natural history societies from the 1830s onward, or to the beginnings of a romantically inspired protection of natural monuments. Toward the end of the century, the increasing anti-urbanism and the nostalgic idealization of wilderness and rural life gave these efforts the impetus of a true mass movement, speeding up legislation of nature and monument preservation, animal and plant protection, and the establishment of national parks. Outdoor activities, such as cycling, hiking, and camping came into fashion. The popularity of the outdoor movement increased still further in the inter-war period; landscape and city planning, as well as safeguarding of natural resources, obtained a higher political priority. It was not before the 1960s, however, that environmental issues triggered another sweeping public mobilization (Hays, 1958; Linse, 1986; Lowe, 1983; Lowe and Goyder, 1983; O'Riordan, 1971; Sheail, 1976).

Whereas these movements showed a gradual (even though discontinuous) growth in the nineteenth and twentieth centuries, *alternative movements* manifest much less organizational continuity. The 1830s and 1840s were a time of social criticism, mass agitations and liberal reform campaigns in both Anglo-Saxon countries. In this context, alternative movements experienced a first, modest bloom as well. Under the influence of Owenism and Fourierism, an unprecedented wave of commune-building spread. The temperance movement, too, had its first peak during the 1840s. Again, it was not until the turn of the century that the spectrum of alternative movements fanned out into a multitude comparable only with their development in the 1960s and 1970s: the "thousand blossoms" of utopian-anarchist and agrarian-socialist movements, the back-to-the-land and back-to-nature movements, libertarian community experiments, sectarian "life-reform" movements (temperance, vegetarianism, nudism, naturopathy, anthropology, rational dress, school reform, and garden city movement, etc.), counter-cultural youth movements and Bohemian settlements, the nostalgic revival of folklore, and rustic arts and crafts. Whereas this fascination with alternative ways of life found a quick end in World War I, in Germany youth movements, commune-building, and millenarian simple-life movements revived anew in the 1920s because of the fundamental crisis of political and economic life (Hardy, 1979; Krabbe, 1974; Linse, 1983; Marsh, 1982; Nash, 1967; Sieferle, 1984; Zablocki, 1980).

What general patterns evolve in the development of all of these movements?

- A first feature is the largely parallel nature of the mobilization phases of the individual movements. Only the peace movement shows independent, additional mobilization phases.

- A second is the largely parallel nature of these mobilization cycles in all three countries (in so far as the individual movements exist already).

- A third feature is the appearance of these mobilization cycles in specific historic periods and specific intervals: a beginning (in the Anglo-Saxon countries) during the period of 1830–50, a second all-embracing wave around the turn of the century (in Germany still continuing in the twenties), and a third still more sweeping wave in the 1960s and 1970s. The intervals between these periods of increased mobilization come to approximately 60–70 years.

These periods coincide with times of an emergent, pervasive mood of cultural criticism. This will be illustrated more in detail in the following section.

DESCRIBING PERIODS OF CULTURAL CRITICISM (MODERNIZATION CRITIQUE)

In the nineteenth and twentieth centuries, moods of cultural criticism swept in three waves across Europe and the United States: in the period of romanticism at the beginning of the nineteenth century which achieved its broadest effects in both Anglo-Saxon countries in the 1830s and 1840s; in the two decades around the turn of the century (in Germany a marked mood of *Zivilisationskritik* still prevailed in the 1920s); and in the 1960s and 1970s. The different historical and national conditions give these critiques of modernization a different thematic direction and a different political weight in each period and country.

The 1830s and 1840s are considered a turbulent period in both Anglo-Saxon countries. The contrasts between the old agrarian and the new industrial era, and between the aristocracy and the rising middle-class elite, overlapped with the tensions arising from the increasing social problems of early industrialization and the experience of cultural crisis disseminated by the accelerated spread of capitalism. Although the latter called forth anti-modern reactions which are fed by pre-modern, agrarian traditions as well as by a general romantic mood, these reactions were embedded in a dominant optimistic belief in moral and social progress which was carried by liberal and democratic groups forcing their way to power. Thus, the high sensibility to the problem of the time gave birth to a comprehensive social, political, and moral reform zeal, still fired by the gradually ebbing spirit of the preceding evangelical revival. This combined with the prevailing romantic element in the thoughts and feelings of that time, to give the various forms of social criticism, utopianism, revolt, and escapism their particular characteristics. It strongly influenced the philosophy of Transcendentalism; and it ignited as well a new bellicose national self-consciousness, for instance in Ireland and the Southern United States (Rose, 1981; Clark, 1955).

The romantic sentiment in Germany reached its zenith around 1800 and found its strongest political expression in the Anti-Napoleonic liberation war of 1813–15. The political restoration initiated by the Vienna Congress in 1815 caused a swift change of the romantic impulse for reconciliation into an idealization of traditional, hierarchical bonds and the sentimentality of the *petit-bourgeois* idyll of the "Biedermeier." The radical-democratic movements of intellectuals and *petit-bourgeois* classes originating in the French revolutions of 1830 and 1848 hardly showed any romantic specifics.

Towards the turn of the century a more pervading wave of anti-modernism spread in all three countries. In Europe, the third quarter of the nineteenth century was, like the period following the Civil War in the United States, a time of turbulent economic expansion which accelerated the transition from agrarian to industrial mass society. *Laissez-faire* liberalism, social Darwinism, fascination by positivist science and technology and a solid belief in material progress dominated the general way of thinking and feeling.

During the 1880s, however, a dissatisfaction with modern culture and industrial civilization spread on both sides of the Atlantic. The prevailing mechanistic conception of the world and the worship of material progress appeared increasingly hollow and empty in the eyes of a new middle-class generation. They rejected the artificiality and prudery of the Victorian or Wilhelminian conventions they sensed as an unreal façade. They also had a clearer view of the ugly side of industrialization, of the mass misery in the slum quarters of the cities, of the social, moral and psychological costs of progress. A realistic and naturalistic social criticism became dominant in the literature of the 1880s and 1890s. The feeling of over-civilization and spiritual homelessness paved the way for a wave of cultural criticism and anti-modernism. A new fascination with the fantastic, with occultism and spiritualism, grew. "Modern doubt" and a "morbid self-consciousness" expressed the feeling of *fin-de-siècle*, as did the melancholic aestheticism of Decadence. Growing anti-urbanism accompanied a revival of pastoral sentiments and a nostalgia for country life, folklore and handicrafts (Hynes, 1968; Krabbe, 1974; Lears, 1981; Marsh, 1982). In the United States, the return to the old republican values of the agrarian democracy promised the solution to the social, political and moral problems of over-civilization (Hofstadter, 1962). At the same time, vitalistic tendencies expanded, leading to an upsurge of enthusiasm for outdoor recreation and sports, a revitalized interest in wilderness, and the spread of a new "muscular spirit" (Higham, 1970). The erosion of conventional morality, however, also called forth massive religious counter-reactions. At the beginning of the nineteenth century, "purity crusades" in England gained a following that grew by leaps and bounds (Hynes, 1968).

All in all, the years before the turn of the century had a markedly pessimistic character, tinged by an atmosphere of crisis, self-doubt, introspection, nostalgia, and melancholy. In the early 1900s, the balance shifted to a regenerative activism in both Europe and America: in the United States to the reform zeal of Progressivism, in Edwardian England to an optimistic, liberal mood of breaking all traditional bonds. In Wilhelminian Germany the feelings of cultural awakening and of moving on the brink of a precipice remained closely interwoven with each other.

The social criticism and the idealistic reform impulse of the pre-war period gave way to a technical functionalism—the "new functionality"—and a withdrawal to private interests in the 1920s. In Germany, however, the political and economic turmoils of the 1920s caused a cultural atmosphere of uncertainty and disorientation which formed a fertile ground for the widespread criticism of modern civilization and a proliferation of anti-modern reactions, *völkisch* nationalism, and salvationism (Linse, 1983).

CONCLUSIONS

The historic materials presented here appear to support the thesis that the mobilization cycles of new social movements and their precursors find an exceptionally fertile ground in times of spreading cultural criticism. Such times heighten public sensitivity to the problems of industrialization, urbanization, commercialization, and bureaucratization. They temporarily upset the hegemony of the materialistic conception of progress, thus giving way to a broad spectrum of anti-modern reactions and reform movements. These phases also provide a short-lived opportunity for the creation of radicalized visions of a non-alienated, communal, and egalitarian way of living. Peace movements similarly profit from such moods, though they also emerge independently for a variety of reasons, such as the reaction to increased international tensions, or as an attempt to ban the experienced horrors of war.

The movements discussed here do not benefit equally from every kind of cultural criticism. Optimistic variants of a romantic-idealistic mood favor emancipatory, egalitarian, and cultural-revolutionary movements. Pessimistic moods of *Zivilisationskritik* favor escapist and nostalgic back-to-nature movements, environmental protection, self-help, and health and therapeutic movements. However, most themes of this middle-class radicalism experience only a shift of accent by the change from optimistic to pessimistic moods of modernization criticism and vice versa. Within the women's movement, for example, the accent may shift from the stress on universal demands as for equality of rights and self-determination to the stress on gender differences and a specific "female superiority."

Our findings regarding long economic waves suggest that optimistic versions of cultural criticism appear rather in times of economic prosperity (as between the turn of the century and World War I or in the 1960s); pessimistic versions appear in phases of economic down-swing and depression (as in the 1830s and 1840s, in the last two decades of the nineteenth century, in part in the 1920s, and again in the 1970s). But, obviously, the periodic appearance of anti-modernism and the new middle-class radicalism it feeds does not run parallel to the Kondratieff cycle (see Figure 26.1). So, one can conclude that neither economic up-swings nor down-swings cause the specific periodicity of recurring waves of cultural criticism. Whether such a periodicity exists at all remains an open question which cannot be answered on the basis of only three historical cases. If such moods spread, however, the economic situation strongly influences the kind and direction of criticism. But this is not all that can be said. There exists a more hidden link between socio-economic processes and these cultural and movement cycles which reveals itself if we look closer at the structural and political characteristics of the three periods in question.

The first wave of cultural criticism emerged in a transitional period, in which the old agrarian structure of society became more and more obsolete, whereas the outlines of the new bourgeois society were still fluid, bringing about new social misery as well as magnificent future prospects. In contrast, the other two waves appeared in fully developed capitalist societies. They were preceded by a long period of economic growth which triggered a rapid and comprehensive process of industrialization of production and everyday life. In both periods the material living conditions improved enormously for vast parts of the population. For the sons and daughters of the new middle classes—especially the liberal and educated—growing up in the boom phase, however, the material promises of industrial progress lost much of their attraction. The consensus on material progress broke down. Instead, the dark sides and the deficits of modernization, as well as the blocked possibilities of further emancipation, came more clearly into view.

But this is only one aspect, the postmaterialist side of the coin. In all three historical cases the emergence of new middle-class radicalism, nourished by the upsurge of cultural criticism, goes hand in hand with a more dramatic breakdown of the established basic consensus of social integration and political regulation caused by unintentional side-effects of economic and social modernization. In the first case, the upheaval of the 1830s and 1840s, the struggle between the supporters of the old, traditional order and the new, bourgeois society gave way to a new liberal order. In the second case, the rapid processes of industrialization and urbanization produced not only unprecedented social mobility and social strains concentrated in rapidly growing urban slums, it also gave birth to an increasingly militant and politically self-conscious working class eroding the hegemonic liberal consensus of the blossoming "Age of Capital" (Hobsbawm). Over a long period of bellicose imperialism, social struggles, economic depression, and the fascist challenge, a new class consensus of Keynesian politics and pluralist democracy established itself in the 1930s and 1940s. The latest wave of cultural criticism goes hand in hand with the breakdown of this post-war consensus in view of social and ecological "limits to growth" and industrialization, of a new technological revolution fundamentally transforming the social structure, and a cultural revolution equally radical in transforming the traditional socio-cultural patterns of orientation and behavior.

What conclusions can be drawn from this? If the latter two cases (the first showing a more diffused pattern) may be generalized upon, cultural criticism and new middle-class radicalism spread in the wake of a period of rapid industrial growth and social transformation, favored by the establishment of a new model of political integration and development promising progress and the solution of longstanding problems and social conflicts. Losing much of its attraction for a successor generation and showing by this time its negative side-effects and new structural problems more publicly, this model, however, is being questioned more and more. The level and the intensity of conflict increase, disseminating feelings of crisis and alienation, but, at the same time, opening up new horizons of alternative models of development and social life ....

The revival of a new wave of modernization critique in the 1960s and 1970s makes it clear that its appearance does not represent a transitional phenomenon that will disappear with the establishment of a full-fledged industrial society. Rather, it accompanies the dynamic of capitalist and industrial development which does not come about gradually, but in discontinuous processes of crisis, disorganization and restructuring. It is not before the 1960s and 1970s, however, that the specific kind of new middle-class radicalism which is fed by the periodic upsurge of modernization critique becomes a major political force in the restructuring processes of a new model of social integration and political development.

NOTES

1. The figure shows an approximate dating following the evidence in the literature on long-wave theory (see Freeman, 1983). The timing of up-swing and down-swing phases by different scholars largely coincides.
2. One substantial difference in the timing of mobilization waves is provided by O'Riordan (1971) and Lowe and Goyder (1983), who identify three instead of two peaks in the history of environmental movements. In addition to the upsurge of environmentalism around the turn of the century and in the 1960s–1970s, they observe another peak in the 1930s. In the United States, however, this was not a mass-based movement, but a new political emphasis on rational planning of resource use. In the case of Britain, this refers primarily to the spread of groups organizing outdoor activities.

REFERENCES

Banks, Olive. 1981. *Faces of Feminism: A Study of Feminism as a Social Movement*. New York: St Martin's Press.

Brand, Karl-Werner, ed. 1985. *Neue soziale Bewegungen in Westeuropa und in den USA: Ein internationaler Vergleich*. Frankfurt/New York: Campus.

Brock, Peter. 1968. *Pacifism in the United States: From the Colonial Era to the First World War*. Princeton, NJ: Princeton University Press.

Brock, Peter, 1970. *Twentieth Century Pacifism*. New York: Van Nostrand.

Brock, Peter, 1972. *Pacifism in Europe to 1914*. Princeton, NJ: Princeton University Press.

Clark, Kitson. 1955. The Romantic Element—1830 to 1850. In John Plumb, ed., *Studies in Social History: A Tribute to G.M. Trevelyan*. London: Longmans, Green and Co.

Evans, Richard J. 1977. *The Feminists: Women's Emancipation Movements in Europe, America and Australasia 1840–1920*. London: Croom Helm.

Flexner, Eleanor. 1975. *Century of Struggle: The Women's Rights Movement in the United States*. Revised edn, Cambridge: Harvard University Press.

Freeman, Christopher, ed. 1983. *Long Waves and the World Economy*. London: Butterworth.

Freeman, Jo. 1983. A Model for Analyzing the Strategic Options of Social Movement Organizations. In Jo Freeman, ed., *Social Movements of the Sixties and Seventies*. New York and London: Longman.

Gordon, David, R. Edwards, and M. Reich. 1982. *Segmented Work, Divided Workers: The Historical Transformation of Labor in the United States*. Cambridge: Cambridge University Press.

Hardy, Dennis. 1979. *Alternative Communities in Nineteenth Century England*. London and New York: Longman.

Hays, Samuel P. 1958. *Conservation and the Gospel of Efficiency: The Progressive Conservation Movement, 1890–1920*. Cambridge, MA: Harvard University Press.

Higham, John. 1970. The Reorientation of American Culture in the 1890s. In J. Highman, *Writing American History: Essays on Modern Scholarship*. Bloomington, IN/London: Indiana University Press.

Hirschman, Albert. 1982. *Shifting Involvements: Private Interests and Public Action*. Princeton, NJ: Princeton University Press.

Hobsbawm, Eric. 1975. *The Age of Capital, 1848–1875*. New York: Scribner.

Hofstadter, Richard. 1962. *The Age of Reform: From Bryan to F.D.R.* London: Jonathan Cape.

Huntington, Samuel. 1981. *American Politics: The Promise of Disharmony*. Cambridge, MA: Harvard University Press.

Hynes, Samuel. 1968. *The Edwardian Turn of Mind*. Princeton, NJ: Princeton University Press.

Klandermans, Bert. 1986. New Social Movements and Resource Mobilization: The European and American Approaches. *International Journal of Mass Emergencies and Disasters*, 4: 13–39.

Krabbe, Wolfgang R. 1974. *Gesellschaftsveränderung durch Lebensreform.* Göttingen: Vandenhoeck and Ruprecht.

Lears, Jackson T.J. 1981. *No Place of Grace: Antimodernism and the Transformation of American Culture 1880–1920.* New York: Pantheon Books.

Linse, Ulrich. 1983. *Zurück o Mensch zur Mutter Erde: Landkommunen in Deutschland 1890–1933.* München: DTV.

Linse, Ulrich. 1986. *Ökopax und Anarchie: Eine Geschichte der ökologischen Bewegungen in Deutschland.* München: DTV.

Lowe, Philip D. 1983. Values and Institutions in the History of British Nature Conservation. In A. Warren and F. B. Goldsmith, eds, *Conservation in Perspective.* Chichester: Wiley.

Lowe, Philip, and Jane Goyder. 1983. *Environmental Groups in Politics.* London: George Allen and Unwin.

Marsh, Jan. 1982. *Back to the Land: The Pastoral Impulse in Victorian England, 1880–1914.* London: Quartet Books.

Namenwirth, Zvi J. and Robert P. Weber. 1987. *Dynamics of Culture.* Boston, MA: Allen and Unwin.

Nash, Roderick. 1967. *Wilderness and the American Mind.* New Haven, CT, and London: Yale University Press.

O'Riordan, Timothy. 1971. The Third American Conservation Movement: New Implications for Public Policy. *Journal of American Studies,* 5: 155–71.

Rendall, Jane. 1984. *The Origins of Modern Feminism: Women in Britain, France and the United States, 1780–1860.* London: Macmillan.

Riesenberger, Dieter. 1985. *Geschichte der Friedensbewegung in Deutschland: Von den Anfängen bis 1933.* Göttingen: Vandenhoeck.

Rose, Anne C. 1981. *Transcendentalism as a Social Movement, 1830–1850.* New Haven, CT: Yale University Press.

Rowbotham, Sheila. 1973. *Hidden from History.* London: Pluto Press.

Schenk, Herrad. 1981. *Die feministische Herausforderung: 150 Jahre Frauenbewegung in Deutschland.* Munich: Beck Verlag.

Schlesinger, Arthur M. jr. 1986. *The Cycles of American History.* Boston, MA: Houghton Mifflin Company.

Sheail, John. 1976. *Nature in Trust: The History of Conservation in Britain.* London: Blackie.

Sieferle, Rolf P. 1984. *Fortschrittsfeinde? Opposition gegen Technik und Industrie von der Romantik bis zur Gegenwart.* München: C.H. Beck.

Zablocki, Benjamin. 1980. *Alienation and Charisma: A Study in Contemporary American Communes.* New York: Free Press.

27

POLITICAL PARTIES

*I*n Western liberal democracies, political parties evolved with the extension of the franchise. As universal adult suffrage was achieved, political parties became a fundamental institution associated with democracy. Providing a critical link between society and government, the rulers and the ruled, they were facilitators of modern participatory politics.

Political analysts have theorized that political parties were vital in making democracies work. Parties were said to perform many important roles in the political process—acting as an outlet for public involvement in politics, providing representation and recruitment, and serving to integrate a variety of interests in society.

While political parties are highly visible and active at time of elections, they have not been crucial players between elections in the policy-making process. In fact, other institutions in the political process such as the executive and the bureaucracy have become the central focus in organizing the public policy agenda. This shift in responsibility from political parties to the political executive has led to hypotheses about the "decline of political parties." John Meisel's article addresses this issue by reviewing the traditional roles of political parties, and explaining why some of these roles have been assumed by other organizations in the governmental process.

John Meisel is Sir Edward Peacock Professor of Political Science at Queen's University, Kingston, Ontario. He has written a number of books and articles on elections, political parties, and politics in Canada. He is a former chairman of the Canadian Radio-television and Telecommunications Commission; has served on numerous royal commissions, task forces, and inquiries; and is a past president of *the Canadian Political Science Association. The reading, "The Decline of Party in*

Canada," appears in Party Politics in Canada.

• • • • • • • •

Anthony King, in a searching paper analyzing the role of parties in liberal democracies, summarizes much of the relevant literature by listing six usually cited functions of parties: (1) structuring the vote; (2) integration and mobilization of the mass public; (3) recruitment of political leaders; (4) organization of government; (5) formation of public policy; and (6) aggregation of interests. He notes that there is a good deal of imprecision in the manner in which political scientists deal with the roles of parties and that the importance of their functions tends to be exaggerated. Nevertheless, he concludes, parties are critical components of the political process and they need to be studied, albeit with greater precision than is often the case.

This article shares King's view and, although it focuses on the relative decline of political parties in Canada, it should not be interpreted as arguing that the parties and the party system are insignificant. Parties clearly still influence critical aspects of politics and, most notably, they influence who occupies the government benches in parliament and who heads the various departments and ministries. The emphasis in this article is on federal politics, although many of the observations also apply to the provincial arena.

Parties still perform the first function listed: they structure the vote in most elections, except at the municipal level. They, to some measure, present options to the electorate about current issues and so can be said to organize mass opinion, although one is often tempted to conclude that they disorganize it. As for the related role of mobilizing the public, a remarkably high proportion of Canadians participate in elections in one way or another, and by no means just by voting. The preparation of electoral lists, staffing the polling booths, and organizing the campaigns on a polling-division by polling-division basis all takes a great deal of effort, most of which is provided by volunteer activists. This not only enables the electoral process to function, it increases the public's knowledge of political questions and facts. It is well-established that a greater sense of partisan attachment is associated with a greater knowledge of politics.

Nevertheless, an increasing number of Canadians have sought to participate in politics and public life outside the framework of parties— in tenants' or neighbourhood organizations or through voluntary associations, from unions to environmental or anti-nuclear groups. There was an upsurge of such "unconventional" politics in the sixties in the United States and to a lesser extent in Canada, but there is some uncertainty about the degree to which non-partisan politics has continued to flourish in North America in the seventies. Although the situation in Canada is a little ambiguous, there is no doubt that the proportion of people in the United States who identify with political parties in the sense that they think of themselves as Democrats or Republicans is steadily declining.

Parties also recruit politicians, although many question whether, in general, politics attracts a sufficiently high calibre of individuals. Data are unavailable on this point but some speculate that other careers appeal to the ablest Canadians and they conclude that we could do with a good deal more talent in the parties. This question raises another, also imperfectly understood puzzle: what characteristics make for a good politician? Indeed, what is a good politician?

By deciding which partisan team forms the government and who is in opposition, parties do organize government in an important way. But there is little doubt that a great many decisions about what is placed on the public agenda and at what time, are forced on political parties by events, non-political decision-makers, and very often the preferences of powerful civil servants, whose responsibility to the politicians is increasingly more formal than real. Even the organization of the government—the way in which legislation is drafted and considered by the cabinet and its committees, the extent to which outside interests are consulted, the manner in which policies are administered—is more likely to reflect the wills of a small number of senior civil servants than the decision of senior party officials, including the ministers. It is indeed questionable whether the government party leader—the prime minister—continues to function as a party person after accession to power or whether the party role and influence are maintained as a successful administration becomes accustomed to power and develops close relationships with senior civil servants.

In short, one must ask whether the parties really play the central role liberal democratic theory ascribes to them in organizing government and in the formation of public policy. And, given the changes in communication and the importance of voluntary associations and interest groups, one wonders about the relative unimportance of parties in the processes which aggregate the interests of various individuals and groups into satisfactory policies.

In seeking to identify the main manifestations of, and reasons for, the decline of party, relative to other political factors, this essay distinguishes between long-run factors, most of which are universal in liberal democracies and appear to a greater or lesser extent in most highly industrialized and post-industrial societies, and those which are of more recent origin and uniquely Canadian.

LONG-RUN REASONS FOR PARTY DECLINE

Rise of the Bureaucratic State

Modern political parties evolved from small cliques of power-wielders when the extension of the franchise necessitated the organization of mass electorates. The greater participation of the public in political life led, in conjunction with other factors, to the emergence of the positive state—one which increasingly participated in virtually every aspect of the human experience. But the "ancestors" of our political institutions and the political parties serving them evolved at a time when governments were dealing with a limited range of problems, and when only a small minority of the population was politically active. Under these conditions parties were able to act as suitable links between the small electorate and the even smaller number of political decision-makers.

The continuous expansion of governmental activities has created mounting problems for the legislative and representative system. Up until the First World War, the Canadian parliament dealt with only a small number of issues, met seldom and required little specialized and technical knowledge to operate. Now the number and complexity of the areas in which the federal government operates are so vast that it is quite impossible for MPs to be abreast of what is going on. At best, each can become reasonably well-informed about one or two areas.

The expansion of government activities and the increasingly complicated nature of government decisions have reduced the capacity of elected officials to deal with many important public issues and necessitated the restructuring of many governmental institutions. Thus MPs and even cabinet ministers are often incapable of fully understanding the problems and options confronting them, and the normal structure of ministries is being supplemented by a large number of quasi-independent administrative, regulatory and judicial boards and commissions not directly responsible to the elected representatives of the public or to party politicians. In short, an important shift has occurred in the locus of power of liberal democracies, from elected politicians to appointed civil servants, whose links to political parties are indirect and increasingly tenuous. This means that parties, supposedly in control of the political process and responsible to the public for its performance, are often little more than impotent observers of processes they cannot control and the results of which they can only rubber stamp.

A good illustration is the case of irregularities in the sale of reactors by Atomic Energy of Canada Ltd., a crown corporation, to Argentina and Korea. There were strong suspicions that bribes had been paid and that the foreign exchange regulations of some countries had been violated.

Enormous commissions were also allegedly paid to shadowy foreign agents. One of the reactors was sold at a loss of over 100 million dollars. The Public Accounts Committee of the House of Commons held extensive hearings and questioned closely Mr. J.L. Gray, president of Atomic Energy of Canada at the time of the sales. His stonewalling of the issue, and that by everyone else connected with the matter, was so effective that the House of Commons committee failed to shed light on the sales and finally had to let the case rest.

Pluralism and the Rise of Interest Group Politics

Before the expansion of governmental activities and the increase in their complexity, the usual pattern of lawmaking was relatively simple. Ministers or the whole cabinet, with or without prompting by their civil servants, decided on the broad outlines of what needed to be done. Civil servants, drawing on expert knowledge and advice, prepared the necessary background papers and draft proposals. These were discussed by the ministers, in the absence of their civil servant advisors, and ultimately presented to parliament for enactment. The basic decisions were essentially those of politicians and their officials. More recently, a more involved process of legislation has evolved, partly because of the need to deal with problems having enormous ramifications, partly in an effort to make government more participatory, and partly in response to the claims of a market-oriented, pluralist society in which political parties depend on the financial support of powerful economic interests or of unions. Before any law or important administrative decision is decided upon, an intense consultation between officials and representatives of various vested interests takes place. There has been a striking increase in lobbying by interest groups who have the resources and capacity to do so. Many important decisions are arrived at through private consultations between civil servants and spokesmen for various vested interests, during which politicians play no role. By the time ministers enter the decision-making process, the die is cast and only minor changes, if any, can be made. The *general* interest, therefore, as aggregated by political parties, tends to receive scant attention and parties are left with little choice but to approve what has already been decided by others. The process of consultation is for the most part totally non-partisan and most ministers engaged in it act as governmental decision-makers, far removed from their party personas. For the government party caucus to disown government policies already decided on after considerable negotiations would be politically harmful and is hardly ever heard of. Convincing testimony of the relative impotence of parties is found in Robert Presthus's study of Canadian interest groups, which shows that the latter spend considerably more time and effort lobbying bureaucrats than members of parliament. Furthermore, it is clear that having recourse to pressure group participation in policy-making is not a feared or temporary phenomenon. The Canadian government, like many others, has institutionalized the practice by appointing large numbers of advisory committees and other bodies designed to ensure the pressure of interested parties in the policy process.

Incipient Corporatism

A related phenomenon received wide attention during the ill-fated, mid-1970s anti-inflation program of the federal government. Although the case is derived from Canadian experience, the phenomenon is not unique to this country. Efforts to control prices and wages required the cooperation of both management and labor. The idea was that federal economic policy would emerge from regular consultations between the government and representatives of labor, industry and business and that a group comprised of these interests would become institutionalized as a permanent consultative body. In the end, this structure was never established. It is difficult to see how this kind of change in the governmental process could have been made without undermining the power of parliament and hence of political parties. Compromises delicately wrought by a tripartite council would not likely be upset by the House of Commons even if members of the majority party wished to repudiate the deals made by their leadership.

Recourse to the tripartite consultative process reflects a tendency toward a new form of corporatism—a process of arriving at collective decisions through the efforts of representatives of the main "functional" interests in the country rather than of its territorial delegates. Because corporatism is usually associated with fascism, it is viewed with suspicion; but there is nothing inevitably authoritarian in it. There are corporatist elements in the usually high regarded Swedish politico-economic system. But whatever its general merits, corporatist institutions supplement legislatures and reduce the importance of political parties ....

Federal-Provincial Diplomacy

Another and increasingly threatening cause of the decline in the importance of parties lies in the changing nature of Canadian federalism. Accommodation between the various regions of the country (and to some extent, between special interests which happen to be in part regionally based) is taking place more and more through two mechanisms which are largely unrelated to party politics. The first of these is the federal-provincial prime ministerial conference, where Ottawa and the provinces hammer out compromises touching virtually every aspect of human experience. Most of these are the result of delicate bargaining on the part of eleven governments which sometimes cannot help but take positions imposed by other negotiators and which therefore cannot be anticipated by legislative caucuses, let alone by party supporters.

The second procedure through which policies are agreed upon by the federal and provincial governments is the regular meeting and consultation among federal and provincial officials. There are now thousands of such encounters annually and hundreds of formally established committees, task forces and work groups in which decisions are made which bind the participating governments. As with prime ministerial meetings, these encounters reach decisions which can be reversed or altered only at great cost—one not likely to be risked by rank-and-file members of political parties.

It can be argued that governments, at the ministerial level, are composed of leading party politicians and that their actions are in a sense those of political parties. This is technically correct, but the infrequent and unfocused expression of party opinion and the almost nonexistent party activity between elections deprive elected officials of any viable contact with their party organisms. There is, in contrast, a striking frequency and intensity of contract between office-holding politicians and civil servants and spokesmen for vested interests. It is no exaggeration to argue that although ministers, and through them, the officials who serve under them, formally reflect party interests, they do not do so in any meaningful way. Between elections, except for occasional and exceedingly rare party gatherings, the cabinet is the party, insofar as the government side of the equation is concerned. Thus, such major policy changes as the introduction of wage control in the seventies and Trudeau's 1983 resolve to play a mediating role between the superpowers were introduced without any party involvement of any sort.

The Rise of Electronic Media

Until the advent of radio and particularly of television, politicians were the most effective means through which the public learnt about political events. In many communities across the country the political meeting was not only an important means of communication but also prime entertainment. Political issues were personalized by politicians who, in addition to adding colour to the consideration of matters of public policy, lent the political process a gladiatorial dimension that heightened its public appeal.

Television has, to a great extent, changed all that. The average Canadian spends several hours a day watching all manner of programs among which political material plays a relatively minor role. The entertainment value of face-to-face politics has declined since there are so many other exciting things to watch. And the public perception of the political process and of political issues that remains is derived from television treatment of the news and of political personalities. Public taste and public opinion on almost everything is being shaped by television programs and television advertising. Politics and politicians are filtered by a medium in which the primary concern is often not enlightenment, knowledge or consciousness-raising but maximal audiences and profits. This has meant that even major political events like the choosing of national party leaders are dominated by the requirements of television. The organization and scheduling of meetings are arranged so that the most appealing events occur during prime time, when they are broadcast, and all other aspects, even the quality of discussion and the time spent on critical issues, are made subservient to the demands of the electronic media.

Television has to some extent wrested the limelight from party politicians; but, on the other hand, it provides a matchless opportunity for the public to witness the party game. Its coverage of the most colourful political events—leadership conventions, elections, and so-called debates between party leaders—furnishes unprecedented opportunities for parties to be seen in action. The problem is, of course, that the exposure is chosen by the media largely for entertainment value, rather than as a continuous in-depth exploration of the dominant political issues and partisan strategies. The focus tends to be on the people who report and comment on political news rather than on the political actors themselves. One result of this tendency is that public opinion on political matters is shaped as much by media intermediaries as it is by the protagonists representing the various parties. Furthermore, the key role of television is changing the character of political leadership. It is now virtually impossible for anyone who is not "telegenic" to be chosen as party chief. His or her presence and style on television can make or break a politician; yet, these are only some (and not the most important) attributes of an effective political and governmental figure.

Investigative Journalism

Although television has come to occupy a key position in the manner in which the public perceives political and party life, it has not eclipsed the more traditional ways of reporting and analyzing news and of entertaining the public. Newspapers and periodicals still receive considerable attention, particularly among the politically most active members of the public. Partly, no doubt, in response to the competition provided by TV and partly because of the intense rivalry among some of the major printed media, newspapers and magazines have recently resorted to numerous ploys designed to attract attention and a wider audience.

Among these, investigative journalism—a return of sorts to the old muckraking days—has been particularly important. Many of the major papers and some of the periodicals have sought to discover governmental lapses and to reveal wrongdoing on the part of local, provincial and federal authorities. These efforts at exposing flaws and shortcomings, errors, dishonesty and inefficiency perpetrated by governments have often led to the establishment of judicial and quasi-judicial inquiries and to the corroboration of the sins unearthed by the sleuthing journalists. The watch-dog function of the print and electronic media is important to the present argument because it can be seen as an encroachment upon, or at least a complement to, the role of opposition parties. They, of course, are the agents par excellence, according to conventional theory, for keeping governments on their toes and for publicizing their misdeeds.

Although opposition politicians and investigative journalists no doubt derive mutual benefit from one another's activities, the recent increase in the role of the media as agents unearthing governmental malfeasance, regardless of how beneficial it may be, detracts from one of the most essential roles of opposition parties—that of criticizing the government. This is not to say the activities of the journalists inhibit or hamper opposition politicians; on the contrary, the latter exploit them; but the relative importance of government debate is reduced when much of the combat occurs outside the party arena—on the printed page or the television screen. One of the questions presented by the new or perhaps revived emphasis in the media on tracking down governmental errors of commission or omission is in fact whether the often vigorous reportorial initiative of the media does not reflect a decline in the energy and resourcefulness of opposition parties. Like many of the arguments presented above, this is a question requiring systematic research.

Whatever the reasons, a considerable challenge of, and check on, governments today originate outside the realm of political parties and tend to reduce the effectiveness of the party system. The media may be able to report governmental failings, but they cannot provide alternative governments—one of the functions of opposition parties. By sharing with others the task of exposing and criticizing official actions (and by often being outdone by them), opposition parties lose some of their credibility as alternatives to the current power-holders.

Opinion Polling

Increasingly widespread use of opinion polls by the small groups of officials and cronies working with the party leader has diminished the need to rely on the knowledge of public attitudes by local militants and elected politicians. The vast, sensitive network of contacts, reciprocal favours, and exchanges of information which characterized the relationship between party leaders and their followers has to some extent been attenuated by the use of scientific sampling, sophisticated interviewing techniques and subtle statistical analyses. While the results are in some respects more reliable, there is also a decided loss: the interplay between public opinion and the leadership exercised by politically informed and concerned activists is substantially reduced. There is likely less debate and argument, since local party people are no longer encouraged to take the pulse of their "parishioners" and to mediate between the grass roots and the leadership. Public opinion, as defined by pollsters, guides political decisions more and political decision-makers are less involved in forming public opinion. Two consequences, at least, are relevant for our purposes: the character of political leadership and of political styles has changed and the party organization is no longer needed as an essential information network.

The Domination of Economic Interests

There is little agreement among scholars about the exact role of economic factors in the sociopolitical realm. Are the forces and relations of production basic causes of all other aspects of social organization or can social organization be manipulated through political means? Whatever one's judgment, one does not need to be an economic determinist to acknowledge that governments have frequently found it difficult to resist certain kinds of economic pressures or to work against certain economic realities. This vulnerability is enhanced by the greatly increased number and power of multinational corporations. These vast, globe-girdling enterprises are rarely dependent on their operations in any one political jurisdiction and are adept at playing one interest against another. The behaviour of the oil companies before, during and after the oil crisis of the seventies is a case in point. Even those who doubt that Canadian industry and business can withstand governmental pressure cannot ignore the fact that the multinationals, recognizing no loyalties other than to their balance sheets, can obviate, ignore, influence and even dominate Canadian governments. A striking example came to light in the autumn of 1977 when Inco, a Canadian-based multinational, which has benefited from lavish tax and other concessions, announced that it would lay off 3,000 employees in Canada. Against arguments to the effect that the company was at the same time using funds provided by Canadian taxpayers to expand productivity capacity overseas, a senior vice-president indicated that "fears of government takeover and other economic recriminations in Indonesia and Guatemala forced Inco ... to cut back production in Canada where massive layoffs could be made with little prospect of serious political interference." This episode provides an illuminating vignette illustrating the impotence of the Canadian government and of Canadian political parties, in the face of economic pressure from industry. This subservience of the political realm to the economic is related to the prevailing value system and dominant ideologies: when parties and governments buckle under economic pressure, they do so because they do not believe in interfering with private enterprise.

One-Party Dominance

Finally, among the long-run, general factors leading in the decline of party in Canada is the very nature of the Canadian party system. Its chief feature during this century has been that it is a one-party dominant system, in which the important alternation is not between different parties in office but between majority and minority Liberal governments. Increasingly, the line between the government and the Liberal party has become tenuous, leading Liberals have become ministerial politicians and the opposition parties have been out of office for so long that they are seldom perceived as being capable of governing, sometimes (according to one scholar) even by themselves.

Canada has long been in a situation in which there has been a serious loss of confidence in the government and in the government party and at the same time no corresponding or compensating sense that the opposition might do better. The latter was perceived as inexperienced, fragmented and disposed to attack on principle everything and everyone who had anything to do with the government. Public opinion polls taken after the 1975 Conservative leadership convention showed a major decline in Liberal support and corresponding upsurge in Conservative fortunes, but the election of a Parti Québécois government in November 1976 reminded Canadians of the woefully weak position of the Conservatives in Québec and of the fact that, in the past, only the Liberals (among the major parties) have tried to find a satisfactory accommodation between French and English Canada. The fear of national disintegration drove many voters back towards the Liberals, albeit with very little enthusiasm. Despite extensive doubt about the Liberals' capacity to provide adequate government (particularly west of the Ottawa River), the Conservatives were able, after the 1979 election, to form only a minority government which was toppled a few months after coming to power by the combined vote of the Liberals and NDP.

This reinforced the already strong sense, among most leading Liberals, that they are indispensable and (since the Canadian public seems to recurrently favour them), nearly infallible in dealing with Canadian problems. The sense of self-assurance—an increasingly important element in the party's physiognomy—has itself contributed a great deal to the decline of party in Canada.

Among the many other consequences of one-party dominance, one requires special notice in the present context. The less favoured parties (unless they are essentially doctrinaire organizations which attract ideologues regardless of electoral opportunities) experience great difficulty in attracting candidates of top quality. Highly successful and ambitious individuals do not, for the most part, wish to forsake promising careers in exchange for a difficult electoral campaign and, at best, an almost permanent seat on the opposition benches. In a system in which parties in power alternate, able deputies know that part of their career is likely to be spent in the cabinet and they may therefore be attracted to a political career even if their preferred party does not, in the short run, seem to stand a good chance of election.

SHORT-RUN CAUSES: THE LIBERAL STYLE

Disdain of Parliament

Prime Minister Trudeau is not, as has often been noted, a House of Commons man. He seems to hold Parliament in low esteem and is on record as questioning the intelligence of his opponents. He seldom uses parliament as the platform for important pronouncements, preferring to deliver policy statements or general reflections on the state of the country in public speeches, television interviews or press conferences. Having entered politics relatively late in life, and having been strongly critical of the Liberals, Pierre Trudeau's personal circle appears to be outside the ranks of the party he now leads, and outside of parliament. The two intimate colleagues who entered politics with him, Jean Marchand and Gérard Pelletier, were also not at home in the House of Commons milieu and have retired from it.

A significant decision of Mr. Trudeau, in the present context, was his move in 1968 to establish regional desks within the privy council office, which were designed to keep abreast of developments and ideas in the regions. A more party-oriented prime minister would have relied on his party contacts and on contacts in the House of Commons rather than on civil servants, and there was much criticism of the prime minister's move in the House of Commons and privately, among Liberal backbenchers. The desks as such have been abandoned but the government continues to bypass the House of Commons on some critical issues ….

Confusing the Public

A certain amount of sophistry is indigenous to politics when it comes to governments justifying their failure or unanticipated changes in their policies and strategy. But the public is not likely to maintain respect for either its government or the whole political system when it is confronted by an administration which, after an election, completely repudiates a major policy stand or when it welcomes into its ranks a former opposition member who has been a vociferous leader against one of its most important pieces of legislation. The Liberal party has done both, thereby weakening confidence in the integrity of our political parties and of their practitioners.

One of the principal differences in the platforms of the Liberal and Conservative parties in the 1974 election was the question of how to combat inflation. The Conservatives advocated a temporary price and wage freeze (pending the development of a permanent policy), for which the Liberals excoriated them, arguing that the public would never accept such controls. Having done much to undermine confidence in officially sanctioned constraints, and having given the impression that Canadians could not be trusted to cooperate in such a program, the government in 1975 introduced its own anti-inflation program, which froze wages and tried (unsuccessfully) to control prices. Not surprisingly, the government that campaigned on a vigorous anti-controls platform encountered considerable opposition when it tried to apply them.

The general language policy of the Official Languages Act of 1969 is one of the most important Liberal government attempts to promote national unity. Robert Stanfield, then Conservative leader, succeeded in persuading his party to follow him in supporting the language bill, but he was challenged and about twenty of his followers broke party ranks. None of them was more implacably opposed to efforts designed to assure that both French and English speaking Canadians could deal with the federal government in their own language than Jack Horner, the member for the Crowfoot constituency in Alberta. Mr. Horner had consistently been one of the most savage opponents of efforts to protect the French language and to create in Canada an ambience agreeable to francophones. However, after unsuccessfully contesting the Tory leadership, Mr. Horner became disillusioned with the leadership of his successful rival, crossed the floor of the House, and ultimately became a Liberal cabinet minister.

It is not always easy to distinguish between our two old parties but some basic diverging orientations do in fact divide them. One is the attitude they adopt towards French Canada. Although the official leadership of the Conservative party has, under Robert Stanfield, Joe Clark and Brian Mulroney, been sympathetic to the aspirations of French Canada, the party has always been plagued by a bigoted wing of members who lacked comprehension of and sympathy for Quebec. Mr. Horner, as a leading member of this group, was a strange bedfellow for the Liberal MPs, the former targets of his venom. While this move gave the Liberals a much needed prairie seat and Mr. Horner a cabinet post long before he might otherwise have received one (if ever), it made a mockery of what our political parties allegedly stand for.

Decline in Ministerial Responsibility

It has been a cardinal principle of the cabinet system of government that individual ministers are responsible for anything that is done by the ministries and departments for which they are responsible. The civil service is supposed to be an anonymous body without political views, obediently carrying out the commands of its masters, the politicians. This has always been something of a fiction, of course, since senior civil servants must provide useful advice and so there is no point in their totally ignoring the partisan and political constraints impinging on the ministers. The tendency for ministers and deputy ministers to see the world in like fashion is particularly pronounced in a one-party dominant system in which the collaboration between a minister and his or her deputy may continue for many years. All this notwithstanding, the principle of ministerial responsibility has had a long and respected tradition in Canada, at least in the sense that ministers, as politicians, have assumed complete responsibility for the actions of their civil servants and their departments. The political party in office has thus been the beneficiary of all the popular things done by the public service and the victim of its failings.

Recent developments have altered the once well-established principle of ministerial responsibility. First, there is a rapid turnover in the various ministries. The result is that few ministers have a chance to master the complex business of their ministry before they are assigned a new portfolio. While an alert and hard-working minister can be briefed fairly quickly by his new subordinates, it takes a prodigious amount of work and insight, and a great deal of time, to be able to become the effective head of a department and to lead it. Until this happens—and many ministers of course never gain the upper hand—the politicians are in a sense the captives of their officials. Ministers may, under these conditions, take formal responsibility for what is done in their name but the real power lies elsewhere ....

Plebiscitary Tendencies

All of the short-run causes for the decline of party mentioned so far were laid at the doorstep of the Liberals. While that party has been an important cause of the process of party attenuation, it should not, of course, be assumed that it is the sole culprit. The opposition parties have been unable to present an acceptable alternative and have failed to convince the public that they could remove some of the ills currently afflicting the country. Nor can party politicians of any stripe be held responsible for the fact that much of the political decision-making has shifted from the conventional sites to federal-provincial negotiations, where parties do not fit neatly.

A recent factor that might possibly further impair the viability of parties is also not of the Liberals' making, although Mr. Trudeau's reaction to it might exacerbate its effect on the place of parties in our system. The Parti Québécois' insertion of the referendum into our political process takes away from the monopoly enjoyed by parties in deciding certain issues. The PQ is of course not the first to introduce direct consultation of the public to Canadians. W.L. Mackenzie King had recourse to this device during the conscription crisis in the Second World War, and two referenda were held before Newfoundland became part of Canada. But the commitment of the PQ government to conduct a referendum to decide whether Quebecers wish to break or redefine their relationship with the rest of the country has brought forth an indication that Ottawa might itself conduct a similar vote.

Referenda normally ignore political parties and emphasize policy options, thereby diminishing the importance of parties in the political process. If they are held very infrequently, and only with respect to such fundamental issues as the nature of the country and its constitution, then they are unlikely to do much damage to the role of parties. But once they are used in one case, it may be impossible to prevent them from being applied to other issues—for example, the reintroduction of capital punishment, or language legislation—and they might slowly usurp some of the functions performed by parties. Any federal recourse to referenda is therefore seen by some opposition members as a potential further encroachment on the traditional role of parties.

CONCLUSION

The above catalogue of factors and developments reducing the relative importance of parties touches only some of the highlights; it is a partial and superficial look at a very complex phenomenon. This article's emphasis on federal politics has, for instance, led it to neglect the all-important provincial sphere and the interaction between federal and provincial party organizations. And our skimming of the high points has led to a neglect of some serious questions posed by these developments. We might have asked, for instance, whether the reason for the Liberal party's role in reducing the importance of parties is to be found in the fact that it is a quasi-permanent government party or in some special characteristics associated with Canadian Liberalism at the federal level. Does the Ontario Conservative party play a similar role in the decline of party in that province?

Our purpose here is not to answer these kinds of questions, important though they are, but to indicate that significant changes are occurring which alter the role played by political parties. If a series of limited advantages is allowed to reduce the overall effectiveness of a major mechanism for decision-making without producing at least an equally useful alternative, then the cost to society may be unexpectedly high. One is reminded in this connection of one of R.K. Merton's celebrated "theories of the middle range":

> Any attempt to eliminate an existing social structure without providing adequate alternative structures for fulfilling the functions previously fulfilled by the abolished organization is doomed to failure.

Now it is true that no one is consciously trying to eliminate Canadian parties or even to reduce their importance, and that Merton was thinking of the return or rebirth of a structure whose function was needed. But the parties' sphere of influence and effectiveness is being reduced, by design or not. It may be to the country's advantage to reassign the functions of parties if they are being neglected: society might find other ways of performing these needed functions. There is a danger, however, that the alternatives may be less satisfactory and in other respects—in the field of individual freedom, for instance—potentially very harmful.

The Canadian party system is far from being perfect, but the world is full of examples showing how appalling some of the alternatives can be. That considerable reform is needed is clear. We can benefit from some of the changes occurring now and from ones which could be instituted. Students of Canadian parties need to decide which features deserve preservation and which require change. And before they are in a position to do that, they must undertake more extensive study of the issues raised here.

28

REPRESENTATION

There are three conflicting ideas about what the role of elected representatives should be: (1) the trustee *model, i.e., that when they vote in the legislature, they should exercise their best personal judgment on behalf of their constituents; (2) the* delegate *model, i.e., that they should vote as their constituents instruct them to vote; and (3) the* mandate *or* party-member *model, i.e., that they should vote as loyal members of their parliamentary caucus, following the line laid down by the leadership of the party. This speech by Edmund Burke is the classical expression of the idea of trusteeship. Although not particularly influential in its own day, it has become the standard source for elected representatives who wish to defend their independence of judgment.*

In evaluating the contemporary relevance of Burke's argument, one should keep in mind the following points:

- *Burke lived in a predemocratic age. In 1774, England was not a democracy and hardly anyone thought it ought to be. Thus, the views of the relatively small number of people who could vote did not have the moral weight now attributed to "the will of the people," and the delegate model was correspondingly weaker.*

- *There were no large, disciplined political parties in Burke's time. The so-called "parties" were little better than small cliques of parliamentarians, and the lines between them were fluid and shifting. These parties did not contest elections with competing ideologies, programs, and platforms. Voting was much more a matter of personal allegiance and patronage than of choosing* between competing sets of policies, so the mandate idea would have made little sense.

Edmund Burke (1729–1797) was born in Ireland. He is best known today for his writings, especially Reflections on the Revolution in France. *He also served for 28 years in the House of Commons, representing the bustling port city of Bristol for one term, 1774–80. He delivered this speech shortly after he had been elected. Interestingly, when it became obvious in 1780 that he had no chance of being re-elected, he withdrew and found another constituency, a so-called "safe borough," where he was sure to be chosen. The voters of Bristol apparently did not appreciate his concept of trusteeship.*

The text is reprinted from Burke's Speeches and Letters on American Affairs. *The first part, which does not deal with representation, is omitted. Note that Burke speaks of another MP from Bristol, whose statements on representation he criticizes. British constituencies at that time elected two MPs to serve together.*

• • • • • • • • •

SPEECH TO THE ELECTORS OF BRISTOL

ON HIS BEING DECLARED BY THE SHERIFFS, DULY ELECTED ONE
OF THE REPRESENTATIVES IN PARLIAMENT FOR THAT CITY, ON
THURSDAY THE THIRD OF NOVEMBER, 1774

… I was brought hither under the disadvantage of being unknown, even by sight, to any of you. No previous canvass was made for me. I was put in nomination after the poll was opened. I did not appear until it was far advanced. If, under all these accumulated disadvantages, your good opinion has carried me to this happy point of success; you will pardon me, if I can only say to you collectively, as I said to you individually, simply, and plainly, I thank you—I am obliged to you—I am not insensible of your kindness ….

I am sorry I cannot conclude without saying a word on a topic touched upon by my worthy colleague. I wish that topic had been passed by at a time when I have so little leisure to discuss it. But since he has thought proper to throw it out, I owe you a clear explanation of my poor sentiments on that subject.

He tells you that "the topic of instructions has occasioned much altercation and uneasiness in this city;" and he expresses himself (if I understand him rightly) in favour of the coercive authority of such instructions.

Certainly, gentlemen, it ought to be the happiness and glory of a representative to live in the strictest union, the closest correspondence, and the most unreserved communication with his constituents. Their wishes ought to have great weight with him; their opinion, high respect; their business, unremitted attention. It is his duty to sacrifice his repose, his pleasures, his satisfactions, to theirs; and above all, ever, and in all cases, to prefer their interest to his own. But his unbiassed opinion, his mature judgment, his enlightened conscience, he ought not to sacrifice to you, to any man, or to any set of men living. These he does not derive from your pleasure; no, nor from the law and the constitution. They are a trust from Providence, for the abuse of which he is deeply answerable. Your representative owes you, not his industry only, but his judgment; and he betrays, instead of serving you, if he sacrifices it to your opinion.

My worthy colleague says, his will ought to be subservient to yours. If that be all, the thing is innocent. If government were a matter of will upon any side, yours, without question, ought to be superior. But government and legislation are matters of reason and judgment, and not of inclination; and what sort of reason is that, in which the determination precedes the discussion; in which one set of men deliberate, and another decide; and where those who form the conclusion are perhaps three hundred miles distant from those who hear the arguments?

To deliver an opinion, is the right of all men; that of constituents is a weighty and respectable opinion, which a representative ought always to rejoice to hear; and which he ought always most seriously to consider. But *authoritative* instructions; *mandates* issued, which the member is bound blindly and implicitly to obey, to vote, and to argue for, though contrary to the clearest conviction of his judgment and conscience,— these are things utterly unknown to the laws of this land, and which arise from a fundamental mistake of the whole order and tenor of our constitution.

Parliament is not a *congress* of ambassadors from different and hostile interests; which interests each must maintain, as an agent and advocate, against other agents and advocates; but parliament is a *deliberative* assembly of *one* nation, with *one* interest, that of the whole; where, not local purposes, not local prejudices, ought to guide, but the general good, resulting from the general reason of the whole. You choose a member indeed; but when you have chosen him, he is not member of Bristol, but he is a member of *parliament*. If the local constituent should have an interest, or should form an hasty opinion, evidently opposite to the real good of the rest of the community, the member for that place ought to be as far, as any other, from any endeavour to give it effect. I beg pardon for saying so much on this subject. I have been unwillingly drawn into it; but I shall ever use a respectful frankness of communication with you. Your faithful friend, your devoted servant, I shall be to the end of my life: a flatterer you do not wish for. On this point of instructions, however, I think it scarcely possible we ever can have any sort of difference. Perhaps I may give you too much, rather than too little, trouble.

From the first hour I was encouraged to court your favour, to this happy day of obtaining it, I have never promised you anything but humble and persevering endeavours to do my duty. The weight of that duty, I confess, makes me tremble; and whoever well considers what it is, of all things in the world, will fly from what has the least likeness to a positive and precipitate engagement. To be a good member of parliament is, let me tell you, no easy task; especially at this time, when there is so strong a disposition to run into the perilous extremes of servile compliance or wild popularity. To unite circumspection with vigour, is absolutely necessary; but it is extremely difficult. We are now members for a rich commercial *city*; this city, however, is but a part of a rich commercial *nation*, the interests of which are various, multiform, and intricate. We are members for that great nation, which however is itself but part of a great *empire*, extended by our virtue and our fortune to the farthest limits of the east and of the west. All these wide-spread interests must be considered; must be compared; must be reconciled, if possible. We are members for a *free* country; and surely we all know, that the machine of a free constitution is no simple thing; but as intricate and as delicate as it is valuable. We are members in a great and ancient *monarchy*; and we must preserve religiously the true legal rights of the sovereign, which form the key-stone that binds together the noble and well-constructed arch of our empire and our constitution. A constitution made up of balanced powers must ever be a critical thing. As such I mean to touch that part of it which comes within my reach. I know my inability, and I wish for support from every quarter. In particular I shall aim at the friendship, and shall cultivate the best correspondence, of the worthy colleague you have given me.

I trouble you no further than once more to thank you all; you, gentlemen, for your favours; the candidates, for their temperate and polite behaviour; and the sheriffs, for a conduct which may give a model for all who are in public stations.

29

CABINETS

It is rare indeed to have anyone talk about the inner workings of a cabinet, especially a former minister. The cabinet process and all its interchange is about the most secretive part of the governmental process. Most ministers are very guarded about their work in cabinet because it is very personal. Richard Crossman, however, a former Cabinet minister in the Labour party in Great Britain, has written a revealing piece about the inner struggles that go on among the people trying to run a government.

He discusses the role of cabinet committees and how collective ministerial responsibility came into being. Also, he indicates clearly that the prime minister dominates the cabinet. With the different powers accumulated over the years, there is no doubt that the prime minister is far more than "first among equals."

He also describes in some detail the power struggle between ministers and civil servants. By now all of us should realize that the legislative process is not simply a parliament passing laws that are in the best interest of society. The legislative process is a power struggle between individuals and groups, all of whom have their own agenda about what laws and policies should be enacted. Crossman's revelation about the minister and civil servants is a classic reading about that struggle. It demonstrates how a powerful department in the bureaucracy attempts to manipulate the minister, raising the old question, "do civil servants rule or serve?"

Richard Crossman, a prominent member of the Labour party, was a cabinet minister in Harold Wilson's government from 1964 to 1969. Before and after, he was also a professor of politics at Oxford University. The reading is excerpted from *lectures that he delivered to an American audience at Harvard University in 1970 and that appear in his book* The Myths of Cabinet Government.

• • • • • • • •

We saw last night that Cabinet proceedings are recorded by the Cabinet Secretariat. They do not take down in shorthand what was actually said because they prefer to record [what] should have been said. They are Platonists, not Aristotelians. If you record what a Minister did say it might not turn out to be a precise instruction. There might be a little fuzziness, a little confusion. We can't afford to have confusion when the Civil Service is being given its marching orders.

Cabinet Minutes started in 1916 in World War I, under Lloyd George's Cabinet and with Maurice Hankey in charge. The system was then developed very rapidly; we already had by the end of World War I a system of decision-taking by the Cabinet, decisions which then became the marching orders for the Civil Service.

THE POWER OF CABINET COMMITTEES

The next stage of this was to extend it from Cabinet to Cabinet committees. Now, as a matter of fact, in 1903 a Committee of Imperial Defence had been founded with Arthur Balfour, the Prime Minister, in the Chair, and with the Chiefs of Staff present. Still today the only Cabinet committee at which officials are present, other than Secretaries, the people who record it, is the Defence Committee. The Chiefs of Staff are present and can take part. I must say, having been there for some years, it is disappointing how rarely they do take part. But they are there and they can. We still have the traditional Defence Committee and the Prime Minister in the Chair, and it still goes on much as it was before.

By the end of World War I there were not only Cabinet Minutes but there were minutes being recorded of 165 committees. You see how they multiplied and grew in war-time. But at the end of the war we returned to normalcy in Britain, as you did in America, and, therefore, we ended many Cabinet committees, and got back to pre-war routine. Indeed, it was not until the Second World War that we started the full committee system again. Then they were rapidly evolved under Winston Churchill, and in the 1945 Labour Government Clement Attlee, who was a formidable man in terms of Cabinet management, retained and developed the whole committee system, not merely as a war-time expedient but as a permanent part of Cabinet Government. These committees are divided into those which the Prime Minister chairs, and those which are chaired by Ministers selected by the Prime Minister, Ministers usually without departmental responsibility, such as the Lord President, Lord Privy Seal, or Minister without Portfolio.

Now, in our doctrine, each Cabinet committee is a microcosm of the Cabinet. May I remind you again that a Cabinet decision is formulated by the Prime Minister and follows his elucidation of the consensus which has been achieved. Now, what happens in the Cabinet also happens in each of the multifarious committees below Cabinet level. Each Chairman has the same responsibility of recording the conclusions and the decision; and the moment that any Cabinet committee's decision is recorded, it has the same validity as a Cabinet decision—unless it has been challenged in committee and the issue accepted by the Prime Minister as one to be decided by Cabinet.

So notice that this really means not only that the committee is a microcosm of the Cabinet but that it can exert within its terms of reference the power of the Cabinet. Six or seven Cabinet Ministers meet together and whatever decision they record is binding with the same binding force as though it had been made by the whole Cabinet in Cabinet session. This is a convenient method of reducing the number of Cabinet meetings and ensuring that decisions are taken in reasonable time.

Notice that I said each of these committees is enunciating marching orders to Whitehall with all the bindingness of a Cabinet decision, unless the minutes record that a Cabinet Minister or his representative present dissented from the decision and wished to have it raised in Cabinet. I should perhaps add that in our Wilson Cabinet (but each PM arranges such things as he wants) a Minister can only appeal from the Cabinet committee to Cabinet with the consent of the *Chairman* of the committee. That is a great limitation on the power of the Cabinet Minister, the fact that he has got to get the consent of the Chairman, who, of course, has been selected by the Prime Minister. He and the PM have ways of seeing that a Minister can't get to the Cabinet even if he wants to. I should personally like to see that changed.

Now you may be interested as to what subjects are discussed in a Cabinet committee. First of all, all legislation must be processed through a Cabinet committee. For example, I have been dealing with pensions. My proposals for the reform of the whole of Social Security are put to the Cabinet committee appointed for this purpose, section by section, not just as a bill, but as policy papers, and discussed at length by this committee. Provided I can get agreement in the committee, I can get the pension plan presented as a draft White Paper and cleared at a single Cabinet discussion. Then it is binding on all members of the Cabinet equally even though they have not been present at the detailed discussions. After that, the Bill must go through the Legislation Committee.

Secondly, though this sounds very generalised, anything is raised or discussed in a Cabinet committee for which a Minister feels he will need the support of his colleagues. Weak Ministers will be constantly putting things to Cabinet committees to get backing from their colleagues, and proud and strong Ministers won't bother their colleagues because they hope to drag them along without discussing it with them. It is always a nice question about your colleagues, whether they will be happier if you bother them with insignificant and secondary issues and insist they turn up on committees and give you their approval, or whether they prefer just to read it in the *Times*, and say, "Well, he's done it again and it's a little bit late to object now."

Ministers differ in their views of how to handle their colleagues. That is why the only definition of what goes to a Cabinet Committee is what a Minister thinks he can't safely get away with without a Cabinet committee. Unless the Prime Minister settles it himself, anything goes to full Cabinet which is deadlocked at a lower level, and this, of course, is owing to the doctrine of collective Cabinet responsibility.

THE LEGEND OF MINISTERIAL RESPONSIBILITY TO PARLIAMENT

You will remember that in Bagehot's time a Minister still had individual ministerial responsibility to the House of Commons. The House could censure and ultimately sack Ministers for failings in their Departments. This has long since disappeared. I mean, it is still there as a legend. But now, very often, the worse a Minister manages his Ministry, the more difficult it is to get him removed because it would be an injury to the prestige of the Government. So the more the House of Commons bellows against the Minister, the stronger usually is the Prime Minister's determination to protect him in order to strengthen the hold of the Government on the House of Commons.

So the old theory that the House of Commons could demand the dismissal of the Minister and he would then be dismissed is largely antiquated. Every Minister is covered by full collective Cabinet responsibility and, of course, that means every Government Department is covered in the same way, in the sense that the bigger the fiasco in the Department, the more tempting it is to cover it up. This is collective responsibility in its modern sense.

Of course, if incompetence is too obvious or too damaging, the Prime Minister, in due course, will have a shuffle, but he will very rarely have it on the ground that a Minister has failed and must be moved. Maybe he will have to be promoted to the House of Lords for greater responsibilities, or to a post in the colonies overseas. In some cases, the Minister will refuse to be kicked upstairs and will voluntarily retire to the back benches. But the reason given will seldom be because he was incompetent or because there was a failure in his Ministry.

Such things occurred frequently in the nineteenth century. We don't let it happen now because we have a collective Cabinet responsibility for the actions of individual Ministers. So a Minister has to make up his mind when faced with a departmental catastrophe whether colleagues ought to be forewarned, or whether it is best to present them with a fait accompli in the Press and tell them they had better damn well see him through. It is a matter of taste how to handle colleagues in that particular contingency.

POWERS OF THE OPPOSITION: "THE USUAL CHANNELS"

Every Cabinet meeting starts with a discussion of next week's business and parliamentary matters. This may be what differentiates us from the Americans. All members of the Cabinet are members of the Commons (or Lords) and are constantly aware of the troubles we are having over the road in the Palace of Westminster, and discussing how they should be handled, and what will be the next cause of trouble.

This is a constant preoccupation of a British Cabinet—its sensitivity to the House of Commons. But, may I remind you, that does not mean its troubles come primarily from the official Opposition. You can't please the Opposition. They can never win, since you can always vote them down. Their views are not important from this point of view. What matters is the view of your own people whose votes you require to maintain your majority.

Having said this, let me add that there is one area where the power of the men who sit on the Opposition front bench is real and can be decisive. That area is the allocation of Parliamentary time, the sessional, weekly, and daily timetables arranged largely by verbal agreements—"through the usual channels." This relationship between the Opposition Chief Whip and the Government Chief Whip is so vital to the working of our Parliamentary system and such a characteristic example of what Bagehot would call "an efficient secret" that I must spend a little time on it.

I have talked as though the Cabinet had effectively destroyed the independent power of Parliament at one fell swoop. Actually the process began, largely by accident, in the 1880s as the result of the skilful work of the Irish Nationalists at sabotaging the working of Parliament. The old procedure had given almost unlimited licence to private members to bring forward the business they desired. Government could only get its business through because of the bi-partisan consensus which restrained the private members from insisting too far on their rights. Since the Irish had no such scruples, the Liberal Government was forced to introduce procedural limitations on private members' rights, including not only the timetabling of particular Bills by means of the guillotine but also Government control of the sessional timetable.

This transfer of power from Parliament to the Cabinet was only possible because both the big English parties wanted to defeat the Irish filibuster. The transfer, in fact, took place with the consent and connivance of the official Opposition, which now emerged as the "Shadow" Cabinet, ready to replace the real Cabinet whenever it got the chance, but equally ready to concede the time the Government required to get its legislation through provided only that the Shadow Cabinet was given a fair chance too. The method of achieving this was to allocate to the official Opposition all the so-called Supply Days which had been previously used by Parliament in order to control public expenditure. Traditionally the House of Commons has always claimed the right to investigate the working of the Executive before approving the funds it needs. Under the new arrangement evolved between 1880 and 1905 Parliamentary control of the Executive largely disappeared. Instead Parliamentary time was divided into three parts: (1) the time the Government requires to get its business, including its legislation, through the House; (2) the time which must be conceded to the Opposition for criticising the Government and stating its case; (3) the time left over, which is allocated to private members.

It is this control of the timetable which enables the Government to dominate Parliament. You will see that it came about not because the six hundred members who make up Parliament suddenly surrendered their rights to the Cabinet, but owing to an understanding between two big Party machines, which decided to handle management jointly by leaving the management of the timetable to the two Chief Whips. Time-tabling (which works in the Lords as well as in the Commons) depends on the tiny group of apparently humdrum Civil Servants through whose continuous day and night mediation the two Chief Whips conduct their negotiations. The Cabinet is naturally content to accept the co-operation of the Shadow Cabinet in getting its business through. As for the Shadow Cabinet, since its main desire is to become the real Cabinet as soon as possible, it has a strong common interest with the Government in preserving a system under which it shares four fifths of its parliamentary time with the Government—thereby reducing to a minimum the time available to private members and rebel groups in either of the two big parties. Thus Cabinet control of Parliament is exerted—at a price. It must obtain the active connivance of the Official Opposition by sharing with it the planning of the timetable, and the responsibility for keeping the debates within the time limits they have agreed upon. This requires the continuous and intimate cooperation of the Government and Opposition Chief Whips "through the usual channels."

There is, however, one very important proviso. In the last resort, even today, the Government remains at the mercy of the Opposition. At any moment, if the Opposition feels driven to do so, it can withdraw its cooperation and bring Parliament to a standstill. The powers which prevent a repetition of the Irish filibuster are genuinely powerful. Even so, if the Opposition gets really nasty, it can soon make life impossible for the Government, which needs to keep a stream of formal business, administrative orders and approvals moving through Parliament in order to prevent a complete paralysis setting in. Thus there does remain an ultimate sanction; and even the most compliant Opposition leadership can be forced to use it if the Government is really outraging Parliament and public opinion outside. There are times in the life of each Parliament when Opposition back benchers have recourse to filibuster and obstruction. But normally the operation of the usual channels keeps business proceeding according to timetable despite these outbursts.

It was, for instance, the operation of the usual channels which assured the Labour Government of the passage of the Kenya Asian Bill, which in the U.S.A. would, I guess, have been ruled unconstitutional by the Supreme Court. On the other hand, it was the withdrawal of cooperation through the usual channels which forced the Labour Government to jettison its Parliament Bill reforming the Lords.

POWERS OF THE PRIME MINISTER

Now I want to explain why I think that Cabinet government has been developing into Prime Ministerial government. Here is my list of the six powers the Prime Minister wields.

1. First of all, remember each Minister fighting in the Cabinet for his Department can be sacked by the Prime Minister any day. We must be constantly aware our tenure of office depends on his personal decision. I remarked last time that he is not a "free" man in the sense that he can, for example, sack all the undisputed incompetents in his team—without upsetting his own position. But even though he is balancing forces in the Cabinet rather than ordering them, he has, in my view, tremendous power—something which any Cabinet Minister is aware of every day of his life. I am aware I am there at the Prime Minister's discretion. The Prime Minister can withdraw that discretion on any day he likes without stating a reason. And there's nothing much I can do about it—except succeed—and so build up my own strength.

2. The second of the powers of the Prime Minister is that he decides the agenda of the Cabinet. Say that I think something is terribly impor-

tant: I must get it through and I've had a row in the Cabinet committee. I register my dissent and ask for it to go to Cabinet. Somehow it does not occur on the agenda week after week. I fume—but the PM has the last word. The agenda is fixed in Number 10; and the two men who fix the agenda—the Prime Minister and the Secretary to the Cabinet—decide what issues shall be fought out, what shall not.

3. Thirdly, the Prime Minister decides the organization of the Cabinet committees. What committees exist, how they are manned—above all, who are the Chairmen—all this is entirely a matter for the Prime Minister. As I mentioned in the last lecture, there is one committee where there are only one or two members, and that's the committee which decides the contents of the Budget—nearly always the Chancellor in consultation with the PM. After that, twenty four hours before the Budget Speech, the Cabinet, as a matter of form, have the proposals presented to them for comment.

But there are many other issues, awkward issues where it is up to the Prime Minister to decide what kind of Cabinet committee the issue is put to. Shall it contain ten Departmental Ministers; shall it be limited to junior Ministers; or shall it be only three Senior Ministers? He's absolutely free in adjudicating to which members of the Cabinet or of the Government the issue shall be put in committee. He can in fact virtually decide whether the proposition is buried without ever coming to Cabinet, or whether it comes with certain amendments, or whether it is given top priority and pushed through intact.

Of course, all this has a tremendous effect on the doctrine of collective responsibility. This is a doctrine which many people in America regard as the distinguishing characteristic of British Cabinet Government, but I am not so sure they all understand how it works today. In Bagehot's time collective responsibility used to mean that every member of the Cabinet had the right to take part in the Cabinet discussion; but after the discussion was over, he was bound by the decision which had been reached. That was the original notion. That's what you find in Bagehot.

Collective responsibility now means something totally different. It means that everybody who is in the Government must accept and publicly support every "Cabinet decision," even if he was not present at the discussion or, frequently, was completely unaware the decision had been taken. As we have seen, collective decision-taking is now fragmented, and many major decisions may be taken by two, three, four, or five Ministers. But the moment they have been taken, *and minuted*, they have the force of a decision taken by the whole Cabinet, and are binding on a hundred-odd members of the Government.

This is an interesting transformation of the old notion of collective responsibility which enormously increased Prime Ministerial power. There is all the difference in the world between a Prime Minister who has to carry twenty colleagues with him when anything of importance is being decided, and a new-style Prime Minister who has appointed one hundred colleagues as his agents, each of them with a specific job to do, and only permitted to hear after the event nine tenths of the decisions for which he shares collective responsibility. It is by this transformation that Cabinet Government, in my view, has been evolved into what I call "Prime Ministerial Government."

4. But that does not conclude the powers of the Prime Minister. To an American audience I need not stress the significance of the fact that he has almost a monopoly of patronage. He personally controls the "Honours list." He has an unchallenged free hand in selecting new members of the House of Lords. This latter gives him a useful device for retiring ageing or incompetent Ministers without disgrace—purging his Government by promotion into the Upper Chamber, which really deserves the nickname of "the best club in the world."

As for other appointments, paid and unpaid, there are many, many thousands which departmental Ministers make. All the important ones have to be approved, however, by Number 10 Downing Street. A Prime Minister at the centre of our centralised Party Oligarchy wields far more effective personal control in the field of patronage than an American President.

5. Even more important than the control of patronage is the control of the Civil Service which a Prime Minister has exercised—again since the period of Lloyd George. During World War I, and up until 1919, the heads of the various Departments in Whitehall were mostly selected from inside the Department; and it was the Minister who made the decision.

Then Lord Rhondda, who was wartime Minister of Food, made a decision rather like Caligula, who, as you remember, decided to make his horse Consul. He made his Private Secretary the Permanent Secretary—the Head of the Department. This so shocked Lloyd George that he sent out a minute which said that in the future all heads of Departments would be appointed by the Permanent Secretary of the Treasury, in consultation with the Prime Minister.

Today all number twos as well as all Number Ones are made by the Prime Minister and the Head of the Civil Service, who, by the way, is now different from the Head of the Treasury. There is now a trinity of power in Whitehall: (1) the Permanent Secretary of the Treasury, who is a very powerful man in his own right because of the unique power exercised by his department; (2) the Head of the Civil Service, who is the Permanent Secretary of the new Civil Service Department; (3) the

Secretary of the Cabinet. These are men, I would say, of equal status and power, and this trinity under the Prime Minister controls promotion to the top jobs in the Civil Service.

The change which began in 1919 completely transformed not only the nature of the promotions in Civil Service but also the power of the Prime Minister. Before this, you were appointed Head of the Department because you knew something about it. This idea that in order to be a good Permanent Secretary of Education you must know about education is long since defunct. The Permanent Secretaries now are professional administrators with minds so trained that they can move from Department to Department, and within a week administer any Department equally skilfully. This is what we call our "Mandarin System."

As I told you, I did Greek at Oxford, and a study of Greek philosophy is an almost perfect training for a Mandarin. It means you know nothing in particular about what you are actually doing but you have a "perfectly trained mind." We have evolved the requirement that if men want to rise to the top, they must mark themselves out as they rise, for example, through the Ministry of Education as being able to run Transport just as well. Non-expertise is the mark of a man who is going to get on in the British Civil Service.

There is one other mark that he requires. He requires a period in the Treasury. This is the "Halmark," if I many say so, of a man doomed to success. A period in the Cabinet Secretariat is pretty useful for promotion prospects, but a period in the Treasury counts for a lot more because ex-Treasury Civil Servants make up an open conspiracy. Everybody who has once been in the Treasury always belongs to it in spirit and can be reckoned on to tell the Treasury most of what it wants to know about any Department in which he serves.

I very early discovered as a Minister that my Department could not keep a secret from the Treasury. Long before I was ready, my plans would be disclosed to the Treasury by my loyal Permanent Secretary on the ground that one must really consider the national good and not be parochial about Housing. That is why the Treasury nearly always wins the battle against a Department.

But let's get back to the Trinity of Power. You can now see why I claim that the Prime Minister has a peculiar and unique power, apart from the Cabinet altogether. He is the only politician to whom these three all-powerful Civil Servants look as their political master.

6. His final power is his personal control of Government publicity. I have told how Government policy is promulgated in Whitehall as Cabinet Minutes. The Government's Press relations are conducted by the Number 10 press department at its daily press conferences. That means

we have a daily, coherent, central explanation of what the Government is doing—an explanation naturally in terms the Prime Minister thinks right.

Anyway, the media of mass publicity tend to personalise politics; and as our politics centre on Number 10, and as much of the news is released from Number 10, you can see how natural it is for the Press to be fed with the Prime Minister's interpretation of Government Policy, and to present him as the Champion and spokesman of the whole Cabinet in the battle against the "shadow" enemy on the other side.

Now I have listed his powers, do you see what I meant by Prime Ministerial government? It does not mean that he is a dictator; it does not mean he can tell his Ministers what to do in their Departments. But it does mean that in this discussion and argument and battle of Whitehall this man in the centre, this Chairman, this man without a Department, without apparent power, can exert, when he is successful, a dominating personal control. This explains why a British Cabinet is always called a "Wilson Cabinet" or a "Macmillan Cabinet." It is because every Cabinet takes its tone from the Prime Minister. The way the Prime Minister conducts it and administers it will give it its particular character. Usually it is dominated by his personality, and, if it is not, this is because he prefers to exert his control in less obvious ways. Attlee, I gather, pretended not to run the Cabinet. Actually, he was a quite ruthless little man, and fairly often he was savage and cruel and even unjust. There are various ways of exercising power and getting your way as Premier, some more dramatic and theatrical than others. All I am saying is that the way a Cabinet works, the way it functions, is determined by its Prime Minister ....

MINISTERS AND CIVIL SERVANTS

The greatest danger of a Labour Cabinet is that its members will be corrupted from being a team of Socialists carrying out a collective Cabinet Strategy into a collection of individual departmental Ministers. The greatest temptation is that I should be too interested in the praise of the Department and too pleased at being told how well I am doing: "Wonderful Minister, you're putting all this Party thing behind you, and really working for the Department—that's so fine of you." And before I know what, I am beginning to lose interest in the causes for which I was sent to fight in Parliament.

Therefore, the battle is really for the soul of the Minister. Is he to remain a foreign body in the Department, inserting into the departments things they don't like, a political dynamo, sparking off things they don't want, things he wants and the Party wants? Or is he to become *their*

Minister, content to speak for them? There is nothing easier than being a departmental success. Nothing easier at all. The Private Office sees to that.

That's one danger—that Ministers may become departmental spokesmen. The other danger we face is that the Departments get together and dictate to the politicians behind the scenes at Whitehall. I have said something about Cabinet committees. I have not revealed to you that parallel to each Cabinet committee is an official committee. Say you have a Cabinet committee consisting of seven Cabinet Ministers to discuss a problem which affects five Departments. There will be an official committee consisting of officials from those five Departments, who will seek, as far as possible, to achieve an official solution which they can recommend to their Ministers, rather than have the risk of the Ministers fighting it out with five conflicting departmental briefs and coming to a collective political decision on their own. Whitehall likes to reach an official compromise at official level first, so that the Ministers are all briefed the same way.

The emergence of these official committees is something which has been going on for the last fifteen years, and I will give you an example of how it works from my own life. At one time I was Minister of Housing, and I was very keen to substitute local income tax for local rates as the main basis of our local taxation. So I made a speech or two about this before I squared my officials. What happened? An official committee was established which did a tremendous lot of work in order to prove that rates were the only practical form of local taxation. And so before I could get to my colleagues and argue the case for the local income tax, every one of my colleagues had been briefed by his officials that there was no alternative to the rates. So that was that! If Whitehall gangs up on you it is very difficult to get your policy through, or even to get a fair hearing for a new idea.

Let me sum up this part of my argument. The effective Minister is the man who wins the support of his Department without becoming its cherished mascot. To do so he has to strike a balance. He needs the acquiescence, at least, of the Department in what he is up to, and for this he needs to be a success in the Department's eye. So he's got to appease them by winning a number of their battles for them in the Whitehall war.

Simultaneously, he must hold his own in the paper war. Every Department wages a paper war against its Minister. They try to drown him in paper so that he can't be a nuisance. Every night, as you know, we receive our red boxes. When I get home to my house in London about ten or eleven at night from the House of Commons, there are one, two, three, four, or even five boxes, which include not only the papers for next day's meeting but the decisions which I have to take that night before reaching the Ministry the next day. The first job you have to do is to prevent yourself becoming a slave of the red box.

By the way, it's no good thinking you can evade this by use of the telephone. At one time I was very irate; I thought, I won't sign this damn stuff, I'll do it all by phone. That has no effect on the British Civil Service. What they care about is the written word. Even the word "yes" or "no" written on paper is enough. So I awake at six and I work until half past eight or nine, working through the boxes so that every decision is taken and sent back to them duly minuted and initialled.

You must never let them defeat you. You must never fail to give a decision back in writing. If you do that, and if you do it having clearly read the documents—and that's important too—then you have some chance of asserting your authority.

Having asserted your authority, the next thing is to select a very few causes and fight for them. The greatest danger of a Radical Minister is to get too much going in his Department. Because, you see, Departments are resistant. Departments know that they last and you don't. Departments know that any day you may be moved somewhere else and they can forget you. It does not pay you to order them to change their minds on everything. For one thing, they can't. There's a limit to the quantity of change they can digest.

Select a few, a very few issues, and on those issues be bloody and blunt because, of course, you get no change except by fighting. I know there are people who believe you can achieve things in Whitehall without a battle with your Department. Well, it hasn't been my experience, and a very good thing too. If I want to change something and they have got their own departmental policy, they are bound to say, "Look, before we are going to change our departmental mind for a temporary Minister, he must show that he really means it. First of all, he must be able to answer all our arguments; secondly, his will power must be sufficient so that when we refuse to do anything week after week he must notice it, he must send for us, he must bully us." There might be a fight and a triumph. It's like a man with a woman in a Victorian novel, if you know what I mean. They are females to our males. They aren't prepared to give way without a good fight before it happens. But you can't afford to have fights on many things. You must have them on one or two or three issues.

In all this, as I have said, it's no good being brilliant or successful unless you have powerful allies. Your officials know whether you are on good terms with the Prime Minister or not. They know whether the Chancellor is willing to give you the money or not long before you do because their information is better than yours. They have an unrivalled grapevine in Whitehall. They brief each other.

Therefore, it's no good being heroic unless you have one or two good big guns on your side, and this explains why Ministers are inclined not to back too many causes in the Cabinet. Why wasn't I fighting for the Right on X or Y or Z? Because I couldn't afford to make too many enemies by espousing causes I wasn't vitally concerned in, when I needed the support of these colleagues in my own departmental affairs. The need to have allies in your own field limits your altruistic activity in other fields. I won't go further than that. I think you will see what I mean.

TASKS OF A RADICAL PRIME MINISTER

... I fancy a Prime Minister could well calculate that the amount of time a strong man can be in a Department and go on fighting is not much more than three years. After that symbiosis occurs of the most danger- ous character. He actually starts getting on with the Department too well. For about three years he remains an active foreign body and there can be a creative friction—a battle out of which something comes. But sooner or later a point is reached where he gets too close to the Department. I would know and care too much about Health after three more years, and then I might be a dangerous person because I might align myself with these Health people against the Cabinet.

This explains this continuous shuffling of a British Cabinet. They are shuffled because the PM did not select his Cabinet Ministers as experts on Health and Defence and so forth, but rather as members of a political team elected to do a definitive collective job. And each is to be inserted into the huge rigid structure of a Department in order to get things moving inside the way the Government wants.

So the PM's task is to keep a watch on his Ministers to see that they aren't getting too respectable, too Department-minded, that they are not developing a Ministry-based independence of the Cabinet.

Secondly, he must be concerned with the machinery of the Government. The Prime Minister has an absolute control here. He can create new Departments; he can chop Departments in half. This constant threat is a wholesome way of keeping the Civil Service on their toes.

Thirdly, he supervises reforms of the Civil Service. We are now doing a major reform with the abolition of the class system in the Civil Service. These are things where the Prime Minister is personally responsible.

I end this second lecture with one question. If the Labour Government has made mistakes and suffered failures, would I attribute these failures and mistakes to the Civil Service? My answer is "no." I am absolutely clear that the chance you have as a Government or as a Minister of changing things in Britain is enormous; provided that the

Government is a team; provided the Ministers are capable of keeping their political drive while helping the Department and working eighteen hours a day. Provided they have these qualities, they have an instrument which is trained to accept change. I said "accept change"—of course, they often fight it. Of course they do, but that's part of their job. But the point is they only fight to the point where you have licked them, and that's all you can ask.

So, when we are looking at the record of a Government, I wouldn't attribute its failings to the British Civil Service. I would say that normally when a Government fails it is not because the Civil Service blocks it, but because the Government team has not had a clear enough sense of direction. A Government which really knows where it is going, a Government which has a series of measures ready, prepared, well thought out, has to hand in Britain an instrument which will enable it to carry out all it wants.

30 BUREAUCRACY

Growth of modern government administration (known also as the civil service or bureaucracy) has paralleled the growth of modern governmental functions. As governments took on more societal responsibilities, more people and organizations were needed for example, to administer agricultural programs, to build roads, to run the public school system, or to dispense unemployment benefits. This is not to say large bureaucracies are found only in modern governments. Indeed, two thousand years ago Chinese "Mandarins" were an integral part of the administration of Chinese empires. However, according to Max Weber, a number of distinctive characteristics accompany the development of modern bureaucracies.

Administrative officials, as opposed to elected officials, represent the large reservoir of resource people on whom public policy-makers depend for technical expertise. These bureaucracies have to become "professional" organizations in that they provide a vocation for the qualified. In theory, they are detached from the political world, and operate in an impersonal and impartial way. Employment in the organization must be by competitive examination to avoid accusation of political patronage and nepotism. At the same time, professional bureaucratic organizations must follow institutionalized procedures for administration that are established to avoid situations of privilege or favour.

While one can, theoretically, construct a large, professionalized bureaucracy that does administer fairly, there is an inherent problem with modern bureaucracies. Because elected officials depend on the expertise and information of bureaucrats, *those bureaucrats and their organizations become very powerful in the policy-making process; and yet they are not responsible to the voters.*

In the reading that follows, Max Weber provides an analysis of modern bureau-cracies and indicates the problems inherent in that organization. Weber (1864–1920) is generally considered the most important sociologist of the twentieth century. The excerpts on bureaucracy printed here are from his masterwork Wirtschaft und Gesellschaft, *translated by H.H. Gerth and C. Wright Mills in* From Max Weber: Essays in Sociology.

• • • • • • • •

1. CHARACTERISTICS OF BUREAUCRACY

Modern officialdom functions in the following specific manner:

I. There is the principle of fixed and official jurisdictional areas, which are generally ordered by rules, that is, by laws or administrative regulations.

1. The regular activities required for the purposes of the bureau-cratically governed structure are distributed in a fixed way as official duties.

2. The authority to give the commands required for the discharge of these duties is distributed in a stable way and is strictly delimited by rules concerning the coercive means, physical, sacerdotal, or otherwise, which may be placed at the disposal of officials.

3. Methodical provision is made for the regular and continuous fulfilment of these duties and for the execution of the corresponding rights; only persons who have the generally regulated qualifications to serve are employed.

In public and lawful government these three elements constitute 'bureaucratic authority.' In private economic domination, they constitute bureaucratic 'management.' Bureaucracy, thus understood, is fully devel-oped in political and ecclesiastical communities only in the modern state, and, in the private economy, only in the most advanced institu-tions of capitalism. Permanent and public office authority, with fixed jurisdiction, is not the historical rule but rather the exception. This is so even in large political structures such as those of the ancient Orient, the Germanic and Mongolian empires of conquest, or of many feudal struc-tures of state. In all these cases, the ruler executes the most important measures through personal trustees, table-companions, or court-servants. Their commissions and authority are not precisely delimited and are temporarily called into being for each case.

II. The principles of office hierarchy and of levels of graded authority mean a firmly ordered system of super- and subordination in which there is a supervision of the lower offices by the higher ones. Such a system offers the governed the possibility of appealing the decision of a lower office to its higher authority, in a definitely regulated manner. With the full development of the bureaucratic type, the office hierarchy is monocratically organized. The principle of hierarchical office authority is found in all bureaucratic structures: in state and ecclesiastical structures as well as in large party organizations and private enterprises. It does not matter for the character of bureaucracy whether its authority is called 'private' or 'public.'

When the principle of jurisdictional 'competency' is fully carried through, hierarchical subordination—at least in public office—does not mean that the 'higher' authority is simply authorized to take over the business of the 'lower.' Indeed, the opposite is the rule. Once established and having fulfilled its task, an office tends to continue in existence and be held by another incumbent.

III. The management of the modern office is based upon written documents ('the files'), which are preserved in their original or draught form. There is, therefore, a staff of subaltern officials and scribes of all sorts. The body of officials actively engaged in a 'public' office, along with the respective apparatus of material implements and the files, make up a 'bureau.' In private enterprise, 'the bureau' is often called 'the office.'

In principle, the modern organization of the civil service separates the bureau from the private domicile of the official, and, in general, bureaucracy segregates official activity as something distinct from the sphere of private life. Public monies and equipment are divorced from the private property of the official. This condition is everywhere the product of a long development. Nowadays, it is found in public as well as in private enterprises; in the latter, the principle extends even to the leading entrepreneur. In principle, the executive office is separated from the household, business from private correspondence, and business assets from private fortunes. The more consistently the modern type of business management has been carried through the more are these separations the case. The beginnings of this process are to be found as early as the Middle Ages ....

IV. Office management, at least all specialized office management—and such management is distinctly modern—usually presupposes thorough and expert training. This increasingly holds for the modern executive and employee of private enterprises, in the same manner as it holds for the state official.

V. When the office is fully developed, official activity demands the full working capacity of the official, irrespective of the fact that his obligatory time in the bureau may be firmly delimited. In the normal case, this is only the product of a long development, in the public as well as in the private office. Formerly, in all cases, the normal state of affairs was reversed: official business was discharged as a secondary activity.

VI. The management of the office follows general rules, which are more or less stable, more or less exhaustive, and which can be learned. Knowledge of these rules represents a special technical learning which the officials possess. It involves jurisprudence, or administrative or business management.

The reduction of modern office management to rules is deeply embedded in its very nature. The theory of modern public administration, for instance, assumes that the authority to order certain matters by decree—which has been legally granted to public authorities—does not entitle the bureau to regulate the matter by commands given for each case, but only to regulate the matter abstractly. This stands in extreme contrast to the regulation of all relationships through individual privileges and bestowals of favor, which is absolutely dominant in patrimonialism, at least in so far as such relationships are not fixed by sacred tradition.

2. THE POSITION OF THE OFFICIAL

All this results in the following for the internal and external positions of the official:

I. Office holding is a 'vocation.' This is shown, first, in the requirement of a firmly prescribed course of training, which demands the entire capacity for work for a long period of time, and in the generally prescribed and special examinations which are prerequisites of employment. Furthermore, the position of the official is in the nature of a duty. This determines the internal structure of his relations, in the following manner: Legally and actually, office holding is not considered a source to be exploited for rents or emoluments, as was normally the case during the Middle Ages and frequently up to the threshold of recent times. Nor is office holding considered a usual exchange of services for equivalents, as is the case with free labor contracts. Entrance into an office, including one in the private economy, is considered an acceptance of a specific obligation of faithful management in return for a secure existence. It is decisive for the specific nature of modern loyalty to an office that, in the pure type, it does not establish a relationship to a *person*, like the vassal's or disciple's faith in feudal or in patrimonial relations of authority. Modern loyalty is devoted to impersonal and functional purposes. Behind the functional purposes, of course, 'ideas of culture-values' usually stand. These are *ersatz* for the earthly or supra-mundane personal master: ideas such as 'state,' 'church,' 'community,' 'party,' or 'enterprise' are thought of as being realized in a community; they provide an ideological halo for the master.

The political official—at least in the fully developed modern state—is not considered the personal servant of a ruler. Today, the bishop, the priest, and the preacher are in fact no longer, as in early Christian times, holders of purely personal charisma. The supra-mundane and sacred values which they offer are given to everybody who seems to be worthy of them and who asks for them. In former times, such leaders acted upon the personal command of their master; in principle, they were responsible only to him. Nowadays, in spite of the partial survival of the old theory, such religious leaders are officials in the service of a functional purpose, which in the present-day 'church' has become routinized and, in turn, ideologically hallowed.

II. The personal position of the official is patterned in the following way:

1. Whether he is in a private office or a public bureau, the modern official always strives and usually enjoys a distinct *social esteem* as compared with the governed. His social position is guaranteed by the prescriptive rules of rank order and, for the political official, by special definitions of the criminal code against 'insults of officials' and 'contempt' of state and church authorities ....

2. The pure type of bureaucratic official is *appointed* by a superior authority. An official elected by the governed is not a purely bureaucratic figure. Of course, the formal existence of an election does not by itself mean that no appointment hides behind the election—in the state, especially, appointment by party chiefs. Whether or not this is the case does not depend upon legal statutes but upon the way in which the party mechanism functions. Once firmly organized, the parties can turn a formally free election into the mere acclamation of a candidate designated by the party chief. As a rule, however, a formally free election is turned into a fight, conducted according to definite rules, for votes in favor of one of two designated candidates ....

3. Normally, the position of the official is held for life, at least in public bureaucracies; and this is increasingly the case for all similar structures. As a factual rule, *tenure for life* is presupposed, even where the giving of notice or periodic reappointment occurs. In contrast to the worker in a private enterprise, the official normally holds tenure. Legal

or actual life-tenure, however, is not recognized as the official's right to the possession of office, as was the case with many structures of authority in the past. Where legal guarantees against arbitrary dismissal or transfer are developed, they merely serve to guarantee a strictly objective discharge of specific office duties free from all personal considerations. In Germany, this is the case for all juridical and, increasingly, for all administrative officials ....

4. The official receives the regular *pecuniary* compensation of a normally fixed *salary* and the old age security provided by a pension. The salary is not measured like a wage in terms of work done, but according to 'status,' that is, according to the kind of function (the 'rank') and, in addition, possibly, according to the length of service. The relatively great security of the official's income, as well as the rewards of social esteem, make the office a sought-after position, especially in countries which no longer provide opportunities for colonial profits. In such countries, this situation permits relatively low salaries for officials.

5. The official is set for a *'career'* within the hierarchical order of the public service. He moves from the lower, less important, and lower paid to the higher positions. The average official naturally desires a mechanical fixing of the conditions of promotion: if not of the offices, at least of the salary levels. He wants these conditions fixed in terms of 'seniority,' or possibly according to grades achieved in a developed system of expert examinations. Here and there, such examinations actually form a character *indelebilis* of the official and have lifelong effects on his career. To this is joined the desire to qualify the right to office and the increasing tendency toward status group closure and economic security. All of this makes for a tendency to consider the offices as 'prebends' of those who are qualified by educational certificates. The necessity of taking general personal and intellectual qualifications into consideration, irrespective of the often subaltern character of the educational certificate, has led to a condition in which the highest political offices, especially the positions of 'ministers,' are principally filled without reference to such certificates ....

6. TECHNICAL ADVANTAGES OF BUREAUCRATIC ORGANIZATION

The decisive reason for the advance of bureaucratic organization has always been its purely technical superiority over any other form of organization. The fully developed bureaucratic mechanism compares with other organizations exactly as does the machine with the non-mechanical modes of production.

Precision, speed, unambiguity, knowledge of the files, continuity, discretion, unity, strict subordination, reduction of friction and of material and personal costs—these are raised to the optimum point in the strictly bureaucratic administration, and especially in its monocratic form. As compared with all collegiate, honorific, and avocational forms of administration, trained bureaucracy is superior on all these points. And as far as complicated tasks are concerned, paid bureaucratic work is not only more precise but, in the last analysis, it is often cheaper than even formally unremunerated honorific service.

Honorific arrangements make administrative work an avocation and, for this reason alone, honorific service normally functions more slowly; being less bound to schemata and being more formless. Hence it is less precise and less unified than bureaucratic work because it is less dependent upon superiors and because the establishment and exploitation of the apparatus of subordinate officials and filing services are almost unavoidably less economical. Honorific service is less continuous than bureaucratic and frequently quite expensive. This is especially the case if one thinks not only of the money costs to the public treasury—costs which bureaucratic administration, in comparison with administration by notables, usually substantially increases—but also of the frequent economic losses of the governed caused by delays and lack of precision. The possibility of administration by notables normally and permanently exists only where official management can be satisfactorily discharged as an avocation. With the qualitative increase of tasks the administration has to face, administration by notables reaches its limits—today, even in England. Work organized by collegiate bodies causes friction and delay and requires compromises between colliding interests and views. The administration, therefore, runs less precisely and is more independent of superiors; hence, it is less unified and slower. All advances of the Prussian administrative organization have been and will in the future be advances of the bureaucratic, and especially of the monocratic, principle.

Today, it is primarily the capitalist market economy which demands that the official business of the administration be discharged precisely, unambiguously, continuously, and with as much speed as possible. Normally, the very large, modern capitalist enterprises are themselves unequalled models of strict bureaucratic organization. Business management throughout rests on increasing precision, steadiness, and, above all, the speed of operations. This, in turn, is determined by the peculiar nature of the modern means of communication, including, among other things, the news service of the press. The extraordinary increase in the speed by which public announcements, as well as economic and political facts, are transmitted exerts a steady and sharp pressure in the direction of speeding up the tempo of administrative reaction towards various situations. The optimum of such reaction time is normally attained only by a strictly bureaucratic organization.

Bureaucratization offers above all the optimum possibility for carrying through the principle of specializing administrative functions according to purely objective considerations. Individual performances are allocated to functionaries who have specialized training and who by constant practice learn more and more. The 'objective' discharge of business primarily means a discharge of business according to *calculable rules* and 'without regard for persons.'

'Without regard for persons' is also the watchword of the 'market' and, in general, of all pursuits of naked economic interests. A consistent execution of bureaucratic domination means the leveling of status 'honor.' Hence, if the principle of the free-market is not at the same time restricted, it means the universal domination of the 'class situation.' That this consequence of bureaucratic domination has not set in everywhere, parallel to the extent of bureaucratization, is due to the differences among possible principles by which polities may meet their demands.

The second element mentioned, 'calculable rules,' also is of paramount importance for modern bureaucracy. The peculiarity of modern culture, and specifically of its technical and economic basis, demands this very 'calculability' of results. When fully developed, bureaucracy also stands, in a specific sense, under the principle of *sine ira ac studio* [impartiality]. Its specific nature, which is welcomed by capitalism, develops the more perfectly the more the bureaucracy is 'dehumanized,' the more completely it succeeds in eliminating from official business love, hatred, and all purely personal, irrational, and emotional elements which escape calculation. This is the specific nature of bureaucracy and it is appraised as its special virtue.

The more complicated and specialized modern culture becomes, the more its external supporting apparatus demands the personally detached and strictly 'objective' *expert*, in lieu of the master of older social structures, who was moved by personal sympathy and favor, by grace and gratitude. Bureaucracy offers the attitudes demanded by the external apparatus of modern culture in the most favorable combination. As a rule, only bureaucracy has established the foundation for the administration of a rational law conceptually systematized on the basis of such enactments as the latter Roman imperial period first created with a high degree of technical perfection. During the Middle Ages, this law was received along with the bureaucratization of legal administration, that is to say, with the displacement of the old trial procedure which was bound to tradition or to irrational presuppositions, by the rationally trained and specialized expert ....

9. THE LEVELING OF SOCIAL DIFFERENCES

Bureaucratic organization has usually come into power on the basis of a leveling of economic and social differences. This leveling has been at least relative, and has concerned the significance of social and economic differences for the assumption of administrative functions.

Bureaucracy inevitably accompanies modern *mass democracy* in contrast to the democratic self-government of small homogeneous units. This results from the characteristic principle of bureaucracy: the abstract regularity of the execution of authority, which is a result of the demand for 'equality before the law' in the personal and functional sense—hence, of the horror of 'privilege,' and the principled rejection of doing business 'from case to case.' Such regularity also follows from the social precon-ditions of the origin of bureaucracies. The non-bureaucratic administra-tion of any large social structure rests in some way upon the fact that existing social, material, or honorific preferences and ranks are connected with administrative functions and duties. This usually means that a direct or indirect economic exploitation or a 'social' exploitation of position, which every sort of administrative activity gives to its bear-ers, is equivalent to the assumption of administrative functions ....

10. THE PERMANENT CHARACTER OF THE BUREAUCRATIC MACHINE

Once it is fully established, bureaucracy is among those social structures which are the hardest to destroy. Bureaucracy is *the* means of carrying 'community action' over into rationally ordered 'societal action.' Therefore, as an instrument for 'societalizing' relations of power, bureau-cracy has been and is a power instrument of the first order—for the one who controls the bureaucratic apparatus.

Under otherwise equal conditions, a 'societal action,' which is methodically ordered and led, is superior to every resistance of 'mass' or even of 'communal action.' And where the bureaucratization of admin-istration has been completely carried through, a form of power relation is established that is practically unshatterable.

The individual bureaucrat cannot squirm out of the apparatus in which he is harnessed. In contrast to the honorific or avocational 'notable,' the professional bureaucrat is chained to his activity by his entire material and ideal existence. In the great majority of cases, he is only a single cog in an ever-moving mechanism which prescribes to him an essentially fixed route of march. The official is entrusted with special-ized tasks and normally the mechanism cannot be put into motion or arrested by him, but only from the very top. The individual bureaucrat is thus forged to the community of all the functionaries who are integrated into the mechanism. They have a common interest in seeing that the mechanism continues its functions and that the societally exercised authority carries on.

The ruled, for their part, cannot dispense with or replace the bureaucratic apparatus of authority once it exists. For this bureaucracy rests upon expert training, a functional specialization of work, and an attitude set for habitual and virtuoso-like mastery of single yet methodically integrated functions. If the official stops working, or if his work is forcefully interrupted, chaos results, and it is difficult to improvise replacements from among the governed who are fit to master such chaos. This holds for public administration as well as for private economic management. More and more the material fate of the masses depends upon the steady and correct functioning of the increasingly bureaucratic organizations of private capitalism. The idea of eliminating these organizations becomes more and more utopian ....

Under normal conditions, the power position of a fully developed bureaucracy is always overtowering. The 'political master' finds himself in the position of the 'dilettante' who stands opposite the 'expert' facing the trained official who stands within the management of administration. This holds whether the 'master' whom the bureaucracy serves is a 'people,' equipped with the weapons of 'legislative initiative,' the 'referendum,' and the right to remove officials, or a parliament, elected on a more aristocratic or more 'democratic' basis and equipped with the right to vote a lack of confidence, or with the actual authority to vote it. It holds whether the master is an aristocratic, collegiate body, legally or actually based on self-recruitment, or whether he is a popularly elected president, a hereditary and 'absolute' or a 'constitutional' monarch ....

14. THE 'RATIONALIZATION' OF EDUCATION AND TRAINING

We cannot here analyze the far-reaching and general cultural effects that the advance of the rational bureaucratic structure of domination, as such, develops quite independently of the areas in which it takes hold. Naturally, bureaucracy promotes a 'rationalist' way of life, but the concept of rationalism allows for widely differing contents. Quite generally, one can only say that the bureaucratization of all domination very strongly furthers the development of 'rational matter-of-factness' and the personality type of the professional expert. This has far-reaching ramifications, but only one important element of the process can be briefly indicated here: its effect upon the nature of training and education.

Educational institutions on the European continent, especially the institutions of higher learning—the universities, as well as technical academies, business colleges, gymnasiums, and other middle schools—

are dominated and influenced by the need for the kind of 'education' that produces a system of special examinations and the trained expertness that is increasingly indispensable for modern bureaucracy.

The 'special examination,' in the present sense, was and is found also outside of bureaucratic structures proper; thus, today it is found in the 'free' professions of medicine and law and in the guild-organized trades. Expert examinations are neither indispensable to nor concomitant phenomena of bureaucratization. The French, English, and American bureaucracies have for a long time foregone such examinations entirely or to a large extent, for training and service in party organizations have made up for them ....

Social prestige based upon the advantage of special education and training as such is by no means specific to bureaucracy. On the contrary! But educational prestige in other structures of domination rests upon substantially different foundations.

Expressed in slogan-like fashion, the 'cultivated man,' rather than the 'specialist,' has been the end sought by education and has formed the basis of social esteem in such various systems as the feudal, theocratic, and patrimonial structures of dominion: in the English notable administration, in the old Chinese patrimonial bureaucracy, as well as under the rule of demagogues in the so-called Hellenic democracy.

The term 'cultivated man' is used here in a completely value-neutral sense; it is understood to mean solely that the goal of education consists in the quality of a man's bearing in life which was *considered* 'cultivated,' rather than in a specialized training for expertness. The 'cultivated' personality formed the educational ideal, which was stamped by the structure of domination and by the social condition for membership in the ruling stratum. Such education aimed at a chivalrous or an ascetic type; or, at a literary type, as in China; a gymnastic-humanist type, as in Hellas; or it aimed at a conventional type, as in the case of the Anglo-Saxon gentleman. The qualification of the ruling stratum as such rested upon the possession of 'more' cultural quality (in the absolutely changeable, value-neutral sense in which we use the term here), rather than upon 'more' expert knowledge. Special military, theological, and juridical ability was of course intensely practiced; but the point of gravity in Hellenic, in medieval, as well as in Chinese education, has rested upon educational elements that were entirely different from what was 'useful' in one's specialty.

Behind all the present discussions of the foundations of the educational system, the struggle of the 'specialist type of man' against the older type of 'cultivated man' is hidden at some decisive point. This fight is determined by the irresistibly expanding bureaucratization of all public and private relations of authority and by the ever-increasing importance of expert and specialized knowledge. This fight intrudes into all intimate cultural questions ....

31

COURTS

*J*udicial review is an integral part of any federal system of government. Judicial review can be defined as the ruling by the courts on the constitutionality of legislation or executive action. In Canada, the practice of judicial review changed considerably with the adoption of the Charter of Rights and Freedoms in 1982.

Prior to 1982, the courts generally exercised a narrow interpretation of the power of judicial review. The British doctrine of parliamentary supremacy prevailed, and the courts rarely intervened to strike down a law of Parliament, for example, ruling it unconstitutional and thus null and void. However, the courts would rule on whether federal or provincial legislation was indeed a federal or provincial responsibility. Sections 91 (federal powers) and 92 and 93 (provincial powers) of the Constitution Act (1867 were used as the basic for decisions. If the courts, for example, decided a federal act was ultra vires, unconstitutional in the sense that it was outside the jurisdiction of the federal government, then obviously it was a provincial responsibility. And the same applied to provincial responsibilities; if those acts were ultra vires, then they were a federal responsibility. Thus, this form of judicial review was compatible with parliamentary supremacy; one level of government, federal or provincial, was always "supreme."

With the adoption of the Charter of Rights and Freedoms, however, judicial review has come to raise another issue—the supremacy of the constitution—because the constitutional rights of individuals are enumerated in the Charter. If individuals feel their Charter rights are violated by either level of government, they can take the *dispute to the courts. Courts are now asked, in effect, to place the disputed legislation of federal or provincial parliaments alongside the Charter.*

F.L. Morton reviews the decisions of the Supreme Court of Canada since passage of the Charter. He suggests that the Court has become more of an "activist" Supreme Court in that it is ruling more frequently on the constitutionality of federal and provincial legislation. This selection is a revised and updated version of the essay which appeared in the third edition of this book. F.L. Morton is a professor of political science at the University of Calgary.

• • • • • • • •

INTRODUCTION

The adoption of the Charter of Rights and Freedoms in 1982 introduced three principal changes in the Canadian political system. First, it replaced (or at least qualified) parliamentary supremacy with constitutional supremacy. Secondly, it explicitly recognized the practice of judicial review—the role of the courts to interpret and enforce the Charter, and to refuse to enforce any statute that conflicts with the Charter. Finally, unlike the 1960 Bill of Rights, the Chapter applies to the provinces as well as to the federal government.

Under parliamentary supremacy, final authority for all public-policy matter—including the protection of civil liberties—rests with Parliament. Under a system of constitutional supremacy, the powers of both the legislature and the executive are restricted by written limitations, which are interpreted and enforced by the courts. Under the latter system a court may overrule the legislature and nullify a law, if it is found to violate a right protected in the Constitution. This is not possible in a system of parliamentary supremacy.

The differences between parliamentary supremacy and constitutional supremacy are not as great as they first appear. Neither is or ever was absolute. Just as parliamentary supremacy was limited by the norms of the "unwritten constitution," the Charter's efficacy ultimately depends upon public opinion. The American experience with racial segregation until 1954—despite the constitutional guarantee of "equal protection of the law"—tragically demonstrates that the existence of a constitutionally entrenched right is no "guarantee" that rights will be respected. Similarly in Canada, the explicitly protected constitutional language rights of francophones in Manitoba were violated with impunity by the Manitoba legislature in 1890. Under the Charter, as before, the ultimate protection of justice in Canadian society is still in the ethical quality of public opinion—the collective commitment of all Canadians to fair play and tolerance of diversity.

Notwithstanding the ultimate power of public opinion, the enhanced status of the Charter does have important practical consequences. Unlike the 1960 Bill of Rights, which was only a federal statute, the Charter is part of Canada's written Constitution. The constitutional status of the Charter, combined with the explicit authorization of judicial interpretation and enforcement in Section 24, means that the Canadian courts will play a much more active and influential role in defining the meaning of the enumerated rights. The 1960 Bill of Rights did not explicitly authorize judicial review, and as a result Canadian judges proved to be very self-restrained in its interpretation. No such ambiguity restrains Charter interpretation. The most important practical effect of constitutionally entrenching rights is to give judges a more authoritative voice than other policy-makers in determining the scope of these rights.

I. THE CHARTER AS A CATALYST FOR A NEW JUDICIAL ACTIVISM

One of the simplest measures of the Charter's impact is to compare the pre- and post-Charter decisions of the Supreme Court of Canada in civil-liberties cases. The outcome of these decisions can be interpreted as tending toward judicial self-restraint or judicial activism. Judicial activism denotes a disposition of judges to interpret rights broadly and a corollary willingness to strike down statutes or exclude evidence in criminal cases. Judicial self-restraint denotes the opposite tendency: to interpret rights in a manner that avoids conflict with legislative decisions or interference with pretrial police investigations. Cumulatively, the outcome of these decisions shapes the relationship of the courts to the legislative and executive branches of government. An activist court uses the power of judicial review to intervene and to influence the making and enforcement of laws. A self-restrained court tends to avoid such interventions.

In the first decade of the Charter (1982–92), the Supreme Court of Canada decided 195 Charter cases. In 65 cases the individual litigant won, in 116 cases the Crown won, and there were 14 cases with no clear winner. This success ratio of 33 percent can be compared to a ratio of only 15 percent (5 out of 34) under the 1960 Bill of Rights (1960–82). In its Charter decisions, the Supreme Court has already declared invalid portions of 41 statutes, compared to just one such instance of judicial nullification under the Bill of Rights. The Supreme Court has also overruled several of its own Bill of Rights decisions in order to rule in favour of Charter litigants in similar cases. Together, the higher success rate, the larger number of nullifications, and the overruling of pre-Charter precedents are all indicators of a new era of judicial activism ushered in by the Charter.

II. IMPACT OF THE CHARTER ON PUBLIC POLICY

Judicial interpretation of the Charter is also changing various areas of public policy. The area most affected has been the Criminal Code and criminal law enforcement. Three out of every four Charter cases deal with legal rights, and they also account for 74 of the Supreme Court's first 100 Charter decisions. The Supreme Court has given a broad interpretation to the legal rights enumerated in Sections 7–14 of the Charter, in effect creating a new code of acceptable police conduct. For example, the Supreme Court's interpretation of the Section 10(b) right to counsel has had a major impact on policing. It has been interpreted to require police to immediately inform anyone they detain or arrest of their right to the assistance of counsel and the right not to speak until such assistance is procured. Police have been told that they cannot persist in questioning a suspect if that suspect asks for a lawyer, nor use tricks such as placing undercover agents in jail cells. If a suspect is too intoxicated to understand the utility of the right to counsel, police must cease questioning until the suspect sobers up. If an arrested person requests a lawyer but cannot afford one, the Court has said that Section 10(b) requires the police to provide one. The cumulative effect of these decisions is to greatly decrease the likelihood of voluntary confessions or incriminating statements, since the first thing a lawyer tells a client is to say nothing to the police.

In a sharp reversal of pre-Charter practice, the Court has established a policy of excluding evidence from a trial if the police do not follow any of the new rules outlined above, no matter how good the evidence may be. This new "exclusionary rule" has forced the Crown to discontinue prosecution in thousands of criminal cases because of lack of sufficient evidence. The net effect of the Court's activism in this area has been to substantially enhance the procedural defences of those accused of crimes—a result applauded by civil libertarians and defence lawyers. The cost has been a proportional decrease in the efficiency of law enforcement and crime control, a trend that worries others.

The Charter decision with the greatest policy impact to date has been the 1988 *Morgentaler* abortion decision. By a margin of 5–2, the Court ruled that the abortion law violated Section 7 of the Charter, forcing the Mulroney government to deal with the politically charged abortion issue.

The government struggled for two years to frame a new abortion policy. The result was Bill C-43, a compromise measure that left abortion in the Criminal Code but allowed therapeutic abortions when a pregnancy threatened the life or health of the mother. The determination of any health threat was left to the woman and her doctor. In this respect, the new policy closely followed the Dickson judgment in the *Morgentaler* decision. In 1990 the House of Commons in a free vote adopted Bill C-43, but it was then defeated on a tie vote in the Senate. As a result, Canada has become the only Western democracy with absolutely no regulation of abortion services.

A lesser known Charter case but one with a major policy impact was the 1985 *Singh* decision. *Singh* struck down the procedures for hearing applications for refugee status under the Immigration Act and forced the government to provide a mandatory oral hearing for refugee applicants. This decision had the unintended consequences of creating a backlog of 124 000 refugee claimants; an amnesty for 15 000 claimants already in Canada; $179 million in additional costs; and a new refugee law that some critics say is more unfair than the original one. The new refugee law took effect 1 January 1989. Eighteen months later, the government announced that the "new" Immigration and Refugee Board would quadruple its capacity to keep up with applications. This would allow the board to hire an additional 280 public servants (to add to the present 496) at an additional cost of $20 million. This increase brought the annual budget of the new board to $80 million.

Another major policy impact of the Charter has been in the area of Sunday-closing legislation. Directly overruling its own Bill of Rights precedent from 1962, the Supreme Court ruled in *Big M Drug Mart* (1985) that the federal Lord's Day Act as enforced in Alberta violated the freedom-of-religion provision of the Charter. Two years later in its *Edwards Books* decision, the Court upheld an Ontario Sunday-closing statute enacted for the explicitly secular purpose of a common day of rest. A majority of the Court rejected the argument that its "effect" was to violate the freedom of religion of non-Sunday sabbatarians whose religious beliefs required them to close on Saturday.

Despite the fact that its law was upheld, the Ontario government repealed the Sunday-closing provisions of its Retail Holiday Act and substituted a "local" option for municipalities. In Alberta, the government was reluctant to deal with what it regarded as an emotional, no-win issue, and also left the problem to municipalities to handle on a local-option basis. Critics say that while the local-option policy sounds good in theory, it does not work in practice. When one community forces its merchants to close while a neighbouring community allows its retail stores to remain open, the retailers in the first community lose potential sales. Research suggests that the resulting economic pressure creates a "domino effect" that forces all municipalities to open, especially in urban corridors such as Oshawa-Toronto-Hamilton and Edmonton-Red Deer-Calgary. The result has been increasingly wide-open Sunday shopping in both provinces.

Another important area of public policy directly affected by a Charter decision was the Canada Elections Act. The act placed strict limitations on independent "political action committee" expenditures in federal elections. Just prior to the 1984 national elections, the National Citizens' Coalition, a conservative public-interest group, successfully challenged these provisions as a violation of the "freedom of expression" provision of the Charter. Because the decision was handed down on the eve of the 1984 elections, the government did not appeal this Court of Queen's Bench decision. While the demise of the anti-PAC clause had little effect in the 1984 election, the subsequently elected Conservative government never acted to plug the loophole created by the decision. This became important during the November 1988 election, which turned into a virtual one-issue referendum on the Mulroney Free Trade Agreement with the United States. The absence of any legal restrictions on nonparty spending allowed pro-free trade groups to spend millions on political advertising in the closing weeks of the campaign. This advertising blitz helped to reverse an 11th-hour surge of anti-FTA sentiment and to re-elect Prime Minister Mulroney and his Tories. Thus a 1984 Court of Queen's Bench judge's interpretation of the Charter's freedom-of-expression provision may have affected the fate of the 1988 Free Trade Agreement, one of the most important decisions ever made by Canadians.

III. IMPACT OF THE CHARTER ON INTEREST-GROUP BEHAVIOUR

The most enduring impact of the Charter may be on the political process through the creation of a new forum for interest-group activity. Historically, Canadian interest groups have concentrated their lobbying activities at the cabinet and senior levels of the bureaucracy. Unlike their American counterparts, they avoid lobbying parliamentary committees and have rarely used litigation as a political tactic. This pattern of Canadian interest-group activity is explained by the "closed" character of the Canadian policy-making process. Unlike the American separation-of-powers system, in the parliamentary system there is very little opportunity to influence public policy in either parliamentary committees or in the courts. In the British tradition of "cabinet government," party discipline negates legislative independence and thus any real power of parliamentary committees. The tradition of parliamentary supremacy relegates the courts to a secondary political role and a more legalistic exercise of the judicial function. Interest groups accordingly concentrate their efforts at this single "access point" of the policy process. The adoption of the Charter of Rights has changed this situation by creating a new access point in the decision-making process. Interest groups which fail to achieve their policy objectives through the traditional political party and bureaucratic channels can now turn to the courts.

A leading example of interest-group success can be found in the area of minority language rights. English groups within Québec and francophones outside of Québec have both used Section 23 of the Charter to gain more favourable education policies from their respective provincial government. As soon as the Charter was adopted, the Québec Protestant School Board challenged the education provisions of Bill 101 in Québec. Known as the "Charter of the French Language" and the centrepiece of the Parti Québécois' legislative efforts to protect French-Canadian culture, the impugned sections of Bill 101 severely restricted access to English-language education in Québec. This policy was ruled an unconstitutional violation of Section 23 by the Supreme Court. In its 1990 *Mahé* decision, the Supreme Court also ruled that Section 23 entitled francophones in Edmonton, Alberta, not only to separate French-language schools but also to administrative control over the instruction, curriculum, and buildings. The impact of the *Mahé* decision has extended well beyond Alberta, since the other English-speaking provinces have had to follow the *Mahé* precedent.

The most publicized instances of interest-group use of the Charter have been the pro-choice and pro-life challenges to Canada's abortion law. Pro-choice groups spent over half a million dollars in legal fees to finance Dr. Henry Morgentaler's successful challenge, discussed earlier. Pro-life groups spent almost as much to support the Charter challenge of Joe Borowski, a tenacious ex-NDP cabinet minister from Winnipeg. Borowski argued that the existing abortion law was too permissive and violated the unborn child's right to life, as protected by Section 7 of the Charter. Unfortunately for Borowski, his case arrived at the Supreme Court just nine months after the Court had struck down the abortion law in the Morgentaler case. The Court ruled that because there was no longer an abortion law to challenge, the Borowski case had become "moot," and declined to answer the question of the rights of the unborn under the Charter.

The best organized interest-group use of the Charter has been mounted by Canadian feminists. Feminists gained a head start on other interest groups by successfully lobbying Parliament for favourable wording of the Section-15 equality-rights provisions while the Charter was still in draft stage. Soon after, the Canadian Advisory Council on the

Status of Women (CACSW) commissioned a study which concluded that, with the adoption of the Charter, "we find ourselves at the opportune moment to stress litigation as a vehicle for social change." The study recommended the creation of a single, nationwide "legal action fund" to coordinate and pay for a policy of "systematic litigation" of strategic "test cases." On 13 April 1985, only days before the equality-rights section of the Charter came into effect, the Women's Legal and Education Action Fund (LEAF) was launched. Its purpose is "to assist women with important test cases and to ensure that equality rights litigation for women is undertaken in a planned, responsible, and expert manner."

Since its inception, LEAF has raised more than $250 000 from private sources and has received a $1 million grant from the government of Ontario. It has also received funding from the Court Challenges Program. LEAF has participated in numerous Charter cases both as litigants and as intervenors. It intervened successfully in both the *Borowski* and *Daigle* abortion cases. LEAF has also enjoyed success in cases involving a "boys only" hockey league in Ontario, the use of original surnames by married women, and the eligibility of adoptive fathers for "maternity" leave. Perhaps LEAF's most important achievement came in the Supreme Court's first major equality-rights decision, *Andrews*, in which the Court adopted an interpretation of Section 15 that favours "disadvantaged groups," precisely what LEAF had argued for.

Interest-group use of Charter litigation was actually encouraged by the Court Challenges Program (CCP) announced in September 1985 by the federal government. The government allocated $9 million over five years to fund litigation arising under the equality-rights, language-rights, and multiculturalism provisions of the Charter. Applications for financial support are screened according to the criteria of "setting of social justice priorities ... legal merit ... [and] consequences for a number of people"; in other words, for maximum policy impact. Selected cases are eligible for $35 000 at each stage of litigation—trial, provincial appeal court, and the Supreme Court of Canada. During its first five-year mandate, the Court Challenges Program funded 150 equality-rights cases and 50 language-rights cases. (The latter included the *Mahé* and *Québec Protestant School Board* cases discussed earlier.)

In 1992, the Mulroney government cancelled the Court Challenges Program as part of a budget-reduction process, claiming that it had achieved its initial purposes. However, most observers believe the real reason was that the Conservatives were responding to criticism that the CCP had a liberal bias in the groups it selected for support. After winning the 1993 federal election, the Liberals announced that they would renew the program under a new name.

IV. IMPACT OF THE CHARTER ON FEDERALISM

A second important impact of the Charter is its centralizing effect on Canadian federalism. Decisions about policy issues that were previously made by provincial governments sensitive to different regional particularities must now meet minimum national standards imposed by the Supreme Court's Charter decisions. Restrictions on Sunday shopping, restrictions on who can practice law in a province, and on the level of minority-language education services—these are all policy areas that have been affected in this manner. While the Supreme Court has acknowledged that provincial differences are a legitimate consequence of federalism, there are several factors that push Charter jurisprudence in a centralist direction. Firstly, the Charter is grounded in a universalistic logic—the idea that every individual should enjoy equal rights regardless of where he or she lives—and this discounts the value of regional differences. Secondly, the interest groups who are most closely identified with the Charter have little attachment to federalism, especially when it conflicts with their policy agendas. The various Section-15 "equality-seeking" groups, for example, almost always argue for the highest possible national minimum standard. Thirdly, the final meaning of the Charter is provided by a national Supreme Court that is much less responsive to local public opinion than are the 10 provincial legislatures. That six of the nine justices are also from Central Canada and that the Ontario Court of Appeal hands down a large number of important Charter rulings are also contributing factors.

This trend is reflected in the number and types of statutes declared invalid under the Charter by the Supreme Court. During the first 10 years, the Supreme Court struck down 18 provincial statutes and 23 federal statutes. While the quantitative impact of the Charter has been roughly equal at both levels, there are some interesting qualitative differences. The invalidated provincial statutes tended to be of a substantive character and more recently enacted. Seventeen of the 23 nullifications of federal statutes were procedural in character and based on the legal-rights provisions of the Charter. With the important exception of abortion and the "rape shield" provisions of the Criminal Code, the federal legislation overturned by the Court has not involved major policy concerns. (Unlike abortion, Parliament succeeded in enacting a new "rape shield" law within 12 months.) By contrast, 13 of the 18 nullifications of provincial statutes were substantive in character, and eight were based directly or indirectly on French-English minority language and education issues—a perennial source of conflict in Canadian politics.

Six provinces have lost legislation to Charter challenges: Québec, British Columbia, Alberta, Saskatchewan, Manitoba, and Ontario. Of the six, Québec has clearly been most affected. The Québec Protestant School Board successfully challenged the education provisions of Bill 101. At the time the Charter was adopted, René Lévesque bitterly denounced Section 23, which was clearly intended to strike down the education policy embedded in Bill 101. "No self-respecting Québec government," he declared, "could ever abandon the smallest fraction of this fundamental right to protect the only French island in the English-speaking sea of the North American continent." Because Section 23 is excluded from the scope of the Section 33 legislative override, Québec had no alternative but to accept the Court's decision.

Three years later, the Supreme Court struck down another section of Bill 101—the "French-only" public-signs requirement. This provision prohibited the use of English in commercial signs—billboards, store-front advertising, and the like. The 650 000 Québec anglophones living in Montreal considered this law oppressive and humiliating, and challenged it as a violation of the Charter right to freedom of expression. Québec nationalists considered the "French-only" rule essential to preserving the "French face" of Québec, and harshly denounced the Supreme Court's decision. The recently elected Liberal government of Robert Bourassa—contrary to promises it had made to anglophone voters in the 1985 election—gave in to nationalist sentiment and invoked the Section 33 legislative override to reinstate the "French only" public-signs policy. This override of the Supreme Court's decision infuriated many people in English Canada, and this negative reaction contributed to the subsequent defeat of the Meech Lake Accord.

The minority-language-rights cases from Québec and the other provinces present the clearest example of how the Court can use the Charter to protect the rights of a minority against the local majority. From a different perspective, however, these decisions show how the Charter, through the Supreme Court, can serve as a vehicle for imposing national standards in policy areas previously under exclusive provincial control. In this sense, judicial review expands majority rule rather than restricts it. The catch is that what is being imposed is the will of a national political majority against what is deemed to be the perverse and unacceptable behaviour of regional majorities in Québec or the West. Put differently, the Charter has created new opportunities for political interests that are weak and unpopular at the provincial level but enjoy support at the national level. Both perspectives show how the policy autonomy of provincial governments has been eroded under the Charter.

V. EVALUATING THE CHARTER'S IMPACT

The Charter has clearly had a significant impact on the Canadian political process and public policy. The judicial decisions and events described are without precedent in Canadian politics, and would be virtually unthinkable without the advent of the Charter. Nor is there any doubt that this trend will continue. The volume of Charter litigation has swelled to over 500 reported cases annually. In the first 10 years the Supreme Court decided 195 Charter cases, more than five times the total number (35) of Bill of Rights cases that it decided between 1960 and 1982. Charter decisions now account for approximately 25 percent of the Supreme Court's annual caseload and show no sign of decreasing. Equally important, this new style of Charter politics has the support of important elites, including the media, intellectuals, lawyers and the law schools, feminists, and other human rights groups. There can be no turning back the clock.

At the time of its adoption, Peter Russell described the principal impact of the Charter as not so much the creation of new rights, but rather a new way of making decisions about rights, in which the courts play a much more authoritative role. Decisions about public policy that were made by elected legislators and civil servants are now often reviewed and revised by judges. Russell described this change as the "judicialization of politics." The preceding sections have provided an overview of what the "judicialization of politics" has meant in practice. Now it is time to evaluate these changes.

Critiques of judicial policy-making through the exercise of judicial review can be classified under two headings. First there is the problem of institutional legitimacy: Is it right for nonelected judges to overrule policy decisions of elected governments? The second is the problem of institutional capacity: Are judges capable of making a good policy choices? The question of the legitimacy of judicial review is an old one. From its inception in the U.S. Constitution of 1787, people have debated how in a democracy, in which legitimate authority is based on the consent of the governed, can unelected, tenured-for-life judges be allowed to overrule the policy decisions of elected, accountable legislatures and executives? Second, there is a more recent concern with institutional capacity. It concedes that judicial review makes some judicial policy-making inevitable, and focuses on the more practical question of whether courts have the necessary expertise to make competent policy choices.

While the entrenchment of the Charter was clearly intended to empower the Court to strike down offending statutes, it did not spell out the precise rules which should govern the judicial exercise of this awesome new power. Under what circumstances should unelected, unaccountable judges overrule the policy judgments of the democratically elected Parliament and provincial legislatures? There is an easy answer to this question: whenever Parliament or a provincial government makes a clear mistake and enacts a law that obviously violates the Charter. The problem is that the case of the "clear mistake-obvious violation" is rare. Neither level of Canadian government is likely to enact laws that violate the core meaning of Charter rights, for which there is general consensus and support. The example of the "clear mistake" allows us to justify the judicial veto in theory, but it is rare in actual practice.

More common is the case which contests the peripheral meaning or "outer limits" of a Charter right. The *Morgentaler* and *Borowski* cases are both typical examples. No fair person can reasonably claim that the right to abortion for the mother or the right to life for the fetus/unborn is *clearly* included in Section 7 of the Charter. The text, its legislative history, and past practice all dictate otherwise. But at the same time, no one can reasonably deny that such meanings might be implied by the broadly worded rights to "life, liberty and security of the person." That is, it is plausible to interpret Section 7 as including either of these specific rights as falling within its outer limits.

To say that Morgentaler's (or Borowski's) Charter claims are plausible, however, is not to say that a judge should accept them and declare the abortion law invalid. To say that a claim is plausible is to say that it might be right or it might be wrong. It is a matter of personal opinion, an issue over which reasonable people can reasonably disagree. But if it is essentially a matter of opinion and not a "clear mistake," why should the opinion of several unelected judges take precedence over the collective judgment of democratically elected representatives of the people? To do so risks placing the Court above Parliament and undermining Canadian democracy.

The antidemocratic character of judicial review under the Charter can be minimized or maximized by two factors. The first is the way in which judges exercise their new power. Do they limit their use of the judicial veto to cases in which there is a "clear mistake-obvious violation"? When they do, it is hard to pin the "antidemocratic" label on the decision. They are merely enforcing the clear mandate of the Constitution. Those who do not like the decision can direct their criticism at the Constitution, not the court.

Another way in which the courts can minimize the antidemocratic character of judicial review is by basing a decision to strike down a law on the narrowest possible reasoning. The Supreme Court's abortion decisions—or nondecisions—are again a good example of this. In the

Morgentaler decision, all the judges except Justice Wilson avoided dealing with the claim that the Charter creates any new rights to abortion. The two dissenters said the Charter did not—and therefore the Court should not—even address the abortion issue. The other four judges in the majority, while they struck down the law, did so for relatively narrow, procedural reasons, thereby leaving Parliament a great deal of room to craft a new abortion policy. When Joe Borowski arrived nine months later, the Court invoked the mootness doctrine to avoid addressing the question of the unborn child's right to life under the Charter, thereby leaving Parliament free to take the first step on this issue.

The other major concern with judicial policy-making under the Charter concerns the ability of judges to make the right—or at least competent—policy choices. Most judges do not have the "tools"—either personal or institutional—associated with effective policy-making in the modern state. Few judges have any specialized knowledge of the policy fields into which the Charter leads them. They thus lack any familiarity with the policy tradeoffs and political accomodations that typically shape a policy area. Few judges are trained in statistics and are thus handicapped in sorting out the conflicting interpretations of sophisticated data characteristic of policy disputes. The judicial process, with its strict rules against hearsay evidence and preference for sworn testimony, is not organized to deal with the fact-finding and fact-sorting, public input, and political accommodation. Nor do courts have the authority to follow up policy decisions or amend them if necessary. The judicial process tends to have a "narrow focus." It is preoccupied with the rights and duties of the litigants, and often misses the interconnectedness of social problems and policy. A change in one area of social relationships is likely to cause unintended changes in related areas. These unintended consequences may create new problems worse than the original. These are all familiar problems for students of public policy, but are hardly typical judicial considerations.

A good example of the potential downside of judicial policy-making can be found in the Supreme Court's handling of the Sunday-shopping controversy. The Court insisted on treating this controversy as a freedom-of-religion issue, when religion is clearly only one—and perhaps not the most important—issue at stake. The corporate character of the litigants strongly suggests that commercial interests are also very much in play. Outside the courtroom, the secular character of the Sunday-closing dispute is reflected in the political coalitions that have formed in both Alberta and Ontario to contest the issue. While church groups are part of the pro-Sunday closing coalition, its real political strength comes from organized labour and smaller, family-owned businesses. Likewise, shopping-mall owners and chain stores, not non-Christian merchants, are the most powerful supporters of wide-open Sunday shopping.

The broader evidence suggests that the principal dispute is not over a freedom-of-religion issue but a socioeconomic or "quality of life" issue. Do the economic advantages of a seven-day retail shopping week outweigh the social advantages of a uniform day of rest where all members of a family—especially in an era of two-income and single-parent families—can be together? What about the freedom of religion of employees and families who own stores in malls? How—and who—is to balance their freedom of religion against that of management?

While there are plausible arguments both for and against Sunday-closing laws, the issue is not simply a question of freedom of religion. Yet this is how the Court has treated it, a predictable consequence of the narrow rights-oriented focus of the judicial process and the ability of litigants to successfully exploit the "tunnel vision" character of the judicial process.

VI. CONSTITUTIONAL SUPREMACY WITHOUT JUDICIAL SUPREMACY

The Charter of Rights has proven to be a mixed blessing, with both positive and negative political impact. The negatives associated with the judicialization of politics should not be allowed to obscure the positive potential of the Charter as a readily available check on police excesses and abuses, heavy-handed government bureaucrats, and overzealous or malevolent political majorities.

Nor are the dangers inherent in the judicialization of politics inevitable consequences of the Charter. As the examples illustrate, they result from judicial fallibility. In some cases judges will be perceived as striking a statesmanlike balance between private interest and public interest, and in some they will fail. The Supreme Court of Canada can exercise its final appellate jurisdiction to correct the Charter "mistakes" of lower courts. But what if the Supreme Court makes a Charter decision that is clearly deleterious to the public interest? A Chief Justice of the American Supreme Court once said that his court was "not final because it was infallible, but infallible because it was final." Is the same now true of the Supreme Court of Canada?

Happily, the answer is no. Constitutional supremacy is not the same as judicial supremacy. While primary responsibility for Charter interpretation is vested with the courts, this does not mean that the courts should or do have the final say on all questions of constitutional policy. While the rule-of-law principle obliges the other branches of government to comply with the decision of the Supreme Court in any particular Charter case, democratic principles prohibit nine nonelected, permanently tenured judges from setting permanent constitutional policy, especially where the Charter meaning is ambiguous and the public-policy impact is clearly unacceptable.

Section 33 of the Charter provides a potential remedy for judicial fallibility of this magnitude. If a court rules that a statute is void because it violates the Charter, Section 33 allows Parliament or a provincial legislature to re-enact the statute by inserting an additional clause stating that it shall take effect "notwithstanding" the relevant section of the Charter. Section 33 is commonly referred to as the "legislative override" power, because it allows a government to override a judicial interpretation of the Charter that it thinks is too harmful to the public interest.

Section 33 has been used very sparingly to date. The Alberta government threatened to use it to protect the antistrike clause of its public employees (firemen, police, etc.) act, but never had to, as the courts subsequently upheld the act. The Saskatchewan government attached the notwithstanding clause to a back-to-work law in order to protect it from an earlier Court of Appeal precedent. This precedent was subsequently overturned by the Supreme Court, rendering Saskatchewan's use of the override unnecessary. Québec, however, has used the Section 33 power to shield itself from the impact of the Charter. To protest the adoption of the Charter without its consent, the Parti Québécois government of René Lévesque routinely attached a "notwithstanding" clause to all Québec laws, past and present. This practice was discontinued in 1986 by the new Liberal government of Robert Bourassa. However, it was the Bourassa government which used Section 33 to reinstate the "English only" public-signs law in 1988 after it had been declared invalid by the Supreme Court. Bourassa's use of the override was very popular among French Québeckers, but strongly condemned by most English-speaking Canadians.

Civil libertarian enthusiasts and the media have portrayed Section 33 in a very negative light, as undermining or "gutting" the Charter. This criticism is overstated, as it rests on two false assumptions: that judges are infallible and that the meaning of Charter rights is self-evident and widely agreed upon. The infallibility of judges need hardly be commented on. As to the second proposition, it suffices to say that almost no Charter cases involve clear conflicts between rights and wrongs, but rather questions of where to draw the outer limits on the application of traditional rights in new contexts. Section 33 is more accurately described as a form of "legislative review of judicial review." Just as judicial review serves as a check on a certain kind of legislative mistake, so legislative review serves as a check on judicial error. Also, when used by a provincial government as in the Québec public-signs case, Section 33 can be used to protect provincial rights against the centralist tendency of the Charter.

Québec's use of the Section-33 override also shows that the effectiveness of judicial review of Charter rights varies according to the state of public opinion. American experience with constitutionally entrenched rights suggests that courts are likely to be "least successful in blocking a determined and persistent law-making majority on a major policy issue." This would apply to the situation in Québec. On the other hand, the impact of and compliance with court decisions is likely to be much greater when public opinion is divided (e.g., the abortion decision) or public interest is low (e.g., the legal rights cases).

What the critics of Section 33 are trying to say is that it is open to abuse, which is certainly true. But what they ignore is that a government that abuses its Section-33 power to violate clearly defined and widely recognized rights must face the ultimate check in a democracy—the judgment of the voters. In this light, Section 33 can be seen as avoiding the American dilemma of allowing constitutional supremacy to degenerate into judicial supremacy. Rather it places responsibility for observing constitutional rights on both legislatures and courts, thus creating a legislative-judicial partnership, the final outcome of which the people shall judge.

ACKNOWLEDGMENTS

Patrick Boyer, from *The People's Mandate: Referendums and a More Democratic Canada.* (Toronto: Dundurn Press, 1992), pp. 1–9 (abridged). Reprinted by permission of the author.

Karl-Werner Brand, from "Cyclical Aspects of New Social Movements: Waves of Cultural Criticism and Mobilization Cycles of New Middle-Class Radicalism," in Russell J. Dalton and Manfred Kuechler, eds. *Challenging the Political Order.* (New York: Oxford University Press, 1990), pp. 23–42 (abridged). Reprinted by permission of the publishers.

Edmund Burke, from "Speech to the Electors of Bristol," in *Burke's Letters and Speeches on American Affairs.* (London: J.M. Dent and Sons, 1908), pp. 68–75 (abridged).

Richard Crossman, from *The Myths of Cabinet Government.* (Cambridge, Mass.: Harvard University Press, 1972), pp. 41–69 (abridged). Reprinted by permission of the publishers.

Brian Dickson, from *Reference Re Manitoba Language Rights,* [1985] 2 S.C.R. 347, as reprinted in the University of Calgary, Research Unit for Socio-Legal Studies, *Leading Constitutional Decisions of the Supreme Court of Canada,* pp. 5–8, 11 (abridged).

Thomas Hill Green, from "Lecture on Liberal Legislation and Freedom of Contract," in *The Works of Thomas Hill Green*, ed., R.L. Nettleship. (London, 1985–88), vol. 3, pp. 365–386 (abridged).

Thomas Hobbes, from Leviathan, printed in *The English Works of Thomas Hobbes*, ed., Sir William Molesworth. (London, 1839), chapter 17. Orthography modernized following *Hobbes Selections*, ed. Frederick J.E. Woodbridge (New York: Charles Scribner's Sons, 1930), pp. 335–340.

Gad Horowitz, from "Conservatism, Liberalism and Socialism in Canada: An Interpretation," *Canadian Journal of Economics and Political Science* 32 (1966): 143–170. Reprinted by permission of the author.

Michael Ignatieff, from *Blood and Belonging: Journeys into the New Nationalism*. (Toronto: Penguin Books, 1993), pp. 3–9. Reprinted by permission of the publishers.

Russell Kirk, from *The Conservative Mind: From Burke to Elliott*, 3rd. ed. (Chicago: Henry Regnery, 1960), pp. 6–10 (abridged). Reprinted by permission of the publishers.

Arend Lijphart, from *Democracy in Plural Societies: A Comparative Exploration*. (New Haven: Yale University Press, 1977), pp. 25–52 (abridged). Reprinted by permission of the publishers.

Juan J. Linz, from "An Authoritarian Regime: Spain" in *Mass Politics: Studies in Political Sociology*, eds., Erik Allardt and Stein Rokkan (New York: Free Press, 1970), pp. 251–71 (abridged). Reprinted from *Cleavages, Ideologies and Party Systems*, eds., Erik Allardt and Yrjo Littunen (Helsinki: The Westermarck Society, 1964). Reprinted by permission of Erik Allardt.

Karl Marx and Friedrick Engels, *Manifesto of the Communist Party*, trans. Samuel Moore. (London, 1888), section 1.

John Meisel, from "The Decline of Party in Canada" in Hugh Thorburn ed., *Party Politics in Canada*, 5th ed. (Scarborough: Prentice-Hall, Canada, 1979), pp. 98–114 (abridged). Reprinted by permission of the publishers.

John Stuart Mill, from *On Liberty*, as reprinted in *Utilitarianism and Other Writings*. (Cleveland: Meridan Books, 1962), pp. 135–38, 205–207.

J.D.B. Miller, from *The Nature of Politics*, rev. ed. (Harmondsworth: Penguin Books, 1965), pp. 13–19 (abridged). Reprinted by permission of the publishers.

Hans J. Morgenthau, from "Realism," in *Politics Among Nations: The Struggle for Power and Peace*, 4th edition. (New York: Alfred A. Knopf, 1967), pp. 3–14 (abridged). Reprinted by permission of the publisher.

Benito Mussolini, from *Enciclopedia Italiana* 14 (1932), and translated in Ion S. Munro, *Through Fascism to World Power: A History of the Revolution in Italy*. (Freeport, N.Y.: Books for Libraries Press, 1971; reprint of 1933 edition), pp. 302–309.

Madsen Pirie, from *Blueprint for a Revolution*. (Toronto: National Citizens' Coalition, 1994), pp. 9–17. Reprinted by permission of the publishers.

Ernest Renan, from "What is a Nation? in *Poetry of the Celtic Races and Other Essays*. (New York: Kennikut Press, 1896), pp. 61–83 (abridged).

Bert A. Rockman, from "Minding the State—Or a State of Mind? in James A. Caporaso, ed. *The Elusive State: International Comparative Perspectives*. Troy,

N.Y.: Sage Publications, 1989, pp. 173–199 (abridged). Reprinted by permission of the publishers.

Richard Rose, from *The Problem of Party Government*, Pelican edition. (Middlesex, England: Penguin Books, 1976), pp. 90–108 (abridged). Reprinted by permission of Macmillan, London and Basingstoke.

Walter A. Rosenbaum, from "The Meaning of Political Culture," in *Political Culture*. (New York: Praeger Publishers, 1975), pp. 3–33. Reprinted by permission of Greenwood Publishing Group, Inc., Westport, CT.

Garth Stevenson, from *Unfulfilled Union: Canadian Federalism and National Unity*, 3rd ed. (Agincourt: Gage Publishing), 1989, pp. 1–19 (abridged). Copyright, Gage Educational Publishing Company. Used by permission of the author and publisher.

Douglas Verney, from *Analysis of Political Systems*. (London: Routledge and Kegan Paul, 1959; New York: The Free Press of Glencoe, 1959), pp. 17–56 (abridged). Reprinted by permission of the publishers.

Max Weber, from *Wirtschaft and Gesellschaft*, H.H. Gerth and C. Wright Mills, trans. in *From Max Weber: Essays in Sociology* (New York: Oxford University Press, 1958), pp. 196–244, 245–250, 295–296 (abridged). Reprinted by permission of the publisher.

ACKNOWLEDGMENTS

Permission to reprint copyrighted material is gratefully acknowledged. Information that will enable the publisher to rectify any error or omission will be welcomed.

Reading 1
J.D.B. Miller, from *The Nature of Politics* (London, England: Gerald Duckworth and Company Ltd., 1962), pp. 13–19 (abridged). Reprinted by permission of Gerald Duckworth and Company Ltd.

Reading 2
Max Weber, from *From Max Weber: Essays in Sociology*, edited and translated by H.H. Gerth and C. Wright Mills. Copyright © 1946 by Oxford University Press, Inc.; renewed 1973 by Hans H. Gerth. Reprinted by permission of Oxford University Press, Inc.

Reading 3
Thomas Hobbes, from *Leviathan*, printed in *The English Works of Thomas Hobbes*, ed., Sir William Moleswoth (London, 1839), chapter 17. Orthography modernized following *Hobbes Selections*, ed. Frederick J.E. Woodbridge (New York: Charles Scribner's Sons, 1930), pp. 335–340.

Reading 4
Ernest Renan, from "What Is a Nation?" in *Poetry of the Celtic Races and Other Essays* (New York: Kennikut Press, 1896), pp. 61–83 (abridged).

Reading 5
Bert A. Rockman, from "The Elusive State: International and Comparative Perspectives," edited by James A. Caporaso, *Minding the State—Or a State of Mind? Issues in the Comparative Conceptualization of the State*, pp. 173–198 (abridged). Copyright © 1989 by Sage Publications. Reprinted by permission of Sage Publications, Inc.

Reading 6
Reference re: *Manitoba Language Rights* (1985). Reprinted in the series *Leading Constitutional Decisions of the Supreme Court of Canada* (edited by the University of Calgary, Research Unit for Socio-Legal Studies).

Reading 16
Gad Horowitz, from "Conservatism, Liberalism, and Socialism in Canada: An Interpretation." *Canadian Journal of Economics and Political Science,* 32 (1966), pp. 143–171.

Reading 17
Neil Nevitte, from "New Politics" in *Introductory Readings in Government & Politics,* 3rd ed. (Scarborough, ON: Nelson Canda, 1991), pp. 161–170.

Reading 18
James Madison, from *Selections from The Federalist,* edited by Henry Steele Commager (New York: Appleton-Century-Crofts, 1949), pp. 9–15.

Reading 19
Richard Rose, from *The Problem of Party Government,* Pelican edition (Middlesex, England: Penguin Books, 1976), pp. 90–108 (abridged). Reprinted by permission of Macmillan, London and Basingstoke.

Reading 20
Patrick Boyer, from *The People's Mandate: Referendums and a More Democratic Canada* (Toronto and Oxford: Dundurn Press, 1992), pp. 1–11 (abridged). Reprinted by permission of the author.

Reading 21
Juan Linz, from "An Authoritarian Regime: Spain," *Mass Politics: Studies in Political Sociology,* eds. Erik Allardt and Stein Rokkar (New York: Free Press, 1970), pp. 251–271 (abridged), and reprinted from *Cleavages Ideologies and Party Systems,* edited by Erik Allardt and Yrjo Littunen (Helsinki: The Westermarck Society, 1964). Reprinted by permission.

Reading 22
Douglas Verney, from *Analysis of Political Systems* (London: Routledge and Kegan Paul, 1959; New York: The Free Press of Glencoe, 1959), pp. 17–56 (abridged). Reprinted by permission of the publishers.

Reading 23
Garth Stevenson, from *Unfulfilled Union: Canadian Federalism and National Unity,* 3rd ed. (Agincourt: Gage Publishing, 1989), pp. 1–9 (abridged). Copyright © Gage Educational Publishing. Used by permission of the author and publisher.

Reading 24
Arend Lijphart, from "Consociational Democracy," *Democracy in Plural Societies: A Comparative Exploration* (New Haven, CT: Yale University Press, 1977), pp. 25–52 (abridged). Reprinted by permission of Yale University Press.

Reading 25
Walter A. Rosenbaum, from "The Meaning of Political Culture," in *Political Culture.* Reprinted by permission of Greenwood Publishing Group, Inc., Westport, CT.

Reading 26
Karl Werner-Brand, from "Cyclical Aspects of New Social Movements: Waves of Cultural Criticism and Mobilization of the New Middle-Class." In Russell Dalton and Manfred Kuechler (eds.), *Challenging the Political Order* (New York: Oxford University Press), pp. 23–42 (abridged).

Reading 27
John Meisel, from "The Decline of Party in Canada," in Hugh Thorburn, ed., *Party Politics in Canada,* 5th ed (Scarborough, ON: Prentice-Hall, Canada, 1979), pp. 98–114 (abridged). Reprinted by permission of the publisher.

Reading 28
Edmund Burke, from *Burke's Speeches and Letters on American Affairs,* edited by Ernest Rhys (London: J.M. Dent & Sons, Ltd., 1919), pp. 68–75

Reading 29
Richard Crossman, from *Myths in Cabinet Government* (Cambridge, Mass.: Harvard University Press, 1972), pp. 41–69 (abridged). Reprinted by permission of the publisher.

Reading 30
Max Weber, from *Wirtschaft and Gesellschaft,* H.H. Gerth and G. Wright, trans., in *From Max Weber: Essays in Sociology* (New York: Oxford University Press, 1958), pp. 196–244 (abridged).

Reading 31
F.L. Morton, from "Courts" in *Introductory Readings in Government & Politics,* 3rd ed. (Scarborough, ON: Nelson Canada, 1991), pp. 374–375.

To the owner of this book

We hope that you have enjoyed *Introductory Readings in Government & Politics*, fourth edition, and we would like to know as much about your experiences with this text as you would care to offer. Only through your comments and those of others can we learn how to make this a better text for future readers.

School _____ Your instructor's name _____

Course _____ Was the text required? _____ Recommended? _____

1. What did you like the most about *Introductory Readings in Government & Politics?*

_____

_____

2. How useful was this text for your course?

_____

_____

_____

3. Do you have any recommendations for ways to improve the next edition of this text?

_____

_____

_____

4. In the space below or in a separate letter, please write any other comments you have about the book. (For example, please feel free to comment on reading level, writing style, terminology, design features, and learning aids.)

_____

_____

_____

_____

Optional

Your name _____ Date _____

May Nelson Canada quote you, either in promotion for *Introductory Readings in Government & Politics* or in future publishing ventures?

Yes _____ No _____

Thanks!

- FOLD HERE -

Nelson

MAIL ⇒ POSTE

Canada Post Corporation / Société canadienne des postes

Postage paid
if mailed in Canada

Port payé
si posté au Canada

Business Reply

Réponse d'affaires

0107077099   01

TAPE SHUT

TAPE SHUT

0107077099-M1K5G4-BR01

Nelson Canada
College Editorial Department
1120 Birchmount Rd.
Scarborough, ON M1K 9Z9

PLEASE TAPE SHUT. DO NOT STAPLE.